Adolfo Natalini
"Four Sketchbooks"

—

From Superstudio
to Natalini Architetti

Forma

EDITORIAL PROJECT
Forma Edizioni srl,
Firenze, Italia
redazione@formaedizioni.it
www.formaedizioni.it
-
EDITORIAL PRODUCTION
Archea Associati
-
PUBLISHING AND EDITORIAL COORDINATION
Laura Andreini
-
TEXTUAL SUPERVISION
Riccardo Bruscagli
-
EDITORIAL STAFF
Valentina Muscedra
Maria Giulia Caliri
Beatrice Papucci
Elena Ronchi
Elisa Martini
-
GRAPHIC DESIGN
Elisa Balducci
Sara Castelluccio
Vitoria Muzi
Isabella Peruzzi
Mauro Sampaolesi
-
PHOTOLITHOGRAPHY
Art&Pixel,
Firenze
-
PRINTING
Tap Grafiche,
Poggibonsi, Siena
-
TRANSLATIONS
Katherine Fay
Katy Hannan
Yolanda Rillorta
Renée Tennenbaum
Maureen Fay Young

Cover:
Adolfo Natalini,
from *Quaderni Neri*

-
Quaderni Cinesi
[Chinese Sketchbooks]
Small lined sketchbooks with black cover and red corners, made in China.
-
Quaderni Estivi
[Summer Sketchbooks]
Sketchpads for watercolour, tempera, and acrylic paintings, "done over the summer"
-
Quaderni Neri
[Black Sketchbooks]
Sketchbooks with hard black cover.

-
Works still under construction are marked with "–" after the start of construction date

First edition: November 2015

ISBN: 978-88-96780-88-6

—

From the *Quaderni Neri*: June 5, 2015

For this book, I gathered together a series of drawings made between 1959 and 2013 for comparison with the photos of the buildings and city areas generated by the sketches.

Not all the drawings are architectural, but they are linked with architecture, sometimes in strange ways. The last series of coloured images brings back a certain nostalgia for painting, and perhaps this closes a circle opened almost sixty years before.

—

27.08.15

While assembling the images and buildings for this book, I felt I was seeing them from far away.

They had become landscapes that I could paint like an enthusiastic amateur.

I used sheets of heavy paper (260 gr/m^2, 75x55 cm) and the tempera paints I bought for my nephew Arno (when he was small) to stimulate a taste for painting; often I dilute them too much, transforming them into watercolours.

The quality of my landscapes is very mediocre, but I had planned to draw other elements on top: plants, cross-sections, axonometric projections, details... symbols taken from the architect's drafting compendium, but other drawings as well: portraits, objects, and people from the artist's repertoire.

After my vain attempts at overlayering and hybridization, I abandoned the idea and the landscapes remained empty, as often happens in architectural photos.

And yet, architectural constructions are full of things, people, days and nights, years, memories and hopes.

—

28.08.15

I had set myself a task for the month of August at the beach: a project of summer paintings on 14 sheets (all that was left of the packet given to me by Gabriele Bertocci at Fabriano) and I had chosen the subjects just as I had selected the projects for this book.

However, I deviated from the original plan: I did not paint Manetstrasse, the Uffizi, the Museo dell'Opera del Duomo, but replaced them with pictures of Calenzano, San Casciano and a *Continuous Monument* floating on the mountain lake in which it had been rooted, and this gave rise to other reinterpretations.

I thought again about the *Continuous Monument*, a project from the heroic period of Superstudio, the images that had become Avant-garde icons, and I tried to imagine others. I also put together images of a *Histogram City*, where volumes with no purpose and without actual dimensions created a contrast with natural landscapes.

-
Adolfo Natalini/Superstudio, 1969-2015, *Monumento Continuo e Niagara Falls* [Continuous Monument and Niagara Falls]

-
Adolfo Natalini/Superstudio, 1969-2015, *Città degli Istogrammi - Utah Desert* [Histogram city - Utah Desert]

Adolfo Natalini/Superstudio
with Arno Bonaiuti,
1969-2015, *Città degli*
Istogrammi sul mare
[Histogram city on the sea]

Lemmario 1

[Lexicon 1]

—

Introduction

01. What is this book? I could save myself by quoting Saint Augustine: "What is time? I know until you ask me; when you ask me, I don't know."
Architects' monographies contain projects and buildings set out according to a certain order (chronological, typological, geographical – I wanted to add topological, but restrained myself in time) – as well as descriptive, theoretical and critical texts. Architects try to explain their intentions (what they wanted to do) and describe what they have done (which rarely coincides with their intentions).
I did not want to write a book, and I was not capable. So, I thought I would limit myself to selecting images and projects from my archives from the 1960s until today, with assorted texts (notes, lectures and interviews) and assemble them together.
The projects have been divided into four sketchbooks: Il quaderno di scuola, Il quaderno italiano, Il quaderno tedesco, Il quadeno olandese [School sketchbook, Italian sketchbook, German sketchbook, Dutch sketchbook]. The texts are in alphabetical order like a glossary or *lemmario* [lexicon]. Naturally as with any rules, there are exceptions.
[08.09.14]

02. I drew up a list of works and for each one I added sketches, drawings, and photos. Each image was a fragment from a theatre of memories. They recalled places, people, days of work and travel, streets and piazzas, skies, water, trees. They brought back voices, phone calls, discussions. These memories were not far away, nor were they close by, but rather like an undulating air curtain, a kind of hallucination or mirage. I would have liked to go back in time, to relive those moments of enthusiasm, worry, and apprehension. Perhaps I would have wished for something different, following other paths or taking other directions. Yet, I found I did not want to change a single thing. I wanted to maintain everything exactly as it had been. I knew that the bricks and stone would have aged (and in fact most had already aged) and that the inhabitants would have modified the houses, enclosing a loggia, adding an awning, changing some doors and windows... and that trees would have grown in the gardens and public spaces, and there would have been a gazebo here, a garden shed there, perhaps a child's swing and garden gnomes.
[10.09.14]

03. I searched for a few fragments of architectural autobiography among my scattered writings, interviews and articles. I wanted to put together an illustrated story of projects and constructions. But, like that never-ending discussion on song writing – what comes first, the melody or the lyrics? Did the story generate the projects with its *kunstwollen,* or did the projects generate the stories in an attempt to freeze them in time?
[17.09.14]

04. I go back through pages and pages of notes and transcriptions. I find the same sentences repeated and rewritten. I ask myself how much of this jumbled mixture of thoughts, lectures, and parts of lessons can be salvaged for this sort of anthology that I want to publish.
On one hand, a catalogue – on the other, an essay. Fundamentally, it is a diary, a kind of autobiography that grows longer each day, or at least I hope so.
[14.11.14]

Autobiografia patetica
[Paltry autobiography]

01. I was born in 1941 in Pistoia, an ancient provincial city in Tuscany (with a marvellous stone piazza and a black and white banded baptistry) in a family that had farmed the land for seven hundred years in Valdinievole. I work as a university professor, and I am an architect by profession... but I am an artist at heart.
At the time of the flood in Florence in 1966, I founded an avant-garde group, Superstudio. We began a movement called *Radical Architecture* and during the hard and difficult years from 1966 to 1978, I worked with the group on the anthropological refoundation of architecture.
I have always been more interested in the humanities (literature, philosophy, and politics) than in science and technology. I owe more to painters and poets than I do to architects.
I live and work in Florence because I love the clarity of Leon Battista Alberti and Brunelleschi, but also the malaise of Buontalenti and Pontormo, and because it is like living in a library. The historical city centre is like Borges' *Library of Babel* or the library in *The Name of the Rose.* Since 1978, I have been designing architectural projects for historic cities and I focus more on the exception than on the rule in the secret hope that an ensemble of exceptions will help to establish a norm...
I am well aware that we should not indulge in autobiographies, but as I get older and understand less and less of the world, I think that in writing and building, what we create are simply autobiographies. We secretly hope that our life resembles that of the universe, or at least, that it is same as that of other beings who, recognising themselves in us and in the stone, will feel part of a building. I have only fragmented memories of the works and heart-rending autobiographies of my *maestri,* which I read when it was too late to go back and love them.
The daily fundamentals of my job are hard work, solitude and a passion for what I do.
If I look back on the twenty years in which I have worked tirelessly day and night, filling pages of black sketchbooks and endless sheets of paper with pens, pencils and coloured pencils; if I think of all the ideas I pursued with my drawings, I feel disheartened over all the things I might have done but did not do.
I remember places glimpsed from a train, streets and piazzas seen in books and never explored. I think of lost hours of sunshine behind closed shutters, summer nights blurred by the lamp that enclosed, in a magic circle on the table, my drawings and the ethereal insects that came there to die.
I think of people I loved, and of conversations I did not instigate, of people I appreciated, dear friends and *maestri,* who died before I had the time to launch discussions that I now feel, could have been uplifting.
All that remains of the life I experienced is nostalgia and some fine, almost illegible lines. I thought the world was a book I was charged to read and write.
I thought that the indescribable construction of the universe was based on a great plan, already written, and that one only had to read and rewrite it to possess it. I drew tiny objects, and rooms to contain them, and containers to take them with me, and more rooms to pile them in, where I could sit among all these things. I designed buildings, streets, piazzas and towns. Sometimes at night, on the typewriter, I would align words, paying more attention to the cabalistic geometry

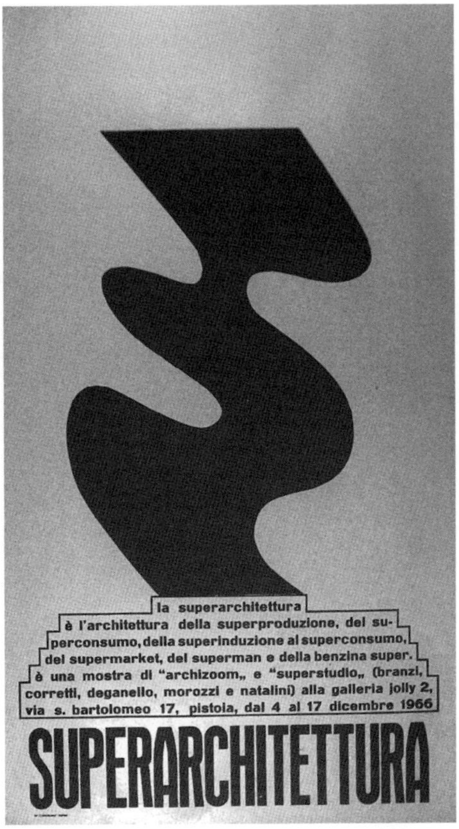

Palazzo dell'Arte
Florence, Degree thesis
by Adolfo Natalini, 1965-66

Superarchitettura exhbition,
poster, Pistoia, 1966

Superstudio and *Hidden Architecture*, Piazza
di Bellosguardo, 1971

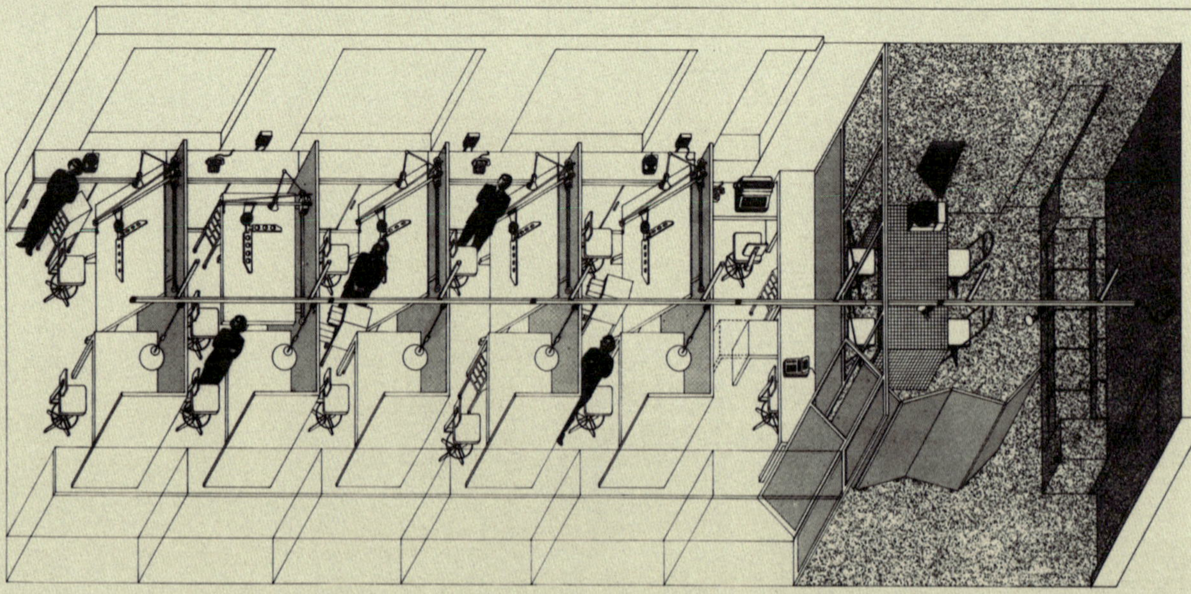

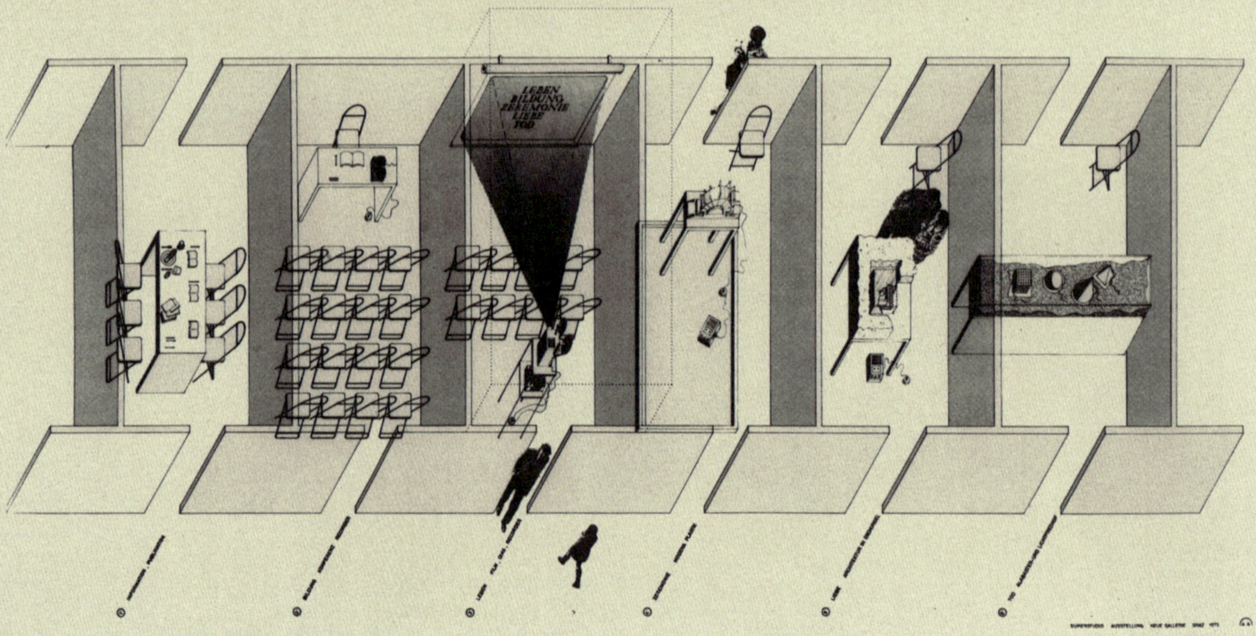

SUPERSTUDIO AUSSTELLUNG NEUE GALLERIE GRAZ 1973

of the lines on the page than to their meaning. Besides, most of the time I was searching for the meaning, but during the hunt I could not bend down to look for the footprints.
If I look forward in time, that I try to guarantee through the expiatory process of this project, I still see objects and rooms, architecture and cities, but more serene and tranquil than those in my past.
The objects I want to draw speak of lengthy, slow moments, of actions repeated without reservation.
The architecture is similar to many other styles I have seen; it speaks through old materials that, only here and there, crumble to reveal concerns and questions.
The streets, the piazzas and the places in the city are the spaces that represent civilised living and the heroism of daily life.
If time is the mobile image of eternity, I would like architecture to be the mobile image of beauty, of the sublime catalyst without which no transformation is possible.
When seeking water with a rod or forked branch, the water diviner searches for a contact with the universe and listens to its voices. Discovering water is his prize for taking part in the dialogue with hidden things.
In old city centres, there is already so much architecture; one simply needs to know how to recognise it to uncover it. Places generate architecture, and in turn, architecture can become a place.
Architecture generated by places with inherent elements tries to communicate through illustration. Linguistic illustration defined by rhetoric (the art of efficient communication) seeks its equivalent in construction so that it may speak (and sing).
Only two of these projects have been built, but all aspired to construction in the same manner. After long years of apprenticeship in drawing, I have now begun to approach architecture through construction. I would like my 'figures' to be built in stone.
[05.02.85]

02. I have carried around with me much of my first twelve years of work, as well as much of what I produced even earlier, when I was a painter in Pistoia with Barni, Ruffi and Buscioni; a great deal also originates from my increasingly stronger affinity with my Tuscan roots...
Everybody shows the signs of life's experience, and the face we have after forty is what we have built for ourselves.
I chose to be an architect – or rather, I try to be an architect – even though often I discover I am very attached to the world of objects (in my dreams I see more objects and rooms than houses and cities); deep down, my aspiration remains what I dreamt of when I was young: to be an artist.
I have never been very clever with my hands (I think my only manual capacity is drawing) and perhaps it is for this reason that I have always been fascinated by handcrafting and art, and all those techniques and skills that give man a certain control over his world at close range.
However, I have a long distance view of time, both past and future, (as a child, I had one short-sighted eye and one far-sighted, so perhaps this is the explanation).
With a close-up view in space, and a far-sighted view in time, I tend towards the classical, but not so that I can "become a part of history more easily" (as you say), if anything, it would be to remain there.
In any case, there is no other place to go.
[From a conversation with Ugo La Pietra 27.01.88]

Superstudio

01. *Fragments from a personal museum*
Our work has always taken the form of inventories and catalogues: perhaps the only form of work possible today is autobiography as a project for one's life.
From 1965 to 1968, we worked with the conviction that architecture was a means of changing the world. Designs were a hypothesis of physical transformations, they were ways to hypothesize diverse qualities and quantities:
The first catalogue was called *Viaggio nelle Regioni della Ragione*.

02. Between 1968 and 1969, we began to be interested in transpositions and metamorphoses: architecture stopped being "specific," it lost its "scale" connotations to become an abstract planning of platonic, neutral and available entities. This work has been collected in the second catalogue: *Istogrammi d'Architettura* [Architectural Histograms].
The catalogue text read:
"In those years it became clear that continuing to design furniture, decorative objects, and other household goods was not the solution to the problems of living, or the problems of life, or the way to save one's soul...
It also became clear that no amount of beautification or declaration could be sufficient to remedy the damages of time, the errors of mankind, and the bestiality of architecture...
Thus the problem was to break away from these activities, perhaps by adopting the theory of minimal effort in an overall reductive process. We prepared a catalogue of non-continuous three-dimensional diagrams, a catalogue of architectural histograms, with reference to a grid that could be transposed to different areas or scales for the edification of a serene and immobile nature in which to identify. The catalogue of histograms led without much effort to the generation of furniture, environments, architectures.... But none of these things matter to us very much, nor did they ever matter very much. The surfaces of these *Histograms* were homogeneous and isotropic: every problem of space and sensitivity had been carefully been removed.
The *Histograms* were also called *Le Tombe degli Architetti* [The Tombs of the Architects]."

03. Between 1969 and 1970, we elaborated an extreme line of thought on the possibilities of architecture as the instrument for attaining knowledge and action through the means of an architectural model of total urbanisation. This work appears in the third catalogue: *The Continuous Monument*.
The catalogue text read:
"For those who believe, as we do, that architecture is one of the few means we have available to make the order of the cosmos visible here on Earth, to put things in order, and above all to affirm the human capacity to act according to reason, 'moderate utopia' consists in the hypothesisation of a near future in which all architecture is produced by a single act, by a single 'design' that is capable of clarifying, once and for all, what motivates humans to build dolmens, menhirs, and pyramids, to create cities in the forms of squares, circles, and stars, and to trace out (*ultima ratio*) a white line in the desert. We believe in a future of 'rediscovered architecture', in a future in which architecture resumes its full powers, abandoning every ambiguous designation and presenting itself as the only alternative to nature. Between *natura*

Superstudio,
the studio in via
delle Mantellate 2/9,
Florence, 1971

Superstudio, Fragmente aus einem personlichen Museum [Superstudio, Fragments from a personal museum], exhibition Graz, Vienna, Innsbruck, 1973

naturans and *natura naturata*, we choose the second term. By eliminating the mirages and fairylands of spontaneous architecture, sensitive architecture, architecture without architects, bioarchitecture and fantastic architecture, we move toward the 'continuous monument': an architecture that emerges equally throughout a single, continuous environment: the earth made homogeneous by technology, by culture and by every other imperialism. An architecture that joins a long history of black stones, of objects that fall from the sky or are built on Earth: meteorites, dolmens, obelisks. They represent cosmic axes, vital elements, the reproductive elements of the relationship between Earth and Sky, testimonies of marriages, tablets of the law, final acts of variable-length dramas.
From the Holy Kaaba to the Vertical Assembly Building, a stone cube placed on earth is a primary act, it is a testimony to architecture as a relational node between technology, sacredness, and utilitarianism; it implies humankind, machinery, rational structures, and history. The cube is the first and last act in the history of architectural ideas. Architecture becomes a closed, immobile object that makes no reference to anything other than itself and the use of reason."

04. Between 1970 and 1971, we started to produce dic-fic projects, architectural critiques. We used architecture as self-criticism, endeavouring to enquire into its promotional mechanisms and its ways of working. The didactic plans are *The Hidden Architecture, Reflected Architecture, Interplanetary Architecture, The Twelve Ideal Cities*.

05. From 21 March 1971 to 20 March 1973, we worked on a series of films about fundamental acts, centreed on the relationship between architecture (as the conscious formalisation of the planet) and human life. Those films produced constitute propaganda for ideas outside the typical channels of the architectural discipline.
The five films are:
Vita educazione cerimonia amore morte [Life, Education, Ceremony, Love, Death].
The presentation text read:
"The major themes, the fundamental problems of our lives have never been touched by architecture. Architecture sits at the sidelines and intervenes only at a certain point in the relational process, when all behaviour has already been codified, furnishing answers to rigidly posed problems. Even if its answers are aberrant or subversive, the logic of their production and consumption does not permit any real upheaval. Architecture does not propose alternative behaviors because it uses instruments that have been created by the system to prevent any substantial deviation. For this reason, both the worker house and the manor house follow the same models and the radical architect and the academic architect are equivalent: the difference lies only in terms of quantity, as the decisions regarding the quality of life have already been made. In accepting his role, the architect becomes an accomplice of the machinations of the system whose approval he seeks. The avant-garde architect holds an even more rigidly fixed role, a bit like a 'young lover'.
At this point, the architect who recognizes, in himself and in his work, connotations of cosmetic activities, of environmental pollution, and of *consolatrix afflictorum*, stops dead in his tracks along a well-paved road. It thus becomes an act of coherence, or a final attempt to save oneself, to concentrate on the 'redefinition' of the primary actions, and to examine what relationships exist, in the first place, between architecture and those actions. This operation becomes a therapy for the elimination of the archimanias...
An attempt to reestablish the anthropological and philosophical foundations of architecture has become the focus of our reductive processes."

06. Presenting a traveling exhibition of our work in the United States, we wrote:
"These [...] are fragments of projects executed from 1966 to 1973 for the modification of the natural and artificial landscape which surrounds us and for the modification of ourselves through ideas. Having continued for years to dream up, on paper, testaments, lovers' promises, immobile (colloquies with fellow-guests of stone), having confided to paper bottle-messages, love poetry, invisible whispers [...] And again: having built, on paper, castles and cities, and inviolate oases amid the sands, and empty houses, or warehouses full of useless objects, or funeral processions [...]
And having for years interrogated the stars on the itinerary to follow, the navigator drew the constellations in the night. Having for centuries interrogated the earth, the farmer drew geometric patterns on hills and valleys, transforming them into mosaics.
Finally, after examining the omens, the founder of the city drew a geometric perimeter on the ground and thereon he built the city. Innumerable cartographers delineated the terraqueous globe, marking invisible boundaries which later turned into paths of blood on the earth and seas. Others drew flags in blood or gold. In this fashion they also made vestments for kings and other dignitaries. (The Native Americans instead executed designs in coloured sand that would only last a few moments after the prolonged magic that made them, the father teaching the art to his son by example.) The marks we left on the paper, or the pieces of photos glued together, and the blueprints of perspectives and axonometrics, and the sheets from the copier, the drawings done with coloured pencils or shaded ones done with the airbrush, were ways and maps for ancient or future journeys. They were paths running through the territory of will and hope. They were plans for journeys, activities, magic calendars, lists of gifts.
They were always projects.
The plans that remain provide evidence of lives never lived, of invisible objects, of lightweight structures. In the beginning, we designed objects for production, designs to be turned into wood and steel, glass and brick, or plastic [...]
Then we produced neutral and usable designs, then, finally, negative utopias, forewarning images of the horrors which architecture was laying in store for us, with its scientific methods for the perpetuation of existing models... Then the images slowly disappeared, as if in a mirror: now there remain only fables and parables, descriptions and speeches. No longer figures, but traces of a mode of behaviour directed towards suggesting the magnificent possibilities of rediscovering and of governing ourselves. The only project is thus the project for our lives and our relationships with others."

[30.04.73 From "Sottsass & Superstudio: mindscapes", in *Design quarterly*, special issue, no. 89, 1973]

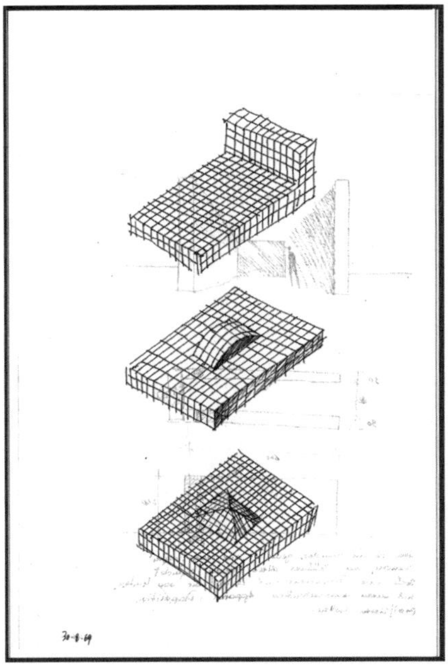

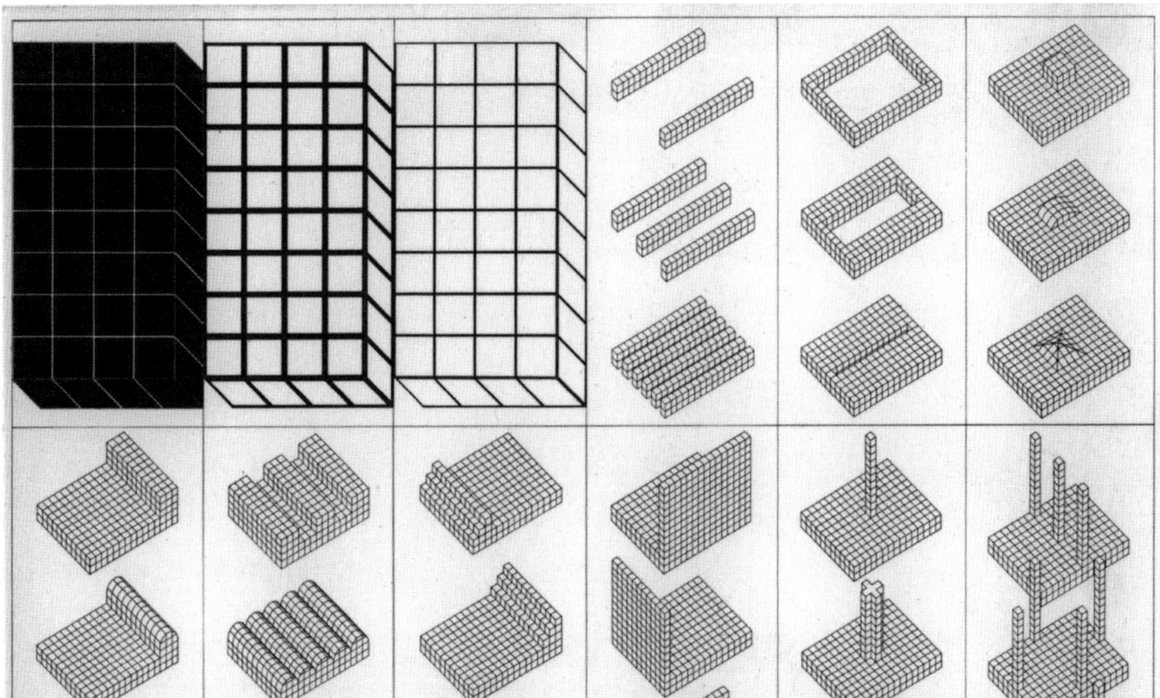

Superstudio, *Histograms,* from *Quaderni Neri,* 1969

Superstudio, *Histogram* catalogue, lithograph, 1969

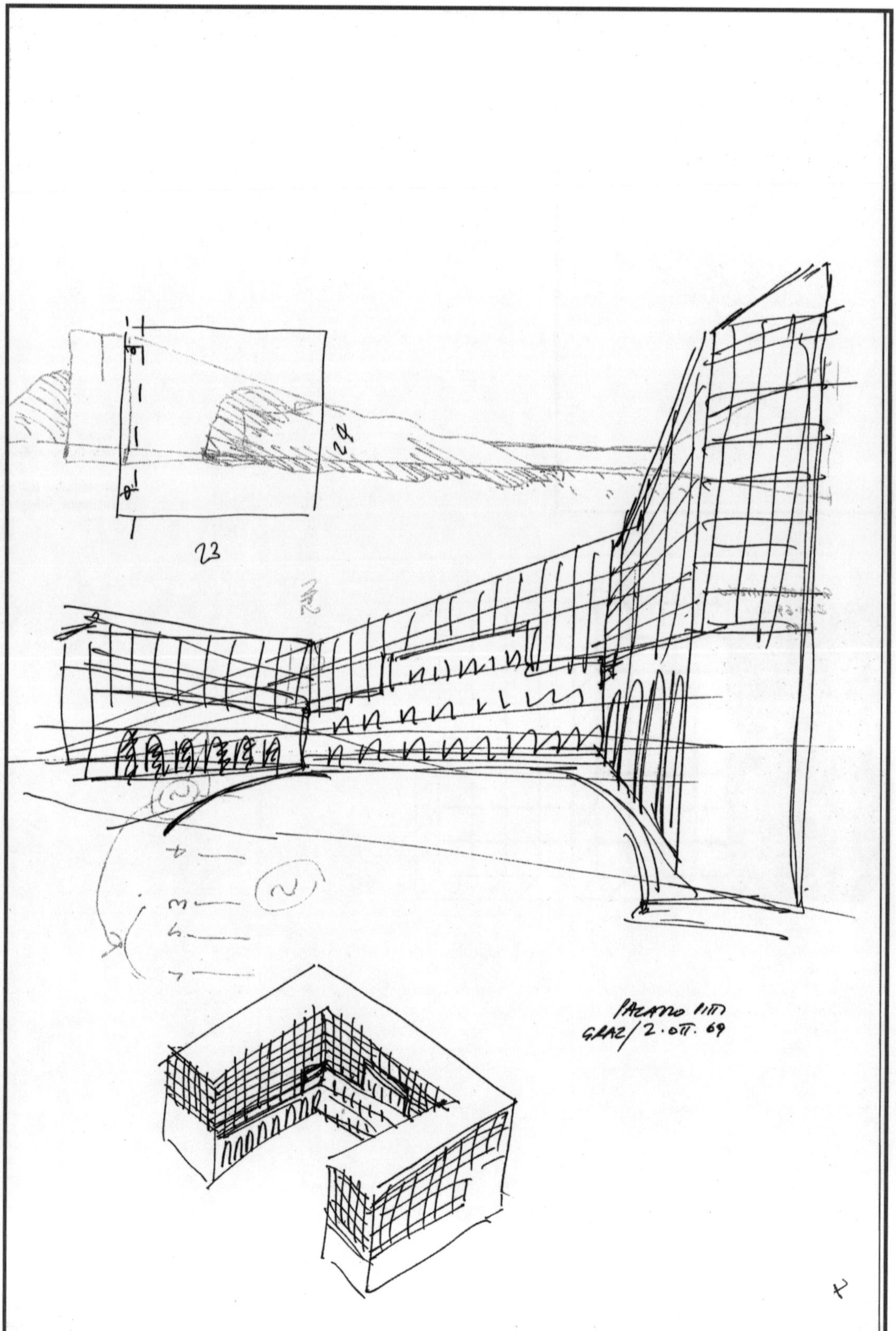
PALAZZO PITTI
GRAZ/ 2. OTT. 69

07. An attempt to summarize ten years of work: "When the projects and images, the texts and objects of *Radical Architecture* were being produced, *Radical Architecture* didn't exist. Now that the label exists, *Radical Architecture* has become extinct. In other words, it cannot be regarded as simply another movement or school with homogeneous, well-defined characteristics, but a series of situations, intentions, and acts.
Its various modes of being included architecture, design, art, communication [...] but also happenings, agitation, philosophy, and politics. The rejection of the discipline and the destruction of its specificity were its liberating techniques. Irony, provocation, paradox, false syllogism and logical extrapolation, terrorism, mysticism, humanism, reduction, and the pathetic were the categories employed, depending on the situation, whilst continuous repositioning, discontinuity (UFO), dialectical overcoming, and 'the Knight's move' (Menna) proved to be the driving forces.
For Superstudio, today, the methods of analysis and action have changed: cultural anthropology, research on man and his intellectual and material creations, attempts at conscious modification of the environment and of ourselves, are all part of a process of permanent education that involves us entirely. Visible evidence of these efforts is thin on the ground (the mirror that endlessly multiplied such images has been smashed to smithereens), but through an engagement with everyday life, the fusion (the identity) between memory and project, work and education, the individual and the political is slowly but surely taking shape.
Through its critical, destructive, and liberating activities, *Radical Architecture* has laid the foundations for this fusion.
Over and above the paper graveyard it has left behind, it is this, we think, that made it worthwhile."

[18.07.77 From "Com'era ancora bella l'architettura nel 1966... (Superstudio e l'Architettura Radicale, dieci anni dopo)", in *Spazio-Arte*, nos. 10-11, 1977]

Superstudio a Middelburg
[Superstudio in Middelburg]

01. On November 4, 1966, the river Arno invaded Florence: this turned into the worst flood of the century, and the water reached a depth of nearly six metres in the Santa Croce area. Superstudio was born on the same day, because, unaware of the water encroaching on the city streets, I spent nearly all day drawing up the first Superstudio manifesto. Then at five o'clock, the water reached my studio. The first person to notice this coincidence was Arata Isozaki in an essay entitled "Superstudio and the traces of the flood". Superstudio was a situationist movement that used the traditional tools of architecture (drawings and projects) to create a critique not only of architecture itself with its current ideas, but also of society in general. Superstudio used the rhetorical devices of metaphor and allegory and the tools of irony and imagination, moving in the no-man's-land between art and architecture in order to be able to make incursions into the fields of politics, sociology and philosophy. This is why it was truly avant-garde, using this term in its military sense (vanguard): a group that goes before the main force, destroying the first defences of the enemy, sacrificing themselves in order to open the way for the rest of the army.
We were trying to destroy the current system so as to prepare a new system free from divisiveness, from cultural colonisation, from violence and consumerism.
We were chasing a utopia: a world and lives freed from work, a "life without objects". Such works of ours as the *Continuous Monument* and *The Twelve Ideal Cities* used a negative utopia; others such as the *Histograms* pointed a way towards rationalism and minimalism, yet others, such as *Atti Fondamentali* [The Fundamental Acts] were a form of existential meditation. In 1973, we considered our duty as a vanguard over. We had not won the war but only a few battles.
We thought it was time to end the destructive phase and to start on a re-constructive phase. So, together with friends and the students at the university here (the Faculty of Architecture in Florence already had 13,000 students, 60% of whom came from places and countries other than Tuscany), we tried for a rebirth of architecture, enquiring into the simple tools of everyday life and extra-urban material culture. We were searching for the roots of creativity and necessity. We looked at elementary needs and desires (dreams).
Then, in 1979, I thought that the time for my apprenticeship, research and studies was over (I was 38), and I decided to become an ordinary architect.
Superstudio existed as a group until 1986, when we celebrated our twentieth anniversary (this is a very long time for an avant-garde group) and decide to disband. You can't be young forever. We are still friends, including Roberto Magris, who died on March 6, 2003, only a few days before this exhibition opened at the Design Museum in London. This current show is dedicated to his memory.
The exhibition has gathered together about 100 drawings made between 1966 and 1973, and some items documenting our research into material culture (1973-1978). There is nothing about our professional work (we designed objects, furniture, rooms, buildings and even trains) and nothing about what surrounded us that was antagonist to our work.
In their book *Superstudio: life without objects*, Peter Lang and William Menking attempt to explain the socio-cultural situation in which Superstudio worked and their relationship to the world of architecture and objects. I believe this book can answer to the curiosity and questions of young people who are rediscovering Superstudio within many avant-garde ideas today (Rem Koolhaas, Leon Krier and Bernard Tschumi were students of mine at the Architectural Association in London in 1970-71)...
It is more difficult to answer the question that these same young people, especially in the Netherlands, ask me: how did Natalini go from Superstudio to the work he is doing today? (His anti-modernism?)
My work today still stems largely from my early work, although it is quite difficult to find its traces...
My work is still anti-utopian, if the only utopia left to us is globalisation. Today architecture has been homogenised by a cynical and useless experimentalism: the only possible reaction is thus a return to order, or rather to tradition (which is a consolidated patrimony of experiments that have had long-term success).
So, we want to oppose the utopia of globalisation with the harshness of small local worlds and a great longing for beauty.
Superstudio's work was needed in the sixties, and what I have done in the Netherlands was needed

Superstudio, completion of Palazzo Pitti, from *Quaderni Neri*, 1969

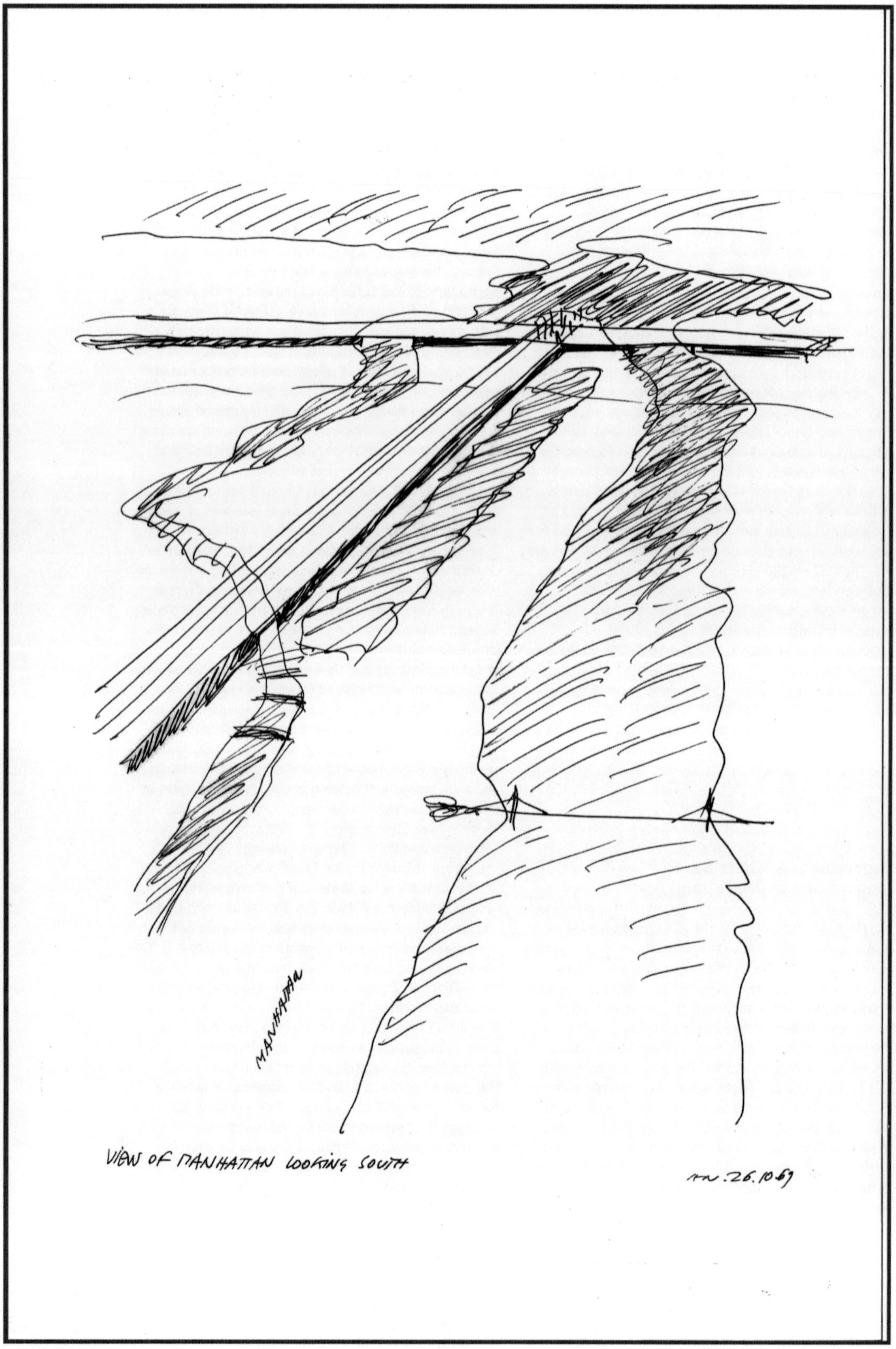
MANHATTAN
VIEW OF MANHATTAN LOOKING SOUTH
AN. 26.10.69

in the nineties and for the beginning of the new century. Then, we needed a revolution, a way of breaking with the established culture of the time; today, all ideologies having departed, we need to work against ultra-liberalism and consumerism, against the too-fast pace of fashion and empty aesthetics void of content, against the cult of personality and useless experimentation.
After our avant-garde years, I thought I had been sufficiently vaccinated against the disease of modernity, and so I have not been touched by the eclecticism of the post-modern movement, nor by the technological baroque of High-tech, and neither by constructivist post-expressionism. Now, I am watching while minimalist chic and functionalism, so exalted by super-modernism, pass by...
Ulysses had himself tied to the mast of his ship so that he could not follow the sirens' calls, but I have not done this, nor have I stopped my ears with wax like his sailors. So, every day I hear the beguiling voices of magazines and the enthusiasm and passion of my students and the people I work with.
I know very well that the fact that I have made the decision to renounce all contemporary experimentation automatically excludes me from the race for success (and celebrity), but I believe that there are much greater values than those consisting of the "new". These values are those of a civilised and dignified city, able to make the change to today's world without losing its heritage of beauty and human dimension. These are the values of a form of architecture calm and with solid bases, that can both reassure us and protect us from the attacks of weather and the human race.
The buildings that I have designed in the last ten years have been based on the idea of resistance against all this. Since 1979, I have been working on Europe's historical cities. I have been faced with differing histories and present situations. Books and journals show me a world in which architecture is capable only of producing novelty and difference, with no attention paid to sites or people, not a really needed architecture, created only to satisfy a desire for self-affirmation, using the methods of marvel created through being different and ugly.
Thus, the only avant-garde position today is to try and re-affirm the uniqueness of every single place, need, hope and the memory of those who have been here before us. Not a search for useless originality, but for a necessary return to our origins. My work aspires to a timeless normality.
I would like to vanish into my buildings. I would like that these buildings vanish into their city context and become a landscape in which we could all live without stress.

[18.09.04 from *Superstudio: the Middleburg lectures*, a cura di V. Byvanck, De Vleeshal: Zeeuws Museum, Middelburg 2005. Adolfo Natalini, translation by Frances Brunton]

Autobiografia architettonica
[Architectural autobiography]

01. *Is it possible to construct an itinerary of your work through projects and constructions, both chronologically, and according to theoretical and linguistic meaning, linked with each individual experience?*

Wow! That is a hefty question! I am sorry that I have been prattling on until now about marginal or private matters (in the end, who is interested in an architect's private thoughts? People are only interested in the architecture, whether completed or not... the rest is material for the analyst, confessor, or patient lover). Between 1966 and 1972, I was completely involved with Superstudio in the neo-avant-garde architectural movement. Now, while waiting for some "supplement" to come and explain to us what and how we were, it seems to me to have been a situationist movement that responded to different situations with different behaviour, while continuing a global (three dimensional) criticism of architecture, culture and society.
Then, between 1972 and 1978, with the Superstudio group, several friends, and a large number of university students, I worked on the anthropological refoundation of architecture, using a range of different disciplines (anthropology, art, literature, philosophy, and politics).
After 1978, I felt that my years of learning and wandering had reached their conclusion, and I began the laborious path towards architecture, detaching myself slowly and painfully from my former travelling companions, and desperately looking for opportunities to design and construct new projects.

[30.10.90]

02. *Constructions*

I began construction projects very late: I was thirty-eight when I began the project for the Banca di Alzate Brianza. I knew this would be a fatal encounter: I was afraid that my ideas would remain frozen in stone as if under the gaze of some Medusa. I wanted to evoke my "figures of stone", but was afraid of making a slip-up between *lapis* (pencil) and *lapide* (headstone). My progress in approaching construction was long and slow: my project designs seemed to be weighed down, insecure and their feet were rooted in the ground. Yet, I felt that it was the only way they could become reality, something tangible among other tangible things, stone among other stone. It was the only way I would have been able to contribute towards that slow transformation in which I felt progressively more engaged. Fascinated by the preparatory work on site, I remembered the rituals of taking possession of the land: tracing the furrow, laying the cornerstone... but also the foundation piles in the Netherlands, and knotted grass in field corners in Japan.
I followed the construction works during the toil and effort, and then saw them miraculously completed. Found it painful to move away, surrendering the buildings to others. I would return to see the buildings and found them younger than I was – as I was getting older. Construction was a job that brought me comfort and reassurance in its choral unity: so many skills working together. Even when I had to defend a building, I felt that I too, was defended in turn. I was surprised by the transformation created by a building in some space, and yet I had never sought traumatic transformations or made incongruously assertive claims. I always sought to leave the lightest of traces, and often I managed to build things that seemed to have always existed there. Basically, I too would have liked to become a landscape.

03. *You are, as they say, on the crest of the wave; to what do you owe your success? Are you satisfied with your career, or would you have preferred to do something else, or more?*

Superstudio,
Continuous Monument in New York, from *Quaderni Neri*, 1969

I don't feel I am on the crest of a wave, no do I feel I have been especially successful. In twenty-six years of total, obsessive and painful dedication to architecture, I have designed a number of buildings that you can almost count on the fingers of one hand. Between 1973 and now, I have taught (in Italy and abroad) about a thousand students for each of those fingers, but only a few have become architects. I have written two books and dozens of pages for specific occasions. Since 1979, I have designed 120 projects, a good number of interiors, pieces of furniture, and objects. My projects have been widely published, but very few have been produced. Success does not depend on the quantity, but in the quality of the work and the capacity to make an impact on the real world, and I do not feel very confident as far as these aspects are concerned. On the contrary, I have so many doubts that I often ask myself whether, given the results, sacrificing so much for my work may not have been a tragic mistake.

However, even though I have not been very successful, I have produced a lot of work: I put this production down to perseverance and tenacity, and after all, "Genie ist fleissig" [Genius is diligence] as the Germans say, and I have worked a lot in Germany.

If I look back at the years between 1979 and today, leaving aside my initial period working on the neo-avant-garde architectural movement with Superstudio and the second period on the anthropological refoundation of architecture, it seems like one, long, uninterrupted workday. If I have achieved anything, it has been due to my daily commitment (almost like breathing), and to the dedication and talent of my few and irreplaceable collaborators: Fabrizio Natalini (with Superstudio since 1971 and with me since 1979), Nazario Scelsi, Gaetano Martella and Marco Magni (to name only those who are currently working in via del Salviatino).

Lastly, I owe a great deal to my friends Vittorio Savi and Pierluigi Nicolin (critics, writers and architects), to Roberto Barni (painter), as well as an increasing inclination towards a certain realism from which so many dreams continue to emerge (despite my efforts to supress them).

[08.92, from the interview by P. Morgera, "20 domande... a Adolfo Natalini", in *Archi & Colonne*]

04. *An architectural autobiography*

I was born in Pistoia in 1941. The family of my father, Adelmo, had farmed the same land for seven hundred years, then my father became a clerical worker and so we moved to several different towns in Tuscany because of his work. My mother had been a teacher, but then dedicated herself to the family. She was very good-natured and her name was Solange.

I went back to Pistoia during my high school years, and there, I found strong friendships and great dreams, and I decided to become a painter. Our group, Barni, Ruffi and then Buscioni, was dubbed "The Pistoia School" by Cesare Vivaldi. Later I thought that perhaps art was not a socially relevant occupation, and I decided to become an architect, as if that would change the world. Between the ages of 20 and 25, I was a passable painter and a bad architectural student.

In 1960, I left my provincial life in Pistoia for Florence, attracted by Brunelleschi, Buontalenti, Masaccio and Pontormo, convinced that Florence was the heart of art and architecture. I have obstinately continued to cultivate these illusions all these years, now and then succumbing to bitter pessimistic reflections like the cycling champion, Bartali, who would say each time he lost: "Everything's wrong; well have to start all over again", but he would keep on pedalling. Perhaps Savi was right when he maintained that in 1534, when Michelangelo left Florence for Rome, architecture abandoned the city as well...

I graduated in Florence in 1966; I had studied from the books by Le Corbusier and Kahn. On the day of the great flood in Florence (4.11.1966) I founded Superstudio, a group of architects who were the initiators of a neo-avant-garde movement now known as *Radical Architecture*, and officially recognised in books and museums. For twenty years, Superstudio was involved in a critical work on the boundary between art and architecture, between sociology, philosophy, and politics, using paradox and irony to construct its premonitory negative utopias: *Continuous Monument, The Twelve Ideal Cities*, and five films in the series: *Atti Fondamentali*. Superstudio demonstrated that it was possible to apply social criticism to institutions and the system using the instruments of art and architecture. In the 1960s, we thought we could change the world, and thought that a revolution was possible by changing social systems and above all, behaviour.

Later we reduced our aspirations, and since it was impossible to carry out a revolution with architecture, we attempted a revolution in architecture.

For many years, I spoke about architecture without involving construction (1966-1973). That is, I spoke about architecture without concretely constructing it. At the end of the 1960s and beginning of the 1970s, we spoke about imaginary, immaterial, reflected architecture... Architecture on paper and conceptual architecture. Drawing and writing assumed a role of regent or substitute for an architecture that was absent, missing, (murder or suicide?) and for an architecture that was still to appear.

We theorised on the correlation of architecture and life (the Superstudio film made in 1972 concludes by predicting that our own lives will form our only work of art), and we established the correlation between the architect and architecture. This sums up my work with Superstudio, avant-garde group, initiator of the so-called *Radical Architecture*: architects without architecture.

Between 1973 and 1978, I focussed on an anthropological refoundation of architecture, studying extra-urban material culture (objects of everyday use and architecture without architects). With my friends from Superstudio, with Alessandro Poli, Lorenzo Netti and Michele De Lucchi, and my university students, we analysed the world of objects, from those for everyday use to industrially manufactured objects. We were architects without architecture who studied architecture without architects.

In 1979, I felt it was time for me to end this period of study and research and decided it was time I became an architect. I used every project design opportunity as an experimental subject, and I focussed on historic cities in Italy and in Northern Europe.

When I was working to become a constructive architect, I began to study cities and their buildings; the anthropological approach of the 1970s led me to focus my interest on actual places, leaving behind the destructive and utopic desires of avant-garde principles. This irritated my travelling companions and made professional architects suspicious, convinced that I was being ironic...

Meanwhile in 1982, Electa published a monography on Superstudio, confirming the historical importance of an experience that was formally terminated in 1986

Proposal for the reconstruction of the area of the Wailing Wall in Jerusalem. Preparatory sketches for information signs from *Quaderni Neri*, 1982

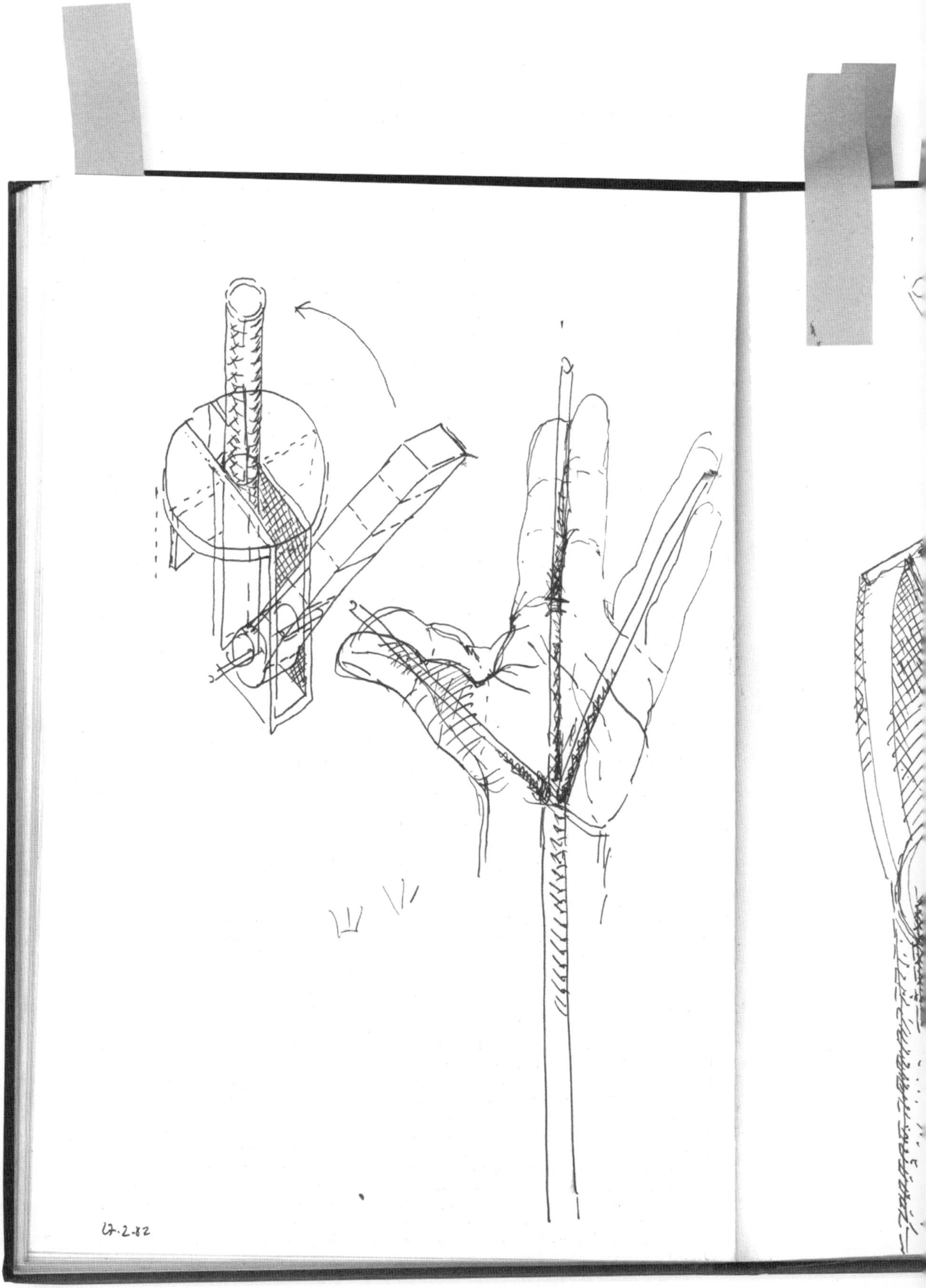
17.2.82

(twentieth anniversary of the floods and the foundation). In 1984, I published *Figure di pietra - Figures of stone*, a collection of project designs and fragments of poetic text. Then in 1989, a book of projects, *Architetture raccontate* which was followed in 1996 by *Natalini Architetti. Nuove architetture raccontate* where Natalini Architetti refers to the studio in via Salviatino where Fabrizio Natalini (same name but not related) and I began working in 1991.
These books contained projects and buildings with an increasingly greater focus on a traditional approach, through movements like the reconstruction of European cities and critical regionalism. In 1989, Pier Luigi Nicolin commented that Natalini had always been an estremist: excessive in his avant-garde radicalism and excessive in his pretentious traditionalism.
I would have liked to be the architect of a small town, or in any case, the architect of my town. I have always thought that architecture was a non-migratory art, like agriculture, and that architects (and human beings in general) should not travel.
The lack of architectural opportunities forced me to look elsewhere, travelling around Italy and abroad. So I worked in Austria, France, and Germany (from 1974, through the 1980s and after) travelling northward as far as Tromsø in Norway, inside the Arctic Circle.
I will try to define the route taken during my attempt to a closer approach to architecture, by listing a few projects.
The projects for the Centre of Frankfurt (the Römerberg zone) and for the area in front of the Wailing Wall in Jerusalem (and later, the reconfiguration of the archaeological area of the piazza in Fidenza) were archaeological projects – in other words, project based on time and memory aimed at making layers of archaeological traces visible in historic city centres.
The house on the corner of the Saalgasse in Frankfurt (completed poorly this year with certain essential parts left unfinished) was an investigation into the possibility of rhetorical figures applied to construction.
The Alzate Brianza and Zola Predosa buildings assessed ways in which locality and construction materials can generate an architecture that, in turn, can generate a sense of place. The large complexes for the market of Pistoia and the sports centre at Gorle (near Bergamo) were experiments in practical architecture, considering the idea of distribution, function and economy as the fundamental core of the project and on the capacity of structuring the building in differently configured parts to answer different needs.
For me, the Teatro della Compagnia in Florence was a (small but extremely important) experiment on how classical architecture can continue to communicate through a "figure theatre".
The project for the Teatro di Rimini (a taxing job that I have been working on with my friends since 1985 when we won the competition) allowed me to broaden my investigations into classical architecture as a generator of urban sense of place (similar to what I attempted in other projects in Karlsruhe and Stuttgart).
Recently, in Leffe (in Val Seriana) I designed a retirement home for the elderly as a reflection on the fragility of life and old age and on the reassuring nature of traditional construction. A similar reflection was the subject for a project in Tuscany for the expansion of a monumental cemetery. In several projects for Florence and surrounding areas, I have been focussing on what Pierluigi Nicolin described as my "obsession for *firmitas* [stability], wavering between Durand-style classical tendencies and a more modern Collage City style..."
Lastly, in Ferrara, "city of a hundred wonders", home of Biagio Rossetti and Metaphysics, I designed the corner of a block in the historical centre, composed of an open pedestrian space to provide visibility for the underlying archaeological elements, and three connected buildings with different configurations. In this project (like all those of recent years), I focussed my attention much more closely on the physical elements, seeking to enter the construction process more intently. I try to study endless details to compile a kind of "architects' manual" that I have always missed, as is obvious in the pages that follow...
This covers the work route followed in the past ten years with Fabrizio Natalini and my very few but exceptional collaborators. Regarding the route we intend to follow in our workshop in Salviatino, that is still an open question.
I have been working in the Netherlands since 1991 (as is described in *Quaderni Olandesi*). The Netherlands is a small and unique country. They have a saying: "God created the world but the Dutch created the Netherlands." The historic cities where I worked are different from one another but share the same desire for survival, renewal and improvement. It would be superficial to think that in German cities, renovation is limited to destruction caused during the war, because much renovation currently underway mainly concerns post-war reconstruction. Just as it is superficial to think that renovation in the Netherlands is limited to recovering land from the sea, because most of the reconstruction relates to buildings dating from the 1960s...
There is a desire for beauty that alternates between nostalgia for the past and the aspiration/hope for a different future. This is translated by a well-ordered, programmed and shared procedure where urban planning and architecture play a risky and cognizant role.
I have kept small sketches of each of these places (some in sketchbooks, others in tiny jotters, and some that are already in the book of sketches published by Motta). In the future, I know that these sketches will recall all these days of work.
An author once wrote that the only true life is that which has been written, and I would add, which has been drawn.
So the drawings and writings are only registrations, exorcisms and incantations against the passing of time...
Between 1991 and now (2005), I have worked in about twenty Dutch cities. During this time, I worked in many other cities in Italy and abroad. However, the Netherlands has a special unified dimension (that is both domestic and heroic in its battle with the sea) that made me feel that all Dutch cities were like a single city despite their diversity.
One unifying element was the unanimous participation of our clients, from the authorities to the community. Projects are developed "in public" with an endless series of directions and corrections which, in the end, made me feel "at home". So my phobia about travelling and my constant feeling of being "foreign" found some slight consolation and became easier to bear. On the other hand, the solitude of constant travel was mitigated by the number of people who worked with me, and in fact, "my" work has progressively become "our" work, gradually involving a greater number of people beginning with Fabrizio Natalini at the Salviatino

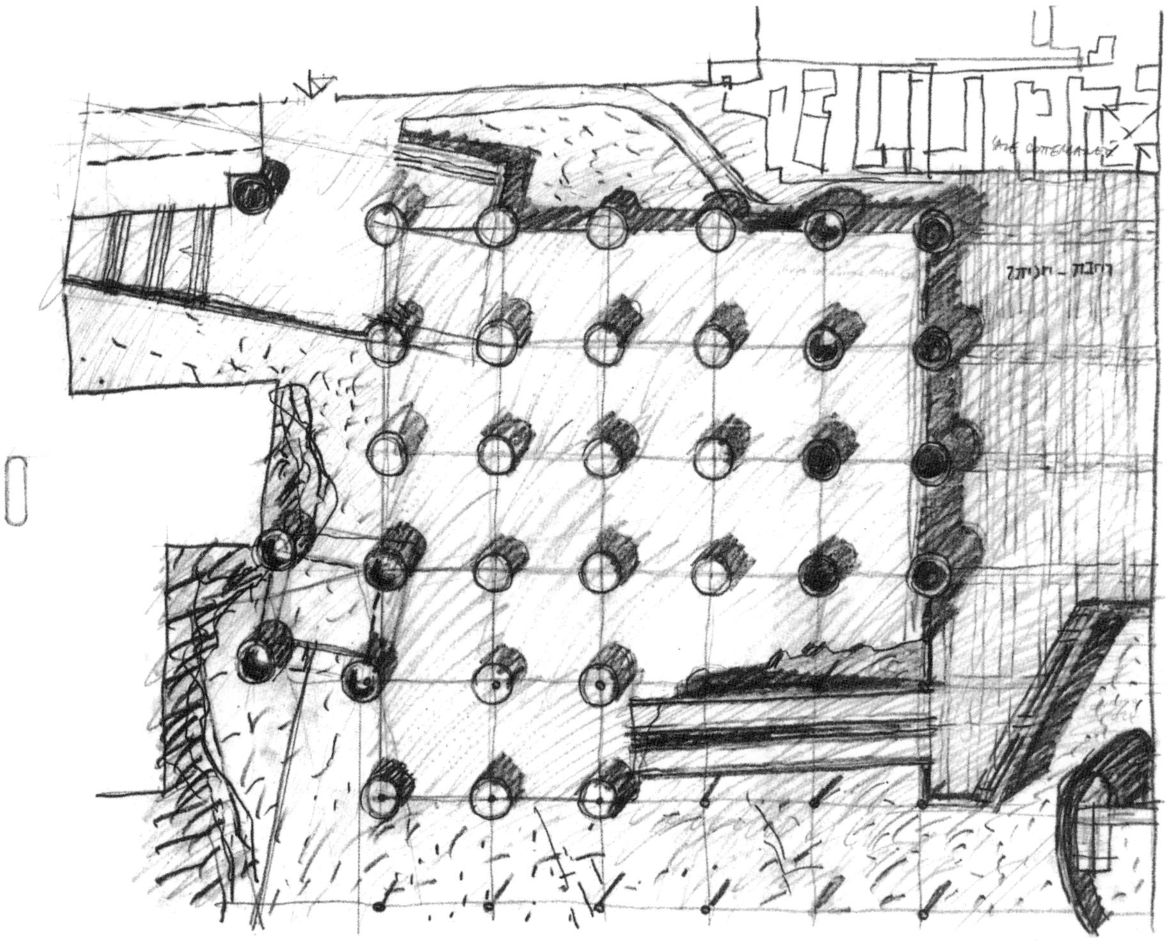

Proposal for the reconstruction of the area of the Wailing Wall in Jerusalem. Preparatory sketches for the upper plaza, 1982

Proposal for the reconstruction of the area of the Wailing Wall in Jerusalem. Preparatory sketches for information signs in archaeological zone, 1982

Proposal for the reconstruction of the area of the Wailing Wall in Jerusalem, Migdal David, from *Quaderni Neri*, 1982

studio in Florence, Corinne Schrauwen in the Bethaniendwarsstraat studio in Amsterdam, and all our collaborators, as well as the structural engineers, installers, specialists, builders, clients, and building control authorities... and so on, as well as whole communities who were called to judge, advise, and modify the projects.
Perhaps this is the reason why I am so attached to the original and very personal beginnings and traces of every project. In the midst of projects and constructions, focussed on interpretation and mediation, but often also conflict and wrangling with the numerous generators of this collective work, my sketched and written diaries keep me rooted to the nascent state, sensations, and emotions, elements seen or imagined, that would otherwise be lost... and with them, I am afraid I would be lost as well.
[2005]

05. *Post scriptum. Projects by Natalini Architetti*
I reread these two autobiographical passages: the first written in 1985, and the second in 2005: I will add some details on completed projects.
Our firm, Natalini Architetti, has built residential complexes, additions to small historical centres in San Casciano (between Florence and Siena) and in Doesburg (on the Ijssel river, in the Netherlands), aimed at providing pleasant, serene housing.
In other projects in Florence and Calenzano, in Pisa, Ferrara and Cesena, after studying the neighbourhoods with their wide variety of residential styles, we focussed our efforts on "an identity in uniformity" (as defined by Giancarlo Cataldi).
In the University Campus projects of Porta Tufi, in Siena, and Novoli, in Florence, we tried to complement the different characteristics of the sites in question. In Siena, close to the city walls, the building is solidly rooted in the hill and opens up the view towards the valley. In Novoli, the University is composed of urban buildings in small blocks, in accordance with the guideline plan set out by Leon Krier.
For the reconstruction projects in the historical city centres of Groningen, The Hague and Zwolle, our buildings are based on the compact city concept, defined by the streets and accessible to the community from public squares. These projects pay homage to great traditional Dutch architecture, recalling the domestic and urban atmospheres of paintings by Vermeer and Saenredam.
The Boscotondo project in Helmond is composed of houses and public administration buildings constructed around a new circular park, and in Haverleij, a residential complex in a kind of fortified castle formation set on a lake. In Roermond, we built a small tower on a river to echo the towers in the historical city centre.
Lastly in Florence, we worked on the projects for the Nuovi Uffizi Museum and for the extension of the Museo dell'Opera del Duomo. The Western Staircase of the Uffizi is incorporated inside a tower. The work on the Cathedral museum is almost completed.
Our other projects are in Germany and other countries further afield.
[14.11.14]

Il quaderno di scuola

[School sketchbook]

—

Painting

1958-1968

In the summer of 1958, I took a night train from Pistoia and arrived in Venice at dawn. Crossing the entire city on foot, from the station to the Giardini, I felt like a pilgrim in the world of dreams, in a dream consisting of stones, water, and light. It was my first time in Venice. I was there to see the Biennale: I was seventeen years old and I wanted to become a painter. Licini was at the Biennale that year, with his *Amalassunte* [Amalasunthas] and his *Angeli Ribelli* [Rebel Angels]. I had written him a letter expressing all my admiration and enthusiasm. Though Licini never answered me (he died in October of the same year), I received many answers from that journey to Venice...

[A. Natalini, *Adolfo Natalini. Architetture raccontate*, Electa, Milan 1989, p. 154]

"Adolfo Natalini has had an intense and very promising career, considering his young age (he was born in 1941, while Ruffi was born in 1938 and Barni in 1939)...
Despite his youth, Natalini has already been painting for ten years and his experiences are quite similar to those of his friends: first figurative art, then action painting, then pop art. And for now he has stopped at pop art, aiming at strict reportage and using his usual photographic style, which, however, is rendered quite personal by his violent, expressionistic use of colour. There are affinities to Americans like Bob Stanley or Italians like Lombard, but Natalini has his own range of colours, harsh and Nordic: dark greens, yellows, violet, brick reds, anti-pretty colours, roughly combined in a grandiose manner, a little bit Mexican."

[C. Vivaldi, "La Scuola di Pistoia", in *Collage*, no. 6, 1966]

"Natalini was only briefly a member of the Scuola di Pistoia, which is a group of painters, and then he abandoned it for architecture, founding the subversive group Superstudio. He left a series of works that clearly belong to the pop movement. People on pedestrian crossings; faces in the middle of a crowd; sprinters crossing the finish line. Strong colour contrasts; attention to photographic technique; the use of sequence. With the vocation of a painter, he has managed to bring the experimental spirit of the avant-garde to the sector of architecture."

[A. Boatto, *Continuità. Arte in Toscana 1945-1967*, edited by A. Boatto, M&M, Montecatini 2002]

p. 27
Armstrong,
tempera on canvas,
diptych,
300x150 cm,
1964

pp. 28-29
Two great runners
Three great runners
tempera on canvas,
diptych,
300x150 cm,
1964

pp. 30-31
Pedestrian crossing
tempera on canvas,
diptych,
300x150 cm,
1964

pp. 30
Double portrait
tempera on canvas,
40x50 cm,
1964

pp. 31
Demonstration
enamel on canvas,
50x70 cm,
1965

Superstudio

1966-1986

A group of avant-garde architects consisting of Adolfo Natalini, Cristiano Toraldo di Francia, Roberto Magris, Gian Piero Frassinelli and Alessandro Magris, (with Alessandro Poli from 1970 to 1972), Superstudio was one of the main initiators of the so-called *Radical Architecture* movement. The group's later work concentrated on an effort to renew the anthropological foundations of architecture.
A rare example of longevity amongst avant-garde groups, the studio conducted twenty years of patient research, through design and construction, into objects, environmental design and architecture.
Superstudio conducted its architectural criticism through theoretical projects, including *One Design*, consisting of: *Histograms of Architecture* (three-dimensional diagrams), *A Catalogue of Villas*, and *The Continuous Momument* (a model for total urbanism); *The Twelve Ideal Cities* (dystopian stories aimed at analysing the lives of individuals in the urban environment); the film series *The Fundamental Acts: Life, education, ceremony, love, death* (an attempt to conduct an anthropological re-foundation of architecture).
From 1973 to 1975, Natalini was a member (co-founder) of Global Tools, a network of workshops for the development of collective creativity. From 1973 to 1978, he devoted himself to academic research and teaching, working on the project *Extra-Urban Material Culture*.
Superstudio's projects and writings have appeared in numerous publications and exhibitions throughout the world.
Selected books: *Superstudio, 1966-1982: storie, figure, architettura*, edited by G. Pettena, Electa, Florence 1982; *Superstudio & radicals*, edited by Superstudio & the Moriyama Editors Studio, Japan Interior Inc., Tokyo 1982; P. Lang - W.Menking, *Superstudio: life without objects*, Skira, Milan 2003; R. Gargiani, B. Lampariello, *Superstudio*, Laterza, Bari 2010.
Selected exhibitions: *Italy: The new domestic landscape*, Museum of Modern Art, New York, 1972; *Mindscapes, Sottsass & Superstudio*, Walker Art Center, Minneapolis and six other American museums, 1973; *Superstudio, Fragmente aus einem personlichen Museum*, Neue Galerie Graz, Galerie nach St. Stephan Vienna, Galerie in Taxis Palais, Innsbruck; *Superstudio Metaphors and Allegories*, Israel Museum, Jerusalem, 1982; *Superstudio 1966-82*, Galleria dell'Accademia. Florence, 1982; as well as several participations at the Venice Biennale, at the Triennale di Milano, at the major design exhibitions and at exhibitions on *Radical Architecture* from 1966 through today (*Architettura Radicale*, Cologne, Ville Urbane, Lyon, Valencia, 2000-2001; *The Changing of Avant-Garde*, MoMA, New York, Frankfurt a/M. 2002-2003; *Future City*, London, 2006, the Biennale of São Paulo, 2010, the Biennale of Venice, 1978, Biennale 2014).
Works by Superstudio are in the collections of such museums as the Museum of Modern Art in New York, the Israel Museum in Jerusalem, the Deutsches Architekturmuseum in Frankfurt am Main, the FRAC in Orleans, the Centre Pompidou in Paris, and the MAXXI in Rome.
In 2001, the Archivio Superstudio was founded in Florence to manage exhibitions and publications. The travelling exhibition *Superstudio: life without objects* began at the Design Museum, London (GB), in 2003, and it the same year it was distributed among three venues in New York: the Pratt Manhattan Gallery, Artists Space, and the Storefront for Art and Architecture. It continued in 2004 at the Williamson Gallery, in Pasadena, California, and the De Vleeshal, in Middelburg, Netherlands, while additional venues are planned.

Adolfo Natalini (Pistoia, 1941): graduated in architecture in 1966, he founded Superstudio together with Cristiano Toraldo di Francia in December 1966.
Cristiano Toraldo di Francia (Florence, 1941): graduated in architecture in 1967, he is a cofounder of Superstudio.
Roberto Magris (Florence, 1935-2003): Designer ADI, he graduated in architecture in 1975 and joined Superstudio in 1967.
Gian Piero Frassinelli (Porto S. Giorgio, Fermo, 1939): graduated in architecture in 1968, he joined Superstudio in 1968. Curator of the Archivio Superstudio since 2001.
Alessandro Magris (Florence, 1941-2010): graduated in architecture in 1970, he joined Superstudio in 1970.
Alessandro Poli (Fiesole, Florence, 1941): graduated in architecture in 1970, he was a member of Superstudio from 1970 to 1972.

p. 33
Superstudio and Hidden Architecture, Piazza di Bellosguardo, 1970.
From left: Alessandro Magris, Cristiano Toraldo di Francia, Gian Piero Frassinelli, Adolfo Natalini (Photo: Cristiano Toraldo di Francia)

p. 34
Lunch on a *Histogram*, 1971 (Photo: Cristiano Toraldo di Francia)

p. 35
Misura furniture series, 1971 (Photo: Cristiano Toraldo di Francia)

pp. 36-37
New New York, from the *Continuous Monument* series, 1969

p. 38
Rockefeller Center, from the *Continuous Monument* series, 1969

p. 39
San Martino alla Palma, from *SuperSurfaces*, 1971

pp. 40-41
The new Modena cemetery, from the *Fundamental Acts* series, 1971-72

FROM: LIFE / SUPERSURFACE
"SAN MARTINO ALLA PALMA" – SUPERSTUDIO 1971

Memory instead

1978

01. *Memory instead of life*
Each year someone engraves an event to remember into a bar in bronze (or copper or aluminium).
The bars are arranged in a row on the wall. The bars of the past years are already engraved with events. Those of the future years only have the date, while the bar corresponding to the present year becomes a medium on which to place "notes on events to remember" (photos, writings...).
A replica of the final bar of life is embedded into the wall of the person's tomb. In this way, the final year – which deletes everything – is replicated.

02. *Memory instead of objects*
Since 1975, I have been teaching a class (conducting actions) at the Faculty of Architecture in Florence regarding simple functional objects: sticks, knives, containers, clothing, chairs, mirrors and coffins. These objects, like the index-fossils of the palaeontologist, can make sense of layers of memory. They constitute the traces or the graphic evidence of behaviours, actions or projects. They bear witness to the past for future reference. They form a mental and material survival kit.
A photograph I once found in a book on the history of furnishings sparked a series of associations in my mind. It was a picture of the interior of a stone sarcophagus, showing the furniture that had belonged to the deceased.
The first association was the use, in death, of the same objects used by the living. The second association was that of living amongst stone objects: in death, the furniture is pushed against the walls.
The third association had to do with rendering immobile the objects of remembrance: memory, like a glimpse of the Medusa, petrified. I began choosing objects to remember; others chose, by their very presence, to be remembered by me. I rebuilt them as if in stone, in a survival chest divided into sections through archaeological rediscovery. I placed the chest in various rooms, confronting it with the surrounding objects and the architecture. Finally, on a beach, removing the sand that covered it, I discovered that the burial mound for the objects was identical to the burial mound for a man that Loos spoke about: "If in a wood we find a mound that is six feet long and three feet wide, with a stone at one end in the form of a pyramid, we become very serious and something inside us says: someone is buried here. This is architecture."

03. *Memory instead of architecture*
For many years my work has been architecture. I have designed, read, looked at, and built (very little). I have described many architectures by means of words and markings. I tried to remember four of them. The dimensional ratios became simplified, the details disappeared, and I forgot the structure and the materials. Once returned to paper, the works no longer had anything in common with the paper architectures from which they had originated. I rebuilt them in refractory clay and fired them. Then I wrapped them in white cloths tied with cords and protected them, one by one, in wooden boxes. The first of these architectures reproduces a Greek urn in the form of a house, found at Argos. The second is a house that I drew when I was five years old. The third is a house I designed when I still very much believed in making architecture. The fourth is a house that I built just when I thought I would not be making architecture anymore.

[A. Natalini, *Adolfo Natalini: La memoria invece*: tre mostre allo Studio Franca Pisani: Firenze, maggio 1978, *I quaderni bianchi*, Studio Franca Pisani, Florence 1978]

p. 42
Memory bars, from *Memory instead of Life*, 1978

p. 43
Survival chest, from *Memory instead of Objects*, 1978

p. 43
Four houses from Memory, from *Memory instead of Architecture*, 1978

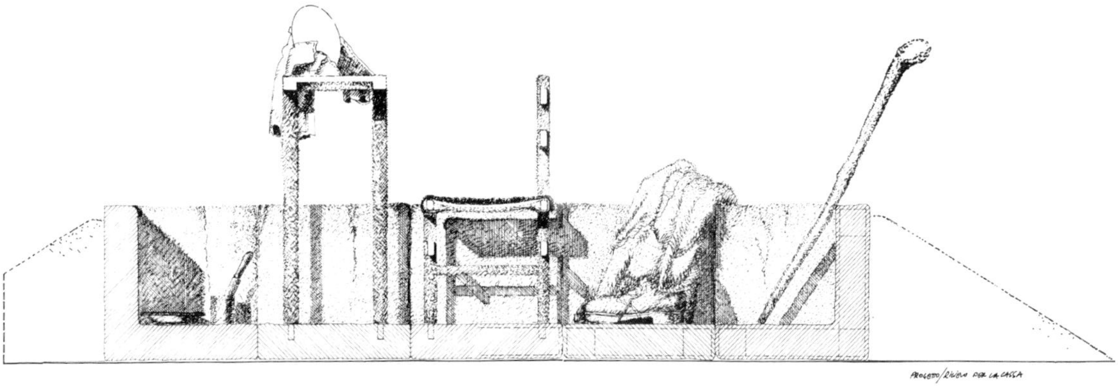

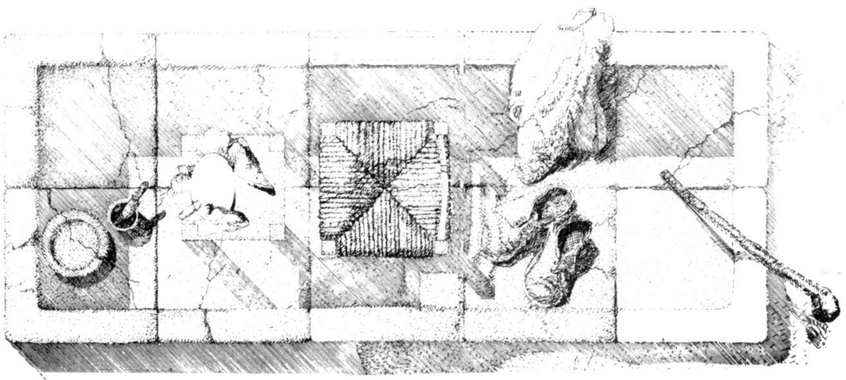

Extra-Urban Material Culture
La moglie di Lot [Lot's Wife] and *La coscienza di Zeno* [Zeno's Conscience]

1973-1978

01. "Since 1973, Superstudio has focused on academic research and teaching, abandoning the limelight and the pages of magazines. Since then, we have held courses on *The Motivations of Architecture*, *The Galaxy of Objects*, *Simple Functional Objects* and *Extra-Urban Material Cultures*. There was little left to destroy of the university system, and thus the programme of the neo-avantgardists, *The technical destruction of culture*, sounded inappropriate.
The dominant culture had already been liquidated: foreign students, students living far from home, working students, adherents of the '68 movement, hippies and Indiani Metropolitani, they all had other things on their minds.
The transformation of the University system, its becoming an educational system of the masses through the process of proletarianisation, its becoming a theatre of social struggle and of the development of political and survival strategies, has turned it into a key location (together with factories, farmlands, and cities).
Our University work consists in the analysis of the act of design (its motivations, how it is carried out and its relationships with the social and environmental context), together with the research of alternative methods and practices. As our field of investigation, we make use of simple functional objects, self-managed processes of transformation (such as agriculture and craftwork) and the extra-urban material cultures. We look at simple functional objects as if parts of a survival kit. We attempt to deeply understand their structure by means of critical inventories, reductive design, and hands-on use. The objects, acting as a mediator between us and the world, become a mental catalyst for processes of self-analysis, in a therapy aimed at unleashing creativity. We study and experience extra-urban material cultures as if they were entries in an enormous encyclopaedia (not exactly Diderot, nor even the *Whole Earth Catalogue*). For two years we studied tools and their relationship to work and to environmental transformations, and now we are examining household objects and their relationship to the lives of humans. For the next two years, we are planning a research project on energy and time (the support and the location of life). We use the anthropological method as a tool for analysis and interpretation.
Direct experience (doing as a way of thinking), hands-on manipulation, usage and behaviour are treated as tools for the reappropriation of ourselves and of the environment."

["Com'era ancora bella l'architettura nel 1966... (Superstudio e l'architettura radicale, dieci anni dopo)", in *Spazio Arte*, nos. 10-11, 1977]

02. At the Venice Biennale of 1978, Superstudio presented two works, a project and an analysis with a very literary double title: *La moglie di Lot* e *La coscienza di Zeno* [Lot's Wife and Zeno's Conscience].
La moglie di Lot consisted of a metal table that held five architectural models made of salt. Water dripping from a mobile structure slowly dissolved the models, revealing meaningful objects within.
"Architecture is to time as salt is to water."
La coscienza di Zeno was a research project on the life and the objects of a farmworker in the Maremma district of Tuscany, an attempt to reconstruct a sense of the process of design and use.

03. "There is no doubt about the date of the foundation of Superstudio, it was 4 December 1966, on occasion of the exhibition *Superarchitettura* in Pistoia. However, there are several versions regarding the date it ceased to exist.
The first version is 1973, after the three exhibitions *Italy: The New Domestic Landscape* at the MoMA in New York; *Superstudio: Fragmenten aus einem personlichen Museum* in Graz, Vienna and Innsbruck; and finally, *Sottsass Superstudio: Mindscapes* at the Walker Art Center Minneapolis and in five other museums in the United States. In fact, we wrote in 1979: 'From 1973, the group was particularly focused on research and teaching [...]: perhaps this is why in 1973 the studio almost completely ceased production of stories and images.'
The second version is 1978. After the period of radical architecture with Global Tools ended, Superstudio worked for the anthropological refoundation of architecture, through research – in the schools and elsewhere – into the extra-urban material culture, between 1973 and 1978. This second life of Superstudio terminated with the double work *La moglie di Lot* and *La coscienza di Zeno*, exhibited at the Venice Bienniale of 1978. *La moglie di Lot* is on display again, thirty-six years later, at this 2014 edition of the Biennale.
The third version is 1986. The exhibition at the Accademia in Florence in 1982 and the monograph published by Electa, *Superstudio 1966-1982. Storie, figure, architettura*, historicise the activities of the studio and bear witness to the existence of a third life that was terminated in 1986, with the consideration that twenty years is the biological limit for an avant-garde group."

[G. Mastrigli "Conversazione con Adolfo Natalini", 2 April 2014, in *Superstudio: the secret life of Continuous Monument*, edited by G. Mastrigli, Venice Biennale, Quodlibet, Macerata 2014]

pp. 44-45
Lot's Wife
Venice Biennale, 1978
(Photo: Cristiano
Toraldo di Francia)

p. 46
Zeno's Conscience,
Venice Biennale, 1978

p. 46
From *Tool catalogue, Extra-Urban Material Cultures*, 1973-78

p. 47
From *Tool catalogue, Extra-Urban Material Cultures*, 1973-78

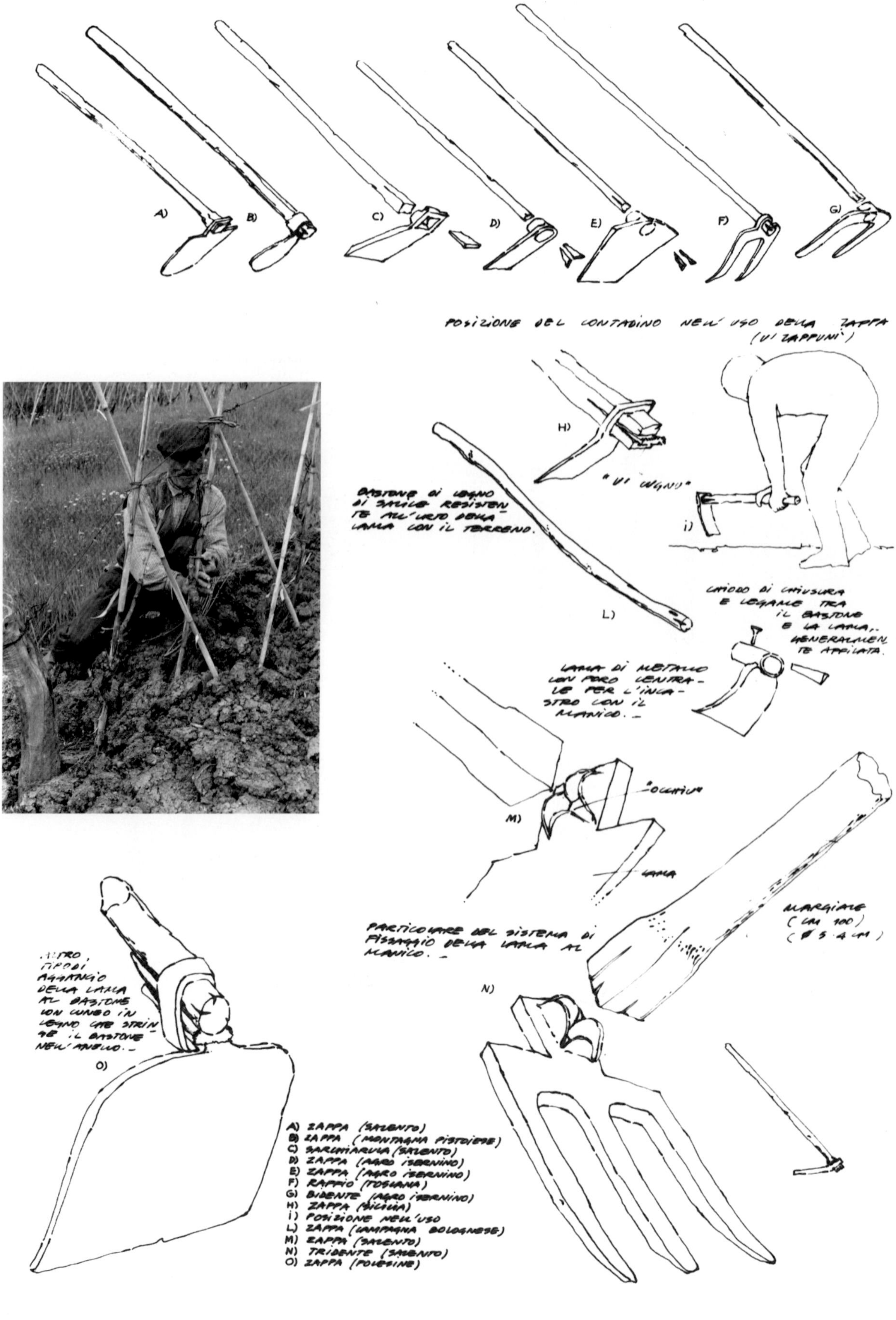
A)
B)
C)
D)
E)
F)
G)
POSIZIONE DEL CONTADINO NELL'USO DELLA ZAPPA
(U' ZAPPUNI')
H)
"U' CUGNU"
BASTONE DI LEGNO DI SALICE RESISTENTE ALL'URTO DELLA LAMA CON IL TERRENO.
i)
L)
CHIODO DI CHIUSURA E LEGAME TRA IL BASTONE E LA LAMA, GENERALMENTE APPILATA.
LAMA DI METALLO CON FORO CENTRALE PER L'INCASTRO CON IL MANICO.
OCCHIUM
M)
LAMA
MARGIALE
(CM 100)
(Ø 5.4 CM)
PARTICOLARE DEL SISTEMA DI FISSAGGIO DELLA LAMA AL MANICO.
N)
ALTRO TIPO DI AGGANCIO DELLA LAMA AL BASTONE CON CUNEO IN LEGNO CHE STRINGE IL BASTONE NELL'ANELLO.
O)
A) ZAPPA (SALENTO)
B) ZAPPA (MONTAGNA PISTOIESE)
C) SARCHIARULA (SALENTO)
D) ZAPPA (AGRO ISERNINO)
E) ZAPPA (AGRO ISERNINO)
F) RAFFIO (TOSCANA)
G) BIDENTE (AGRO ISERNINO)
H) ZAPPA (SICILIA)
i) POSIZIONE NELL'USO
L) ZAPPA (CAMPAGNA BOLOGNESE)
M) ZAPPA (SALENTO)
N) TRIDENTE (SALENTO)
O) ZAPPA (POLESINE)

A
B
C
D
E
F
G
H
A) FORCA IN LEGNO (MONTAGNA PISTOIESE)
B) FORCA IN LEGNO (CAMPAGNA BOLOGNESE)
C) FORCONE (TOSCANA)
D) ANTICA FORCA (EMILIA - ROMAGNA)
E) ANTICA FORCA (EMILIA - ROMAGNA)
F) FORCA (MONTAGNA PISTOIESE)
G) FORCONE (POLESINE)
H) FORCONE (CAMPAGNA BOLOGNESE)
I) SISTEMA PER PIEGARE LE FORCHE IN ABRUZZO.-

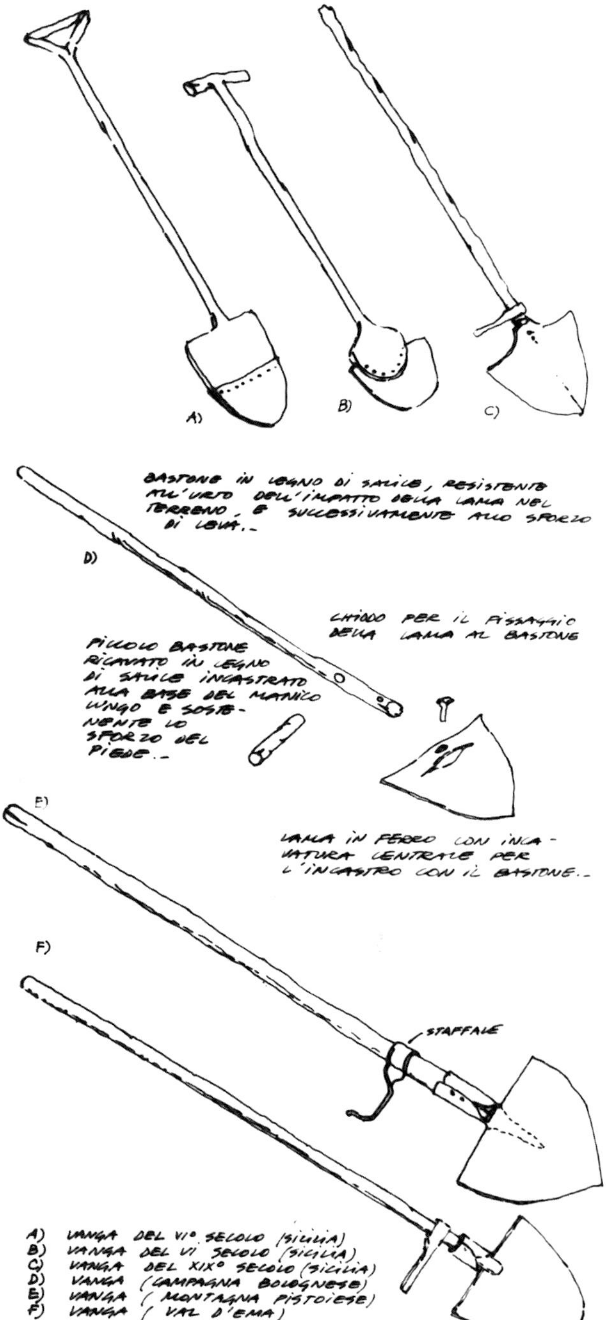
A)
B)
C)
BASTONE IN LEGNO DI SALICE, RESISTENTE ALL'URTO DELL'IMPATTO DELLA LAMA NEL TERRENO, E SUCCESSIVAMENTE ALLO SFORZO DI LEVA.-
D)
CHIODO PER IL FISSAGGIO DELLA LAMA AL BASTONE
PICCOLO BASTONE RICAVATO IN LEGNO DI SALICE INCASTRATO ALLA BASE DEL MANICO LUNGO E SOSTENENTE LO SFORZO DEL PIEDE.-
E)
LAMA IN FERRO CON INCAVATURA CENTRALE PER L'INCASTRO CON IL BASTONE.-
F)
STAFFALE
A) VANGA DEL VI° SECOLO (SICILIA)
B) VANGA DEL VI SECOLO (SICILIA)
C) VANGA DEL XIX° SECOLO (SICILIA)
D) VANGA (CAMPAGNA BOLOGNESE)
E) VANGA (MONTAGNA PISTOIESE)
F) VANGA (VAL D'EMA)

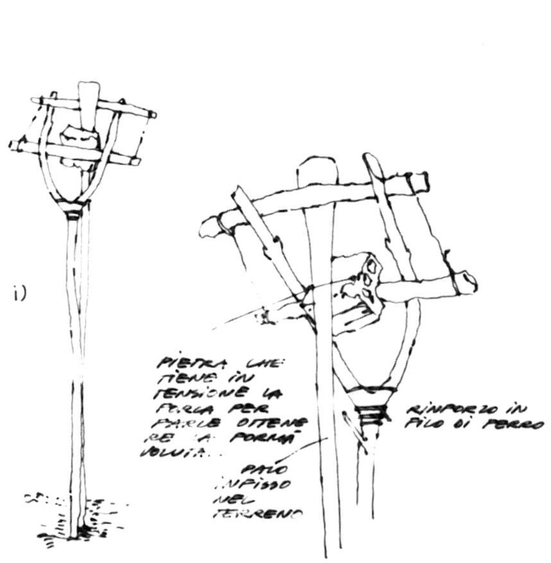
I)
PIETRA CHE TIENE IN TENSIONE LA FORCA PER FARLE OTTENERE LA FORMA VOLUTA.
PALO INFISSO NEL TERRENO
RINFORZO IN FILO DI FERRO

In the vicinity of the area of the Wailing Wall in Jerusalem

1980-82

On the invitation of the Israel Museum of Jerusalem we worked (from January 1980 to March 1982) on a project for the reorganization of the Wailing Wall area of Jerusalem. The West Wall of the Temple Hill (a wall with many names, the Wailing Wall or, as the Jews call it, Western Wall, *Hakotel Hamaravi*) is a meeting point of peoples, men, histories, memories, dramas and hopes. The Temple itself has been twice destroyed (on both occasions on the same day: the ninth day of month of Av) and this section of the enclosing wall has been a place of devotion for Jews until the sixth century. At certain periods access has been made difficult, at other times it has been blocked altogether. Following the reunification of Jerusalem in 1967, a vast piazza of 20,000 sym was created in front of the Wailing Wall, in place of the narrow court-like space of about 3.60x20 m which had existed there as a place of devotion for centuries before. At the same time, a vast archaeological site was opened up, in continual expansion, and divided from the piazza by the access ramp leading to Temple Hill. Based on specifications provided by the Ministry of Religious Affairs, various projects have been elaborated: by Louis Kahn (1967), Isamu Noguchi, Moshe Safdie (1974, carried out in part) and finally by Maestro and Fisher. Despite all these projects, the area is still an open wound in the ancient city which calls out for attention.
Four possible approaches:
1. An urban fabric of places, houses and streets, with the area for prayer in a street running alongside the wall. Objection: Jewish tradition would be against a place of prayer as a substitute for the Temple; at most only the beginnings of a construction would be accepted, to be completed only when the time is ripe.
2. A piazza for large-scale events and ceremonies, giving off a more intimate area for prayer and defining and delimiting the archaeological area. Objection: this would create divisions and contrasts between the different uses of the same places.
3. Extension of the archaeological area to include the whole piazza, providing a lightweight structure (permanent or temporary) for public events and placing the area of prayer at the level of the Herodian road and of the underground spaces. Objection: the area of prayer has never been at this level and temporary structures would look out of place in the stone-built city.
4. A synchretistic scheme, bringing together ages and places, demands, needs and desires. A project built around allegories and metaphors, with the stone used both as tool for construction and sign: an eloquent architecture, a diagram to decode, following perhaps the instructions of the mysterious measurer foretold by the prophet Ezekiel: "And be-hold, there was a man, whose appearance was like the appearance of brass, with a line of flax in his hand, and a measuring reed."
So, though eloquent architecture often turns out more like stuttering architecture, we decided to run the risk. The archaeological zone is extended to the whole piazza and organized by means of a grid. At the intersections we placed "indicators": vertical elements, a cross between tree, column and sign, carrying information about the level of excavation and findings (alluding also to an infinite vertical and temporal extension of the horizontal surface of the piazza). In the area facing the Wailing Wall, at the grid intersections we placed structural elements ("pillars") carrying a platform on two levels. The lower level ("the lower piazza") is destined to be the area of prayer, concentrated on the Wall but protected by a second wall with openings towards the underlying archaeological levels. The upper level ("the upper piazza") is a place for celebrations, ceremonies, meetings and public events. At the grid intersections on the upper piazza "shade towers" stand up, in the guise of perforated stone cylinders, giving light and ventilation to the archaeological levels below and also creating areas of shade and points of meeting. They also provide support for meditation and carry urban connotations: the result is a city at many levels, crisscrossed by the sun, the wind and the steps of men. Access to the area of prayer is via a ramp crossing the underground spaces or via a second (double) ramp from the upper piazza.

Access to the Temple Esplanade is via the Magrabite Gate and a stair contained within a curved volume built against the wall. On the Temple Esplanade a rock is within a dome which is within the wall of seven arches, which is within the wall of the tem-ple which is within the walls of the city, which is within (at the centre, on old maps) the world. The open space in front of the wall is therefore both inside and outside; outside the Temple, inside the city, but at the same time inside the Temple and outside the city. The holy places are places apart, yet at the same time they are places of union. The open space is a place between the holy and the secular, a place between past and future, between memory and hope, ruin and design. The design is therefore about a zone that is both inside and outside space and time; an intersection of space, an interstice of time. We are working between spaces and between times.

[A. Natalini, *Figures of stone*, Electa, Milan 1984]

p. 49
Jerusalem, Near the Wailing Wall, from *Quaderni Neri*

p. 50
Jerusalem, Light and Ventilation Towers from *Quaderni Neri*

p. 51
Prayer area

p. 52
Information signs

p. 53
The Wailing Wall and prayer area

p. 54
Walls and towers, Axonometric view

p. 55
The wailing wall and shade towers

pp. 56-57
Arial photo showing layout

p. 57
Axonometric view

p. 58
The upper plaza with ventilation towers

p. 59
The archaeological zone with information signs

Project
Adolfo Natalini with David Palterer;
Client
Israel Museum, Jerusalem.

HA'KOTEL MA'ARAVI
THE WESTERN WALL JERUSALEM
597

LE TORRI DEL VENTO E DELLA LUCE
COME CASE SUL SULLA PIAZZA.
4.12
399

28.3.82

JERUSALEM - il muro del pianto - zona della preghiera
585

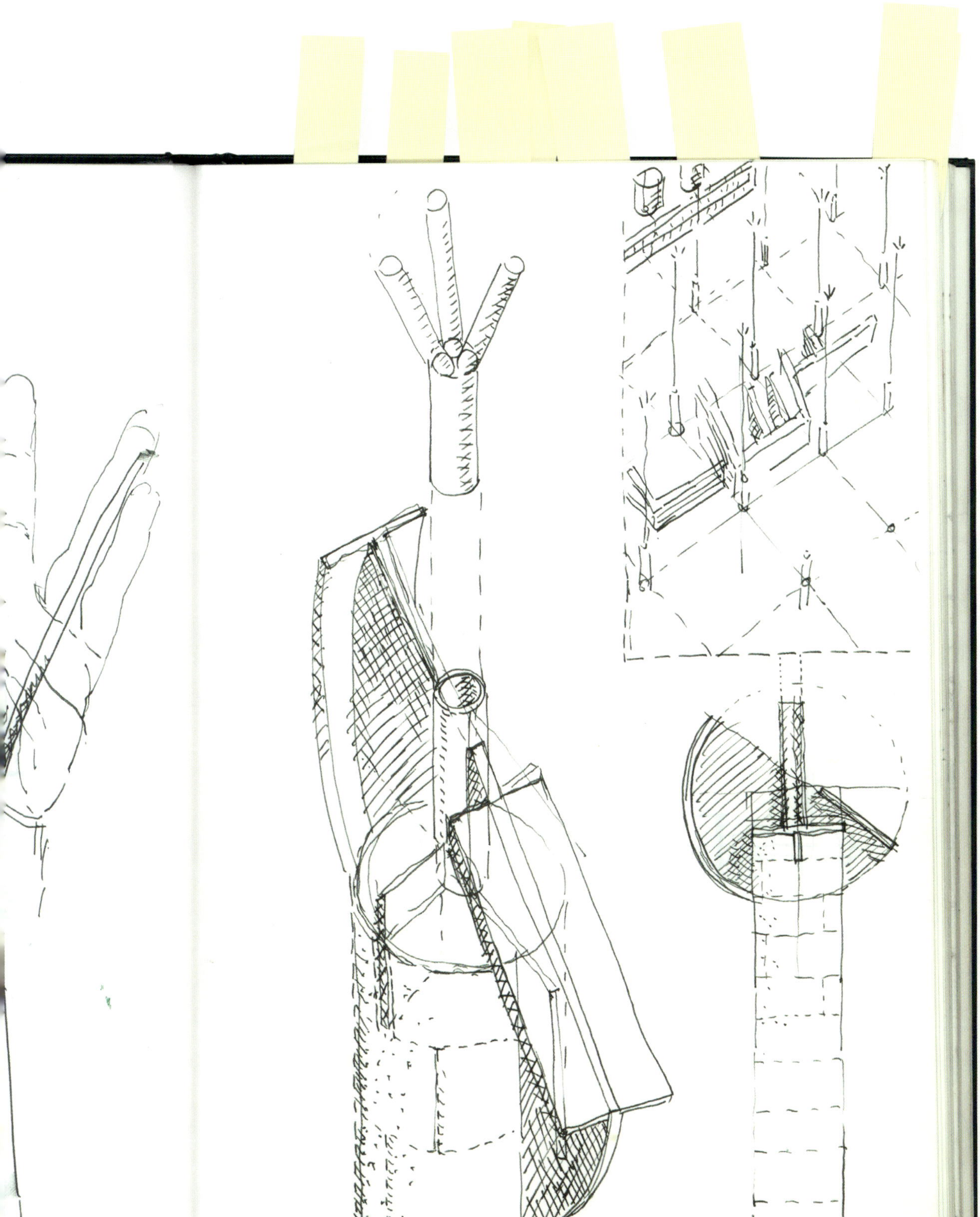
572

Fi→MIL
17.3.82
JERUSALEM
584

583

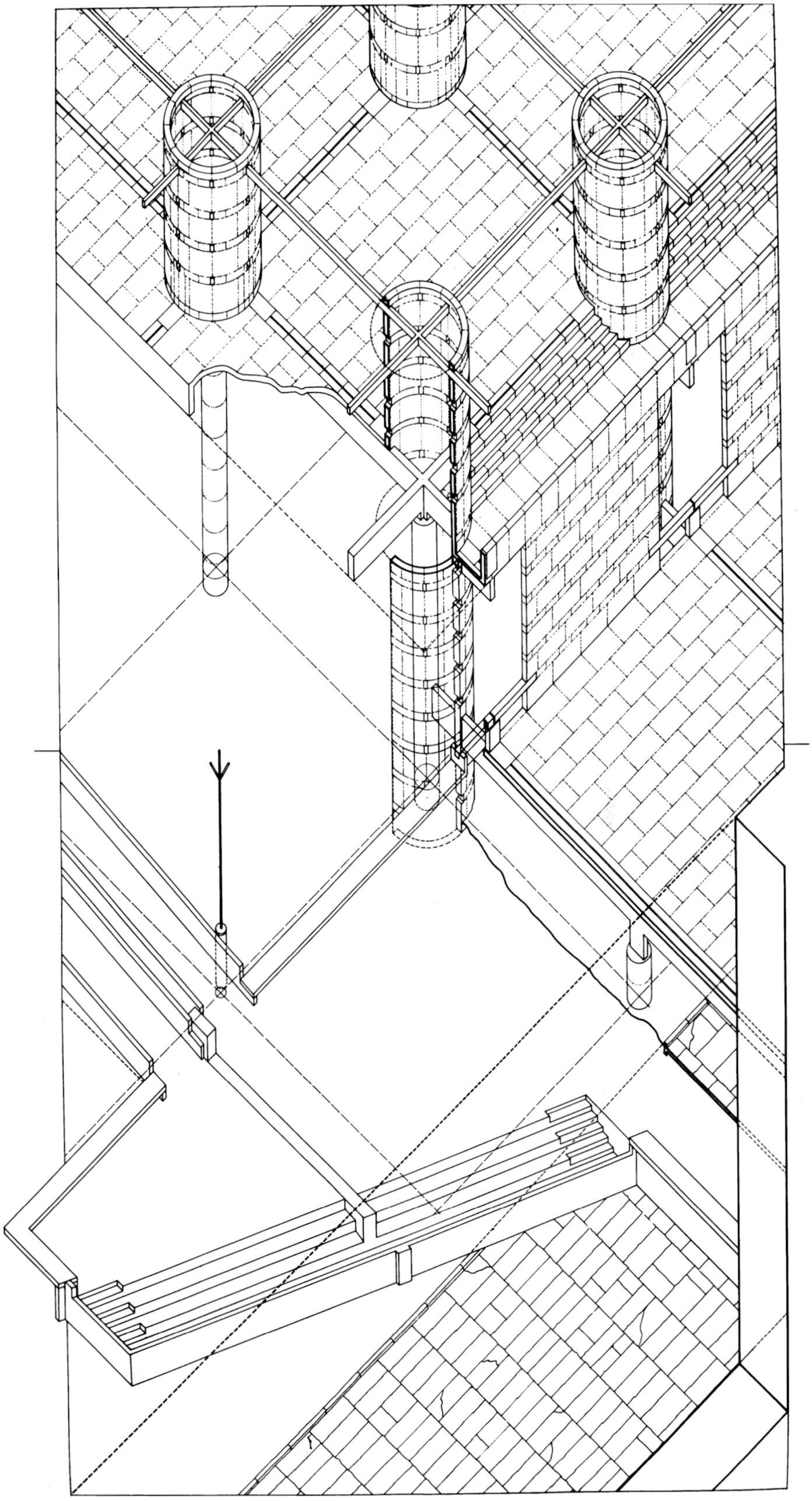

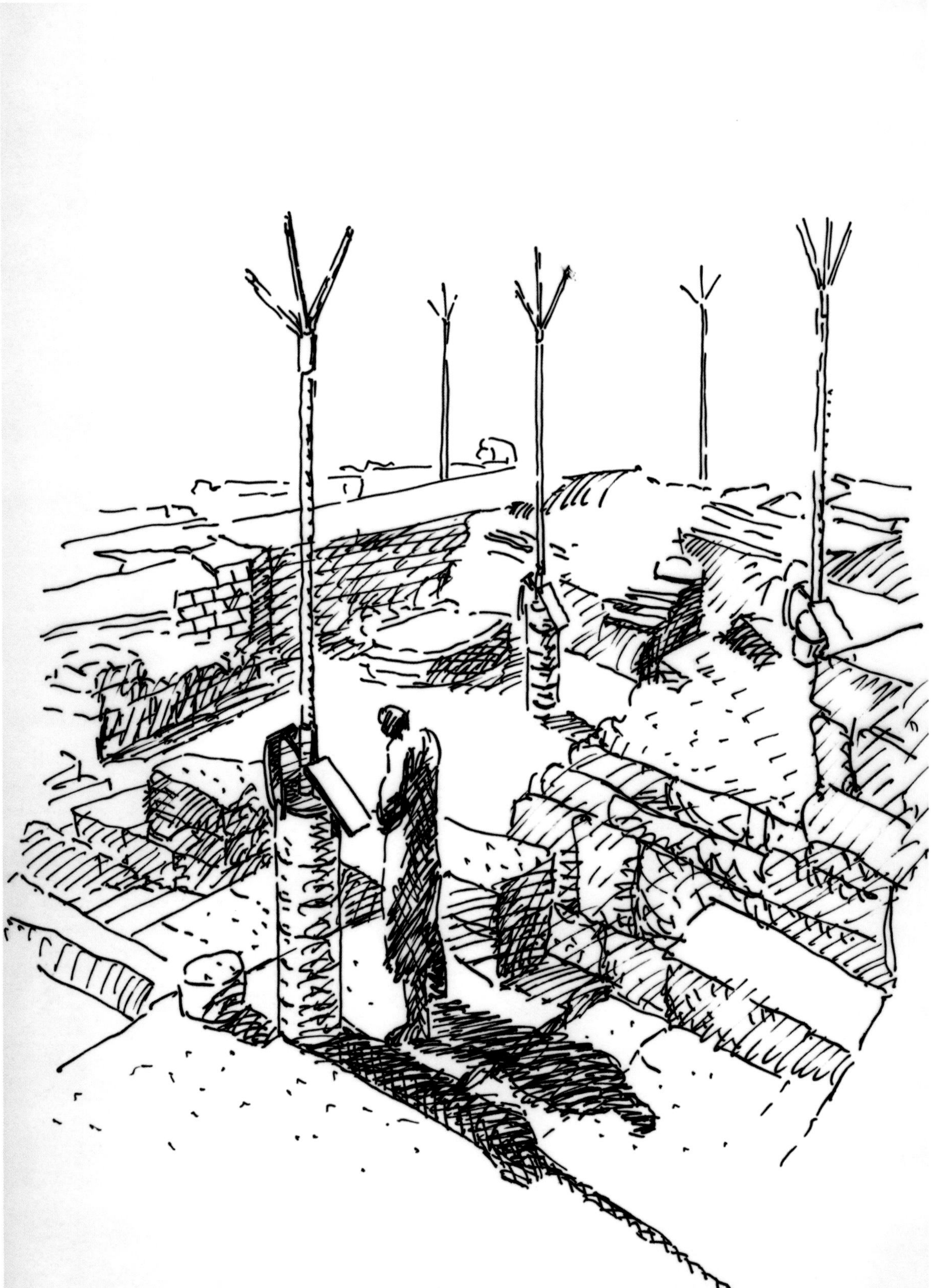

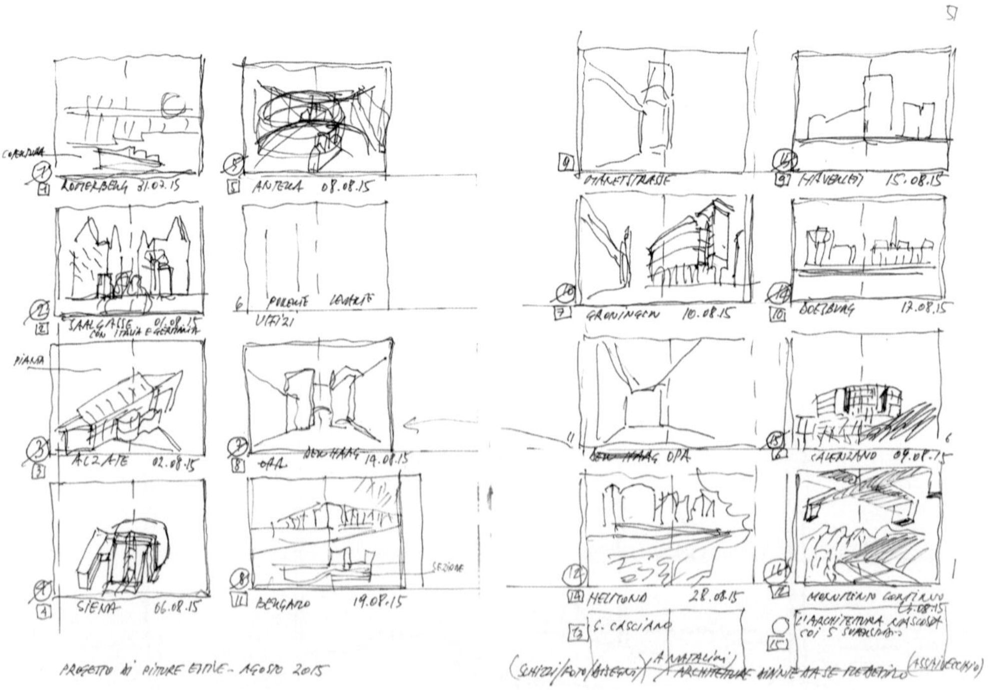

Shadow line

When you look at the buildings of Zola Predosa and Alzate Brianza and the Frankfurt and Jerusalem projects, you have the impression of finding yourself before wonderful inhabited ruins that keep the potentiality of the projects alive.
These buildings retrieve history in places that have forgotten it, town where there is no town any longer, and the countryside where this is about to disappear. The strength of these projects consists in holding together apparently opposite terms by creating a tension between them until a new balance is created through the practice of the project. If you want to find a sense in Adolfo Natalini's research, be careful not to be deceived by the much celebrated and presently very fashionable "abstract furies" of Superstudio, or by the excessive normality of the Dutch works. Rather, examine the central part of his path.
As it happens with Quentin Tarantino's *Pulp Fiction*, where to make sense of the movie, you should not let yourself be fooled by the almost incomprehensible beginning or by the apparently trivial end. Indeed, the key to comprehension is unexpectedly provided in the middle of the movie: the killing of a man exiting the bathroom.
As it clearly appears in the book *Figures of stone*, between 1978 and 1984 Natalini's path is marked by acceleration. The intertwining of the first direct building experiences, the first projects about historical towns and a strong theoretical and conceptual tension lead him to an architectural practice with a strong perspective, as Manfredo Tafuri perfectly anticipated in his *Storia dell'architettura italiana*. Tafuri highlighted the tension of Natalini's works between "monumentality and surreality, nurtured by a derisive attitude typically connected with his Tuscan origins and that allowed him develop sophisticated tools for deconstruction and assembly."
A plurilingual architecture reminding of Gadda's style, capable of melting learned Italian and dialects into new linguistic configurations strong enough to shatter commonplaces and demolish comforting ambiences.
From these four projects an architectural practice appears that, through self-deprecating humour, acquires the iconoclastic strength required to perform the act of criticizing the dominant language.
The best results are to be found where dismembering differences are held together as the poles of a constellation that stays alive in the ceaseless tension of the elements involved. Thanks to the subtle use of derision, the works of these years appear vulnerable yet energetic and free from manneristic repetition. These are works where a merciless innocence turns contradictions and limits into a promise for the future, a promise of happiness.

[M. Navarra, "Terre di confine-un racconto di fondazione", in *Linea d'ombra: 1978-1984; Adolfo Natalini tra il Superstudio e l'architettura*, edited by M. Navarra, Lettera22, Syracuse 2013]

p. 60
Adolfo Natalini,
Project for summer paintings from *Quaderno di Tre Estati*, 2015

p. 61
Adolfo Natalini/Superstudio,
Continuous Monument floating over the lake, 1969-2015

p. 61
Adolfo Natalini,
Bank head office in Alzate Brianza, 1978-2015

p. 62
Adolfo Natalini,
Completion of the Antella Cemetery, 1998-2015

p. 63
Adolfo Natalini,
Urban addition in Doesburg, 1999-2015

p. 64
Adolfo Natalini, *San Lorenzo Hotel in Bergamo*, 2009-2015

Lemmario 2

[Lexicon 2]

—

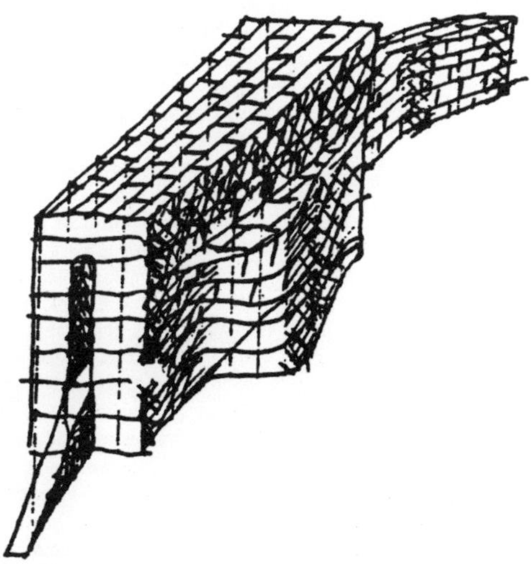

Architettura d'avanguardia e architettura di resistenza
[Avant-garde architecture and architecture of resistance]

01. The architecture that surrounds us in the real world is made up of classical architecture (monuments), traditional architecture (residential fabric), and some rare examples of experimental architecture. The architecture of the virtual world (printed or digital in books and magazines) is more experimental and in a lesser measure, classical. Traditional architecture appears only in illustrated travel and geographical books, rarely in urbanistic or anthropological texts. It almost seems as though a paper world, generated by the desire to be different, has placed itself in contrast with the world as it was and how it should be, in a logic of necessary continuity. It almost seems that architects wish to continuously cause conflict between previously built works and the new, constantly affirming a need for the new rather than a desire for continuity. It seems that only the new carries any value, or rather, that new is the only value.
Traditional architecture constitutes the great majority of the constructed landscape. Avant-garde architecture forms only a very small percentage. Traditional architecture is the norm, avant-garde is the exception.
In many cases, the quality of traditional architecture is so low that it cannot be considered architecture, but simply building construction. In certain cases of high quality design, architecture can be seen as appropriate to the locality, the history, and the social and cultural community for whom it has been built; it is good solid design, useful, handsome, and able to exist with dignity alongside other styles of architecture, producing streets, towns, and places that make lifemore pleasant in general.
Because of its experimental nature, avant-garde architecture often meets with failure, creating a *fiasco*. But when the commitment and talent of the architects lead to successful experiments, they result in exceptional buildings that are sometimes beautiful, sometimes solid, sometimes useful, but rarely all three together, and always in contrast with the surrounding landscape. Lastly, when the experiment is successful, it is hard to demonstrate the necessity.
On glancing through books and magazines, it would seem that avant-garde architecture is the only style that exists and that traditional design has disappeared. On the contrary, traditional architecture does exist, and has no need to gain ground in real life, but perhaps it simply needs to reconquer its place in the media world. Architectural magazines and articles bear an ever-increasing resemblance to newspaper reports, focussed only on the innovative, because only the new makes news (like disasters, crime and wars). Traditional architecture will gain ground only when this need for sensationalist news ceases; we have a desperate need of normality.
We need architecture that is appropriate to the sense of place and the inhabitants, that can stand up to time and trends; and that reassures us against the rapid transit of time protecting us from the attacks of the seasons and the world. We need solid, protective, reassuring architecture that is decorous and civilised. We need places where the form evolves slowly over time according to need and desire. Naturally, traditional construction can contain every necessary technological innovation that makes life easier, while it is difficult for an avant-garde construction to incorporate necessity and memory. With its liberating and destructive vocation, avant-garde design produces oblivion (amnesia). Traditional architecture does not aim at a picturesque or imitation antique style,

On previous page:
Bank head office
in Alzate Brianza (Como),
sketch, 1969

Bank head office
in Alzate Brianza (Como),
perspective, 1969

but uses the consolidated language of tradition, grafting new elements when necessary. Traditional architecture is not Disneyworld or tourist village design...
The greatest European architects (Lutyens, Perret, Berlage, Asplund, Muzio, Behrens, Aalto...) have demonstrated how it is possible to construct using the old and the new. The limits are those imposed by necessity. Traditional architecture aims at building places where humans feel at home, or as Heidegger put it, "dwelling in peace on earth beneath the sky." Today we can call this architecture "architecture of resistance."

["Architettura d'avanguardia e architettura di resistenza", 2007]

02. *Like during the era of Radical Architecture, when in a hostile cultural climate, you were involved in the construction of a parallel culture?*

The work of the neo-avant-garde and *Radical Architecture* was "cultural guerrilla warfare" against the body of current ideas. However, today it is another type of action aimed at re-establishing a system of values that I feel are completely rejected by current architectural culture. While the work of neo-avant-garde and *Radical Architecture* was an attempt to overcome what was the scene of architectural theory and practice, I feel that my work today is an attempt to slow down a rash and excessive precipitation. I cannot remember who, but somebody observed that all artists who start off as revolutionaries end up as firemen: this may be the reason why, having started as an avant-garde designer, now I have to become a traditionalist. Then, as Giuseppe Verdi used to say, "Let's take one step back, that will be progress."

[25.10.97, from an interview by E. Gonzo and A. Vicari, in *Costruire in Laterizio*]

03. *Avant-garde and rear guard*

The avant-garde has the task of exploring and clearing the terrain for the main body of the army. It is composed of determined, daring men who move at night with a knife between their teeth ready to silently slit the throats of their enemies...
A troubling term with a military flavour that introduced a warlike and conflictual expression into the history of architecture. As if architecture were constantly at war.
I would like to think of it as a pacific occupation, like agriculture. The avant-garde is focussed on destructive action and prepares the terrain for the main army who will carry out all the work: defeating the enemy, destroying infrastructures, and scorching the earth.
And then, the rear guard arrives: they take care of the wounded, bury the dead, and rebuild the roads and bridges. However, if we observe carefully, all three sections of the army move in the same direction.

[11.12.00]

04. *Tradition*

I think that the work I do is marked by a kind of nostalgia for something that does not exist but that could exist, that perhaps resembles something that has existed, in the same way that, as we grow older, we begin to resemble our fathers more closely.
After all, the biologists tell us that life has no meaning, that the only reason for life is to transmit the DNA from one generation to the next, and that we are immune carriers of DNA, which, on one hand may seem insignificant, but on the other, is related to eternity.

["Narrate, uomini, la vostra storia", 2006]

Computer centre
in Zola Predosa (Bologna),
perspective, 1969

Arte e città
[Art and the city]

01. *Urban sculpture*
Pistoia is a city filled with sculpture, from Gruamonte and Giovanni Pisano to Marino Marini. The centre of Pistoia, a windy, stony city, is a sculpture in itself, from the sharp prism of the Baptistry to the sunken bastion of Castel Cellesi. But here, like all the other towns in Italy, it seems there is no longer any room for art. In their attempt to base their work on scientific, sociological, economic, functional and technical principles, urban planning and architecture have removed the concept of art, the divine catalyst of every transformation.
In historic times, the builders of the town and its architecture were artists – the names are illustrious: Arnolfo, Brunelleschi, Francesco di Giorgio Martini, Schinkel...
Then gradually the different skills grew apart, to become specialised occupations, but still working in collaboration until the end of the 19th century, and the early decades of the 20th century (figures like Muzio and Sironi in Milan, or Gio Ponti, Martini and Campigli in Padua). Then, architects began to think that art was simply decorative or ornamental, so Loos wrote his *Ornament and Crime*... For urban planners, lost as they were in their parascientific delirium, art did not even exist. And yet, at the end of the 19th century, Camillo Sitte wrote his important work entitled *City Planning According to Artistic Principles or The art of building a city*. However, silence fell on this book and its wise teachings. We had to wait until 1966 and Aldo Rossi's book, *The architecture of the City*, to rediscover a new expression of urban elements as a work of art.
An attempt by an urban elite to occupy the territory artistically. Demarcation (see animals).
An attempt to date a territory helps break the excessive weight of history and affirm a personal presence with art that we were not able to achieve with architecture (art by proxy?)
"In the artificial context of nature, art ran the risk of being perceived as the plant fossilization of modernity, like exhibition pieces of a natural history of form and a paraphrase of the landscape [...] However, in the urban context, sculpture always has a historical index effect, like the marking of time." (Walter Grasskamp).
Talking of art in architecture was still taboo in the Seventies despite the experimental value of the neo-avant-garde movement. At the beginning of the eighties, with the fall of the ban of modernism (as defined by Portoghesi), architects began to use terms like art and beauty (and to think that two thousand years before, Vitruvius had defined architecture as the union of *firmitas, utilitas, venustas*) [strength, utility and beauty]. Apparently, some form of reconciliation had occurred and although the beginnings were not very promising, there is some hope for the future. For decades, in an attempt to flee their responsibilities as far as beauty was concerned, architects and public administration tried to avoid dealing with art in any way. For example, they systematically avoided the 2% law that established that an investment in art equal to 2% of the total cost was mandatory for all public works. They engaged in violent confrontation with artists during the construction of museums, and these conflictual relations often led to disaster... There were at least fifty years of separation: let us hope that reconciliation will take less time.
As art gradually disappeared from buildings and urban areas, architecture aspired more and more to become sculpture... In short, having removed or killed art, architecture attempted spectacular suicide by disguising

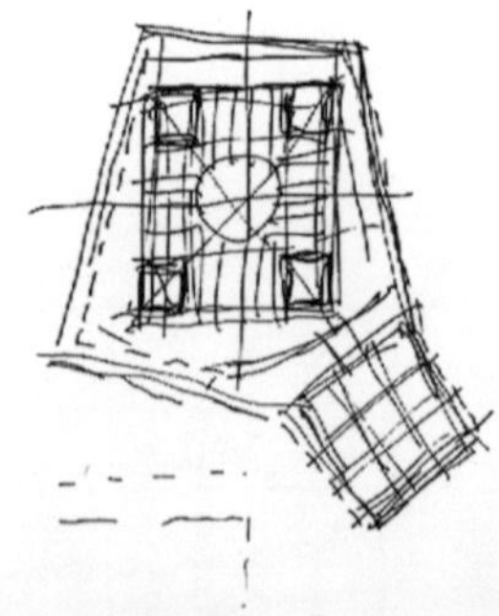

University Campus in Novoli, Florence, 1993-2003, Library and library tower

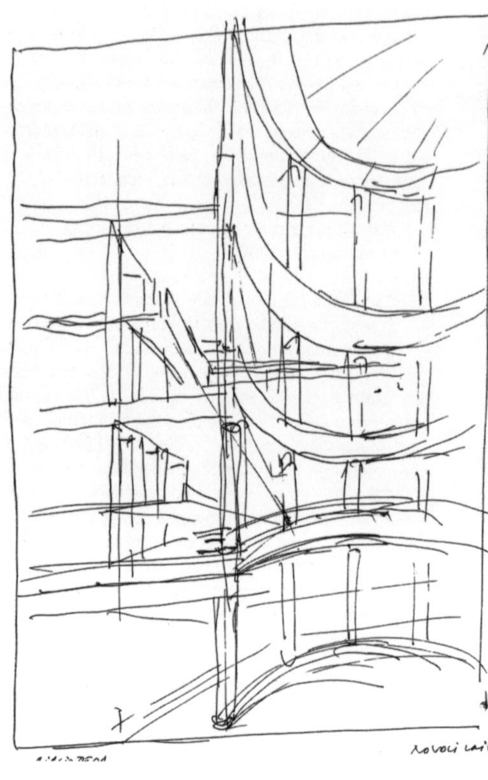

University Campus in Novoli, Florence, 1993-2003, Light well in the library

itself as sculpture and painting.
But why had art and sculpture disappeared? In 1945, Arturo Martini wrote in *Sculpture, a dead language*: "Poetry, music, architecture and painting were translated like ancient languages into the successive vernaculars, adhering to life. Only sculpture has remained static over the centuries, a courtly and priestly language [...] Sculpture remains what it is: a dead language that has no vernacular, but we turn to it in solemn occasions and for commemorative purposes."
"Reign of shadow and architecture: the true architect is the poet of the void (shadow) that the solid (light) sustains as a horizon. Whereas for sculpture, shadow remains an accident, as an echo is for sound." However, Martini was not speaking about the death of sculpture; he was referring to the death of statuary. Martini complained about the narrow-mindedness of sculpture associated with the human figure: "If I want to create an apple..."
Campigli replied: "Make a banana, it is more expressive."
Sexual allegory... the shadow was missing.
Sculpture needs the city and the city needs sculpture. When I think of Pistoia, I think of Pisano's pulpit, the terracotta frieze by Della Robbia on the Ospedale del Ceppo, and *Giro del sole* [Around the Sun] by Roberto Barni When I think of Florence, I think of Pontormo's *Deposition from the Cross,* and of the whole crowd of stone statues in Piazza della Signoria. When I think of Ferrara, I think of the Duke's horse; in Rome, the *Fountain of the Four Rivers...*
In short, in every city, I have found extraordinary motionless inhabitants, but who were able to show me the way in frenetic travels through time. Art has always represented a social service, from altarpieces to palaces. to fountains. The city is the place for exchange and services, and therefore, the place of civilised life. It is the maximum expression of our culture. The elimination of art removes its wealth. However, perhaps we should say that today what is lacking in our cities is architecture and urban planning.
Urban planning and architecture must return to become the art of building our cities. Alongside plastic arts, painting and sculpture, they must rediscover their rightful pace in our cities and buildings; they must return to play their role in civic art. As Camillo Sitte wrote: "However, major plazas and thoroughfares should wear their 'Sunday best' in order to be a pride and joy to the inhabitants, to awake civic spirit, and forever to nurture great and noble sentiment within our growing youth." [*City Planning According to Artistic Principles* (1889), translation G. Collins, Crasemann Collins. London Phaidon Press. NdT]
Today we think of the city like a monster, an archipelago of fragments, clumsily united by infrastructures and services. We have a schizophrenic vision. Centre, outskirts, city, countryside. I am fighting against this separatist concept in favour of a multicentric city, but each one based on good sense, each one equally wonderful...
I propose urban art, an art for rebuilding the city. Splendid in style. In this reconstruction, artists and architects should work together, each in his own field, without intrusion or conflict, but learning from one another. To finally form a new figurative image of the city. Architecture is born from a place, it is composed of an infinite number of elements, it is described using rhetorical figures of speech, (metaphors, allegories).
The figures of architecture are made of stone...
If a protective deity watches over every place (*genius loci*), a protective deity watches over the city as well. The city, said the poet, is the stone face of a god.
[28.11.98]

University Campus in Novoli, Florence, 1993-2003, portico

University Campus in Novoli, Florence, 1993-2003, facade

Boscotondo, Helmond

01. This project is part of a series of projects and constructions that I carried out in the Netherlands where we have been working since 1991. The Netherlands is a very well organised country with strong control over land and water. There are landscaping experts who structure the land, urban planners who organise everything, and the architects are called in only at the end; their task is to give form to what has already been decided. In this case, the project involved redeveloping a decommissioned industrial area adjacent to the historic centre of the town of Helmond, close to Eindhoven. What you see on the right is the local castle that houses the town council, in front is a small park and the historical town centre. There is a large canal that was formerly navigable, but is only used for leisure craft today. Then there is our trapeze-shaped area. We thought of creating a large circular grassed area with a small wood (it was later called Boscotondo) with a diameter of 120 metres. Surrounding the green area is an apartment complex for the elderly; other houses are built along the canal and, in the top right-hand corner, is a large, two-storey underground parking building, above which is the town council building with the new council meeting room, a multiplex movie theatre, and a small museum. The buildings are very simple in design. The residential units are designed to resemble the classical three-window Dutch home, as closely as possible. The external aspect features very simple geometries, in a consolidated style; the units are built in brick and stone, artificial stone and pre-oxidised copper cladding.
We won the Helmond contract in 1995 to redevelop a decommissioned industrial area adjacent to the historic centre, and Boscotondo was inaugurated in October 2001. The local inhabitants are very happy with the result. Each time I returned to see the site, I never knew what it would look like because brick and stone change with the sun and rain. The roofing and some of the public buildings are in green pre-oxidised copper, and change constantly to a blue like a piece of sky, or a green like huge prehistoric animals, as Roberto Barni would say: he is the artist who planted 7-metre tall green bronze trees at Boscotondo, with people and domestic animals in the branches.
["Narrate, uomini, la vostra storia", 2006]

Città/Campagna
[City/Countryside]

01. *Florence is a city rich in extraordinary architecture. It is the city of Brunelleschi, Leon Battista Alberti, Michelangelo and Leonardo. What impact did this have on Adolfo Natalini, student and then young architect, while he was studying and shortly afterwards?*
Before I talk about Florence, I would like to mention the city where I was born. Every time I say I was born in Pistoia, I say it for two good reasons: firstly because I first saw the light of day in the Ospedale del Ceppo on May 10th, 1941, and also because, after wandering around the cities of Tuscany for a long time, it was in Pistoia that I opened my eyes to the city and its architecture in about 1958, when I began to make daily sketches, a practice that I still use today to observe the world around me. It was in Pistoia that I saw the great facade of San Giovanni Fuorcivitas, with its horizontal bands, the architrave by Gruamonte, and pulpit by Giovanni Pisano with its richly carved biblical stories, in the church of Sant'Andrea. It was there that I saw the great piazza with the Palazzo del Comune, the Cathedral and the Baptistry, (and from there the enchanting labyrinth of the mercato della Sala) and the Law Court with its historiated courtyard and bench of justice. Then, just outside the city, the countryside with the houses solidly built into the road walls as far as the banks of the Ombrone.
I have happy memories of the city when I used to wait to see the shadows of the animal busts grow long on the marble Romanesque facade of San Pietro, and I have moonlit memories of the sound of our adolescent footsteps as we talked in the street at night, discovering the world. Back then, the Piazza del Duomo was paved in white stone, and the shadows were engraved between the cracks in the stone, until the shadow disappeared from the facade of the Cathedral to hide below the Cathedral loggia, and then moved up between the pillars as far as the statue of San Jacopo on the roof of the church...
I went to Florence in 1959, and enrolled at the Faculty of Architecture. My family moved to Florence, but for four or five years I continued to return to Pistoia where I had my beginnings as a painter (with very dear friends like Roberto Barni, Gianni Ruffi and Umberto Buscioni; the art critic, Cesare Vivaldi, had christened us "the Pistoia School" in 1966).
In my first year in Florence, I methodically and conscientiously visited the city, my red Touring Club guide in hand, incited to this obsessive behaviour by professor Marchini who demanded a solid knowledge of Florence for his History of Architecture exam: I will never be able to thank him enough.
I have kept fragments in my mind, some small – others magnificent, from this discovery of the city: the Cloister of the Scalzo, tiny, with a light that seems filtered through an aquarium, but made wonderful by the monochromatic paintings of Andrea del Sarto...
the climb up into the dome between the two shells of the Brunelleschi Cupola, almost like clambering through the huge body of an animal, emerging finally out on the balcony, half-way between claustrophobia and agoraphobia and certain streets among the favourites of Rosai, like via Toscanella and via San Leonardo.
The city was a network of dark streets that opened up to mysterious cavities: entrance arches and courtyards, and endless theories of different perspectives where a leaning wall or a protruding shutter always opened up a new world.
However, made immune to the architecture and almost unable to see the true lines because of the confused regurgitation of avant-garde notions and the bad teaching of the modern style in my class, years passed before I was able to see the city again...
I learnt to talk in Montecatini, to walk in Siena, to read and write in Florence, to swim and ride a bike at Forte dei Marmi, but I learnt to see in Pistoia.
At the age of seventeen in Pistoia, I understood the fascination of adventures in the mind, the incredible beauty of travelling in my own bedroom and my own city. I learned to model my ideas and to use them.
I learnt the pleasure of story-telling in the evenings in the piazza, or at a table at the Globo after closing hours, or on a neighbour's front steps...
The discovery and acquaintance with Renaissance architecture will have had a certain importance

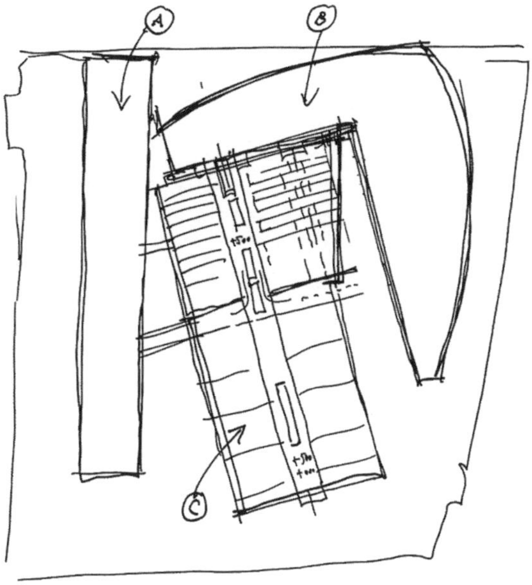

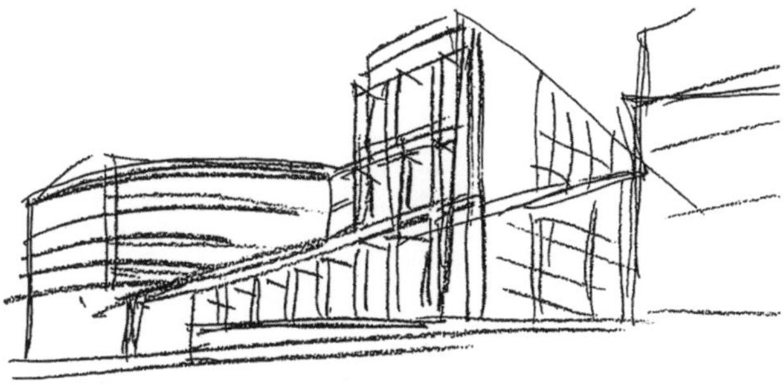

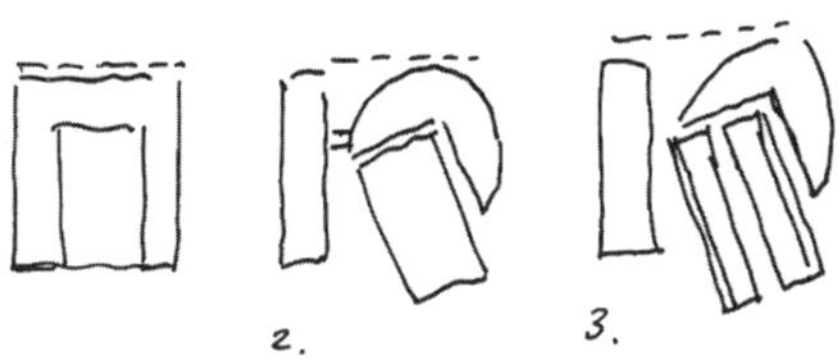

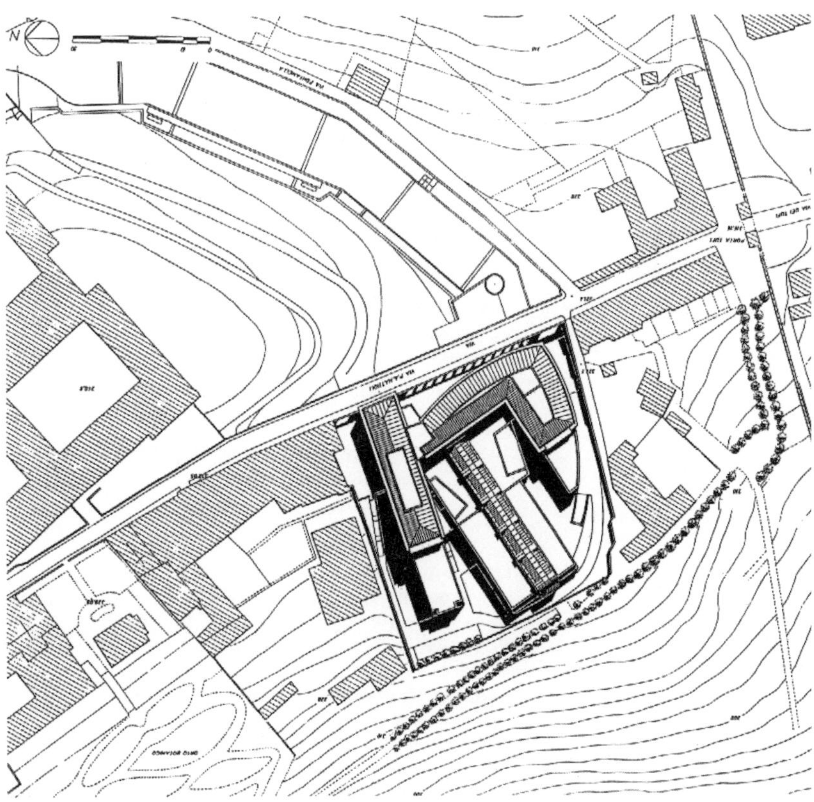

University Campus
in Porta Tufi, Siena,
sketches, 1996

University Campus
in Porta Tufi, Siena,
Layout, 1996

in the development of Natalini the architect. In what form and through which buildings and artists in particular?

In Florence, very gradually and with a lot of resistance, I learnt to love Leon Battista Alberti and Brunelleschi, undecided between their clarity and the anxiety of Buontalenti and Ammannati (in the same way that I continue to be undecided between my passion for Masaccio and another passion for Pontormo).

The Pazzi Chapel and the Loggiato degli Innocenti, the Rucellai Loggia and Palace, but perhaps in a more visceral way, the Holy Sepulchre in San Pancrazio and the Library of San Marco (by Michelozzo), have been in my mind for years like a guideline, naturally along with Palazzo Non Finito and the Casino Mediceo Buontalenti...

Among my projects, from the Teatro di Rimini onward, my debt to Leon Battista Alberti (and Rossellino) and the Tempio Malatestiano appears increasingly more apparent. Biagio is present in the Ferrara projects, in Vicenza, Palladio (also because of the physical vicinity) but perhaps even more, Scamozzi...

Perhaps the Tuscan landscape as well – from your writings and you projects, it is obvious that you are very fond of Tuscany – did its landscape contribute to your education?

My father's family worked the land in Valdinievole. My first memories are of the countryside in this area, certain long light effects in the mornings, the humming of summer afternoons, the feeling of walking barefoot along certain dirt roads and grassy lanes. Other country landscapes near Pistoia remain fixed in my memory, taking long bike rides to make careful but clumsy sketches.

Then in 1970 I went to live in the country, first in the house at San Martino alla Palma, then in Doccia, high up in the hills and battered by the wind (the house was called *Il Chiasso* [Noise] because of the noise the wind made in the chimneys) and I lived there until 1986... I worked for almost ten years with my friends of Superstudio and with my university students on *Cultura materiale extraurbana* [extra-urban material culture] as an attempt at an anthropological refoundation of architecture. This was a necessary refoundation process of building (of architecture in general and of my own architecture in particular) because I felt it was based on few and weak foundations...

The countryside that I grew up in, the landscapes of my memories and those I found in the words and images of my friends (farmers and artists) are strongly rooted within me. Today the rural landscapes I love appear in certain projects where I have finally found the courage to use well-worn words and forms linked with everyday existence... with a certain discretion, as always happens with things that are close to your heart.

[30.10.90, from an interview by P. Scaglione, in *d'A*]

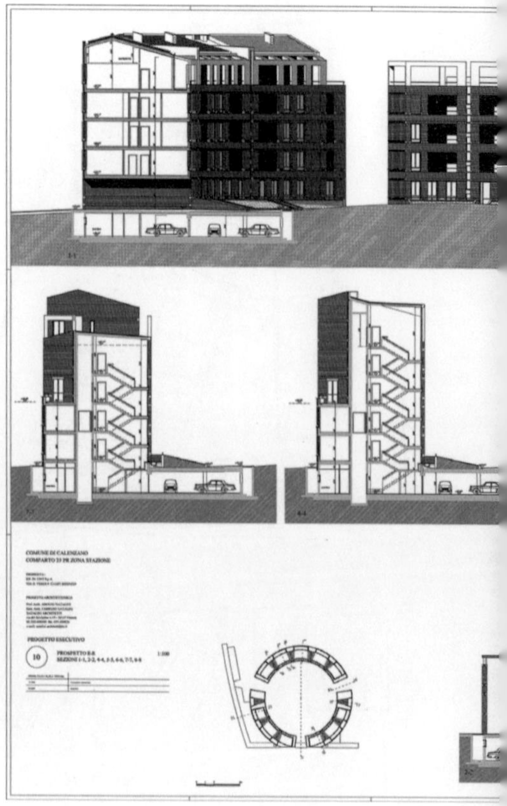

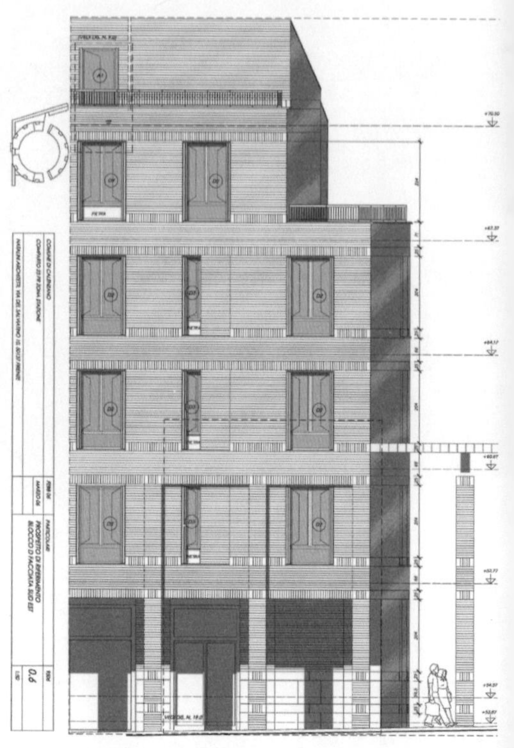

Anello Residential Complex and Park at Val Marina. Redevelopment plan in Calenzano (Florence), 1995-2009, cross-section and details

Didattica e Università
[Didactics/Teaching and University]

01. *The Minerva lecture hall*

According to Greek mythology, Minerva sprang out of Jupiter's head armed from head to foot. Jupiter had been struck by a terrible headache: Vulcan came to his aid with a drastic remedy, he hit Jupiter on the head with his hammer, splitting his skull, and out sprang Minerva fully armed. So from the metal forging work of Vulcan and

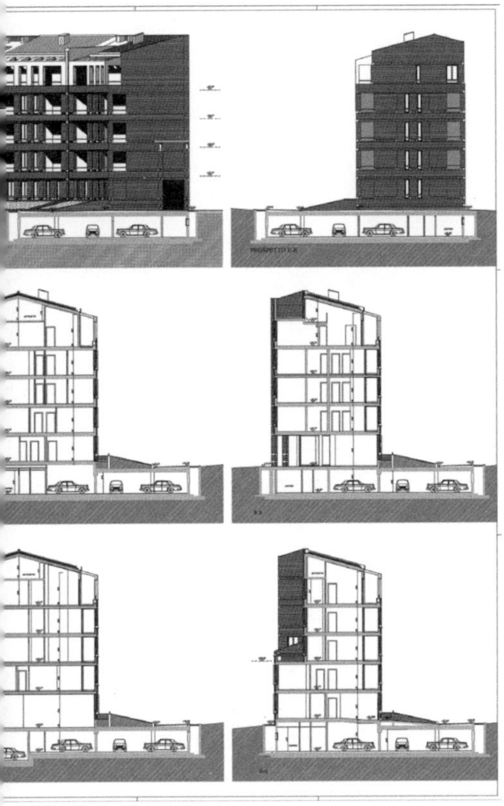

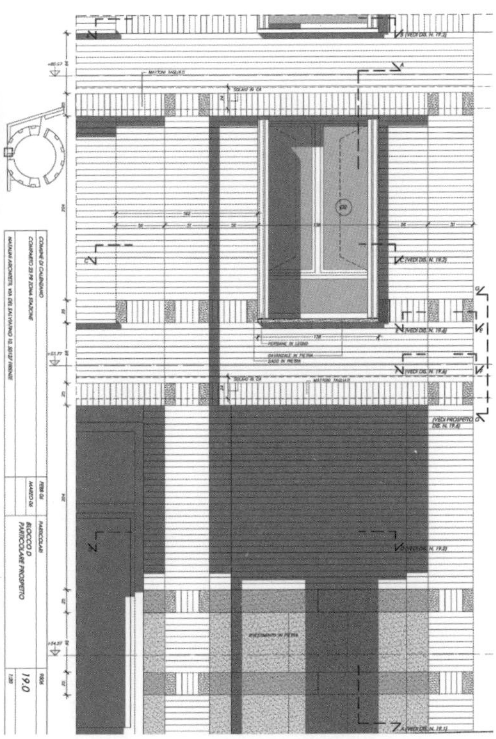

the power of Jupiter, was born the wisdom of Minerva. Frightening and beautiful is Arturo Martini's *Minerva* standing in the entrance to the Sapienza University in Rome. Another *Minerva*, less frightening (and unarmed) gives her name to the lecture hall on the ground floor of the building in via Ricasoli, home to the architectural Faculty in Florence.

The hall was built by Paoletti in 1785 as the assembly hall for the architectural school of the Accademia.

The tall windows and plaster copies of classical statues bear witness to the long years when art was taught as part of the architectural syllabus. At least, that is what I envisioned as I sat there as a student, sometimes gazing at the long crack in the vaulted ceiling, imagining the large battle scenes painted by Fattori floating down from his studio above, where he taught painting. When I began to teach in this lecture hall, I often thought of other generations of students and artists who had followed courses of painting, sculpture, engraving, and more recently, architecture, in these rooms.

The crack in the ceiling has been repaired now. No more paintings will come floating down.

The large plaster statues are protected by a wooden wall: only the upper parts can be seen, and of their feats, their glory and tragedy, there is only a partial and frozen glimpse. Dust has made them even more dramatic: they seem to be lit from below. The *Minerva* has disappeared behind the large screen for slide show lectures.

It is as if art has been removed from this large room. Floods of light still come in through the tall windows.

A few years ago, somebody thought it was a joke to fire a rifle against the windows: there are some bullet holes and spider-web fractures like Duchamp's *Large Glass*.

The Minerva lecture hall is a large rectangular space (about 12 x 22 metres, 10 metres high) with a worn terracotta floor and white walls with narrow grey moulding at the top. Students enter through a huge wooden door, so tall that every time a student is late for lectures, opening it slightly to slip in, he seems very small against the door, like a painting of the gates of Hades. Against the back wall, a podium, a desk, a few tables, an incongruous blackboard and a slide screen create the stage for lessons in architecture. The name of this course is Architectural Project design 2 so one would suppose that it follows the Design1 course, before continuing with other design courses (3, 4, 5...).

This means my course follows that of another person and precedes others in teaching architectural design.

This implies an idea of progression, a closer approach to architecture, a linear progression where the starting point (lack of knowledge) and the finish line (knowledge) are clear.

However, is the progression truly linear, and is there only one objective?

We could imagine that each course (the first, the second, etc.) is always a repetition of the same attempt to approach architecture, either with a tiger's leap or slowly and steadily like a tortoise. A different form of repetition, with a series of leaps, preceded by moments of concentration and waiting, followed by just as many moments of confusion and disappointment (the prey escaped) but perhaps with a final instant of enthusiasm and satisfaction.

Is the leap different each time, or is the objective different? With the project, we are not trying to approach only one single type of architecture.

We are surrounded by different types of architecture: historical examples from ancient cities, more recent styles for the 19th century, modern design from the Thirties,

contemporary styles, and those we can expect in the future (technological, minimal, traditional, immaterial?). As well as the various chronological differences, there are also architectural styles from different places: from the urban centres or the suburbs, from different countries, from the countryside, the mountains, the coast... all different in style, size, materials...
The Design course limits its field of investigation to the historic city centre and proposes a series of replacement and completion exercises.
Parts of the city (a block, a building) are used as pages to be read and rewritten. Generally this refers to building interventions between the Second World War and the Sixties, when the reconstruction emergency and a firm tough faith in the potential of anything new, cut off any ties with the historic areas. Demolition and reconstruction are proposed in an attempt to recover the lost sense of the city.
In other cases, contemporary projects that have not yet been built are analysed to propose completion ideas. In all cases, the objective is to learn the language of the city, to be used as an antidote against diversity and particularism. The urban architectural language declares its desire to live together (*civitas*), not so much as the construction of a new language ("novelty is but oblivion", according to John Donne) but the learning of the language spoken by the city in which we are working.
It will be a learning exercise in observation and imitation; then perhaps we will arrange phrases and words in a different manner (maybe even compose some verse...).
It will be a new language without effort or intentionality (because all of us are different) but always based on – and traceable to – a common language, an urban *koinè*.
This course is aimed at teaching how to design a decorous and well-considered city with "appropriate" architecture. Books and magazines show us another panorama (because only diversity and monstrosities are newsworthy).
Our projects will focus on normality, but without seeking to establish methods or define rules and regulations...
We place our faith in the understanding of the gods and heroes who observe us from over the wooden panels in this lecture hall, and we invoke the wisdom of Minerva.

["Per un nuovo ciclo di lezioni di progettazione architettonica 1994-1995"]

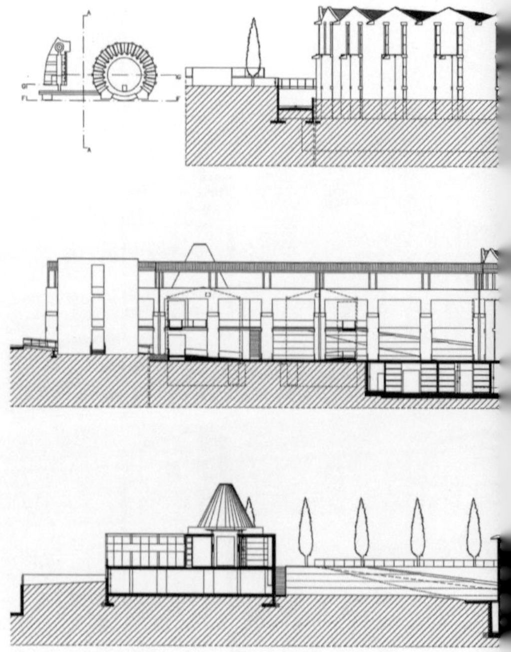

02. *Schools*
Architectural Faculties have become monstrous and as such, they produce monstrosities.
How else can we describe a body of twelve thousand students in Florence, (fifty or sixty thousand throughout Italy) who are desperate to study this art, and what about the endless reams of printed paper crammed with in-depth or superficial analyses, detailed surveys, prefigurations of strange or tiny objects, vast building projects, cities and territories?
Monstrous and monstrosities because of the size, (the Leviathan and Jonah's whale are a *homunculus* and an anchovy in comparison...) the vast interests at stake, and the dramatic lack of coordination between intention and results.
This situation would be very different if schools (university Faculties) were smaller (less than a thousand students in each school) and were spread out over the whole country, with Faculties in all those small and medium-sized historic cities that have so much to teach apprentices learning the art of building cities, and (professional or amateur) architects. In fact, there is a great need for pragmatism,

Completion of the Misericordia Cemetery in S. Maria dell'Antella, Bagno a Ripoli (Florence), 1998-2008, sezioni

Completion of the Misericordia Cemetery in S. Maria dell'Antella Bagno a Ripoli (Florence), 1998-2008, details of round chapel and circular courtyard

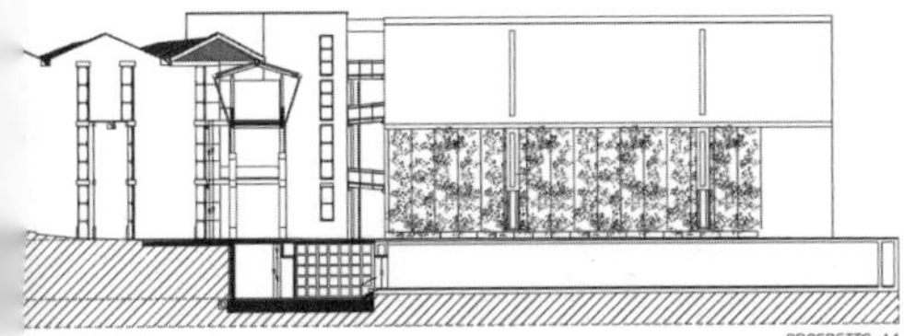

PROSPETTO AA

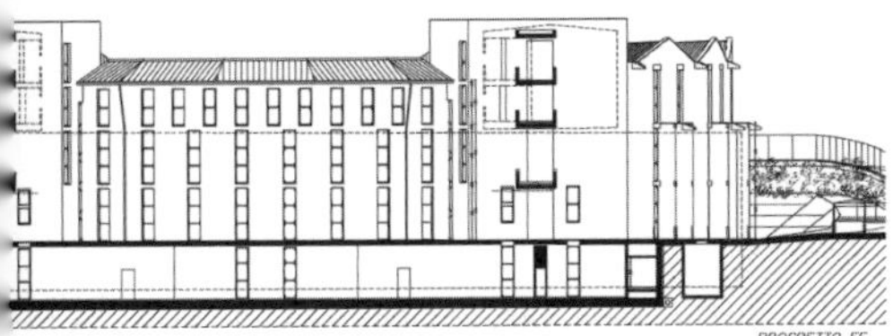

PROSPETTO FF

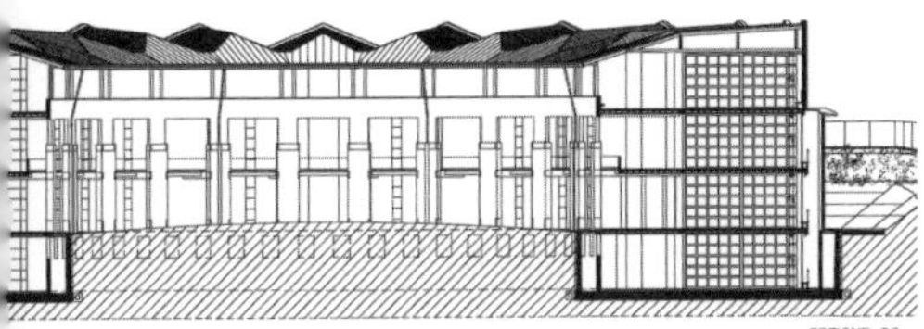

SEZIONE GG

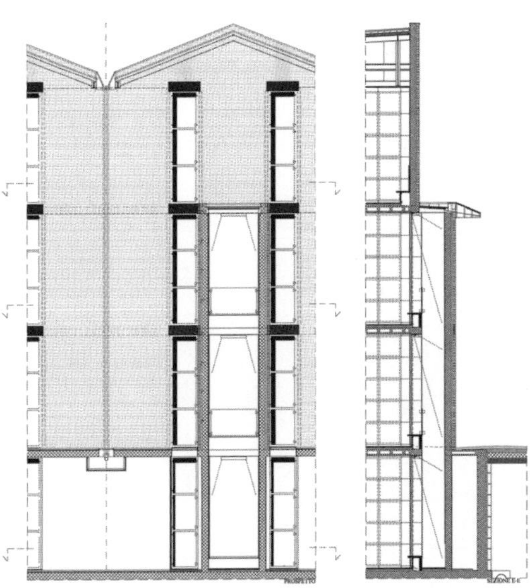

for being rooted in a local community composed of houses, streets and piazzas, for familiar and recognisable cities from which the risky intellectual journeys of the mind take the architect travelling around the world, even before venturing forth by car, train or plane.

The cities where the main Architecture Faculties are located have been almost completely covered by student research: there are areas in Florence where so many projects have been accumulated that the paperwork is almost as voluminous as the buildings they refer to. This often leads to seeking innovative solutions, breaking rules, in a romantic drive for something new (where new often spells lack of attention).

As an alternative to these flights from the city, many students focus on some small or medium aspect of their home town (or nearby) for their thesis work, in an attempt to transfer to an actual and familiar terrain (often interiorised) those fragments of knowledge that they have managed to absorb in the midst of the crowds, the chaos, and the shortcomings of the school.

Statistically, such large numbers of students offer vast possibilities of meeting a multitude of young people, with extraordinary ability, motivation and talent (even though architecture and art do not happily accept the idea of *enfants prodiges*).

Carlo Scarpa maintained that a student's work could not be considered architecture because students do not yet possess the instruments and knowledge necessary. Yet, in many cases, this work is so charged with passion that it is able to pass over any inevitable shortcomings and it closely approaches true architecture. Visionary capacity combined with modest and diligent application in design, an obstinate desire to try and retry different ways and solutions, associated with fragments of various skills, can compensate a lack of technique and rules, balancing out insufficient experience with poetic motivation or tenacity.

03. *Learning from Florence*

Florence was the city of Great Architecture, and it was architecture that gave Florence its splendour, more than the Arno and the hills. Then, the architecture left Florence (perhaps when Michelangelo left for Rome) and in recent times, the traces of great architecture have been scarce and almost invisible: decent decorous buildings replaced architecture between the 1860s and the 1930s, but then even this disappeared and now we have to be content with a few hidden exceptions.

If the city centre and the hills continue to be magnificent, it is only because olive trees and stone are strong enough to withstand stupidity and decay, but the outskirts of Third World cities are no worse than ours.

This is why Florence has a strong need of architects and the new town development plan; a widespread need for quality opens up new spaces (although limited) for reconstruction in the city. Florence has a glorious School of Architecture, even though its reputation is linked more than anything else with the stories about the Florence railway station and the legendary Scuola Fiorentina. I have never been able to see the Scuola Fiorentina (perhaps because I am from Pistoia) but the Faculty of Architecture is dramatically visible. Although it has grown well beyond its physiological limits (its size is unbelievable) divided in addresses, trends, and a thousand different streams, the faculty is beginning to recover its centrality after years of problems. It transmits fragmented knowledge to its students, but is still capable of inspiring their minds. The faculty is inside the city. It occupies former convents,

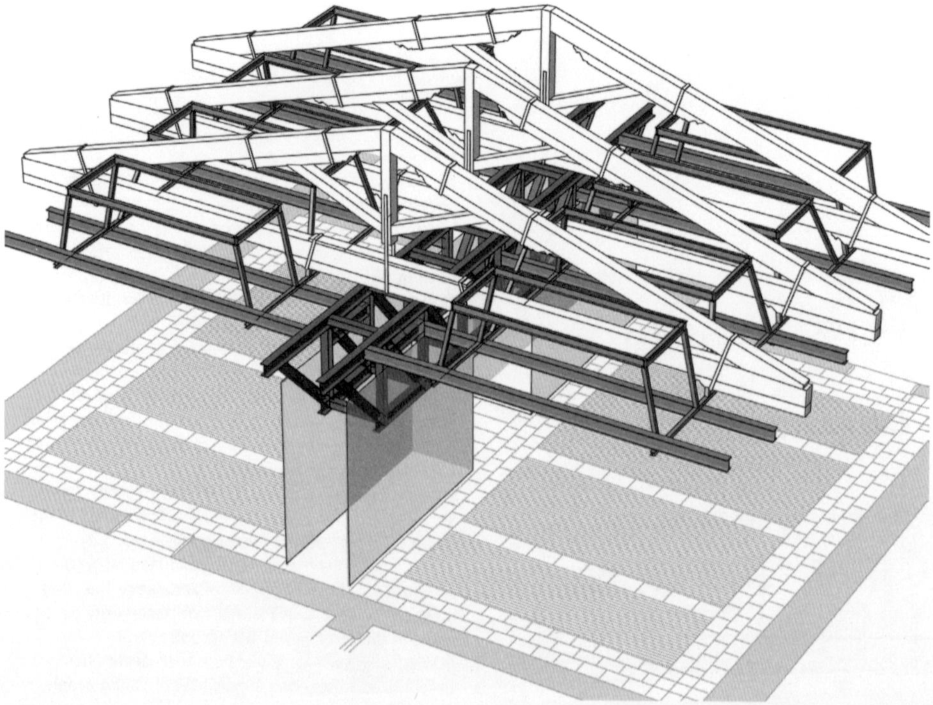

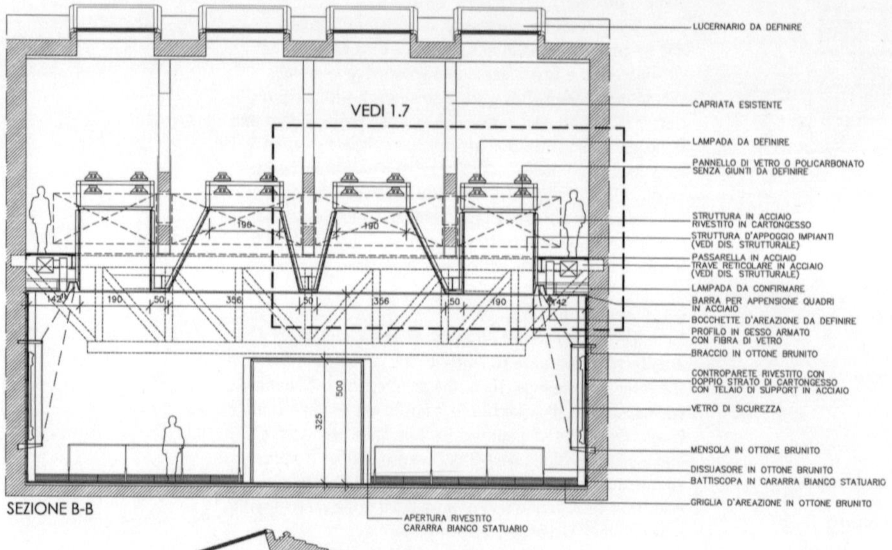

SEZIONE B-B

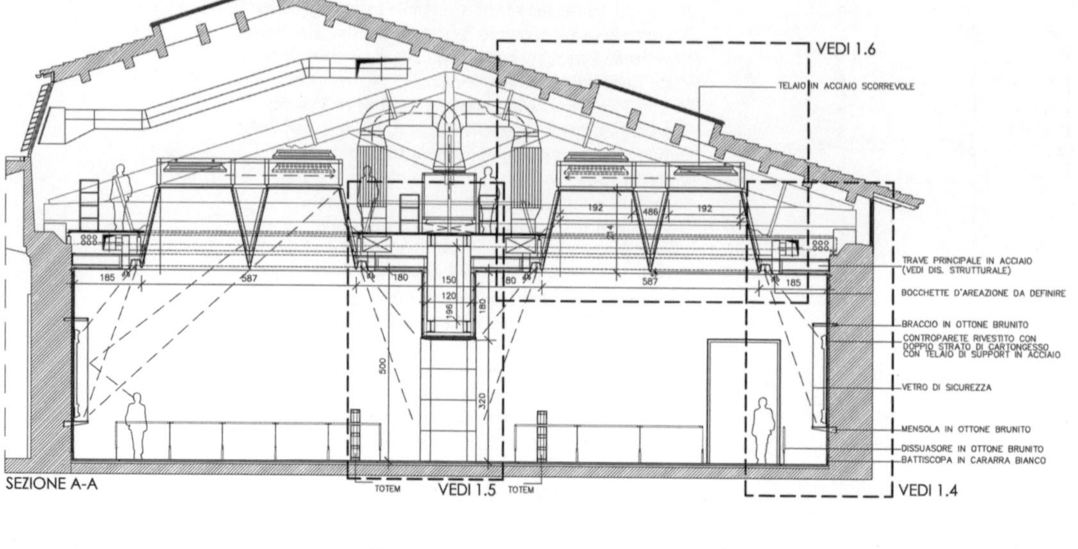

SEZIONE A-A

palaces, jails, linked by the streets and piazzas that the students wander along in their transfer from one point to another within an even greater network of other streets, piazzas, palaces, houses and stations...
The faculty compels the students to read the city.
In turn, the city dramatically asks the faculty for instructions on how to escape its current dire architectural and urban poverty.

[A. Natalini, *Adolfo Natalini. Avvicinamenti all'architettura*, edited by A. Boschi, A. Castellana, S. Follerà, Pontecorboli ("Quaderni di progetto", 2), Florence 1996]

04. *Minerva Lecture Hall. Second lesson*
The program requires that students provide a kind of personal file, a folder containing a self-portrait, their curriculum, and a selection of works from previous years. A kind of autobiography of the young (aspiring) architect. Every form of architecture contains an autobiography (but not vice-versa).
Some architects have written their autobiography trying to explain their personal approach. (Reading of several pages from: Aldo Rossi, *Autobiografia scientifica*, Pratiche, Parma 1990; *Alvaro Siza: scritti di architettura*, edited by A. Angelotto, Skira, Milan 1997; Renzo Piano, *Giornale di bordo*, Passigli, Florence 1997).
These architects talk about simple, fundamental things. They describe their physical involvement with their work. They do not expound theories; they describe their work like a sequence of acts, played out during a long day without interruption...
What autobiography do we expect from our students?
A story about a life and a project: to become an architect. This is by no means an entrance exam, nothing like the questions asked of your aspiring faculty colleagues...
The architects from whose autobiographies we have just read some extracts do not present theories or methods. If we did that during our course, then an entrance exam with its questions and answers would be justified...
At the beginning of each course, the professor should provide a summary of the course content. Instead of this, I will read the beginning of the first lesson by Jean-Nicolas-Louis-Durand.

[31.10.97]

05. *I remember that during one lesson, at the beginning of the course you said that you did not intend teaching a project design method, but would demonstrate how you reacted in relation to each problem.*
During the protest years, Ivan Illich was very popular with his book *Deschooling Society*. Illich sustained that education is an induction, in that that it does not lead out (*ex ducere*) a person from his world to expose him to a much wider environment, but is conceived to simply guide, induce or lead towards. You study architecture to become an architect, the classical educational method or the method for specialisation is anything but a leading outward. In this sense, the route that you call discontinuous can be your salvation compared to this other distorted form of education. Perhaps it is because of this non-linear path, and because I have walked in a kind of garden of forking paths that led in different directions, like the garden in the story by Borges, that I do not have a specific method, no theoretical scaffolding. Perhaps it comes from my chronic weakness, or perhaps it is precisely for this reason that I managed to escape the dismal fate of specialisation.

... a transversal path that crosses through various disciplines...
This discontinuous route opens up perspectives, it allows you to investigate a range of territories to search for what is perhaps your specific territory, it is a system where you might think you lose something in depth, but you gain it in breadth or extension.

...perhaps this can be introductory or preparatory during a certain stage of training?
We could say that it is the most appropriate learning path for exploring a range of different worlds, while searching for the one that is most suited to our work and our activity. Once you have made this choice, then you can begin another path to deepen your knowledge.

Today Natalini Architetti has also become a school of thought for project design formation: what do you think of the so-called "Nataliniani"?
I have never had any ambition to found a school. At the University, I try to transmit my work experience, but more with the aim of helping to avoid mistakes than giving examples that can be reproduced. Every project is born from a specific place and opportunity; it has a unique identity and I have never believed in "methods". I often repeat to my students: "If you imitate my work, you will ruin yourselves", and the only model that I suggest is to be dedicated to your work and to be passionately involved in the places where you build.
I have a work habit with Fabrizio Natalini that has been in place for thirty years, but, apart from having the same name, I would not call him "Nataliniano". In the people I work with, I always find it interesting to notice the different personalities that emerge in the small flashes of freedom that we are conceded in the cast-iron restrictions on a job.
In the end, as with my old unforgettable Superstudio companions, I have been lucky to work with people whose only point in common was that they were different.

[25.10.97, from an interview by E. Gonzo and A. Vicari, in *Costruire in Laterizio*]

06. My work as an architect and as a professor can by no means be termed a high-powered career. I have worked as an architect for forty years and even now, I still do not know what direction I should be taking, much less whether I am able to teach you what you should be doing. In any case, this is a job where nobody teaches anything to anybody else; each one can limit themselves to talking about what they have created in the hopes that it might be useful to somebody else. If nothing else, at least to avoid the mistakes we have made in the past. How do you become an architect? You become an architect through trial and error, through opportunities, attempting to transform them into necessities. I would not really know what else to say.

07. *Teaching*
I entered the faculty in 1960 and I have not left yet. I have taught for forty years but I have not yet understood what I should be teaching nor how I should be doing it. I have simply talked about what I know, my research, my experience, and how I built some of my projects. I have tried to transmit to my students my love for places, things, buildings and people. I have tried to infect them with my enthusiasm for this art and this profession, but I have also tried to warn them about the dangers. I have pointed out the wonders of great architecture and the compact city. I have suggested

Working plan for the Nuovi Uffizi, Florence, 2003-2011, Axonometric view of the Sala Botticelli

Working plan for the Nuovi Uffizi, Florence, 2003-2011, Cross-section of the Sala Botticelli

that beauty is the only catalyst that made every transformation possible. I have tried to teach through examples, indicating a course of dignified normality.

Disegno
[Design]

01. *On drawing*
If you ask me about drawing, like Saint Augustine I would have to answer: "I know until you ask me; when you ask me, I don't know." Yet, I have spent my life sketching and I cannot imagine architecture without images and figures, and these images become real only through drawing and construction.
I have sketched a great deal. I have traced endless little marks and I have watched them line up on pages like tracks left by insects.
I remember as a boy I lived near the sea and I would go to the beach to look at the tracks made by dung beetles that we used to call "shit-rollers"... when I lived in the country, after it had snowed, I would go and look for footprints left by animals. Years later, it seems that the marks I leave on these pages look like those tracks. I always have a whole arsenal of pens in my pocket (one fine, one thick) and an Indian ink pen, a soft pencil, and some coloured pencils (four) and even a white wax crayon to cover any disasters, and a mechanical pencil-compass combo that cost me a fortune. I am always afraid I do not have the right equipment... and I take along a sketchbook for sketching, and if I could, I would take another one for writing, and a load of other gadgets... then maybe, with all this equipment... I don't draw or write anything at all. But I wouldn't like to risk forgetting some idea, if it should come to light...
I have used sketching the way a fisherman uses a net. I have spent days weaving these nets, and many more mending them. For many long nights I have cast the nets, waiting until, like unpredictable twisting fish, ideas are caught in the net.
I have used drawing like a hunter sets his traps. With the patience learnt from my farmer grandparents, I prepared the soil; with the steadfast patience of a farmer, I continued to work the soil day after day, even when it seemed that the season was not right for harvest. With the patience of a brick-mason, I laid one brick on top of another to build a curved wall, transforming it into an enclosure to collect my ideas.
Then I understood that it was precisely my obsessive operations that were generating these ideas, or rather, making them visible to the world.

[06.06-01.07, "Una conversazione con Adolfo Natalini pittore e disegnatore", in *Il Fuoco*, nos. 12-13]

02. In 1954, I began sketching on a very regular basis, as if it were a task I had assigned myself, using the small Fabriano sketchpads with the blue covers. But I used to draw on any kind of paper, preferably on used paper (I used the back of drawing sheets found at school, old forms, and wrapping paper). I drew my own hand, sketches of classmates, landscapes, portraits. By 1958, I had learnt to draw very well but I am no longer able to make drawings like those I used to sketch on old grey wrapping paper. I began to paint, then I enrolled at the Architectural Faculty and at University, they taught me another type of drawing, precise and regular, which I had never been able

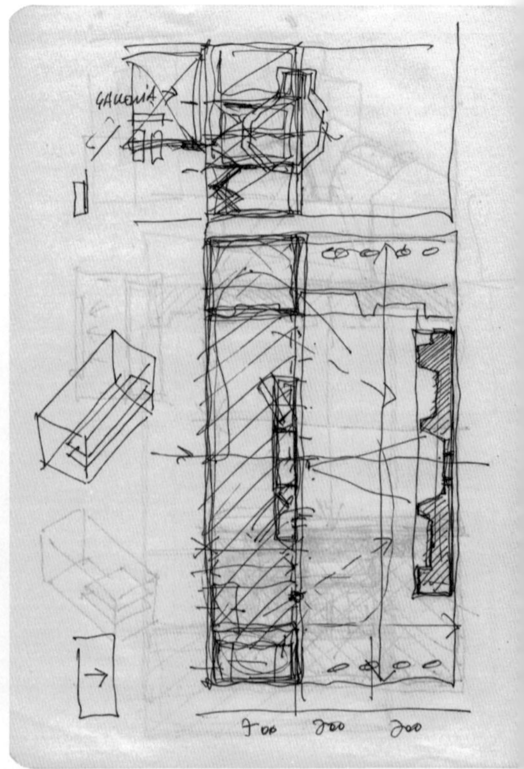

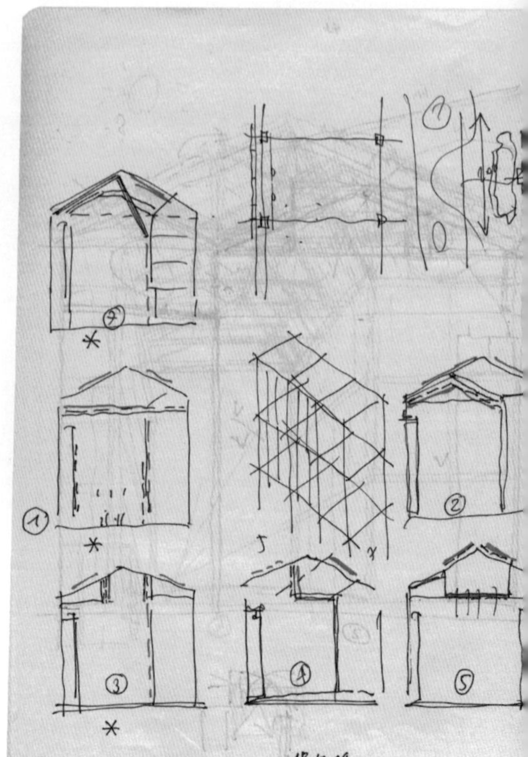

Extension of the Museo dell'Opera di S. Maria del Fiore, Florence, 2001-2015, Sketches of the cathedral facade room

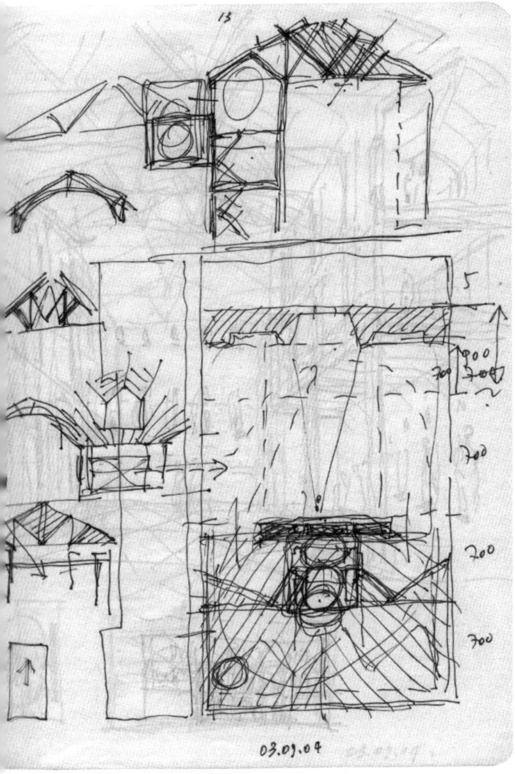

to draw before. I learnt to keep my drawings and ideas in order, like books in a library.
The drawings of other people began to be part of my own. I started to use transparent paper, (tracing paper, butter paper, onionskin paper) to trace drawings derived from others, modifying them to create something new. Transparent sheets could be overlaid like the days of the week: I would have liked to preserve all the others within each drawing, and I hated to lose even a single line.
Around 1964, I started to use spiral-backed sketchbooks. I have only kept a few of them, but I have one, dating from 1968-69, with my first drawings of *Histograms* and the *Continuous Monument.*
I also liked big checked exercise books with a hard cover: they were like registers in which I would mix writings, accounts and sketches.
In my checked registers, I find a large number of schedules, (jobs, drawings to do, letters and texts to write) and inventories (work and drawings I hoped to publish).
The registers contained a kind of double-entry book-keeping system with a mixture of money, drawings and ideas.
In 1974, I began to use the "black hard-cover" sketchbooks: I bought the first books from Rowney in London and they were too beautiful to sketch in. They had hard black imitation leather covers and smooth pages in a light ivory colour. The pages were perforated so they could be detached, but I never removed even a single page... I have had them in various sizes: A4, half-size (booklet) and quarter-size (sketchbook).
I tried using other sketchbooks covered in Florentine print paper: I loved the red and green covers, and when I made photocopies, the edges formed a beautiful decorative border.
Then when I could no longer find Rowney books, I started to use Daler: the pages were not such good quality, but at least they were not detachable, so were not as delicate.
Lastly, I bought Vang sketchbooks (that were Flying Eagle books manufactured in China, imported to Munich by Vangerow and then re-imported to Florence by Leoncini).
I bought up a stock of them in case they ran out, and then I asked myself: but will I have time to fill them all?
I used the *Quaderni Neri* like a portable studio that allowed me to work at home and when I was travelling, without unplugging the receiver from my source of ideas.
So I feel that life has been one single uninterrupted workday.
I numbered the sketchbooks and each page, almost always adding the date under drawings and writings to form a kind of illustrated diary.
In my first sketchbooks I rediscovered the projects for *La memoria invece* (about objects, life, architecture) a series of works between art and auto-anthropology with which I concluded my avant-garde period with Superstudio and started along the laborious journey of my approach to architecture.
Then I rediscovered almost all my projects from the studio in via San Gallo and the Natalini Architects projects from the studio at the Salviatino. Almost, but not all, because now most of my drawings are on transparent sheets (A3 butter tracing paper) and when I travel (no suitcases only cabin luggage) I take smaller and lighter sketchbooks, lined *Quaderni Cinesi* with a black hard cover and red corners and spine.
The projects are mixed with things I have seen: in books, in the mirror, in my rooms, in cities or the countryside.
The *Quaderni Estivi* appeared in recent years (I started taking vacations in 1997), with coloured sketches and watercolours. The *Quaderni Estivi* are a blend of sketched figures, landscapes, and architecture, mixed in a kind of childlike

contentment. It is as if the boundaries between different things have finally disappeared, like those between one day and another, or between a memory and a project, liquefied by the colours of summer like pigments in water. The sketchbooks (numbered like their pages) give a certain order to my thoughts, perhaps only a chronological order, but I feel it is the only kind possible, something like the authors in my library ranged in alphabetical order.

[04.08.01, da "Giustificazione dei Quaderni Neri" in *Adolfo Natalini-Disegni 1976-2001*, Milan 2002]

03. *Your sketches and preparatory drawings are strongly expressionistic. Strong incisive markings; the intense colour of somebody who loves to paint. When beginning a project, what role do you assign to preliminary sketches, or in any case, gestural expression, given that many of your final designs contain freehand interventions, both in line and colour?*

Drawing is the means that I find most suited to me: I have never been a theoretician and I never manage to pre-figure something in my mind without seeing it on the page, (I never remember any of my dreams except perhaps for some nightmare). I approach a project from several sides, each time engaging in a full body contact with the place, the program, and the limits.
In this combat, all means are acceptable: a distorted view of poets and writers who have investigated the area, barefaced copying of what already exists, the chess knight's jump over the adversary, metaphors and allegories, the most efficient arsenal of local constructors to outflank enemy lines...
The weapons I have available in this battle (which is more like Jacob's wrestling with the angel or a battle of love) are few, and among these, drawing is the most important. Drawing allows me to be a lot quicker, and at the same time, it forces me to stay rooted to the page and the project for long periods. I draw like a fisherman who casts his net and waits, or a farmer who works the soil, plants his seeds and waits... however, I certainly do not expect illumination or inspiration. (It has been a long time since I gave up on my Muses and they have indignantly turned their backs on me). But drawings produce other drawings, and these, other drawings again, and in this way, gradually the labyrinth appears and the project emerges. In short, the drawing leads me to the traces of the project, and while I am stalking the wild game, the project emerges (it is patently obvious that I am no hunting expert).
Perhaps my marks are strong because I have a heavy hand (I have never been a refined artist) and the colours are intense because I use only a few bad quality pencils without much colour; the colours are deepened because I change my mind and correct mistakes (my pencils often go back over previous traces or I try to cancel them with new lines). In a certain sense, a project is an entire preliminary sketch of the construction (even though there are tons of executive drawings created with appropriate instruments) and the construction is only the preliminary stage for the life that will exist inside and around it...
My lack of certainty always makes it difficult for me to finish a project; I keep working at it even when it is perhaps too late: this explains the manual interventions that occur at every level and my preference for traditional type constructions that allow me to tamper even during construction on site.

[30.10.90, from an interview by P. Scaglione, in *d'A*]

Facciate/Finestre
[Facades/Windows]

01. The project for a facade may seem a marginal aspect, but it is something that concerns public art, and the image of the city.
If the interior of a house is the private dominion, its exterior is always public, exposed to everybody's sight; it is part of the street, the piazza, the urban interior. The façade is the separating element (the skin, the membrane) between interior and exterior, between public and private. Just like the human face, it has openings to allow communication; the eyes, mouth, nostrils, ears are the orifices of the body that permit a relationship with the world around us, and in the same way, windows, doors, loggias, balconies, and porticoes permit a relationship between the house and the city.
"Architecture is the art of positioning windows", states a Spanish definition from the 19th century. It may seem diminutive, but if we think of a well-ordered city, where the plan of the streets and piazzas is well-defined, where the street alignments and heights are pre-established, and where a shared architectural language (a *koine*) exists, then the rhythm of the openings, their arrangement, size and aspect is the deciding element (naturally together with material and colour...). If we look at the history of architecture, it may seem that there has always been a trend towards increasingly larger openings, from the closed cave to the buildings made of glass... However, if we look at history from a longer perspective, we will note that the first shelters (like the Oldwerry windbreak in Africa) from the campfire of the nomadic hunter-gatherer to stable shelters (huts, pile-dwellings...) showed an evolution from the open dwelling to the enclosed, from control of the environment using energy (fire), then using building materials (wood, stone).
Therefore we can see there has been an "oscillation" from open to closed and back to open, and so on...
Until the arrival of a progressive reclosing with bioclimatic architecture compared to the generalised curtain wall system.

[07.04.00, *Lezioni*]

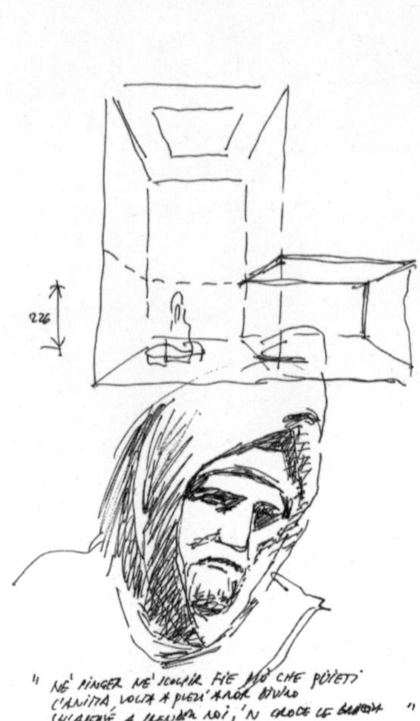

Extension of the Museo dell'Opera di S. Maria del Fiore, Florence, 2001-2015, Sketches for the Sala della Pietà, from *Quaderni Neri*

Il quaderno italiano

[Italian sketchbook]

—

Bank head office in Alzate Brianza (Como)

1978-1983

This is the first of a series of designs worked out between the end of 1978 and summer 1983 (see also *Lotus* no. 37). The aim was to explore the possibilities of effecting crosses and hybrids between traditional and sophisticated construction techniques, between classical language and vernacular language.
The vocabulary of this building is contemporary (open floor layouts, continuous facade, sun-shields) with simple elements markedly characterized, but at the same time evoking techniques and languages (from the Romanesque of the Como area to Terragni) and strongly historicized architectural features (pillar, pilaster, ashlar cladding). The place: no longer countryside but not yet city. A place without image or memory... But the place itself of the building is indeed a memorable place. It's the place of the masterbuilders of Como and of Romanesque, with its dichromatic decoration and semicircular apses and with pilasters and lobed pillars. The place of Terragni, with his heroic youthful frenzies, the place of the absolute geometries of the Casa del Fascio and of the slender pillars of the Sant'Elia kindergarten. The place also of the Rotonda d'Inverigo by Cagnola, and of the villas of Brianza resting on the hillsides with their calm and dignity. The place of the Torre d'Alzata and of Villa Odescalchi... And also the place of bank buildings, first of all the Ca de Sass of Muzio (Milan), with its portico crushed with granite, and of numberless other bank buildings, dignified, rich with dignity, rich with inner calm made to preserve without ostentation and made to endure in materials over which time flows without trace... Finally, feeling the eyes of "engineer" Gadda on me, given the place ("This happy land denominated Breanza"), I wished to avoid giving him an occasion for wondrous descriptions of "ville, villette, villule" or tirades against "20th century functionalism"...
The building stands on a deep site (50 x 150 m) between a busy road (the state highway between Como and Bergamo) and a small local road, on the edge of the township of Alzate Brianza.
A rectangular parallelepiped 12 metres wide and 40 long is set diagonally across the plot and at its end are two triangular prisms housing all the services. The bearing structure is all external to the building and is clad in two-tone bands of stone.
The same cladding is applied to the triangular prisms of the services and to the corrugated block emerging from the structure. The corrugated block (a kind of "articulated" cylinder) emphasizes the public lobby, board room and, reflected in the pond, the cylindrical volume of the semi-underground caveau. On the front facing the state highway a parallelepiped emerges from the ground, inclined in relation to the main one and containing the caretaker's lodge. Overshadowed by the structure, the continuous facades are fully glazed with narrow profiles of black neoprene.
On the reflecting facades transparent windows open. By day the building appears as an exoskeleton shading a reflecting and impenetrable body. By night the relations are inverted and the building reveals its interior lit up with the shadows of its structure standing out against it.
At night only the great cavity of the triangular prisms appears, containing the stairs, and the various colors of the curved bodies of the service floors appear like delicate inner organs...
The diagonal position, imposed partly by needs of space and exposure, displays the building foreshortened from the road, increasing its plastic and dynamic effect. I've always preserved a grateful memory of the lessons on mineralogy by Professor Rodolico and I've often used as a guide for unlikely trips his volume *Le pietre delle città d'Italia*. So, from my first visit of inspection, I found myself observing the morainic hills, among familiar names between Baveno and Montorfano. Then the excavations found a great "erratic" (which I'd have liked to preserve whole)... The cladding is in slabs of polished *serizzo* and light streaked granite: this produces a strongly marked combination of two colors enhanced by different treatment of the surfaces (polished and opaque).
The cladding is detached from the walls and structures following the ventilated wall technique: the gaps of seven millimetres between stone and stone are let open. A series of special pieces of greater thickness form the quoins on the prisms and the mouldings of the pillars. Now that the building has been laboriously completed, I'd like that it would be possible to say, like Palladio of his Basilica, that here "the material is all of stone living and hard" and that the stones have been "laid and bound together with supreme diligence."

Architectural project
Adolfo Natalini
with Gian Piero Frassinelli, Fabrizio Natalini;
Structural project
Studio Alessandro Chimenti;
Mechanical installation design
Enzo Giusti;
Electrical installation design
Studio tecnico Lombardini;
Project manager
Gilardoni.

First prize in a competition invite, 1978.

Final project and working plan, 1979;
Construction, 1980-83.

Tercas Architettura Prize, 1986;
International prize: *Stone architecture award*, 1987;
Prize *Marble Architectural Awards (Maa Italy)*, 1988;
Prize in Italian competition: *Granite design*, 1988;
Selected for the European Architectural Prize in Barcellona (*Mies van der Rohe Prize* – official European Union prize since 2001), 1988.

Photos: Mario Ciampi

CASSA RURALE ED ARTIGIANA DELL'ALTA BRIANZA

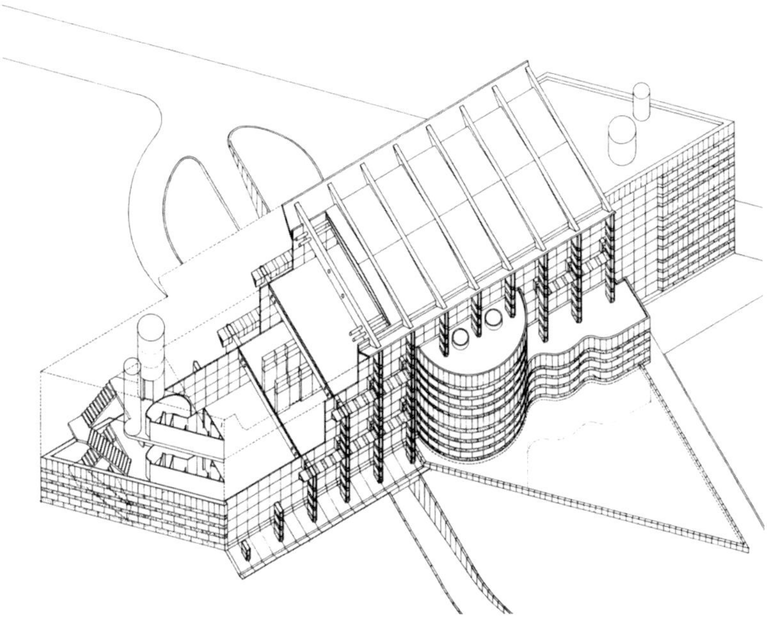

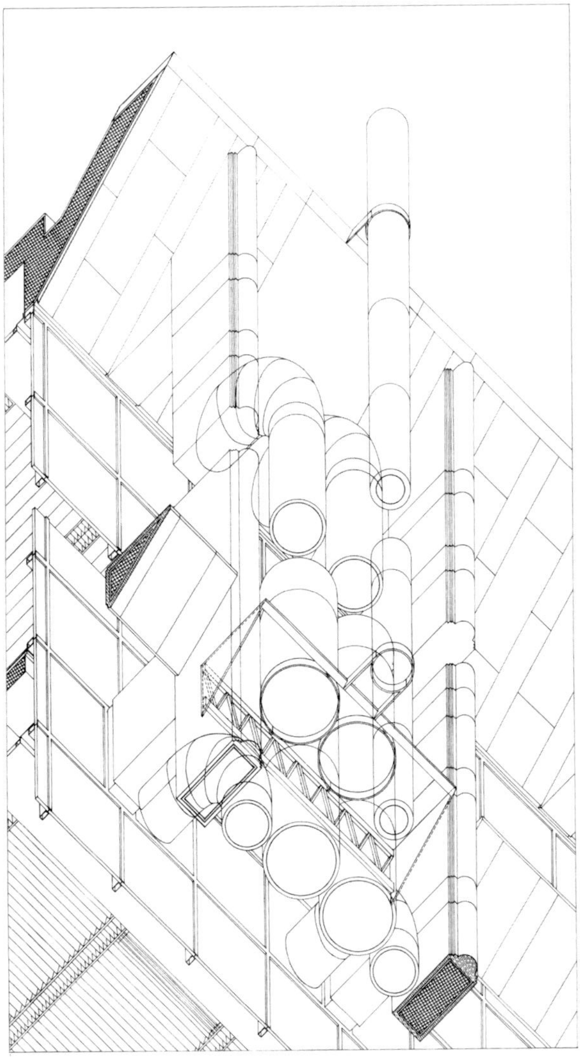

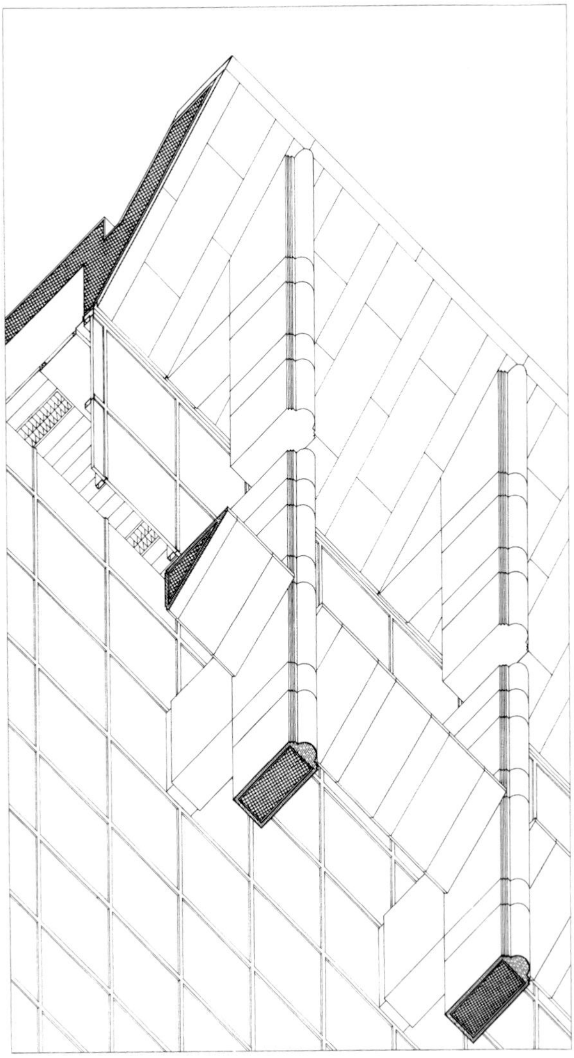

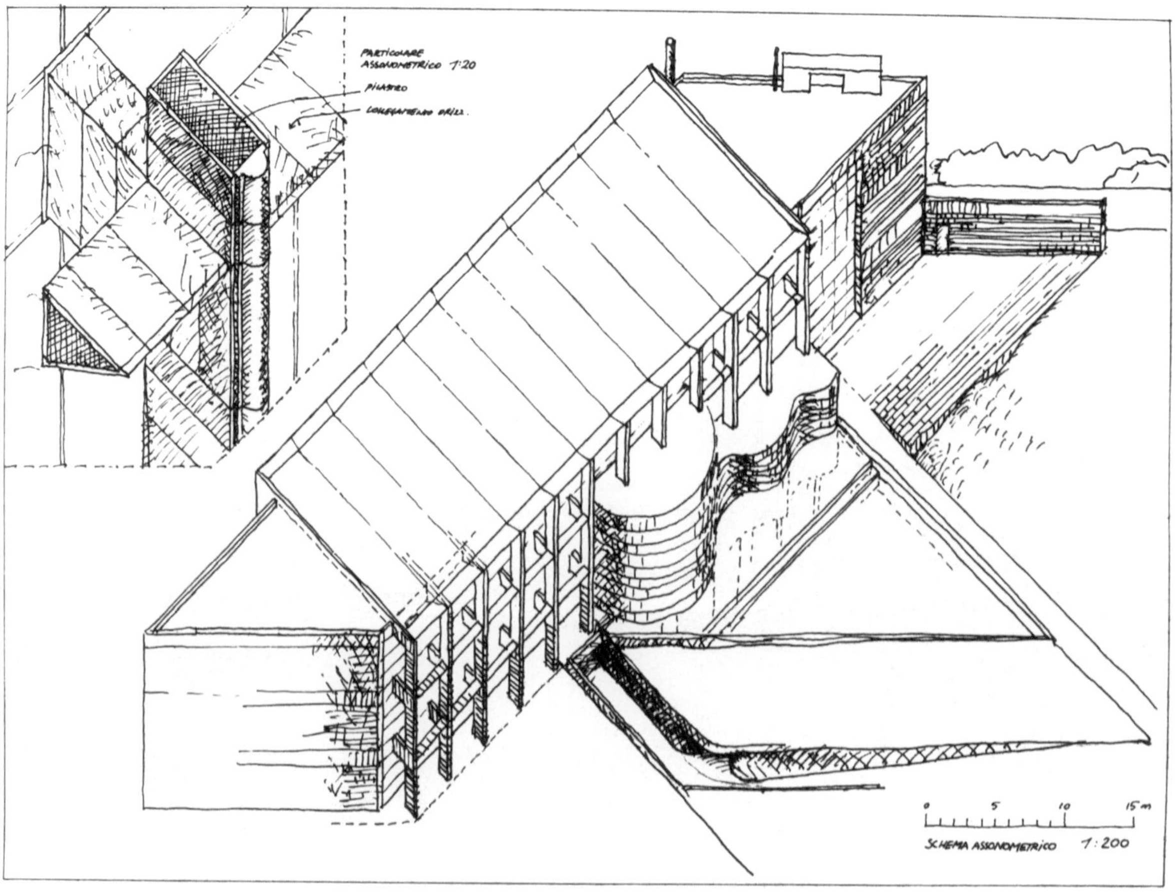
PARTICOLARE ASSONOMETRICO 1:20
PILASTRO
COLLEGAMENTO ORIZZ.
0 5 10 15 m
SCHEMA ASSONOMETRICO 1:200

PROSPETTO EST NORD EST

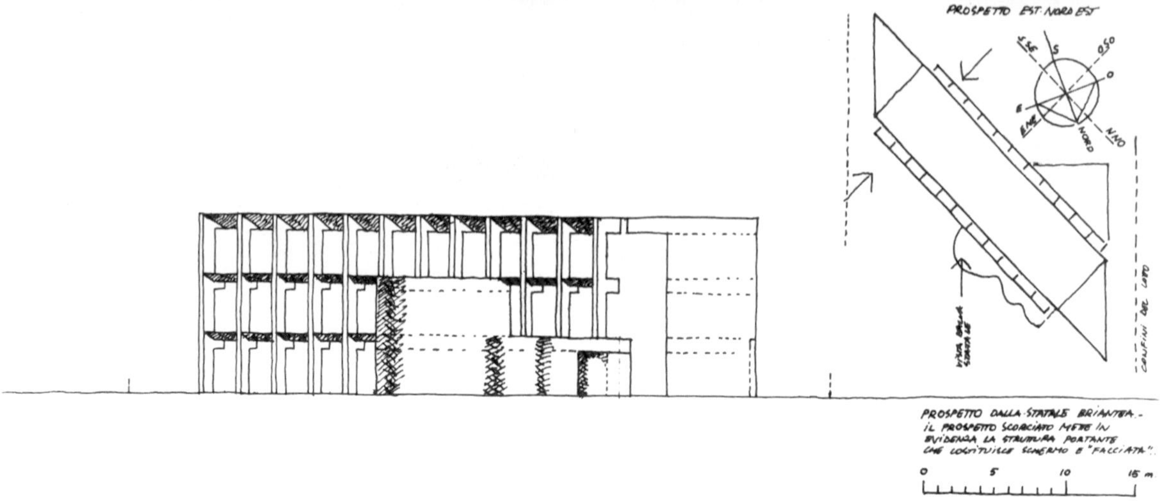
CONFINI DEL LOTTO
PROSPETTO DALLA STATALE BRIANTEA.-
IL PROSPETTO SCORCIATO METTE IN
EVIDENZA LA STRUTTURA PORTANTE
CHE COSTITUISCE SCHERMO E "FACCIATA".
0 5 10 15 m
PROSPETTO E.NE 1:200

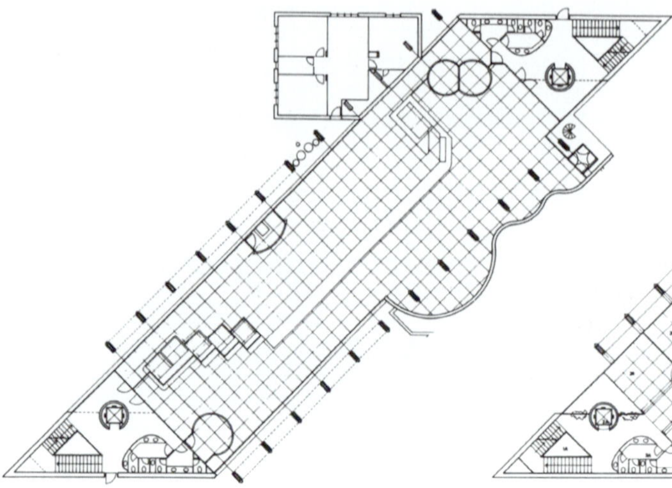

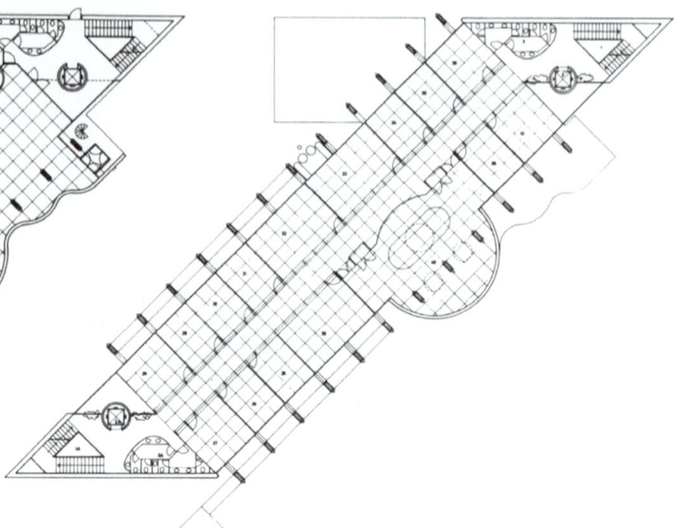

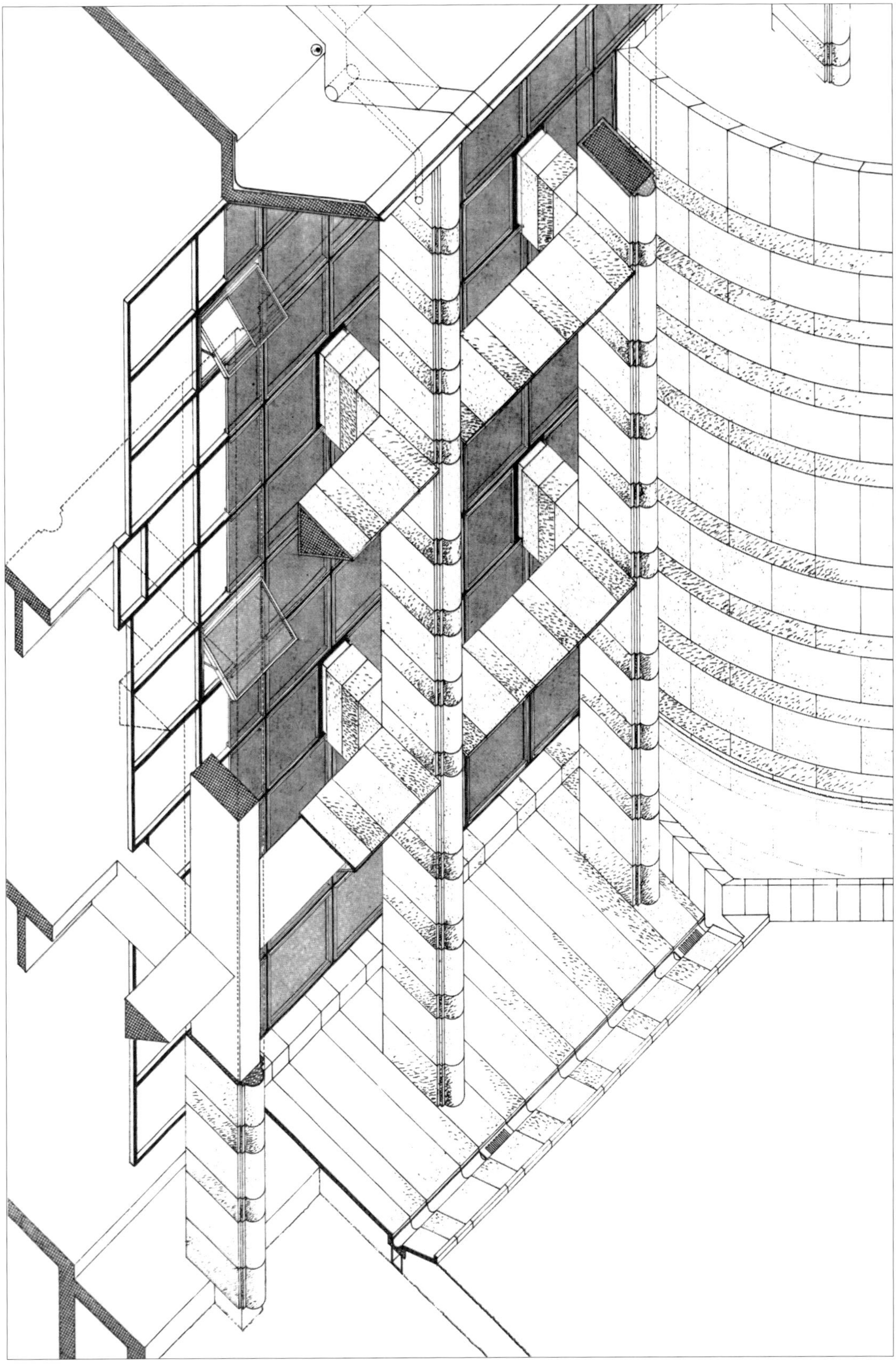

Computer centre in Zola Predosa (Bologna)

1979-1981

Carlo Francesco Dotti's eighteenth century model of a hay loft marked and still marks the Bolognese plain with a series of works of architecture giving shelter under varying structures to hay, farm implements, machines. Our building with its links to this tradition shows how architecture can contain machines (but not vice versa), that traditional techniques can live happily with the most sophisticated ones, that the wisdom of ancient materials can easily tolerate new ones, that history serves to give hope for the future and that, finally, the countryside, the city and industry can be united by the logic of poetry.
The country landscape, industrial buildings and the motorway are the components of this site.
The countryside still retains a large proportion of its preindustrial character thanks to its vast dimensions and the depth of the culture that has shaped it.
Its regular fields, the farmhouses, the large hay lofts with their roofs supported by brick pillars have shaped the countryside so as to maintain control over all events, changes, destructions. This new building is the completion of an industrial complex already in existence whose buildings belong rather to the local architectural tradition than to any industrial logic.
The Autostrada del Sole [Highway to the Sun] and a road bridge form two sides of the site; the existing buildings form the other like a barrier between it and the fields, giving the idea of a courtyard.
The new building is a parallelepiped of rectangular shape at a 45° angle to towards the direction of the road bridge, and closes the third side of the courtyard.
Since it was not possible to equal the large size of the sloping roofed-warehouse on the opposite side, the interior perspective has been widened by the use of triangular prisms containing service units and with a large single-planed roof sloping towards the inside of the courtyard. The roof, a characteristic component of this building, is supported by pillars in brickwork with cast concrete elements.
The outside pillars serve as a sun screen and form two arcades, one of which functions as a passage between the parking lots and the building complex. A square area paved in porphyry, marked by lines in terracotta tiles, that give physical evidence to the two directions of the construction (with an inclination of 90 degrees – the old section – and 45 degrees – the new one) serves as a link between the various parts of the building.
Under the shelter of the roof and the pillars, the building itself has continuous facades of anodized aluminium in two dark tones with a rather special design. All technical elements (fire escapes, any mechanical structures, etc.) are in metal painted red. The three interior floors are structured in different manners. The lower floor contains the computer machinery itself and is the most closed-in (with brick walling and arched windows) for safety reasons. The intermediate floor (offices) is organized along a spinal-cord corridor with a series of sections for files (in brickwork).
The upper floor has an arcade facing the inside courtyard, with perforated openings onto the sky and the surrounding countryside.

Architectural project
Adolfo Natalini,
Roberto Magris;
Structural project
Alessandro Chimenti;
Mechanical installation design
Enzo Giusti;
Electrical installation design
Studio Tecnico Lombardini;
Project manager
Roberto Magris.

Preliminary project, 1979;
Final project and working plan, 1979;
Construction, 1979-81.

In 2001, the Municipal Administration placed a restriction on the building because of its strong architectural importance

Photos: Mario Ciampi

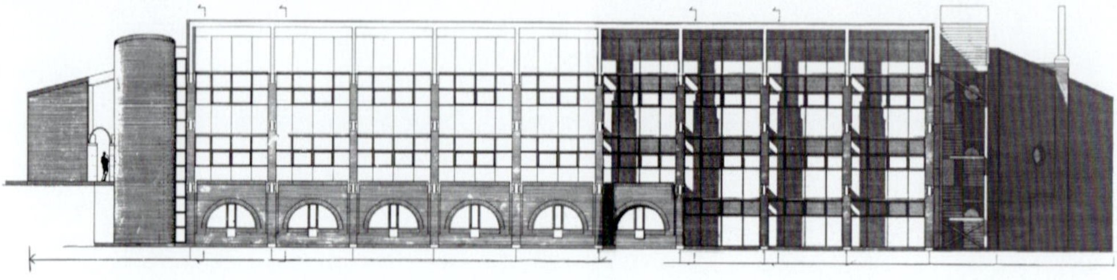

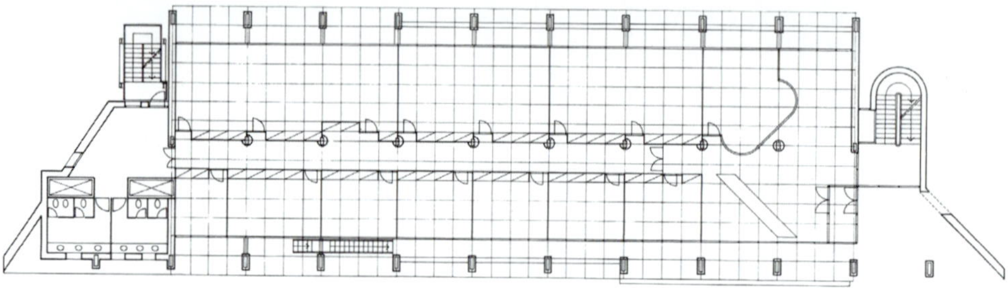

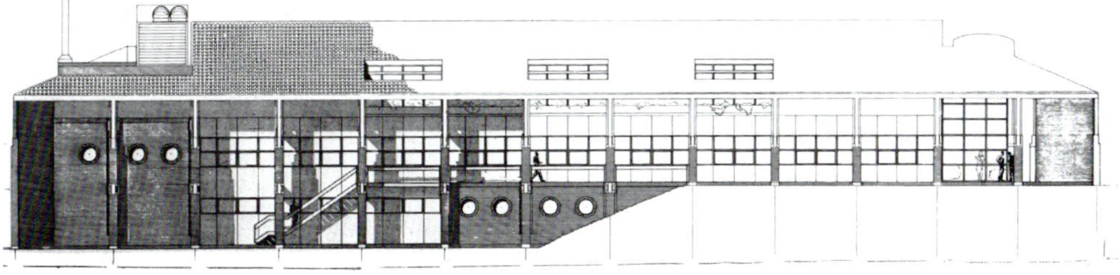

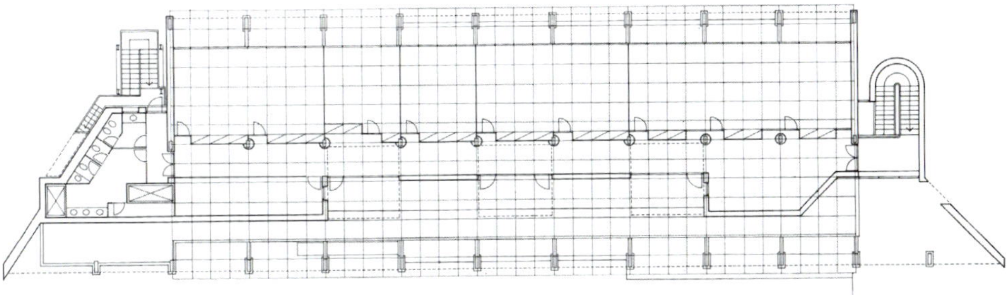

University Campus in Novoli, Florence

1993-2003

The Social Sciences Centre, which includes the three Faculties of Law, Political Science and Economics, is part of the University of Florence building plan.
The localization in the former Fiat industrial area at Novoli, established by the town development plan, will contribute to the vast process of decentralization and urban rebalance in Florence. In accordance with Leon Krier's guideline plan and the Recovery plan proposed by Gabetti and Isola, the complex is subdivided into seven buildings, positioned on a north-south axis between viale Guidoni and a new piazza.
The offices of the dean, plus three buildings for teaching and research purposes are located on the corner formed by via Forlanini and viale Guidoni.
The library is situated between viale Guidoni and the piazza, thus closing the perspective of the north-south axis. The student centre and administration buildings also overlook the piazza. All the buildings are connected by double height porticoes which form the University avenue, terminating with an open loggia below the library book tower. The piazza leads to the large public park, also accessed from the walkways that cross the avenue. Each of the various buildings constitutes a block, according to the guideline policy with blocks that vary in size from 70 x 50 to 36 x 16 metres: the larger blocks form the teaching and research areas, with lecture rooms on the ground and first floors, while on the upper floors, the research areas are arranged around central courtyards. The library building also occupies one of the larger blocks and is divided into two connected building units, one of which contains the library for the three faculties and the other the book tower.
The smaller blocks are aligned with the buildings that house the administration offices, Dean's office and Student centre. Although they have different characteristics, all are designed as "urban buildings" with a plain linear structure aligned with street layouts and a clear division between the ground, upper and top floors. The porticoes, surface finishes, openings and colours combine to create an urban image that is both dignified and restrained. The porticoes and the lower floors are faced in stone, while the upper floors have a red plaster finish with prefabricated artificial stone elements. Roofing is in copper.
The Library building occupies one of the largest blocks and is composed of two connected structures: one contains the library for three faculties, and the other is the library book tower located at the end of the porticoed University avenue. It is connected with the large piazza leading to the park.
The tower is a stone parallelepiped with a double-height open loggia on the ground floor (perhaps this resembles the granary of Orsanmichele before the loggia was transformed into a church?).
The library has a trapeze-shaped perimeter with a large curved glassed wall that welcomes students and teaching staff approaching from the avenue.
The building is designed like a huge cube of books with a central circular light well. The study areas are located around the external perimeter and the light well to provide the maximum number of individual places for study. The library is composed of three floors, one serves as the entrance and the other two for reading rooms, while the books are arranged on six floors because each reading room has double-height ceilings. The reading desks are in direct contact with the windows and the light, and are surrounded by open bookshelves. The students are able to circulate freely among the bookshelves and study close to the light sources. Naturally, the library is equipped with the latest technology and internet connection, but the project was designed to focus mainly on the potential of the books, space and light.
When designing the building, the architects researched many libraries of the past such as the Boullée library at the Uffizi museum, the Asplund library in Stockholm and the Kahn library in Exeter, then directed their focus on the library of the future. The design was based on the number of books, kilometres of shelves required (about 30 km) the number of users and staff, the square footage of the flooring and the cubic air space, but as well as these calculations, great attention was paid to the quality of the environment and the quiet tranquil atmosphere. The aim was to create peaceful isolated surroundings for study, while providing Novoli and Florence with a complex with refined urban design.

Architectural project
Natalini Architetti (Florence), Adolfo Natalini, Fabrizio Natalini;
Interior design
Adolfo Natalini with Fabrizio Natalini, Remo Buti with Silvia Cilembrini and Fabio Leoncini;
General project
Fiatengineering SpA;
Project management
Fiatengineering SpA

Preliminary project, 1993-94;
Final project, 1996-97;
Working plan, 1997-98 (in collaboration with Fiatengineering SpA);
Construction, 1997-2003.

Photos: Pietro Savorelli

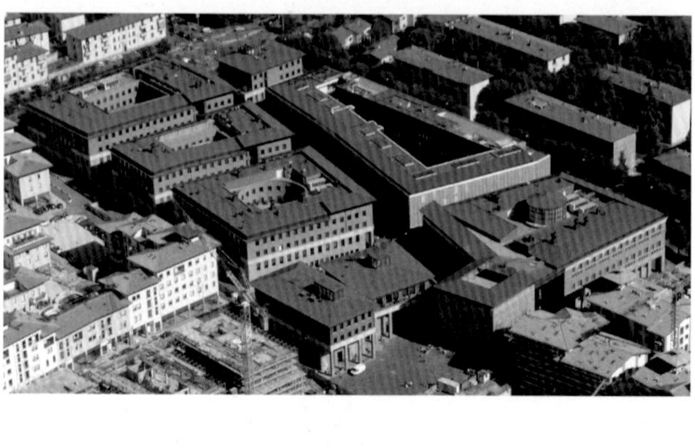

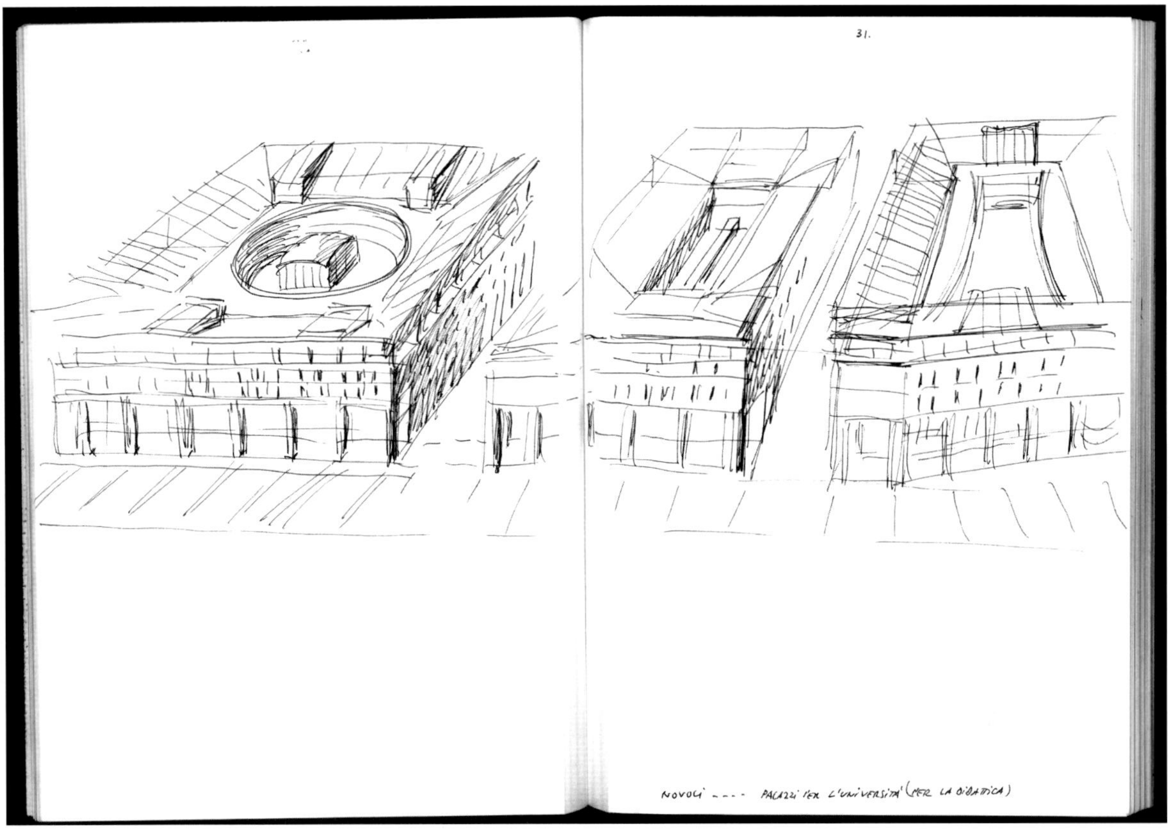

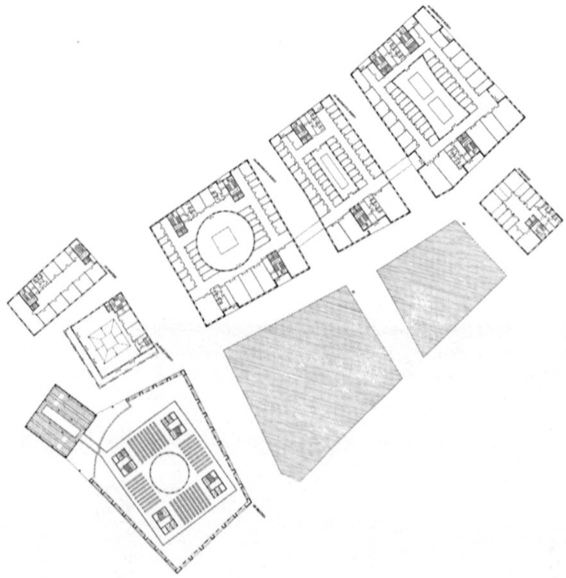

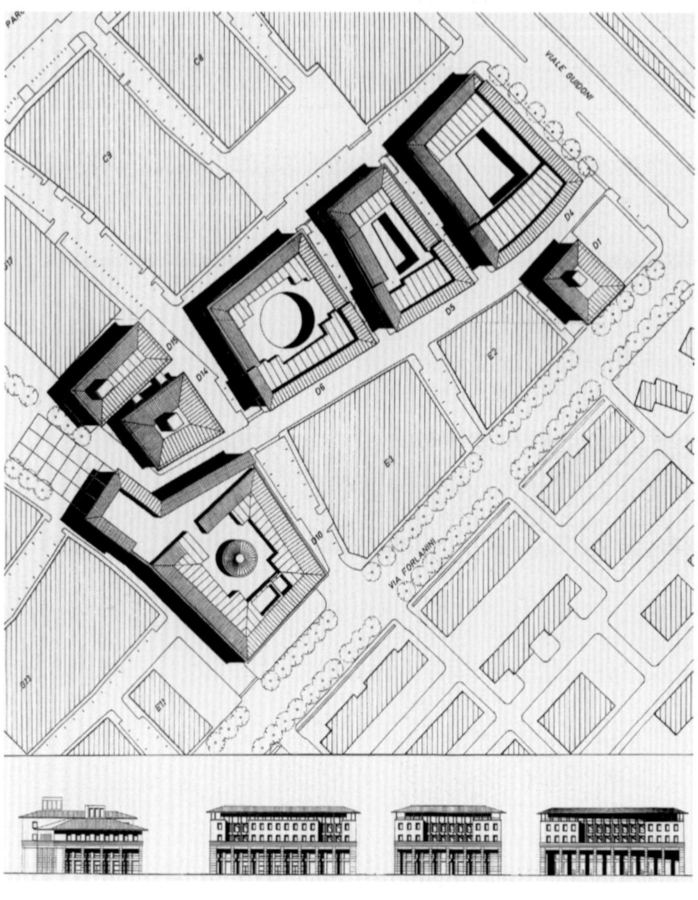
VIALE GUIDONI
VIA FORLANINI

University Campus in Porta Tufi, Siena

1995-2001

The building which used to house the pediatric clinic at Porta Tufi was situated in a visually crucial position for the profile of Siena, and it was one of the most obvious "out of scale" elements of the city. The hypothesis of its restructuring, with its partial demolition and reconstruction. Seemed extremely onerous and not very satisfactory. After examining the various alternatives for its restructuring, the feasibility study proposed replacing the existing building with a new one, which was to become the premises for the Schools of Jurisprudence and Political Science of Siena University. The building is divided into three bodies: a rectlinear body at right angles with via Mattioli, for the studies of the Faculty; an L-shaped building, with a position similar to that of the pre-existing surrounding buildings, assigned as to the Library; and finally a rectangular body connected to the one just mentioned, laid out on two levels, with a flat roof and crossed by a gallery containing the stairs, reserved for the classrooms. The three bodies are connected by the pre-existing wall which looks onto via Mattioli, most of which is open and transformed into an entrance portico, with a perforated screen which maintains the unity of the street front, while at the same time opening it to the new buildings. The new complex appears as a group of differently articulated building units, open towards the valley and positioned in such a way that they follow the level curves of the ground. The overall disposition of masses was broken up into a series of elements, dimensioned in accordance with the surrounding buildings, therefore capable of forming a new urban border which can easily be integrated with the proposals for the improvement of the valley edge by means of a walkway across the hill, as foreseen in the town development plan.
From the higher street level we therefore enter a large portico which con-stitutes a quiet waiting area. Going along the portico we reach the entrance hall, with large windows looking onto the valley, and the professors' studies, the library and the classrooms open onto this hall. From the entrance hall two tong stairways lead to the amphitheatres, in front of which we find a large area for the students and another group of classrooms. In the study wing, facing the entrance hall, we have the offices, staffrooms and meeting rooms. The technical areas, the stores, a number of service rooms and the car parks are situated in the lowest of the three bodies. The buildings are clad in *cotto* and travertine, with some stamped concrete elements. The gallery roofing is in green copper.

General project and architectural project
Natalini Architetti (Florence),
Adolfo Natalini,
Fabrizio Natalini;
Collaborating team
Nazario Scelsi,
Adrian Blanchard,
Giovanna Potestà,
Damiano Pica,
Stefano Tozzi,
Angelo Torre,
Giulia Chiappi,
Tommaso Barni;
Bioclimatic design consultant
Marco Sala;
Structural project
Alessandro Chimenti,
Massimo Vivoli;
Installation design
Luigi Michelozzi,
Mauro Martini;
Project management
Adolfo Natalini,
Project management assistant
Romano Olmi;
Client
Università degli
Studi di Siena;
Construction company
Grassetto SpA, Tortona.

Preliminary project, 1995;
Final project, 1996;
Working plan, 1996-97;
Construction, 1997-2001.

Photos: Pietro Savorelli
and Giovanni Chiaramonte

P

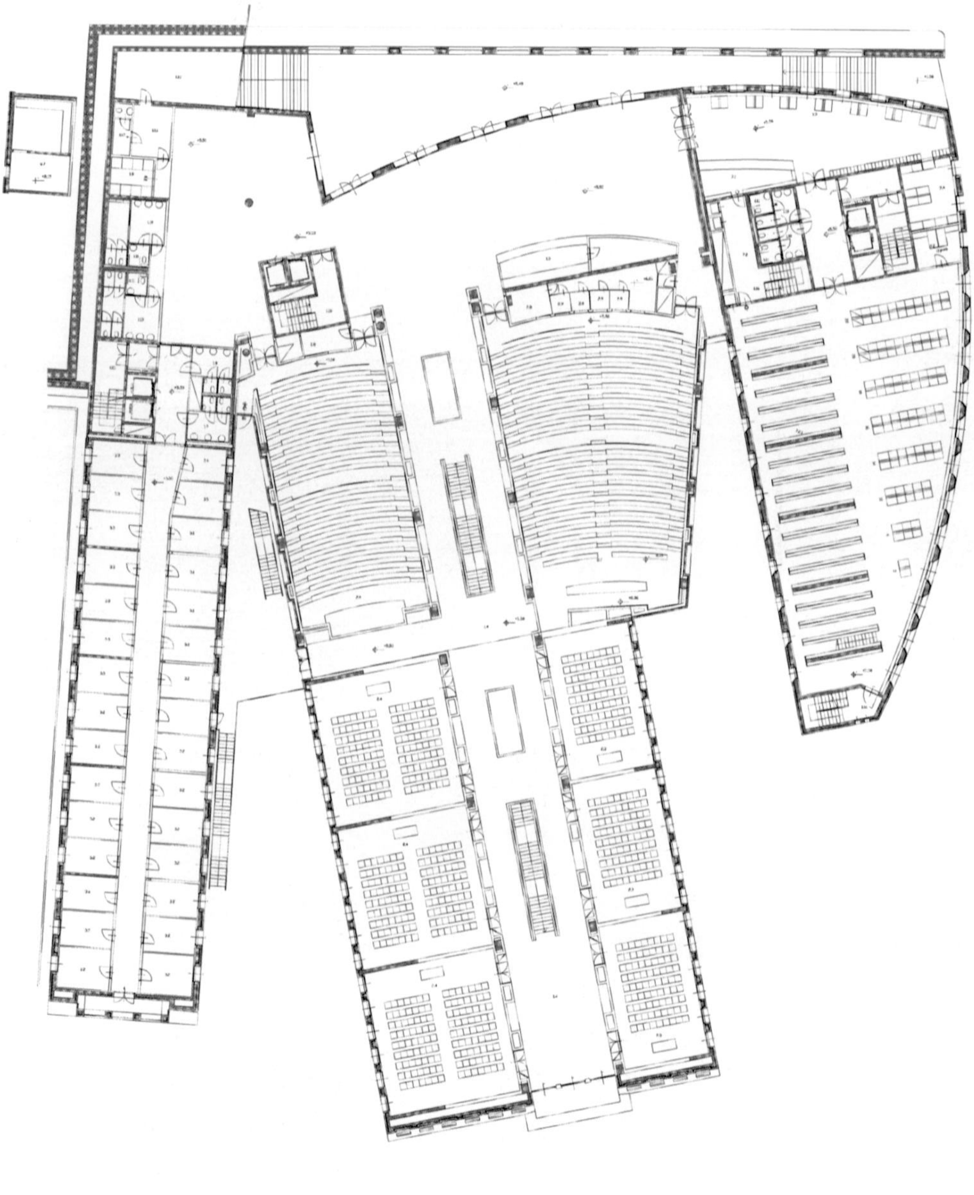

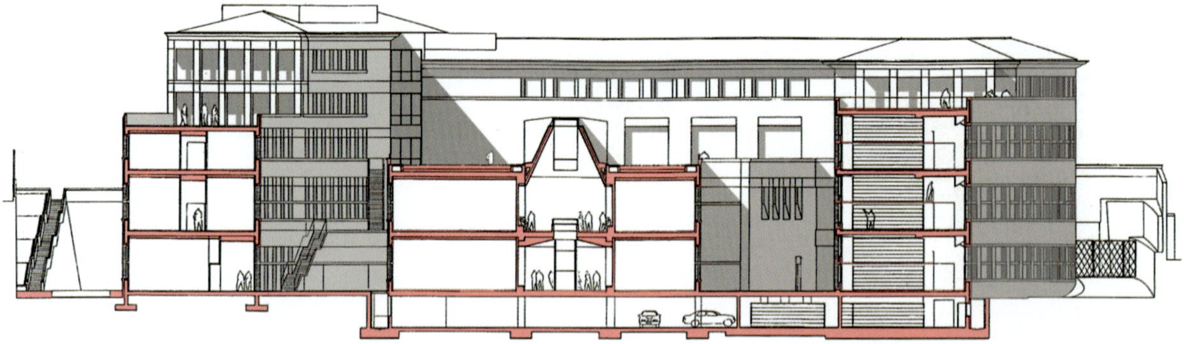

SEZIONE B-B

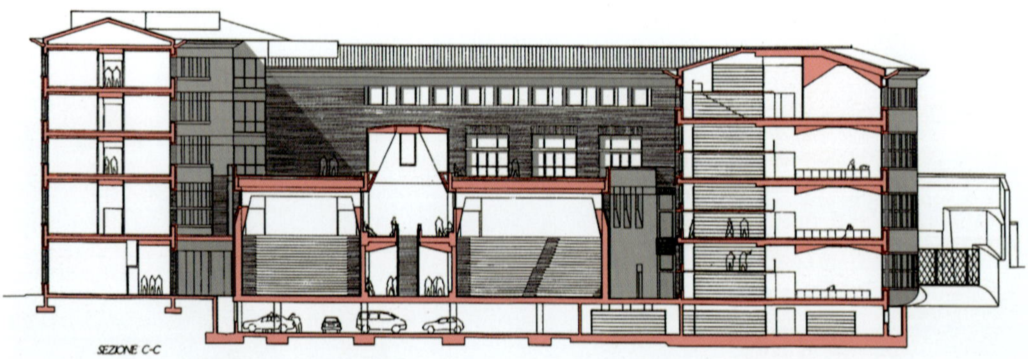

SEZIONE C-C

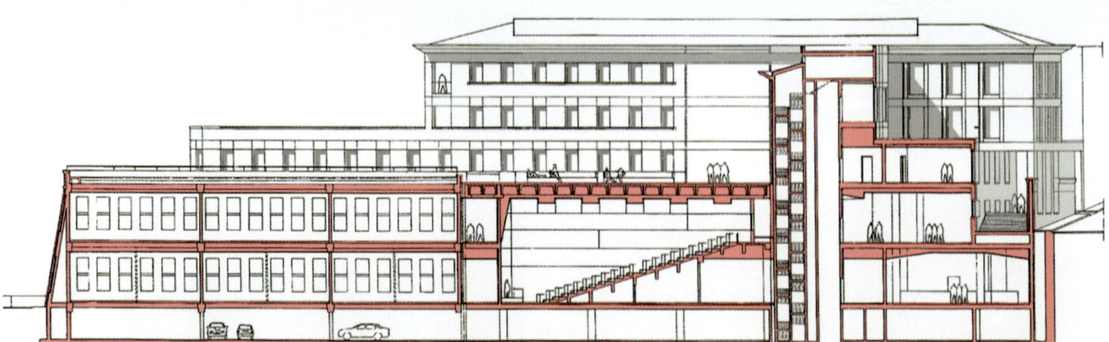

SEZIONE 4-4

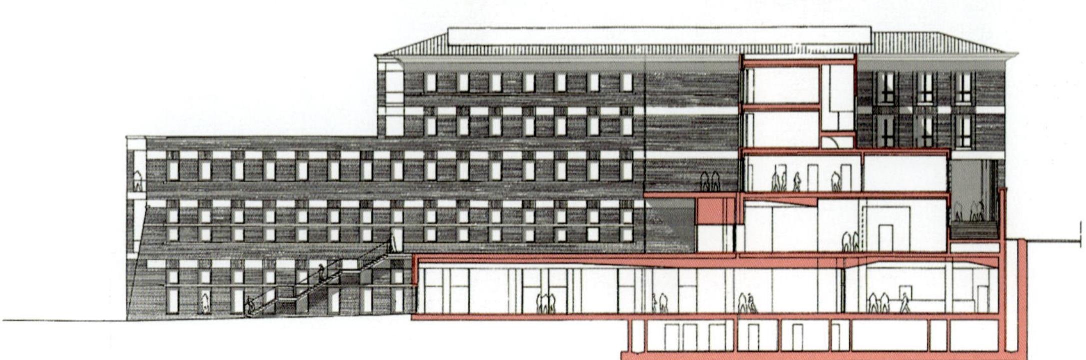

SEZIONE 2-2

Anello Residential Complex and Park at Val Marina Redevelopment plan in Calenzano (Florence)

1995-2009

Anello and Parco di Val Marina is the name given to the urban redevelopment of a decommissioned industrial area divided into two parts by the access road to the Calenzano railway station: the eastern side houses the constructed area with a circular building complex (Anello di Val Marina), while the western side is composed of a public park.
The constructed area is composed of a residential complex with 131 apartments, protected from the roadway towards Prato by a double-height portico that houses retail stores and public welfare offices on the ground floor.
The building also includes underground garages for 152 vehicles and public parking for the station, private green areas and public park.
The building is composed of a single, large, five-storey circle that provides all apartments with spacious views over the internal courtyard green space as well as external views overlooking the public park and private planted areas. On ground level, service companies and public facilities are planned along viale Matteotti and the service road of via di Prato, with an established quota of residential apartments of various sizes on the upper floors in the vicinity of the private green spaces.
A double-height portico on the external perimeter along via di Prato and the road to the station (viale Matteotti) links the different buildings and provides overhead protection for the pedestrian access to the future aboveground subway station.
The complex is composed of two different facades: the first is an austere closed exterior that protects the apartments from surrounding environmental noise pollution, while the inner facade is open and welcoming, with views overlooking the internal green space in the common area for residents' use.
At street level the circular structure in encased by double-height porticoes, which serve a dual purpose: to protect public walkways and to act as a sound barrier.
Once again, architecture is able to take inconvenient restrictive aspects and transform them to become creative elements of the project.

Architectural project
Natalini Architetti;
Structural project
Enrico Baroni,
Alberto Mariotti;
Installation design
Luigi Tavoni,
Daniele Tavoni;
Project manager
Mario Daneri,
Carlo Savelli;
Client
Istria Soc. Coop,
Leonardo da Vinci Soc. Coop,
Nomopao Soc. Coop.

Photos: Mario Ciampi

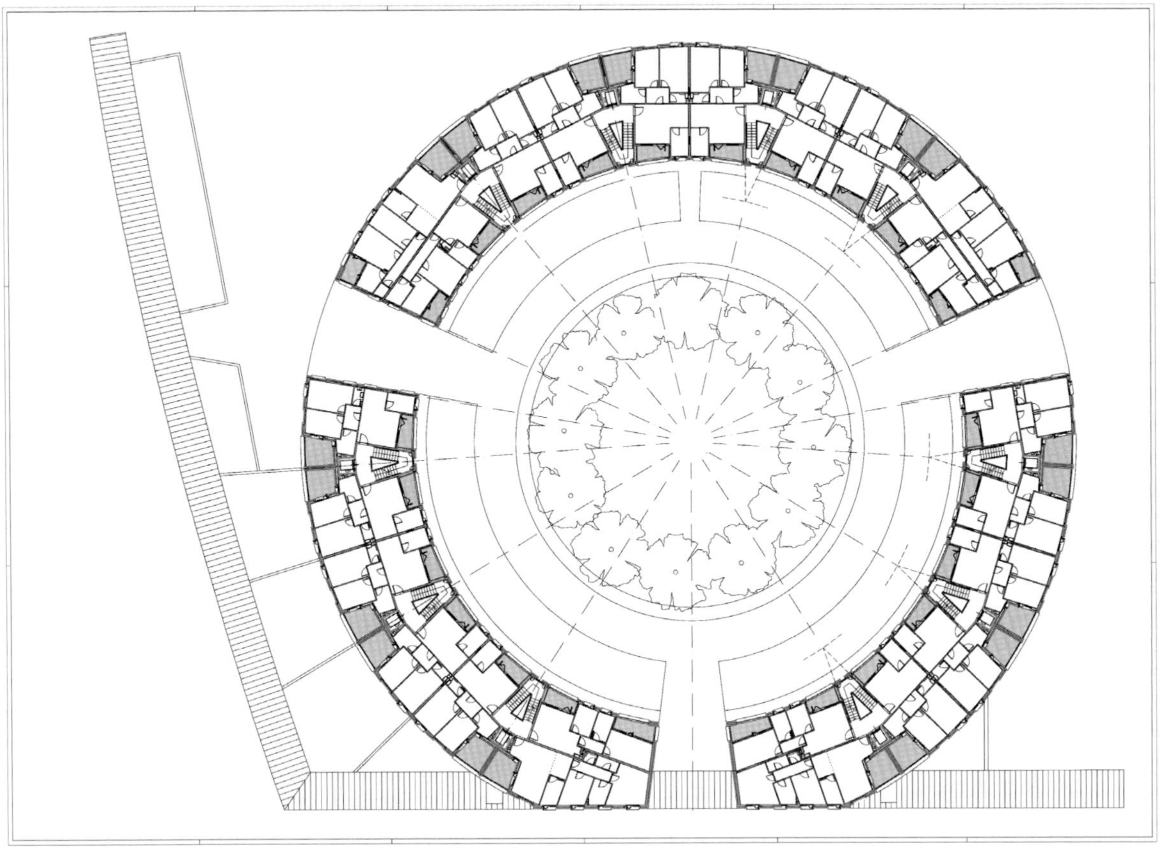

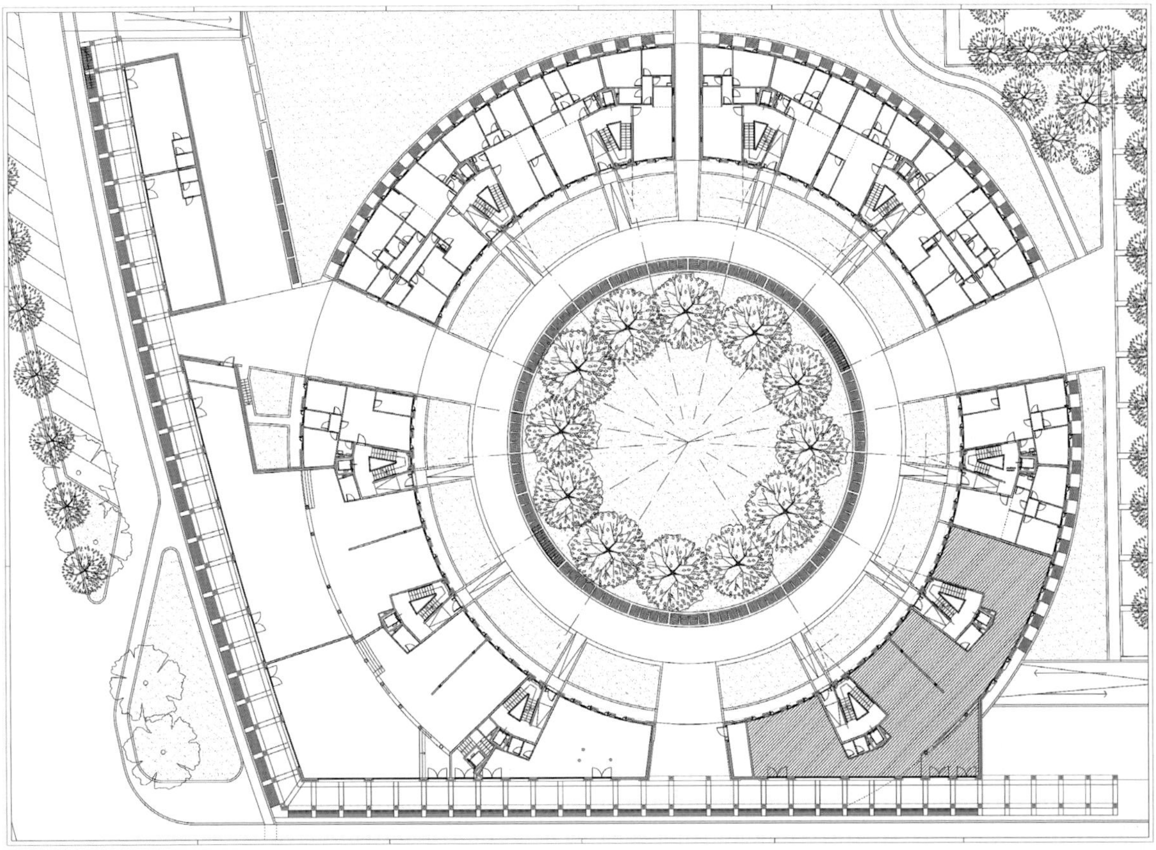

Completion of the Misericordia Cemetery in S. Maria dell'Antella, Bagno a Ripoli (Florence)

1998-2008

I began to design the project for the Misericordia Cemetery in Antella on June 27, 1966, taking part in an architectural competition on the day I graduated. Others won the competition, (I took second place) and the construction was started, but later suspended. On June 27, 1988, the Misericordia Confraternity assigned me the task of completing the cemetery, and I have been working on the project since then, continuously modifying the plans according to new requirements. Over this long period, I have visited the cemetery very often, because during this time my mother, (who died in 1992), my father (in 1995) and my wife, who died in 2008, have all been buried here.

The project was designed as a meditation on the passage of death; therefore, it was conceived as a sacred place, but also a study in civil architecture. It was aimed at completing the existing structure while attempting to reconcile the various styles with an architecture deeply rooted in the sense of place and its history.
The Misericordia Cemetery is a monumental cemetery (famous for the works of artists like Galileo Ghini and Ammanati Piombanti, and for the tombs of well-known figures) but it is located in an extremely beautiful little valley crossed by a small river. The cemetery has a "sober monumental" beauty that needed to be respected and expanded.

The completion project provided for two new additions (the round courtyard and the open courtyard connected by a portico) that were organically integrated with an existing structure and together they create a dialogue with the landscape, the hills and the river.
The additions were not designed to be camouflaged: although different from the pre-existent structures, they respect the general layout composed of long walkways that overlook enclosures and more intimate areas, like the chapels with burial crypts.
The additions are embedded in the topography of the location (to reduce the visual impact) following the course of the river and traces of ancient roadways.

The portico links the pedestrian walkways on various levels, to connect the round courtyard and existing buildings with the floors below ground, at ground level and on the second level, while it is interrupted on the first floor to create a large portal that marks the continuation of main walkway through the monumental cemetery.

From the public pathways, the chapels are set around the circular courtyard; they have a series of openings in the back walls to provide natural light and to give mourners an external view. The roofing, the small votive shrine with overhead lighting and the vertical openings that shed lateral light on the crypt walls create an environment that is respectful and dignified but not bleak or oppressive. The chapels have a trapeze-shaped floorplan that widens towards the exterior with the openings and the votive shrine. The round courtyard is designed to form a semi-circular raised hill with a blessing altar set beneath a glassed roof.

The open courtyard is aligned with the level of the first floor of the round courtyard and the connecting portico. The portico provides access along a new metal grid walkway that links up with the central route between the chapels and leads to the circular Misericordia Chapel with its cone-shaped roof.
The chapel represents an emerging sign of the new profile creating a solemn conclusion to the complex in the direction of via Montisoni and forming the new entrance to the cemetery.
The open courtyard is composed of a large grassed slope that follows the natural gradient of the land. From the portico, this green slope leads the eye towards the landscape and the hills, with an expanded panoramic view of the curve of the round courtyard.

Alongside the open courtyard is a triangular area with burial grounds divided by two paths in cross formation. This area features an oval shaped hill with gentle slopes that blend with the surrounding landscape. Green planting defines the new perimeter of the cemetery and screens the detention basin on the south-west side. The basin has been planted to create a passage between the cemetery and the surrounding areas destined for green crops and paths for nature walks.

Plain and simple architectural language has been used, because when confronted by the tragedy of death we have a desperate need of normality.
The porticoes, loggias and chapels have a familiar aspect and are built using traditional local materials: walls in white clinker (with different textures and small stone inserts), painted walls, grès and stone flooring, and galvanized metal structures for the loggias. Porphyry slab paving has been used for the walkways, with porphyry blocks for vehicle routes, laid to provide adequate drainage. The paths through the burial grounds are in mixed conglomerate material.
Even the Misericordia Chapel resembles a small house: because of its proportions, furnishing and the light that floods in from above, it is transformed into a place of silence and prayer (perhaps the circular form may remind some of the San Galgano Chapel at Montesiepi...).

Architectural project
Adolfo Natalini,
Fabrizio Natalini;
Collaborating team
Nazario Scelsi;
Project manager
Adolfo Natalini;
Project and structural project managment
Alessandro Chimenti,
Massimo Vivoli;
Project and installation design project management
Luigi Michelozzi,
Mauro Martini;
Client
Venerabile Confraternita della Misericordia di S. Maria dell'Antella.

Photos: Mario Ciampi

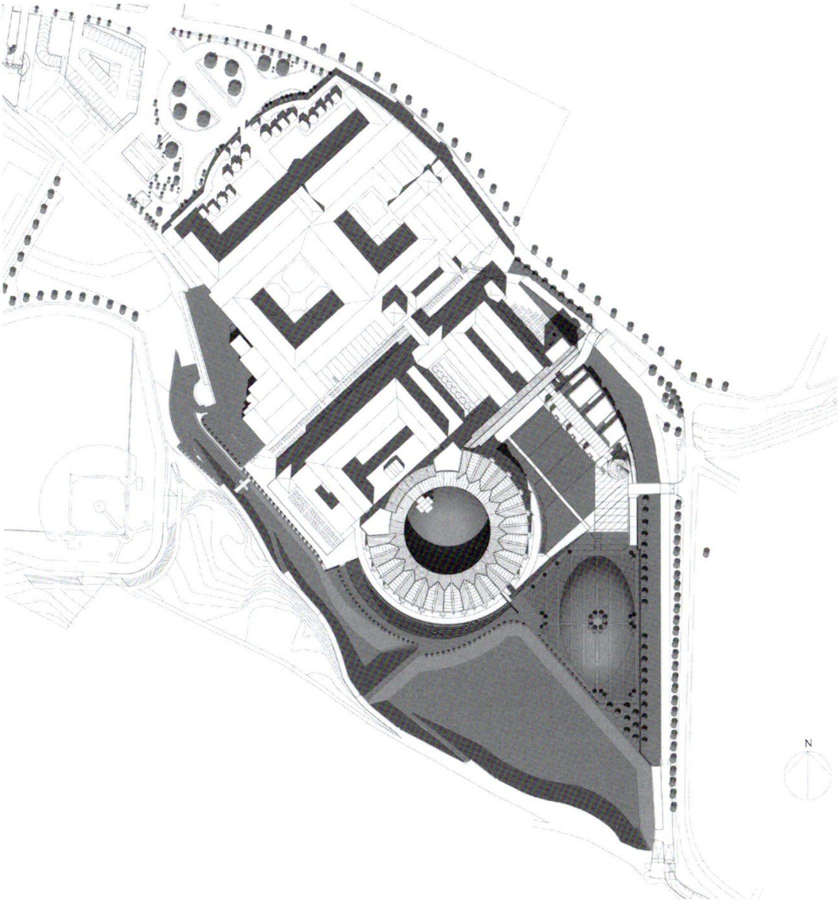
N

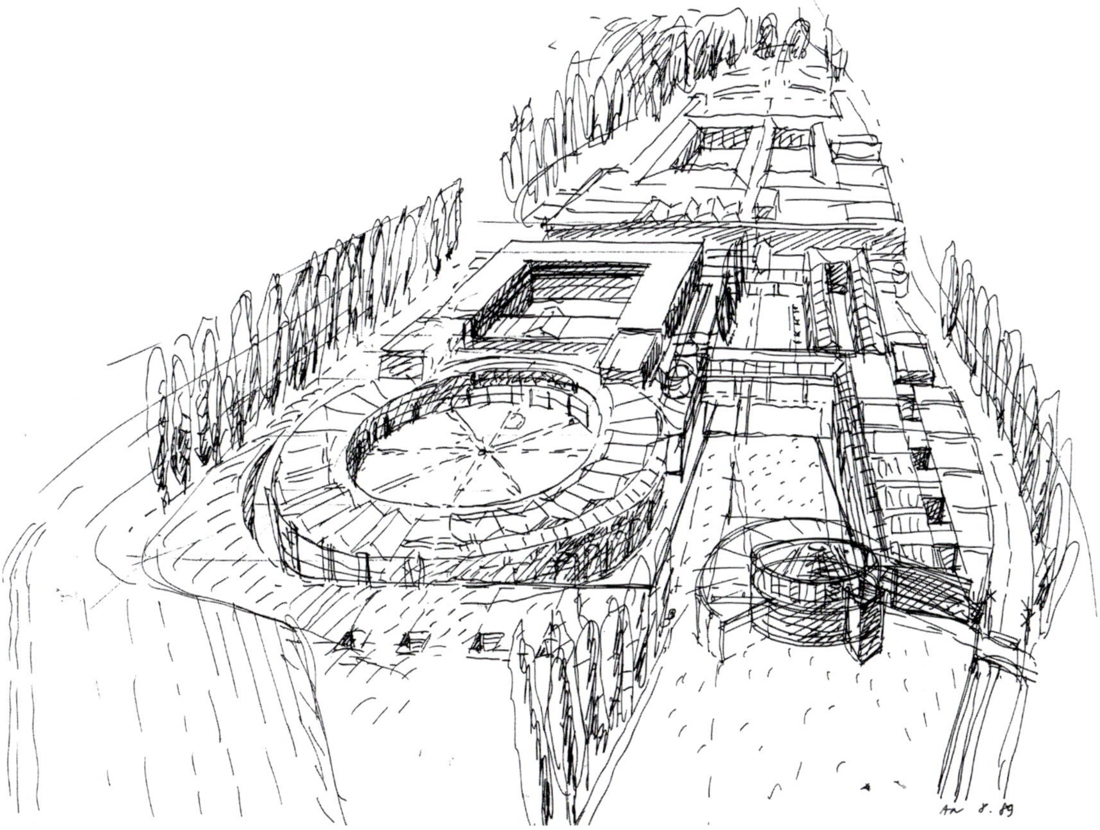
An 8. 89

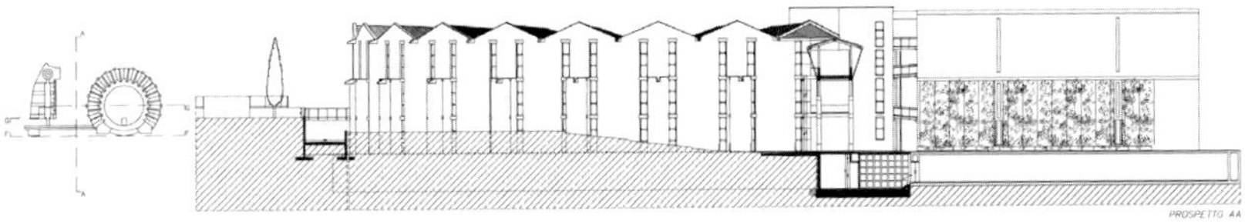
PROSPETTO AA

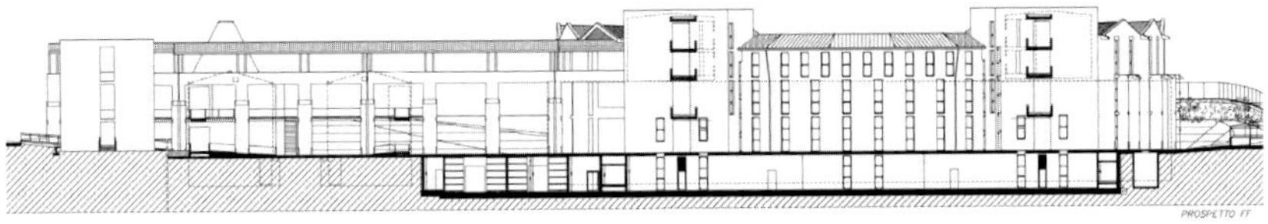
PROSPETTO FF

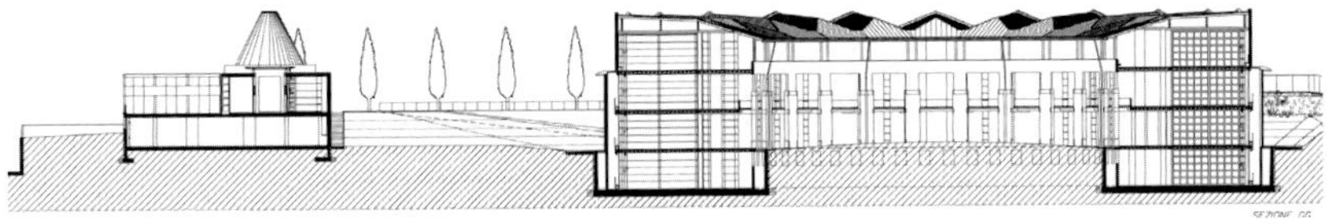

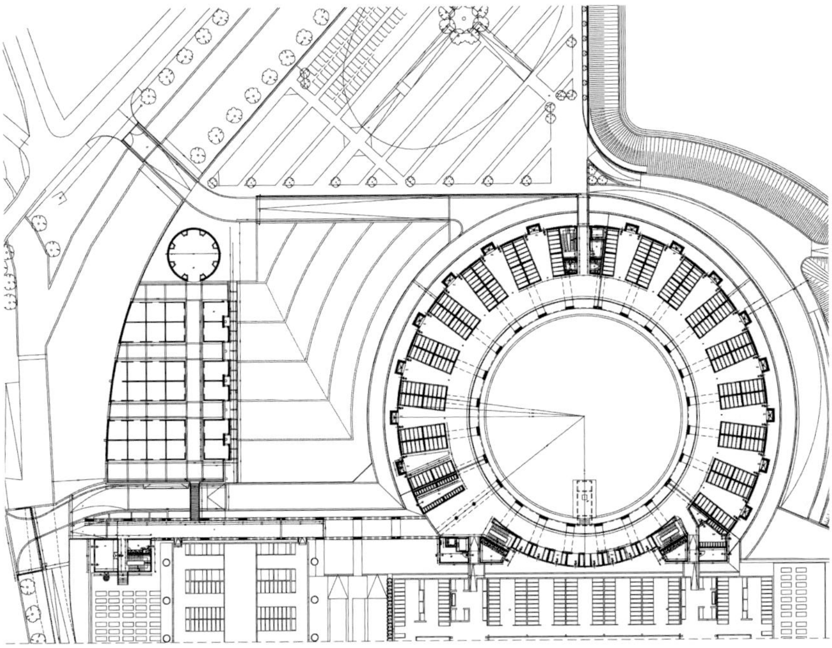

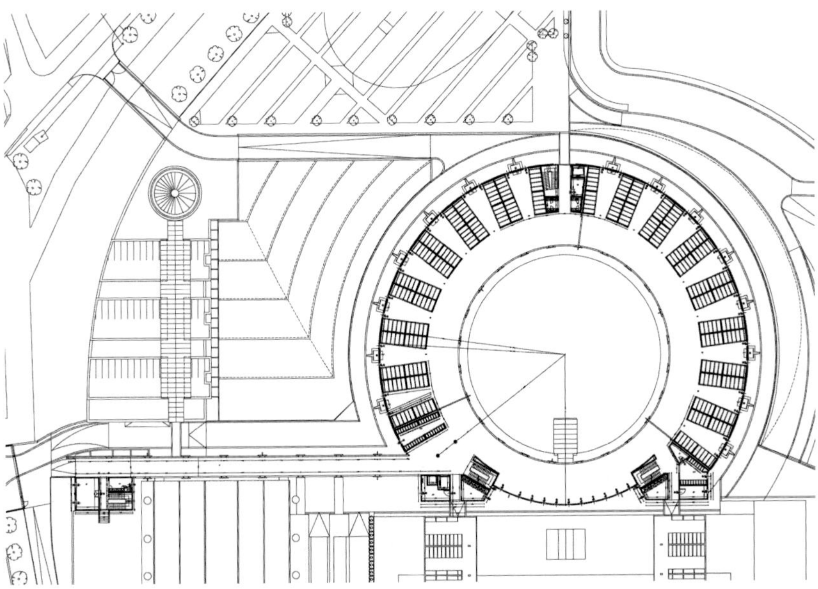

Urban renewal of the former Stianti industrial plant in San Casciano Val di Pesa (Florence)

1998-2008

The Officine Grafiche Stianti was a very important industry in the economy of San Casciano Val di Pesa. For a long period, the buildings located along Borgo Sarchiani, were one of the main features of the town's skyline.
In the words of Repetti: "The air and gentle climate of the whole territory... is excellent and distinguished figures and families would spend leisure time here in the hills of San Casciano during the period of the Republic of Florence." [Translator's translation]
The healthy atmosphere and gentle rolling hills are the most important features of this walled town that, placed by Florence as protection against possible enemy attacks from the direction of via Cassia, dominates Val di Pesa from above. Despite the destruction that occurred up until the Second World War, the urban layout of San Casciano has remained unchanged. The lines of the 14th century town walls are still clearly visible with their polygonal layout, corner towers and keep: a diamond shape cut through the centre by a crossroads. Outside the gates, the ridges are divided by small valleys with winding rivers and are scattered with small towns that have developed around the access roads (San Casciano resembles a kite laid on the hills with Borgo Sarchiani forming its tail...).
The Officine Grafiche Stianti, was a closely built complex along Borgo Sarchiani, one of the many ancient roads leading from the town. However, although the presence of the industry made a strong contribution to the welfare of the community, by no means did it add to the quality of the architectural heritage. When the plant was relocated, it was obvious that the area should be destined for residential and public use. We created our project, carefully designed on site, keeping in mind the exposure, topography, local history, the remains of the factory, and traces of other projects (those underway as well as those that had been abandoned). We tried to maintain the difficult balance between what had previously existed and what could possibly be built, while respecting the historical identity of San Casciano and protecting the integrity of its architectural traditions.
Once the Officine Grafiche factory buildings had been removed, the historical structure of the Stianti company was rebuilt internally maintaining the original features as far as possible. On the ground floor, the building is crossed by a public walkway from Borgo Sarchiani, which passes through the internal courtyard and continues towards the lower level of the complex.
The construction of the new residential complex was planned along three lines developed on three parallel levels in Borgo Sarchiani, sloping down towards via Terracini. With this intervention, we wished to recreate an urban fabric that resembled a natural addition to the historic buildings in the direction of the valley. Although they maintain a regular layout, the new buildings are arranged along the curves of the different levels of the terrain. Attached to the foundations for the parking area, the ground floor apartments are separated by private courtyards connected by public pedestrian walkways designed to create a close community spirit. The underground area contains the cellars and private parking spaces belonging to the residents who have access through a central underpass to and from via Terracini. The buildings are limited to four storeys above ground in relation to the highest elevation, and contain 152 apartments of various sizes. Despite the regular layout, the facades feature recessed spaces, terraces and loggias on different levels recalling the diversity and clever configurations of houses in ancient medieval towns. The materials used for the facades are traditional for this region: the "towers" and ground floors are faced in stone; roofing is built on wooden beams covered with terracotta tiles, with copper guttering and drainpipes.
Part of the area is destined for public services that include a multi-storey car park (with private garage spaces and bus terminus) and a piazza on the roof with planted green areas. Inside, pedestrian walkways and elevators are clearly indicated for easy access from all areas in the parking building. The bus terminus entry and exit access is in via Terracini with one way traffic in an anticlockwise direction. The parking building and bus terminus on the via Terracini side are screened by a rampart faced with stone masonry interrupted by rows of inlaid brick.
The piazza, the various pathways and green spaces are an integrated part of the project; they were designed to recall the complex network of pathways in the ancient centre of San Casciano.

Post Scriptum: To date (July 2010) the Palazzo Comunale designed in 1998 by Gae Aulenti has not yet been built, and no short-term plans are foreseen. The area between the residential area and the walls has not been completed. Certain works on the roof of the underground parking area are still underway. This remains a project that has been interrupted. The missing elements seem to share the melancholic atmosphere of dereliction. However, we must not lose hope...

Architectural project
Natalini Architetti;
Structural project
Gianfranco Bucciarelli,
Cladio Totti;
Installation design
Massimo Vignozzi,
Luca Benelli;
Project management
Gianfranco Bucciarelli,
Cladio Totti;
Client
Unica S.C.A.R.L.
Cooperativa Pian di Mezzana.

Photos: Mario Ciampi

50

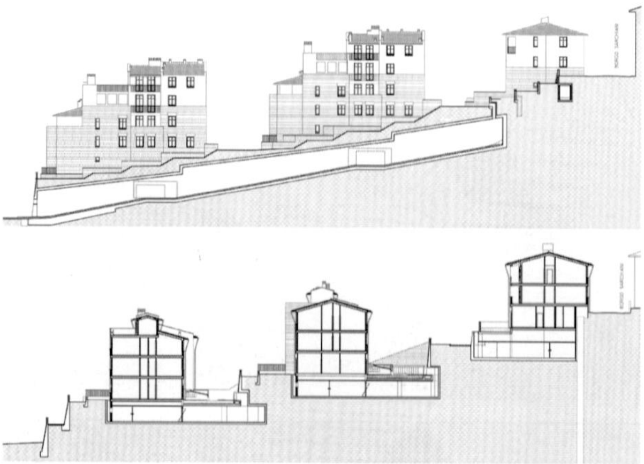

PIANTA PIANO TERRA 1:500

The new Western Staircase in the Uffizi Museum, Florence

2003-2011

Marginal comments on certain contributions to the Nuovi Uffizi project

I would like to begin with a thought on the concept of "new" by quoting John Donne, the 17th century English metaphysical poet who wrote: "Novelty is but oblivion"; and in *Ecclesiaste* we find "Nihil sub sole novi" (there is nothing new under the sun).
But even without aspiring to innovation, this was a very difficult project because my generation had many great masters, so terrifying that we can neither love, nor forget them: when I was a young architect, I met Le Corbusier and Louis Kahn, and shortly afterwards I made a pilgrimage to see Scarpa's restoration of the Castelvecchio museum, Albini's project for the Tesoro di San Lorenzo and the work by BBPR on the Castello Sforzesco. A native of Florence, I often visited the Rooms of the Primitivi collections restored by Scarpa, Gardella and Michelucci, and for years, I wondered why it had never been possible to carry out restoration work in the Uffizi Gallery, so badly in need of renovation. Naturally, what was needed was a hand like that of the magnificent three, or perhaps it would take destruction like that which occurred during the war to convince the Uffizi administration that some renovation was necessary... and in fact, this did happen in part following the criminal bombing in via Georgofili in 1993, which rekindled the interest in the great Uffizi Museum that seemed to have been dormant for years. But, as Buontalenti wrote to his prince during the renovation work on the Baptistry: "Florence is a city that has a good eye and a caustic tongue, and whatever work is done, if it is discovered that what is placed on top is no better than what was destroyed and covered beneath, something new will be built around it..."
On the subject of the building of the Uffizi, Vasari wrote: "I have never built walls for anything as difficult or dangerous, constructed on the river and almost in the air..."
Claudia Conforti (C. Conforti in *Vasari architetto*, Electa, Milan 1993) commented, "he won the challenge and, as happens at the conclusion of any great endeavour, the winner is brushed by the wing of melancholy", and Vasari wrote: "I have nothing more to say except that I am feeling very melancholic."

[C. Enggass, *The Life of Brunelleschi*, Electa, Milan 1993]

Centuries later, a new challenge was launched with the project for the Nuovi Uffizi. As with every intervention on an ancient building, the designers found themselves faced with a dilemma – the choice between conservation and renovation, and a further choice between simple upgrading and addition.
But the Uffizi is a parchment on which so many illustrious hands have written a page of history, that new writers are filled with humility, and are rather reticent to add their signature under such outstanding names. Therefore, the policy of the project was limited in every aspect to what was strictly "necessary and sufficient". However, this does not signify a presumed mimetic intervention: "where it was and how it was before", (this system has already created so much damage in Florence in the areas close to the Uffizi), nor does it mean modern radical-chic minimalist design. The most appropriate solution was sought each time: the project, generated by opportunity, always aspires to necessity. Within the SINTER work group, coordinated by Engineer Alessandro Chimenti, my intervention concerned the two new vertical connection systems located at the ends of the two wings of the Uffizi building.
The Western Stairway, now completed, is located in a small courtyard close to the Lanzi Loggia.
It is composed of a stone tower with large openings and contains the staircase faced with burnished brass. Partial glass roofing and a series of large windows protect the courtyard and provide light, transforming it into a new internal space, where the modern and antique create a subtle dialogue.
The Eastern Staircase will rise in a symmetrical position in the area between the remains of the former church of San Pier Scheraggio and the staircase of honour designed by Vasari, in a large space also lit from above and extended in a tower facing towards the historic Piazza del Grano.

Elementary observations on glossary terms.

In his *Dictionary of Received Ideas*, under the item "Architects", Flaubert wrote: "All are morons. Inevitably they forget to put stairs in their houses." Well, we did not forget the stairs at the Uffizi. The Eastern and Western Staircases had to obey the rules of distribution, itinerary and safety measures: we could not build them in antique style and we did not want to make them seem too new. The Western Staircase is composed of a tower inside which the stairs rise in a sequence of different flights between two enclosed shafts (one for the elevators, the other for service equipment) and two corner structures. The tower is located in a small trapeze-shaped courtyard and is attached to the shorter side. The dictionary definition of "well hole" is the centre void between the flights of stairs, and the "stringer" is the partition that separates the two flights. In our staircase, there is no well or partition, simply a solid tower of stairs, half way between the English "Staircase Tower" and the German "Treppenhaus" or stairhouse.
The Eastern Staircase will form a flight of stairs inserted in the void between the remains of the former church of San Pier Scheraggio and the works by Vasari.

Working plan
SINTER s.r.l.
Alessandro Chimenti;
Structure and restoration
Alessandro Chimenti,
A. Moroni;
Working plan, installation design
Enzo Giusti;
Architectural consulting
Adolfo Natalini;
Lighting design
Piero Castiglioni;
Archaeological consulting
Riccardo Francovich;
Client
Ministry of Cultural Heritage and Activities;
Directorate General for Architectural Heritage and Landscape.

Photos: Mario Ciampi

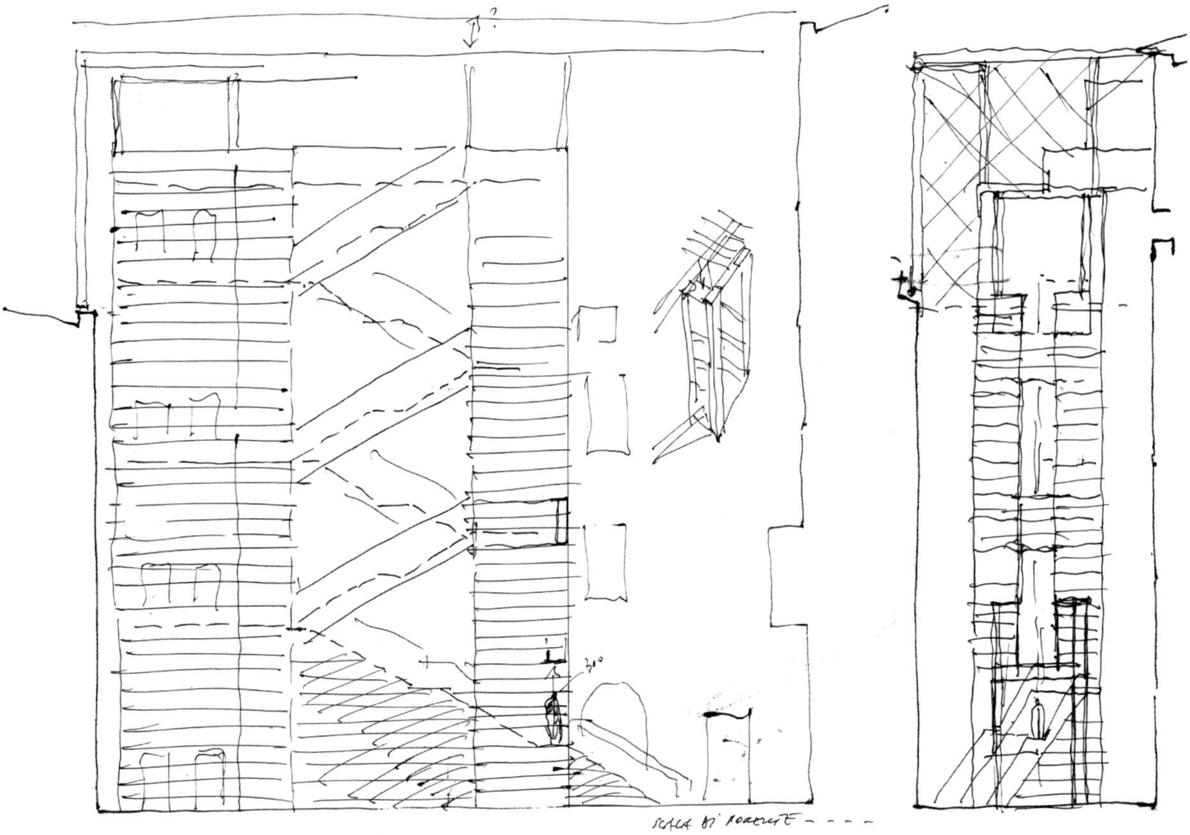

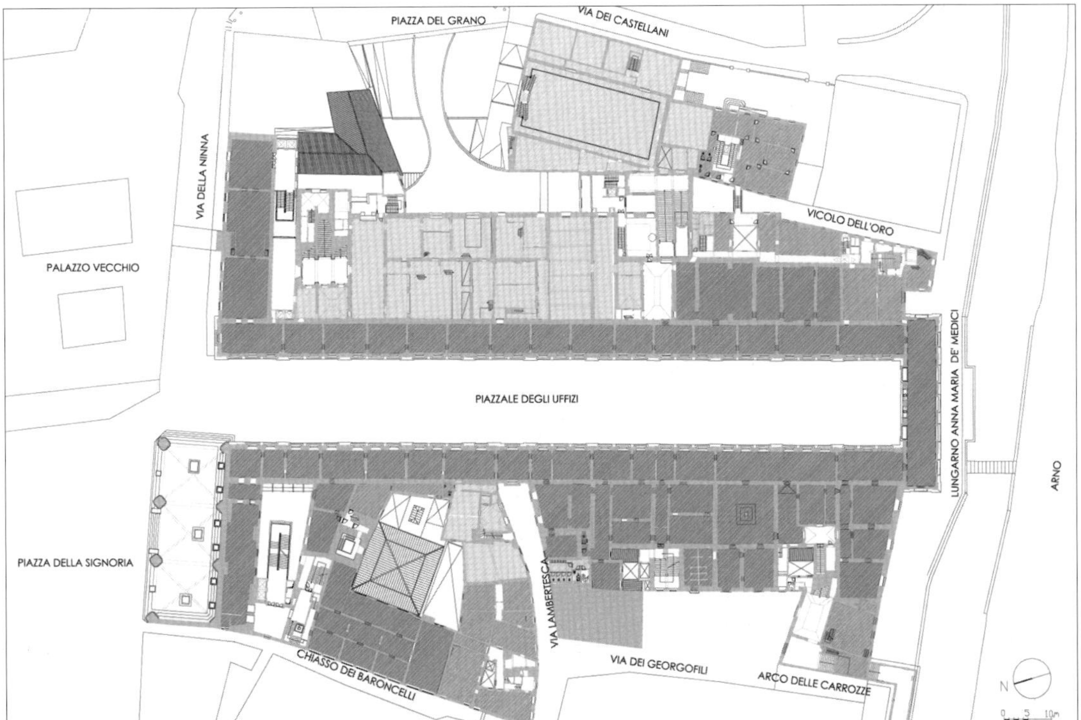
PIAZZA DEL GRANO
VIA DEI CASTELLANI
VIA DELLA NINNA
PALAZZO VECCHIO
VICOLO DELL'ORO
PIAZZALE DEGLI UFFIZI
LUNGARNO ANNA MARIA DE' MEDICI
ARNO
PIAZZA DELLA SIGNORIA
VIA LAMBERTESCA
CHIASSO DEI BARONCELLI
VIA DEI GEORGOFILI
ARCO DELLE CARROZZE
N
0 5 10m

13.01.04

Extension of the Museo dell'Opera di S. Maria del Fiore, Florence

2001-2015

Our project was composed of three tasks: to partially restore the museum, stage the former Teatro degli Intrepidi (an 18th century theatre later converted to a garage) and create further interstitial spaces.

La Sala dell'Antica Facciata [Cathedral façade room]
We tried to preserve the large empty volume of the Theatre maintaining a space lit from above in order to associate the architectural concept with the works that adorned the cathedral.
Although inevitably the original works have been removed for conservation and replaced with copies, there is a constant exchange between the Museo dell'Opera and the Piazza del Duomo, and little by little, the works migrate from the exterior to the interior. Our aim is to recreate the same light and the same positions, now inaccessible, for which the statues were created. An exact model of the original medieval facade of the Cathedral has been installed in the Sala del Teatro [Theatre room], constructed with architectural elements in lightweight materials. Certain works have been placed in their original positions on the facade together with copies of the most famous statues displayed on pedestals under the huge model to provide a closer view.
The reconstruction of the facade gives viewers the possibility of seeing the sculptures in their original context. This authentic model recalls Brunelleschi's remarkable perspective invention where the Baptistery was portrayed from the door of the cathedral. Just as Alberti stated: "nothing painted may ever seem like the true when there is not a certain distance for seeing it..." [L. B. Alberti, *The Ten Books of Architecture*, tansl. by J. Leoni edited by J. Rykwert, Tiranti, London, 1965]we could also say that no object will seem true if removed from the real distance from its observer.
Part of the former 18th century theatre is occupied by a structure composed of three superimposed galleries, faced with white statuary marble, with a red resin finish on the floors and contrasting walls, like the niches of the bell tower. Works from Giotto's Bell Tower are displayed in an architectural structure with a series of openings opposite the reconstruction of the medieval façade. The sculptures are placed on a raised podium about 120 cm above floor level in order to recreate the viewing angle in an upward direction. On the opposite wall is a display of the sculpted panels from the bell tower.

La Sala della Pietà [The Pietà room]
Created in the Sala di Bonifacio VIII [Boniface VIII room], this space is composed of a preparatory section, and a full height end section that houses a group of statues.
This unadorned space is lit from above through a velarium that filters the light from the skylight. The marble group Pietà is in slight contrast with the plaster finish of the end wall, enclosed between the light grey side walls and stone slab floor. The side wall marble panels are treated to lighten the surface colour gradually as the walls rise towards the roof.
A central stone podium, evoking an altar table, allows Michelangelo's Pietà to be appreciated in its religious context. The solemn nature of the display is emphasised by the austere stone bench in the centre of the room.

The project also includes new intermediate spaces recovered between the theatre and the other buildings. A new floor has been created in the Sala di Bonifacio VIII and the space between the former Theatre and the Museum has been reconstructed to create a gallery that is practically invisible from the exterior.
The new spaces generated by this project house the models of the Dome, Brunelleschi's work shop and the choir by Bandinelli. Between the Dome Gallery and the Sala del Coro [Choir room] is a double height space that provides an overhead lightwell into the Sala della Pietà.
Different systems have been used inside the complex according to each individual space. Part of the restoration work and structural consolidation includes new uses of the volume occupied by the former garage. Two new staircases were added to the main historic stairway to improve the distribution of museum access and escape routes. The roof over the main room has been completely replaced with a metal grid system equipped with an upper skylight and large coffers similar to the openings in the new white marble facade of the galleries.
The extension work has more than doubled the space of the Museum.

Having completed our task, we can contemplate a visit to view the project and we would like to echo the words of Ghiberti describing his doors : "it is the most singular work that I have ever made...and finished with all art, measure and skill..." [*Dictionary of Italian Literature*, Peter Bondadella. NdT]

p. 149
The Sala del Paradiso seen from the Column of Saint Zanobi

p. 150
The Sala del Paradiso (the hall containing the earliest façade of the Cathedral)

p. 151
The Galleria del Campanile

p. 152
View of the façade from the Galleria del Campanile

p. 153
Layout of the three floors and the Sala di Michelangelo

Architectural project and staging
Natalini Architetti, Guicciardini & Magni Architetti Studio Associato;
Structural project
Leonardo Paolini;
Electrical installation design
Giancarlo Martarelli;
Mechanical installation design
Roberto Innocenti;
Project management
Adolfo Natalini;
Client
Opera di S. Maria del Fiore.

Photos: Mario Ciampi

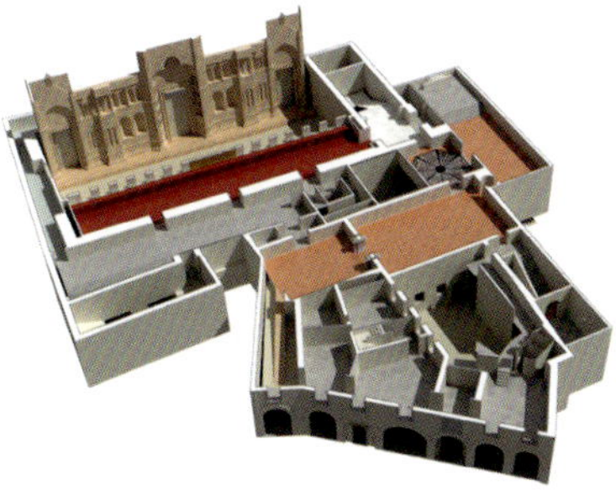

The San Lorenzo Hotel in the Città Alta, Bergamo

2009-2013

"Nothing is built with ruins, but everything is built on ruins." Ruins and projects share the melancholy fate of absence: of something that has gone forever in the case of ruins, and of the expectation of something that may perhaps never come in the case of projects. Here, on the northeast corner of piazza Mascheroni in Bergamo, on the site where we have designed the extension to the San Lorenzo Hotel, the ruins appeared beneath several strata of earth. As in an ancient palimpsest, the superimposed writings were brought to light like fragments waiting to be re-read and interpreted.

The existing hotel was restored and an addition to it was designed as an organic development, respecting the historic city's atmosphere and drawing on a contextual architectural language: not a nostalgic reconstruction but an evocation.
The new building thus begins from the existent and is developed partly on the square, by folding in plan to rejoin the part built against the side of the church, and to recall the old corner buildings whose traces can be found in the underlying archaeological area. In this way we created an inner cloister, reducing the length of the front overlooking the square and saving the view towards Maresana Hill.
On the square, the hotel's image is made up of three elements: the restored front of the existing building (facing south), that of the addition, and the long, restored historic wall. The first is plastered, the second in architectural bronze and glass, and the third in unrefined stones. These three juxtaposed elements refer to the different phases of construction, creating on the square a front in which different periods of time coexist, as in the historic city itself. The new construction is developed on the north and east sides of the area, with the curtain wall being rebuilt on piazza Mascheroni and via Boccola.

For over ten years I have observed the twofold beauty of Bergamo: that of the old city clinging to the hilltop, and the wider beauty of the new city around the Sentierone. I have walked for hours along the city's streets, from its lowest levels right up to the citadel; and through the upper city at night, trying to lose my way to discover more and more hidden corners, walls and doors.
Piazza Mascheroni had lost its status as a square after the demolition, and the extension of the San Lorenzo Hotel has attempted, if only to a minimal extent, to redefine its lost borders. Looking at the finished work, it seems that the square has recaptured a sense of its limit and measure, as well as a further source of satisfaction in the reflections of the evening sun on the hotel's new bronze walls, and in the shadows charged with memories and surprises that fill its underground spaces.

Architectural project
Adolfo Natalini /
Natalini Architetti;
Structural project
Marco Verdina;
Installation design
Alessandro Nani;
Interiors
Guglielmo Renzi;
Project management
ArcheoProject;
Client
HCB.

Photos: Mario Ciampi

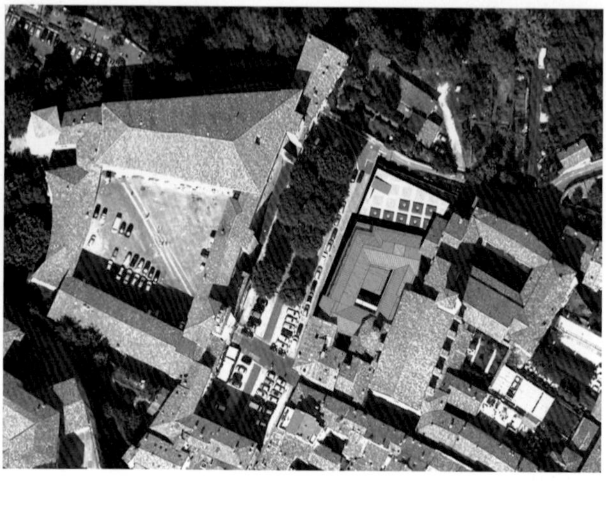

RELAIS
SAN LORENZO

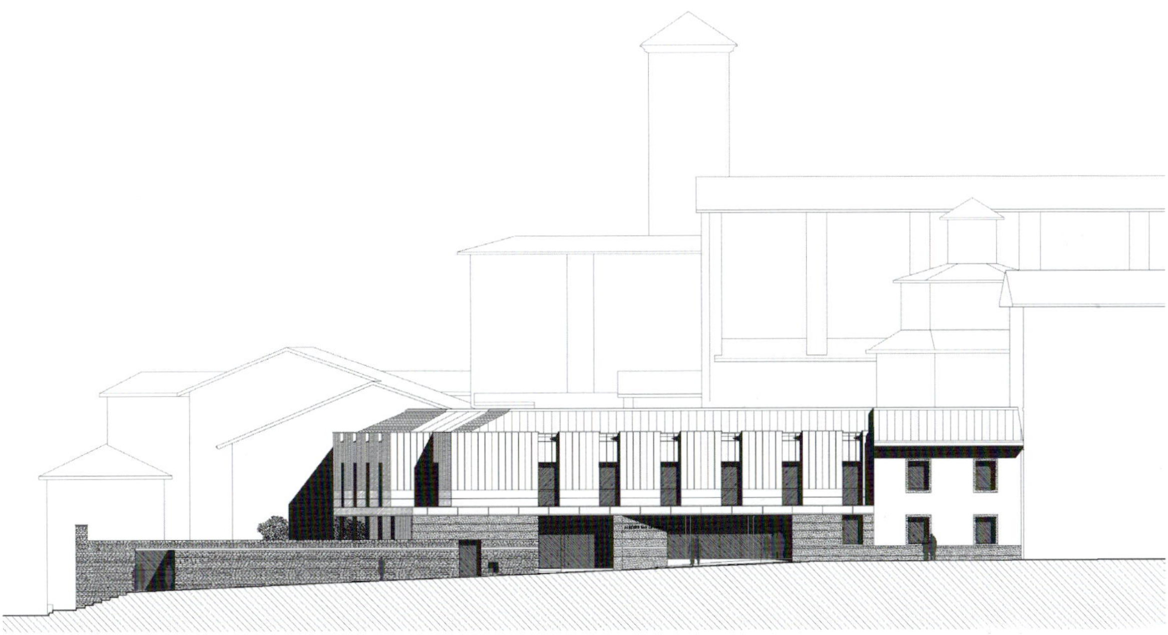

Lemmario 3

[Lexicon 3]

—

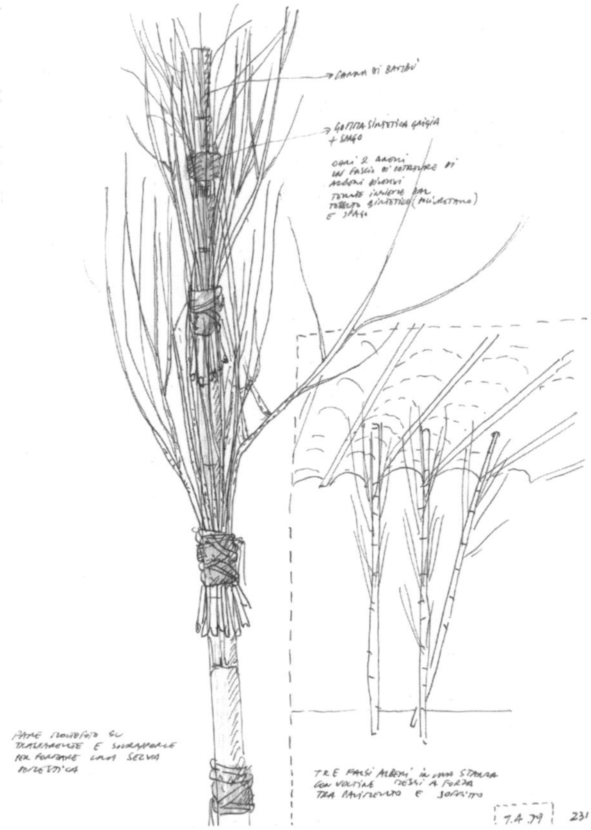

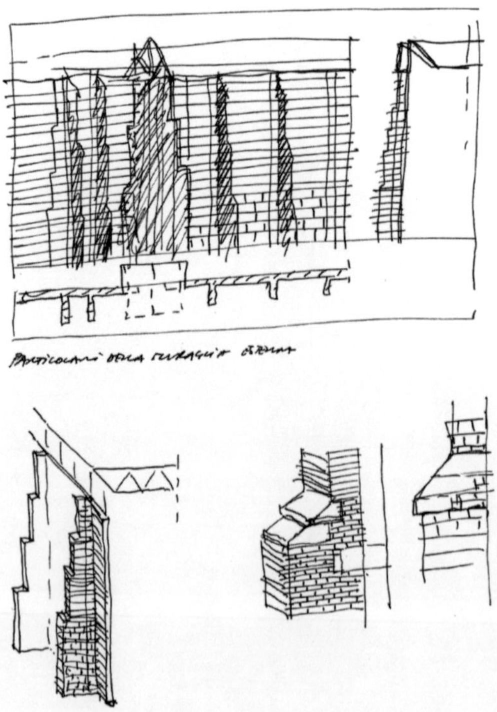

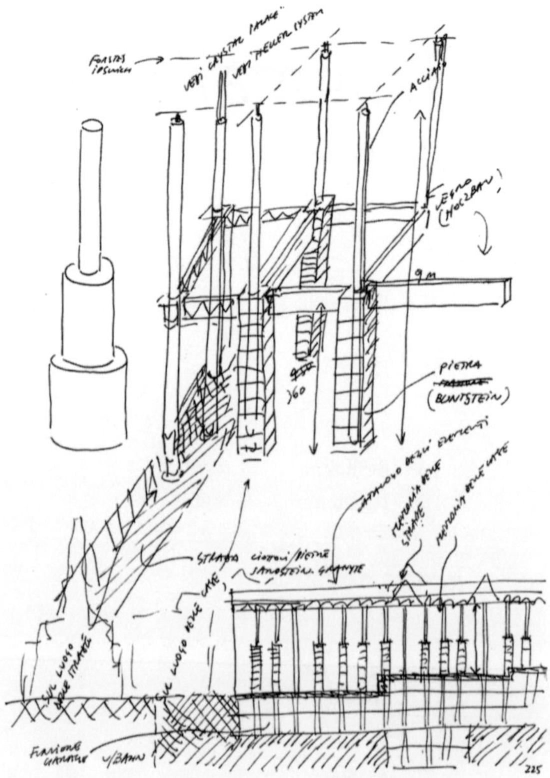

Figures of stone

01. *Do you mean to respond to the crisis of architecture with Figures of stone? In one passage you write: "One evening at Stonehenge I felt as if I were in a cloister of the earth's own teeth, and those teeth were made of stone."*

Figures of stone is not a definitive answer. It is only a series of poetic expressions or, more simply, my notes in a diary where writings are mixed with drawings and occasional constructions. It's a record of my travels and research on architecture. I collect projects dating from 1979 to 1983, and this was my partial and temporary response to a situation of permanent crisis. After all, we are used to living with crises that arrive constantly, one after the other, and it seems we will never be free. Now my response to situations of turmoil and doubt similar to the ones we experienced in those years would be different. Now I'm trying to create projects and constructions that help me to understand the dilemmas in which I operate, and what I am trying to draw, write and describe is to some extent different from *Figures of stone*. Stone remains the solid core of architecture, however, the permanent and reassuring part. All things considered, I work without a lot of certainty or reference points and I seek reassurance in the most solid and permanent part of architecture.

02. Basically, I only wrote that book, *Figures of stone*, to set down my personal reflections on architecture, the same concepts that I was teaching in those years at the University. It was a sort of summing-up of my experience acquired between 1978 and 1984, during the passage between drawn architecture and built architecture. It was an attempt: not so much to found a theory but to express a poetic ideal. So, in order to respond correctly to your questions, I would have to express the same poetic ideals I had then, and this I cannot and do not want to do. The work I do today is anything but an expression of poetic thought. In *Figures of stone* I had various chapters entitled *Places*, *Elements*, *Figures*, *Construction*, *Time* and *Memory*, in which I developed some of my ideas about architecture. The projects and buildings taken as examples illustrated these theories. Now, however, I find myself in what seems a very different situation. The projects I am able to build contain in themselves, albeit in an undertone, a series of analogous statements, while what I am writing are only some notes in the margin. Substantially, to answer your questions appropriately, I would have had to make a series of poetic statements, similar or contradictory to those to which you referred, while now I'd rather answer your questions with actual buildings, architecture, pieces of construction, hoping that they can have the same eloquence as my expressions of poetic thought. I realize, however, that these constructions, just because they differ from one another and are scattered in distant places, are less and less eloquent or, perhaps I should say, speak different languages, making them difficult to understand.

You belong to a generation of architects who expressed themselves more by manifestos than by actual production. Writings and drawings contend for supremacy in the definition of your work (you have often written of "architecture glimpsed" and said that what you have produced was only an "approach to architecture"). At this point, do you think it's more essential to write a book or to build a work of architecture?

I think our job today is to build architecture that can be read like a book.

[25.10.97, from an interview by E. Gonzo and A. Vicari, in *Costruire in Laterizio*]

On previous page:
Project for Römerberg reconstruction in Frankfurt, sketches, from *Quaderni Neri*, 1979

Project for Römerberg reconstruction in Frankfurt, columns, angels, structures, from *Quaderni Neri*, 1979

Firenze
[Florence]

01. All this talk about the beauty of Florence testifies to its dramatic absence.
There is a neurotic desire for beauty that derives from a now deeply ingrained powerlessness to create it.
We want to persuade others, and at the same time convince ourselves, of the beauty of Florence as a consolation for our inability to prepare and follow through on the production of new beauty.
Florence is beautiful in its hills and in the way it nestles in a valley cut by a capricious and sometimes disastrously violent river (a far cry from the silver stream of the *chansonnier*). It was made beautiful by its builders, both celebrated and anonymous, between the 13th and the 15th centuries, only a little in the 17th century, even less in the 18th, for about ten years in the 19th and three (1930-1933) in the 20th... and after that?
After World War II, perhaps the only notable architectures have been the reconstruction of the bridge at Santa Trinita and the Room of the Primitives in the Uffizi...
Then, for more than half a century, the architectural history of Florence has been a chronicle of missed opportunities, of plans not carried out, of bidding competitions dropped, of projects left unfunded or abandoned. The reconstruction of Por Santa Maria (which was supposed to be "where it was, the way it was"), Sorgane reduced by half, the squalid outskirts (Piagge, Novoli), the competition for the Fortezza, the one for the University in Sesto, the office center at Castello (in the'70s), the Murate ('80s), up to the plan for tripling the Uffizi.
When in 1960 I moved eastward from my provincial hometown of Pistoia, I naturally went to Florence, attracted by Brunelleschi and Buontalenti, by Masaccio and Pontormo, thinking that this was the city of art and architecture: I have gone on stubbornly deluding myself all these years. I feel some embarrassment having to talk about architecture in a city that has refused architecture for more than half a century, and so I prefer to talk about something easier to understand: beauty. Beauty is not the purpose of the transformations, but it is the catalyst of every transformation. Not the end, but a means.
Three things are necessary for every transformation: a power, the economic means and a vision. We have to see that they exist and coexist. La Pira had a vision when in his speech before a meeting of mayors from all over the world on 2 October 1955, he said: "[...] And, before I finish my speech about the value of cities for the destiny of the whole civilization, please let me take an overall look at the millenary cities, which, like precious gems, beautify the lands of Europe and Asia. Gentlemen, we would need the inspired speech of the prophets to describe them: Tobiah, Isaiah, Jeremiah, Ezekiel, St. John. Péguy's brilliant definition can be applied to every one of them: being the city of man, the outline and prefiguration of the city of God."
[25.03.03, from "Ascolta il tuo cuore, città"]

02. *The difficulties of architecture in Florence*
In 1403 Leonardo Bruni wrote in his *Laudatio Florentinae Urbis* [Praise of the City of Florence]: "Florence is of such a nature that a more distinguished or more splendid city cannot be found on all the earth. If you take pleasure in antiquity you will find many traces and relics of that... and if you are a lover of things modern, none more magnificent or more splendid can be seen than its new buildings." Vittorio Savi wrote in 1988: "In 1534 when Michelangelo left Florence forever, architecture understood that it no longer had any reason

to inhabit Florence, and soon abandoned the city."
Today, architecture is absent from Florence, perhaps it lives somewhere else. This is a bitter condition, a tragic one.
For anyone who travels the city and its outskirts today, the question arises: where is the architecture of this century? It can be found in the various guides entitled *Modern architecture in Florence*. The search will be a desperate one. With the maximum of good will we could draw up a list: the Nervi stadium, the railroad stations by Mazzoni and Michelucci, the School of Air Warfare by Fagnoni (built in the'30s), the reconstruction of the bridge at Santa Trinita by Gizdulich, the Room of the Primitives at the Uffizi (Scarpa, Gardella, Michelucci), the Giovannozzi Foundry (built in the'50s), Sorgane (Savioli and Ricci), the Church on the Motorway by Michelucci ('60s), the Nuova Italia headquarters by Scarpa and Detti. After that, nothing much has been built, there have only been a few hidden or partial projects (interiors, shops, restorations...).
The historic city seems unable to renew itself. Architecture has been given tasks concerned with invisible changes, where it is possible to avoid the suffocating weight of laws and prohibitions passed with the intent of protecting the city from the abnormal "mass" of speculation, but that have also had the effect of suffocating any possibility of revival through beauty... The newer parts of the city (the outward expansion) is left to the ordinary squalor of construction, as if it were not worthy of architecture, as if it lacked any hope of recovery in that sense.
The public administration trusts in the risky and frustrating practice of competitions, in the history of missed opportunities. From the competition for Por Santa Maria after the war, that saw the victory of a solution of compromise on the vague idea of "where it was, the way it was" (Berenson) to the competition for Fortezza da Basso in 1967, where the three winners were ordered to come up with a common project and, in the meantime, a fourth architect, Spadolini, who had not even participated in the competition, was given a contract to construct the temporary pavilion.
Giovanni Klaus Koenig called it the law of Florentine competitions: "Those who do not participate in competitions in Florence have a better chance of building than the winner." The competition for the office center (in the'70s), the one for the University... either had no outcome or the projects built were greatly different from the projects that won. There have been very few exceptions: the Sports Pavilion and the Government Archive.
The competition for the Murate project (1988) was first contested by the union of architects and later held at the first level with 50 competitors and 10 winners; there was to be a second level but it was never held.
Things go even worse when there is no competition...
For the contemporary art museum there was the offer made by Olivetti to sponsor a project by Wright (1958): the offer was refused. Then, on the occasion of an electoral campaign (1960) there were the projects for Villa Strozzi by Michelucci, Irvin, Scarpa, Gardella, Meier, Isozaki, Hollein: all lost; only the Limonaia was built, posthumously.
For the projects of the Art Center in Rifredi, four architects were appointed, but gradually eliminated due to ferocious infighting and finally the office project was designed and abandoned.
Lastly, the competition for the exit of the Uffizi, where the winning project by Isozaki still has not been built.
Florence seems to remember architects only as testimonials to its good intentions, linked more to the image than to actual construction...
[17.11.98]

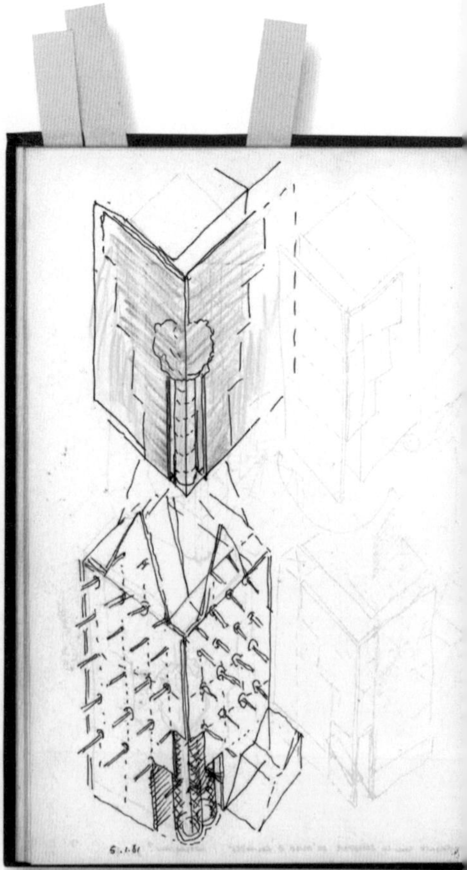

House in Saalgasse, Frankfurt, first project, sketches, from *Quaderni Neri*, 1981

House in Saalgasse, Frankfurt, second project, sketches, from *Quaderni Neri*, 1981

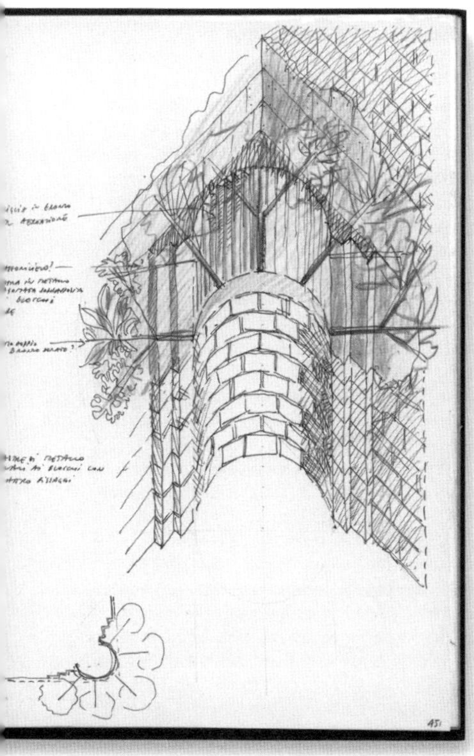

03. *Florence is a city rich in extraordinary architecture. It is the city of Brunelleschi, of Leon Battista Alberti, Michelangelo and Leonardo. What did this mean for Adolfo Natalini as a student and, later, as a young architect, during the years of his studies and immediately after?*

In my first year in Florence, I visited the city conscientiously and methodically, clutching my red Touring Club guidebook, prompted to this maniacal activity by Professor Marchini, who insisted for his examination in History of Architecture that his students have thorough knowledge of Florence: I can never thank him enough.

Many large and small fragments of this discovery of the city are embedded in my memory, like the Scalzo cloister, a tiny space where the light is filtered as in an aquarium, but rendered vibrant by the monochrome paintings of Andrea del Sarto, and the ascent into the Cupola, between Brunelleschi's two domes, almost an exploration inside the body of a great beast, emerging finally on the Lanterns, between claustrophobia and agoraphobia, and certain roads beloved by Rosai like via Toscanella and via San Leonardo.

The city was a network of dark streets along which the mysterious cavities of lobbies and courtyards could be glimpsed, offering an infinite sequence of different perspectives where the tilt of a wall or the angle of a shutter kept opening new worlds.

But, rendered insusceptible to the architecture and almost unable to see it in the confused revivals of the avant garde movement and the defective teaching of modern art in my school, years were to pass before I would see the city again...

The discovery and study of Renaissance architecture must certainly have had some importance in the education of Natalini as an architect. In what form and through which buildings and authors, mainly?

In Florence I learned very slowly, and with considerable resistance, to love Leon Battista Alberti and Brunelleschi, torn between the clarity of their ideas and the angst of Buontalenti and Ammannati (just as I still feel torn between my passion for Masaccio my fascination with Pontormo).

The Pazzi Chapel and the Loggiato degli Innocenti, the Loggia and Palazzo Rucellai but perhaps even more profoundly the Holy Sepulcher at San Pancrazio and the Library at San Marco (by Michelozzo), have been my guiding lights for years with, of course, the Unfinished Palace at Casino Mediceo by Buontalenti...

[30.10.90, from an interview by P. Scaglione, in *d'A*]

04. *Florence and Architecture*

Vittorio Savi once observed that when Michelangelo left Florence for Rome, architecture too abandoned the city...

There was a brief return when Florence was the capital of Italy and Poggi was its architect...

Then we have the solitary triad of masterpieces: Michelucci's railroad station, the Nervi stadium, the School of Air Warfare by Fagnoni. The marvelous inventions of Mazzoni, who was the architect employed by the railroad, have been hidden for years, and his archive is in Rovereto. The dignified architecture of Ugo Giovannozzi (the buildings on via Valfonda and the La Fondiaria building) have been ignored,

the fine constructions of Gamberini and the urban sculptures of Michelucci, Ricci and Savioli lumped under the generic label of "Tuscan School".
Indeed, the most impressive achievement of the postwar years was the reconstruction of the Santa Trinita bridge by Gizdulich.
The architecture gave way to the restoration, a necessary activity like the maintenance of household hygiene but one that can hardly be called creative.
Flashes of creativity appeared at the end of the '60s, at the time of the flood of 1966, with what was dubbed *Radical Architecture*, a neo-Avant Garde in architecture that arose in the Architecture Department of the University of Florence with the Florentine groups Archizoom and Superstudio and that would proliferate rapidly, gaining widespread international fame.
Now, a vast historical revisitation of the movement is in progress, with exhibitions at the MoMA, and the Pompidou and in other museums, but is probably only one of the many episodes of nostalgia for the fantastic '60s.
After working for twenty years in Europe, between Germany and the Netherlands, now I have the opportunity to work in Florence, with the University Campus of Novoli and other projects.
I feel like I am working in a foreign city, where I do not understand the language, the laws, the rules...
Yet, though forever a migrant, I have always been here, in the city, at the University, struggling to understand the language and desires.
I have discussed the destiny of the city and its architecture at length with my artist friends, with Vittorio Savi, critic and writer of architecture, with the students here at the University, with a number of public administrators (including Franco Camarlinghi, Stefano Bassi, Guido Clemente), but I've never been able to draw any conclusions.
What is the destiny of Florence? What treatments will waken it from its state of suspended animation? Must we accept it in its lethargy and irremediable decline, and love it as it is, in its inevitable corruption so similar to that of our own fragile bodies, or can we – must we – do something?

[11.12.00, from an interview by R. Cassigoli, in *Il Corriere della Sera*]

05. *On Florence*
In the early years, I explored every inch of the city with curiosity and passion. I loved it, but I never felt loved by the city.
Florence is a hostile, cruel city, always ready to crush one under the weight of its great past.
It is a city that has acquired an unrivaled position but is ill-disposed to change, stingy with recognition.
Amid its stones, one always feels like an intruder, an unwelcome guest or an accidental tourist. Its monuments combat a geometrical war with each other and against every new arrival. Florence is itself crushed by the shadow of its Cupola.
I wanted to be the architect of this city but I had to give up the idea and seek opportunities in other cities and other countries. Every place I've gone I tried to learn a language that would enable me to communicate through appropriate architecture.
From Florence I learned a great deal about measure, about proportions, about hierarchy, but also about the need not to appear through diversity.
From Florence, I received a lesson in modesty.

[2005]

Germania
[Germany]

01. I have traveled widely in Germany far almost ten years, since '79, due to architectural assignments in Frankfurt, Mannheim, Stuttgart and Karlsruhe. To be precise I started travelling north in 1974, when I built the house of Rainer Krause, pharmacist and collector, in Lübeck, Westphalia.
Travellers usually head for the south, towards warm seas; I have on the contrary always gone north, all the way to Tromsø and to *Ultima Thule*, retracing the paths, in the opposite direction, of the ancient invaders and visitors (the Svears, the Vikings, Goethe, Nietzsche, von Humboldt)... In Germany I was fascinated by the melancholic countryside, the large and orderly forests, the compact cities with their pointed roofs. Those houses seemed an expression of the "living on the land, pacified, under the sky" that I had discovered in the books of Norberg Schulz. Houses rooted to the ground, made in wood and brick, projecting towards the sky with fantastic, fearless profiles. In our country the eaves of the houses always cast a shade, and the roofs conclude the building's ascent in a serene but definitive manner: in the north the outlines of the houses form embroideries against the sky (I was to love them even more in the following decade, in the Netherlands). I have familiarized with cities precisely starting with the houses, those dark and orderly houses, all savagely different, every one with its own name, often proudly displayed. In Frankfurt, building the corner house on the Saalgasse (the house with branches), I sought to create a hybrid between my culture and theirs, with Friedrich Overbeck's painting *Italy and Germany* in mind.
I had meditated for a long time, painfully, on the destruction and reconstruction of German cities. In almost all old cities one finds a book with photographs showing the city as it was before 1940, as it was in 1945 and how it is today. This cruel comparison inspires nostalgia or total repression. In many German cities my projects have faced ruins (the Römerberg and the Karmeliterkirche in Frankfurt); in others they have involved reconstruction (the multimedia museum of Karlsruhe, the theater in Stuttgart). Some cities appeared to lack sense and plan, others were cosmic diagrams of ideal cities: Karlsruhe with its radial plan centered on the castle tower; Mannheim with its Cartesian chessboard inscribed in a semi-circle.
I see them again every month when flying to the Netherlands; they appear to me among the clouds, like a light-house or a friendly presence. But after ten years I could no longer stand feeling a foreigner, a *gastarbeiter* or a welcome guest, and decided to seek architecture only in my land, within a radius of 50 km from my new studio in Salviatino: I wanted it to be my home and workshop ("Illa domus, illa mihi sedes, illic mea carpitur aetas").
But things did not go just as I planned: in '91 I began working in the Netherlands and in '93 I was asked for a project for Leipzig. Thus I resumed my trips to Germany, this time to the eastern part, towards Leipzig, Dresden and Berlin. I had faced ruins on other occasions, but never so vast and so black from distant fires...
Leipzig was a proud city, once again splendid by the construction of the Grunderzeit, with intense trade, full of books, music (for 27 years Bach was the director of the local Thomaskirche choir) and with Europe's largest station. The city, dense with heavy stone buildings and sculptures, was almost razed to the ground by the bombings; the rubble was then removed and the wounds cleaned, but not healed.

The blocks have holes, here and there a corner, a central element is missing. In some cases vast areas were leveled to make room for large gray concrete tenements, human hives based on the examples, never properly understood, of Le Corbusier and other heroes of the *Modern Movement*. This is where the change commenced, *Die Wende*, with citizens who gathered in the Karl Marx Platz to protest; in the papers this became the "city of heroes". The first time 1 saw Leipzig an icy winter sun cast long shades on the urban voids and the missing parts of the buildings were filled with darkness like empty orbits. There were few cars in the streets and the smoking Trabants sputtered at the intersections.
The shop-windows were empty and dusty. In the town hall we were shown a map of the city, where the areas one could build were marked: old closed factories, abandoned buildings, parts of the city destroyed by the war and never rebuilt. The city map appeared filled with colored dots, like a new bombardment.
Three years later the city was an immense building site. The cranes formed a colorful forest in the old center; many buildings have been restored, the gold covering ancient decorations seemed too shiny and the colors too bright, awaiting the patina of time to seem real. A myriad of new constructions have sought the path of urban reparation, but have almost always got lost between Scylla and Charybdis (between postmodern and high-tech). Outside the city the new trade fair proudly asserts the rebirth of Leipzig as a place for exchange and trade. I was asked to build two town blocks near the historical center, as replacement of old factories. I have sought the elements for a possible project in the city. I found them in the city blocks, in the passages, the courts, the corner towers, in the dignified and severe facades, in the endless variety of windows, doors and roofs.
I sought to rebuild blocks made of houses, offices, shops, of parts that were recognizable but integrated, places for life, for work but also open to the city and to a curious visitor. I wanted to make room also for surprise and marvel, as this is what I had encountered in the many courtyards and passages that had appeared before me when I explored the city. "The architect sought to create a block as urban architecture, with a dignified exterior and a pleasant interior, open to the passage of the inhabitants. He listened to the city, seeking to learn its language; other words he brought with him from old European cities; now he awaited the dialogue to begin." In the project for the Contemporary Art Gallery the dialogue was established with the villas, the gardens, the park, with the idea of art as inhabitant of those rediscovered places. In my projects for Leipzig I have wanted to make the results coincide with the ideas. On the other hand neither theory nor method have been my strong points. But perhaps, as they said in *Hamlet*, "though this is madness, yet there's method in it." Now that the Dorotheenhof is built, I stop to look at the stone pavement with the large passages to the oblong court, that faces the green area of the school, the brick walls of the offices, those in plasterwork of the dwellings, the corner tower, the zinc roofs with varied and variable profiles against the sky. I look at how all the different walls match, and how the corner tower dialogues with the square and how it calls one's attention to the fact that it was recently built, but nevertheless suggests a new demand for dignity and figuration, that reconnects it to the old city. Under the gray sky the block is compact and severe. But as soon as a little blue appears above, the roofs seek, with their points, to comb the sky; the court opens to the trees and to the noise of the water in the two fountains, where Roberto Barni's bronze animals drink.

["Progetti per Lipsia", in *Area*, no. 36, January-February 1998]

Grattacieli
[Skyscrapers]

01. *The echo of the collapse and the sight of the billowing dust of the ruins of the Twin Towers still reverberates in our memory and already the press is publishing the names of the self-appointed candidates for their reconstruction. In this frenzied haste, the Italians were among the first. It's like a never-ending show: countless repetitions of the destruction and immediately afterward the spotlights are focused on the reconstruction race. Professor Natalini, shouldn't we reflect a moment on what is happening?*

In 1969, when I was designing the *Continuous Monument* with Superstudio, I imagined a great Cartesian plane, uniform and isotropic, evenly crosshatched to represent the infrastructures, structures and surfaces in a sort of metaphysical and minimalist delirium. In 1971 in New York and Chicago I observed that reality had exceeded our imagination and the infinite latticework on the glass skin of the skyscrapers revealed a harshness and a cruelty that our neo-Platonic fantasies could never have imagined. In recent years, the catastrophic pictures of contemporary architecture have revealed a new generation of cutting-edge architects to me and I was struck by the fact that they were being taken seriously as we never were back in the Sixties. Their deconstructivist, unlovely, jumbled fantasies, products of the deepest sleep of reason, dominated the architectural scene and it seemed as if there were no longer any limits. Then came the pictures of 11 September 2001 in New York, and they too exceeded our wildest imagination. The collapse of the Twin Towers made us realize how fragile ours were, but above all how horrible the fantasies of the architects had been.
If we think of how many died and how many more will die, we can no longer fall victim to the fantasies of the architectures designed and built to seem on the point of collapsing. Winston Churchill, after promising the British "blood, sweat and tears" added that, however, everything had to go on normally – "business as usual": I don't think he would be able to say the same words today, even with a big cigar in his hand and his watercolors on the easel.
We need a measure of time and silence to process this level of grief. For anyone who buried one of his loved ones there, a hot meal can be some consolation, but it might be better to postpone the gala dinner for the rebuilders for some time.

Some took this opportunity to sing the De Profundis for skyscrapers. I'd like to know your opinion on the subject.

The evening of 10 September, a program appeared on an Italian television show (Great Events in History) about the Japanese kamikaze pilots. The September issue of *Domus* that arrived at my studio a few days after 9/11 was devoted to towers and skyscrapers and featured articles with titles like "The Irresistible Charm of the Skyscraper" and "How to Design a Skyscraper". The juxtaposition was disturbing: the human capacity to destroy and rebuild, in response to a faith so absolute as to border on fanaticism.

Le Corbusier wrote in 1934: "The skyscrapers of New York are too small... they are romantic: a gesture of pride. But they have killed the streets and made the city mad. Skyscrapers are unreasonable from top to bottom." Personally, I've never liked them; I love the tall buildings of Northern Europe with their rooftops combing the clouds, but I don't understand those buildings that seem to go on forever.
Buildings come from the earth and from the earth they draw their force. It is right for them to climb as high as logic can support them, but after a certain limit they need so much help (mechanisms, systems) as to force their inhabitants into a completely artificial lifestyle. And anyway, why climb so high to see a view if I can't open the windows to feel the breeze?

[28.10.01, from the interview by M. Pisani, in *L'industria delle Costruzioni*]

Immagini
[Pictures]

01. *Pictures by an architect*
When presenting a project or a construction, there is no need to say a single thing because the architecture speaks for itself. Thus, a presentation can be like a silent movie with just a few essential subtitles, perhaps accompanied by some live music.
But the pictures are immobile: there is no movement in the light, none of the animation provided by people or animals, nothing happens, no one is living, eating, sleeping, loving or dying there.
All we can see in pictures is the "spirit of geometry", some color perhaps, a few recognizable materials.
There are none of the surprises and fears, none of the worries and wondering, none of the accounting of square feet, no information about distributions and functions.
There is nothing of the needs and dreams, of the fear of failure or of the laborious construction with the hundreds of lurking dangers, the possible enemies of beauty, the harsh reality of the budget or the confusing maze of bureaucratic regulations.
What is left of the drawings?
Perhaps nothing more than a few traces of the passion and the trepidation of a gesture repeated or a line in search of impossible perfection.
What is left of the construction?
The clash of different wills remains, the compromise of conflicting needs and struggles. The stones remain, and could speak if their architect had given them his voice. But the stones that remain have no need to speak if someone is living serenely among them.
I hope that is what happens to mine.
The architect disappears in his work and the work disappears or remains in the background of the lives of the people.

[29.06.05]

Laterizio
[Brick]

01. *You gave the brick an unusual architectural style. What fascinates you about this material: its long lasting durability especially in the long run, its quality, its city feel...?*

In the 1980s when I was taking my first steps in architecture through construction works, I studied this material lengthily.
Working with brick led me to anthropological literature and studies on architectural wefts, that show how small and natural elements continually and visibly manipulated interact with architecture. Bricklayers don't use measuring instruments but think in terms of "hands", where each "hand" of bricks is in reality a row. I have always thought of architecture as being massive, whether as a superimposition of inert materials or a removal (excavation, cave) even if it involves a minimum of interlaced and light-weight materials. Paraphrasing the title of a famous book, for me lightness in architecture is unsustainable. I've always thought of architecture as characterized by gravity and heaviness. Working on and observing Italian and North European architecture, I learned many things about the ability of the brick in configuring small and big constructions alike as well as its capacity for the building of small residential structures (like the house of the practical pig) and also extensive breakwaters. The buildings of Zola Predosa, Gorle and Ferrara were the first experiments with the material and on the design of special pieces using terracotta (with Ferrone at Impruneta), that were also parallel with my experiences.
Old catalogues, manuals and the skilful constructions in Emilia Romagna, Lombardy, Germany and the Netherlands were my textbooks and sources of inspiration.
I used the wisdom of traditional buildings to make up for my lack of experience.
Finally, the durability in the long run (as you say), the quality and colour of the material and entire brick cities like Siena and Ferrara have fascinated me and continue to do so.

[26.09.03, from an interview of C. Donati, in *Costruire in Laterizio*]

Linguaggio/Lingue
[Style/Language]

01. *Architectural Style*
Projects of the Natalini Architects propose classical and reassuring concepts. They are familiar buildings, close to the images people have of a house, from their memories and experiences. They are realistic projects without any "nostalgia for the future."
Looking back, this architecture may seem nostalgic. It is not. It is realistic architecture based on "critical rationalism", an architecture that makes use of the best available: types, morphology (image), technology... It does not look back nostalgically to the past but uses its legacy and experience, unlike "contemporary" experiments, an architecture infused with "nostalgia for the future", aimed towards a future we do not know, and filled with risks that the unknown (non-knowledge) implies: unacceptable risks for peaceful living.
The sights of a historic city have a high degree of complexity that comes from the integration of various functions, from the hierarchy of public and private spaces to the coexistence and superimposition of buildings that have different styles. Historical changes have been slow and constant over time until the middle of the 20th century, so as to allow an evolution of style that groups together different buildings in one

Reconstruction of a city block on Manetstrasse in Leipzig, 1993-1994, from *Quaderni Neri*, courtyard

Reconstruction of a city block on Manetstrasse in Leipzig, from *Quaderni Neri*, street view, 1993

145.
ZIMMERSTR. RICHTUNG DOROTHEENPLATZ
9.1.94

163.
193.
1.94
9.1.94

big family. New interventions in a historic city must be undertaken with continuity, using the new language only when absolutely necessary.
Traditional and contemporary materials may mingle and overlap according to necessity. The architecture we propose inspires serenity and dignity similar to the historic city in complexity and humanity. The architecture we propose does not seek an element of surprise but seeks to build a fixed setting where one can take walks, meet others, buy, eat, work, and live daily lives peacefully. Perhaps the happiness we aspire to have is not that of the architect, but we would like to remind you that the buildings are *made by* architects and not *for* architects, and historic towns are not built *in* the city but *for* the city or *against* the city and we root for the first hypothesis.
Our buildings are very simple but obtain richness and complexity by fitting in with the others and blending with the landscape. Public and semi-public external areas are treated as small squares; the volumes, façades and materials are inspired by tradition, with a number of small variations on the theme.
The multiplication of theories and styles of contemporary architecture, and the richness and variety of techniques and materials together with the quest for individual expression and novelty, have destroyed the unity and autonomy of the city.
A historic city, even with the variety of its buildings, is uniform and comprehensible.
Historic centres of Europe are a wonderful example of how different buildings can exist together, and how streets, squares, and public and private spaces are brought together to form a living organism, moderate and comprehensible.
In the contraposition of the historic centre and the suburbs, which have neither rules nor memory, we would like to support the idea that the entire city can be treated equally as a "bearer of sense". In the contrast between architecture and nature, we would like to find a harmonious integration where each of the two achieves its best.
Finally, to counter the proliferation of styles, we can attempt to create a common style based on the metamorphosis of tradition.
Our projects offer different types of architecture, which are at the same time solid and dignified, brought together not only by the use of the same material but also by the desire to be relevant to the places and people, resistant to time and trends, insured against the rapid passing of time and able to protect its inhabitants from the rigours of seasons, and men, united by a desperate need for normalcy.
[2008]

02. *Languages*
Architects have the extraordinary good fortune to be able to speak languages. They can speak at least three. The first is composed of words and is used to express wishes, explain complicated matters and justify errors and omissions.
The second consists of the drawings and designs, light sketches on sheets of paper that represent an existing world or one that may be possible. Signs collected slowly in the folds of time, are able to put some order in events over a long time span.
The third are constructions, objects, rooms, houses and cities. Materials set in order, channelled energy, scenarios for the life of people. Buildings go beyond their creators and narrate dreams and drawings; they speak without words and in the best scenarios they can sing. But even when silent, when appearances are mute and motionless, they speak for the many who have designed and built them. In time, they tell the stories of the inhabitants and visitors, and maybe, of their destroyers.
But there has not been any Pentecost for architects: they were not given the gift of tongues. It was rather a conquest that was gruelling because of the long and difficult journey, and painful because of the sacrifices to be made.
To be able to speak a comprehensible language, the architect should make many sacrifices that are full of infantile stuttering, idioms, puns, tics and quirks of rhetorical phrases and effects.
He must renounce the technical jargon and latest formulas, and must be able to use simple and strong words that can be heard above the noise in the midst of distractions.
[A. Natalini, in *Identità dell'architettura italiana*, Diabasis, Reggio Emilia 2004]

Lipsia
[Leipzig]

01. *Manetstrasse, Leipzig*
This is a 1994 project where I was asked to replace a historical building close to the old city centre with a block of mixed houses and shops. Leipzig is a really beautiful city, mostly built with stone, during a period when the economy was on the uptrend in the so-called Gründerzeit. In Leipzig, as in all the other German cities, they sell some extraordinary books with photos of the city before and towards the end of the war and how it was rebuilt. Most of the German cities were rebuilt in the most philological manner possible whereas other parts were done in a bizarre and modern style. If we compare the photos taken before and after, the conclusion is always the same: it was better before. When I went to work in Leipzig, at the start there were still the ruins of the war. Some blocks had been destroyed, others remained empty, and in other places they had rebuilt houses that were mostly huge prefabricated buildings in cement – the Plattenbau, that desperately resembled the Unité d'Habitation of Le Corbusier. The Germans were convinced of this type of model and had built these huge, absolutely unlivable housing units which they later started to demolish. Now they are thinking of preserving them since they thought it right to keep a token of this period of grand illusions and great hopes in which socialism had risen to power. The ruins are extraordinarily fascinating and they say that good architectures make good ruins. In these two pictures by Bellotto, the ruins still conserve a memoir of the architectures. In the first, the tower of a demolished church, you see each of the bricks and there is also a man climbing up a flight of stairs: it was like a sign of hope and resurrection.
In Leipzig, as in every city in which I worked, I tried to learn from the city. I tried to rediscover the figures of the city which in this case were the walkways, towers and corners of the remarkable buildings of this late-19th-century city. I tried to build a small composite block that could be crossed in two directions, where on a main road there were shops and offices. At a corner

Reconstruction of a city block on Manetstrasse in Leipzig, from *Quaderni Neri*, street view, 1994

Reconstruction of a city block on Manetstrasse in Leipzig, from *Quaderni Neri*, courtyard, 1994

there was a kind of tower which dialogued with a small square and on the internal courtyard there were housing units. The architecture was composite: the houses and the offices were configured in a certain way and the shops in another, but all aspired towards normality and aimed to speak a language of places. The buildings were then organized in a regular manner following the line of the road and divided into a basement, first floor and an attic. In the constructions of Northern Europe the roofs are beautiful and important: it is as if the roofs, with dragon back profile, combed the clouds. The skies in Northern Europe differ from ours which need a different type of treatment. In the various pictures we saw, the inside and outside of the block were visible: in a certain way some parts tried to give an industrial image similar to what was there before; in other cases, the buildings tried to relate with the best aspects of Leipzig's postwar reconstruction. The red building in brick on the left, considered a masterpiece of the prefabricated technique, remained where it was and I thought that it was appropriate to establish a dialogue also with it.
In Leipzig I built a block along the boundary of the historic centre trying to interact with the architecture of the old centre and with the reconstruction of the former DDR: the city of stone on one side and that of massive prefabricated buildings on the other. I tried to put into practice what I had learned over the ten years of German projects: solidity and folly, the domestic features of Biedermeier and the Bismarck *pathos*. The block is composed of different parts, with a big open courtyard and curved walls. It is made of brick and stone, with white plaster on the courtyard, and fantastic grey zinc roofs that will forever tend to resemble the grey winter skies.

[*Narrate, uomini, la vostra storia*, 2006]

Luogo/Contesto
[Place/Context]

01. *First fragment: place/site*
The sights of a historic city are very important. They are stratifications of oriented memories, nodes of relationships, which are (or should be) scenarios of a civilized life. Sights of a historic city are complex places: sometimes we miss out on their true sense because of our scarce connection to the city or for the countless disturbances that make it hard to interpret. These places already contain many architectures which make it often difficult to add more. The *genius loci* (or more simply, the environment) requires the sensitivity of the water diviner (or more simply, a thorough analysis in different directions). Do not just read the city; you have to "feel" the city with the intention of understanding its sense. The reconstruction of the sense of the city is the goal of every "architectural discovery". Usually delimited by boundaries or maps, places/sites are posed to the designer as immutable data, such as closed loops in which to place the project... But places/sites are far from what is described and mapped. They are layers of oriented memories and contain traces of events and transformations. They retain traces of buildings that have existed, and paradoxically, those buildings that will rise. Places/sites are also nodes of spatial grids, where all configurations of the contours, the tensions of distant, visible and invisible but connected places converge. Places are also weather stations, where you change horses, provided that time moves only in one direction... For those who discern it, a place tells you what it is and what it wants to become.

[A. Natalini, *Figures of stone*, Electa, Milan 1984]

02. ***A_*** *The first time I heard about a place having an identity was more than 30 years ago when I was a student of architecture during one of your fascinating lectures. How has your rapport with places changed in all these years and in what manner are they present in your method of designing?*

With the Superstudio we had crossed avant-garde territories (an experience that has led me to avoid the disease of modernism). Between 1973 and 1978 we had started a series of research on the materials used in suburban areas, a study on anthropology, design and architecture.
This research focused our attention on places and relationships that bound them to the production and use of manufactured products. We were looking for roots of creativity and felt committed to founding once again, anthropological architecture.
We backtracked and looked closely, and envied the eyes of children or of the Aranda aborigines of Australia. So when we reread Heidegger through the writings of Norberg Schultz on *genius loci*, we seemed to have found a big brother coming to our aid. In 1979 I began a long series of projects for Italian (and European) cities based on the identity of places. I was studying traces recorded from memory and my visits, more emotional than scientific, explored the different geographical, historical, and human dimensions.
As architecture should be rooted in places, I was aware of the uniqueness and diversity of each place from which we derive the need for each piece of architecture to be different. This need seemed to undermine every theory and methodology: architecture cannot be taught. But my role as a teacher ("the mission of the learned" according to Fichte) forced me to teach it. So I tried to convey my passion for places and tried to understand, as in the words of Louis Kahn, what the place is meant to be. But more than a teacher, I have always been a student (exams never end) and have always tried to learn from what I was teaching.
In all these years my relationship with places has not changed. If some of my projects seem indifferent to the places then it means that these projects were wrong and weak. I've always tried to speak the language of the place in the vast variety of Italian regions, Germany, the Netherlands and elsewhere: from Jerusalem to Tromsø, and lastly Thule.
Sometimes I am successful, and on other occasions I limited myself to stuttering, but I've always sought an architecture that talks, with a stubborn will to listen and communicate. If something has changed, it is only in being more resistant to the spirit of the times (but he who espouses the present will soon be a widower) and with greater respect for stratification, hybridization and common ideas, and let's say with an extraordinary desire for normality.

B_ *If I have to think about the role of architecture in the context of the construction of a contemporary city in Europe, I think of a fire that was constantly stoked in the 1980s, with the flame left to gradually dwindle. What are the reasons for the prevalence of universal languages in a country like ours where a project does not start from scratch but from a cultural wealth that others envy?*

From concurrent architecture to a globalized context. In the 1980s in the movement for the reconstruction of the European cities, regional criticism placed the idea of context as the basis of the project.
Then other research trends occupied the media scene. Here I would like to make a distinction between architecture that builds human environment and design for communication between the real world and the virtual one (paper or digital)... I do not want to be repetitive: I will try to answer the question even if it is wrongly posed. There are manifold reasons for the predominance of abstract styles separated from the contexts, which are not universal (if so only in the sense of a universal folly). The first and most perverse reason is trend.
If novelty is given a value, then novelty is privileged and pursued. Since the first connotation of novelty is diversity, then architecture must be detached from history, places and humans. It seeks diversity through enormity: gigantism, technical and economic absurdity, the illogical, irrational and inhuman.
A second reason is the inability to accept architecture's role as a service, its normal fate. Architects are no longer content to be masons who know Latin (in the words of Loos) and aspire to the role of an artist or a hero, forgetting that true heroism lies in living daily life.

03. *Designing with respect for the place in mind: the value of onsite surveys, the relationship with history, the role of techniques and materials. But when dealing with the issue of style and the power of the signs that we draw on the sheet paralyzes us, what are the ways in which traces of the past become an expression of a new identity? In reality, as we move from passive protection of superintendents to the development of new forms of identity?*

Traces of the past.
"Nothing is built with ruins but everything is built over ruins." I will repeat myself once again, this time by quoting Borges. Each project insists on lands that are accumulations of traces, ruins and other projects. As in every living thing DNA is constructed in the past, able to modify tangibly, foreshadowing future developments. Attention to context, empathy with places along with technical reading and analysis allow us to understand what the place is and maybe also "what it wants to be"... but between that and the summary of the project is a logical gap, a lapse. The plan, constraints, and different needs all play their parts in the transformation of the site and construction of the project. We try to superimpose new signs to existing ones, aiming at continuity. We try to pass on the legacy that has been entrusted to us while bearing in mind the parable of the talents... The complexity of reality does not allow us to identify a methodology.
The statutes of the discipline, rules on proper building... all these are constantly changing as we change.
"Things fall apart; the centre cannot hold; mere anarchy is loosed upon the world," as written by William Butler Yeats between the two wars.

[23.02.13 from S. Follesa, "A tempo e a luogo. Dialogo con Adolfo Natalini"]

04. *After Cristian Norberg-Schulz and Paolo Portoghesi, you wrote the most interesting things about sites, at least until 1983. What about today?*

I am very indebted to the books of Norberg-Schulz; through them I discovered Heidegger and many other subjects, which I did not know existed.
My relationship with sites has become for me, more and more important and visceral since I confront them every day, especially in historic cities. I realize that by learning more about technique and construction, my relationship with the sites grows deeper. At first it was basically a listening relationship: I tried to feel the place and hoped to give it a response. Now I have more sophisticated instruments that allow me to articulate more appropriate answers for the place which remains the cornerstone of my architectural style. Maybe I will never build an image as an architect or a style, as we used to say in the past, because of my extreme interest in places that are different, by nature, and which constrain buildings to diversify to be able to be in tune with each other. The result is a process aimed at the construction of architecture, not an architect.
I try to make architectures that fit into the context, to react, rather than invent. So I force myself with continuous training because each time the place requires me to read and learn. I would have loved to work all my life in the construction of the same place. I would like to work on my home town, Pistoia, or another Tuscan city, in a relationship similar to the one of De Carlo with Urbino or Schatner with his bishop. In working for years on the same site that ultimately belongs to you, its modifications really respond to logic. Unfortunately I move frantically from place to place looking for opportunities to build and every time I always have to start over.

And yet Michelangelo claimed that we are repainting the world. The site then, could be the whole world...

Maybe at the end of history or before this, I will realize that all the places are the same and I am constructing the same architecture or better yet a series of fragments, which when put together make one building.
Sometimes I suspect that my work on exceptions is just this way: discover the rule confirmed by a series of exceptions.

[02.05.86, from an interview by M. Pisani]

05. *City regulations*

Every civilized coexistence is based on a body of rules: what rules govern the physical progress of the city? Plans, implementation of rules and building regulations are necessary but not sufficient. A look at a contemporary city (Florence after the war, for example) is enough to prove it. The legislation, rules and layout define the uses, quantities and locations. There is no indication as to quality, nor is there a proposal or control. So any discussion on quality is entrusted to the good (or bad) intentions and decisions of individuals. The rules of professional conduct require the architect to work according to "science, consciousness and diligence," and maybe we should insert an article specifying that science must be based on the Vitruvian triad, *firmitas, utilitas, venustas* and also *propinquitas* [propinquity] (appropriateness of context).

[From the Presentation of a book on projects for the reconstruction of the area along the Arno river at the Ponte Vecchio, 1996]

06. *You define yourself as a provincial architect but most of your building sites are kilometres away from your offices. How do you gather the best from our local culture and translate it without aberrations in a European scale?*

On job opportunities in different European cities, I am confronted with the need to learn the local language each time. I've always thought that architecture is inherent in the place that is why my buildings must speak the language of the place. I do not believe much in globalization, so I prefer to think of the endless beauty of differences. I never work on places inhabited by the "noble savage," but I always work in places where the cultural stratification is so dense and complex that it is very easy to extract some elements of great importance. The problem for me is not so much the gathering of the best of our local cultures, or my Tuscan culture and translating it into a European scale, but being able to lose my identity and acquire from time to time, the identity of a local architect. This does not mean that I believe I am Zelig nor could I ever be Pessoa with his infinite heteronyms. My ambition is to sometimes be the architect of the small provincial towns where I work. Having failed to be the architect of this extraordinary city of the province where I was born, that is Pistoia, from time to time I try to be reborn in each of these cities.

Going back to the previous question, given the need to forge a close and intimate relationship with the site, then passion intended as tension between what you do and what you love becomes an important component of the project.

In one of the previous questions, I was reminded of one of my favourite expressions: "architectures and objects of affection." Basically what continues to keep me tied to places is this movement of affection, desire to join, and willingness to participate or be a part of it. Perhaps this feeling of alienation (procured by moving from one place to another) leads me to adhere as closely and as long as possible to the place where I am called to work. Affection is a passion that seems obvious. I once read, or perhaps it was Hobbes that said: "The only passion I know is fear" and on another occasion I found a phrase uttered by a young artist who was asked by a great artist: "How do you approach your work?" And the young man responded: "Each time trembling with fear."

[25.10.97, from the interview of E. Gonzo and A. Vicari, in *Costruire in Laterizio*]

07. For years I worked in historic cities in Italy, Germany and the Netherlands trying to learn from them. I learned that each one is different and requires passionate attention. Among the few things they have in common are the presence of monuments, urban form and expansions.

Monuments are permanent elements, the anchors of collective memory. The strength of the monuments lies in their permanence and ability to modify their function without losing their meaning.

The urban form (structure) is its historic structure, made of paths and tracks, roads and squares, and public and private buildings arranged hierarchically.

Tracks remain while the fabrics can be modified or replaced. Expansions rarely have an urban form: their structure is usually too simple, devoid of stratification and order. In many cases, the structure is arbitrary (formless) and does not allow changes: you can only demolish and rebuild in a never-ending process.

The different images are always and only contemporary and do not stand up to the times.

[*Dai miei Quaderni Olandesi*, 2006]

08. *Architecture continues to express itself through the three Vitruvian principles of utility, beauty and solidity that meet the needs of the body, soul and time. Which of these values is a priority and as a final analysis, what is architecture for Adolfo Natalini?*

Next to the Vitruvian triad of *firmitas, utilitas, venustas*, now is the time to add a fourth term, that of *propinquitas*, adhesion to places and what is close to us. None of these values must take priority: it would result in unbalanced and deformed architecture.

If architecture builds a fixed stage for men, and if modification of the earth to make it habitable and inhabiting it means living at peace on earth and under the sky (to use the words of unforgettable teachers), architecture will be immobile and serene since life is already too fast and variable.

In *Figures of stone* I argued that architecture is born from places and composed of many elements (and it's up to us to precariously choose the most relevant) and talking "figures". Twenty years will not be enough to be able to give it a definition.

I try to construct a building appropriate for the places and people, and which is solid, reassuring, calm and dignified (or should be) as the cities they belong to.

It was said before that every place has its own architectural style, but does a universal architectural style exist that can be adapted to any site?

Universal architecture does not exist. For example, there is automobile manufacturing and there is the construction of roads. A car factory manufactures vehicles that may go to Italy, France or maybe even to Sweden. It's an object that functions and moves as long as there is even just one road it is able to go on. It does not care about its so-called context. Its general context is vast but it is not geographical, and that's the market. However, he who builds roads must go there, to see its terrain and adapt its artefacts maybe by resorting to "works of art" (tunnels and viaducts).

I think that architecture is more similar to the construction of roads, it must adapt to the place and not to the construction of automobiles. On one hand there is architecture and on the other is design, mostly overlooked by that of the context. Its contexts are much wider; think of the fashion system and objects. In my opinion, architecture is more local.

[26.09.03, interview by C. Donati, in *Costruire in Laterizio*]

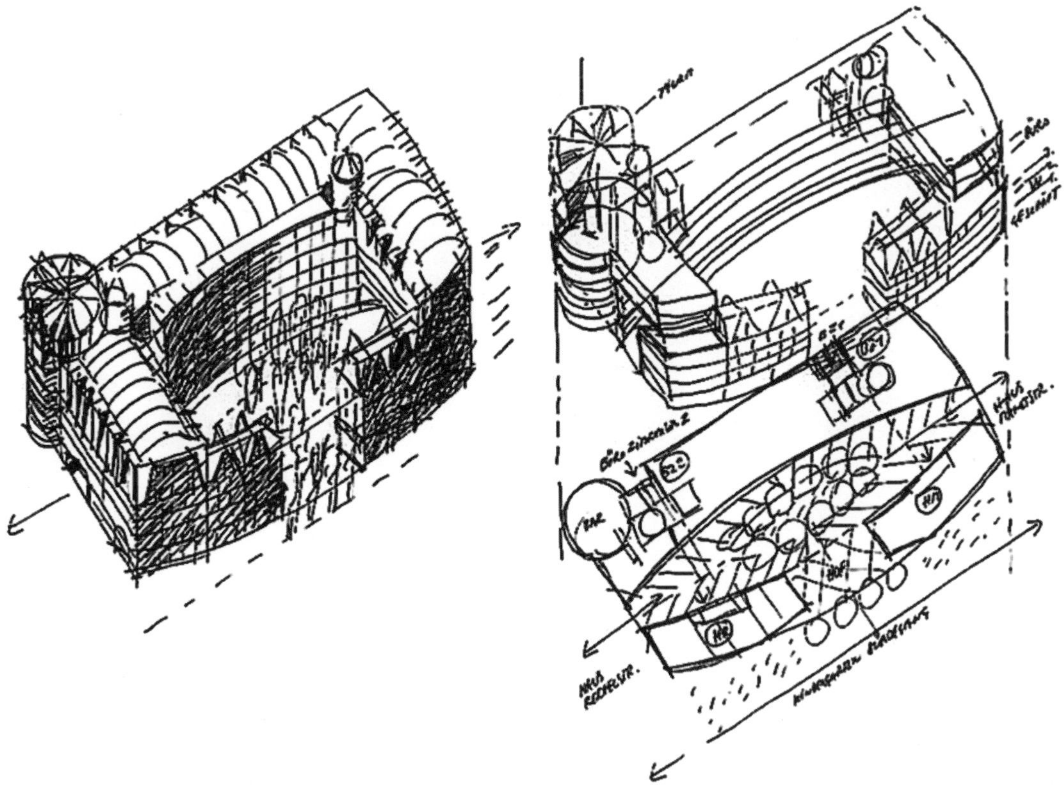

Reconstruction of a city block
on Manetstrasse in Leipzig
Axonometric perspective
from *Quaderni Neri*, 1994

Reconstruction of
a city block on Manetstrasse
in Leipzig, 1993-1994,
View of a model by Franco
Gizdulich, photo Mario Ciampi

Reconstruction of a city
block on Hofmeisterstrasse
in Leipzig, sketch,
from *Quaderni Neri*, 1993

Il quaderno tedesco

[German sketchbook]

—

Project for the reconstruction of the Römerberg, Frankfurt

1979

In the center of Frankfurt, between the Cathedral and the Nikolaikirche, stretches a no-man's-land stretches out, well-paved, flower-bedded and furnished with benches, tables and pergolas, scattered with mysterious cubes of red brick disposed in long rows. These cubes are the only visible portion of the pillars, which, underground, bear the weight of the two (or three) floors of garages which in their turn lie above two storeys of U-Bahn. Thus, the mysterious red-brick cubes mark the points where the pillars will rise to support a cultural center, a modern building of several storeys in height, designed by the architects who won the relative competition. Following the same project, they have already built the Technische Rathaus, another modern building on one side of this large space.
In the spring of 1944, there were only ruins here. The Allied air-force had treated the medieval town center, with its little streets, its Wechmarkt and Alte Markt like a megalomaniac town-planner or a ravaging politician would do. All that was left of the medieval center were ruins, vestiges of the Rathaus and of other Fachwerk (wooden buildings). In the same place, a few Carolingian remains told of the deeds of the Emperors. Even further down, very few Roman remains were a reminder of the Roman camp: this place is still called Römer today. The first time I saw this place on a windy June evening, the paving-stones and the Cathedral had the same reddish light. In the mysterious rows of brick cubes was a waiting for architecture.
In the mysterious series of brick cubes, arranged in calm rows on the temporary roofing, there was the force of a hidden architecture that might be unleashed like a spring.
Looking at drawings of the site, and plans and diagrams of the innumerable influences that have been superimposed during the centuries, the web of memories became so thick as to stop even the wind blowing off the Main. The place was full of presences and voices: the archeological garden with its Roman and Carolingian stones, the layout of the medieval city, which many would have liked to bring back after the violence of the war (perhaps in order to delude themselves into thinking that nothing happened and that the war had never passed – the famous "hygiene of the world supposed to suppress the weak – both men and things"), the Cathedral and the Nikolaikirche, and the fountain of Justice and the Römer, but also the new buildings and the proud and perfect skyscrapers of the banks (a three-dimensional diagram of the financial market), and the great under-ground garage efficient and silent as a Mercedes, and the aseptic project for the cultural center, full of Reformist good sense... There was already so much architecture in the place that it seemed absurd to add more. There was also a subtle sensation of death and destruction in the great emptiness and in this unnatural calm, almost like a great house with a dead body buried in the cellar (a great house, with the dead body under the floor, the broken columns, and no roof – blown away by a hurricane or never finished, because the builders had fled).

The building is a large pillared hall (Säulenhalle) which can be used for exhibitions, parties, meetings, boozing sessions, trade-shows and business. The building continues and completes the existing under-structures (U-bahn and car parks), making use of the provisional roofing as flooring at staggered levels. The facades of dwellings on the Römerberg are reconstructed in rusted steel (Corten) in the original positions and dimensions. As one ascends the staircase behind the facade it is possible to look through the unglazed windows: not reconstruction but evocation. All the external walls are of masonry in local red sandstone (Buntstein) with buttresses featuring white marble elements. The flooring, with its regular granite slabs, shows the layout of the medieval street system with its original paving. Arranged on the pre-existing system of pillars of the car parks, 203 steel pillars support a reticulate roofing. The pillars are cylindrical with a constant external section. In the areas once occupied by the streets they are left visible while in the areas once occupied by dwellings they are cladded with stone to a height of 4.80 metres and above that they are bare. The difference in treatment of the pillars, seen in perspective, conjures up the phantoms of streets and dwellings. In correspondence with the old street layout, glazed prismatic elements recreate on high the glimpses of skies of the past. The roof is like a raised square of memory. A covered wooden bridge crosses the roofing diagonally, suspended over the transparent elements, and is used as a panoramic pathway. Access to it is from a staircase on the Römerberg, behind the mock facades in steel or by an internal escalator. As one walks through, the roofing looks like a rolling landscape where broad brown areas allude to the destroyed houses while the transparent prisms are an allusion to the forgotten streets.

p. 179
Römerberg, columns and walls

p. 180
A page from *Lotus*, n. 32, 1982

p. 181
Plan and cross-section from *Quaderni Neri*

pp. 182-183
Römerberg, arial view

p. 184
Römerberg, internal view

p. 185
Römerberg, cross-section, plan

pp. 186-187
Römerberg, wall with Berlin and Chinese flags.

Project
Adolfo Natalini;
Collaborating team
Roy Barris,
Martine Bedin,
Giovanni De Carolis,
Demetz & Ploner,
Chris Stephens.

A. Natalini, La ricostruzione del Römerberg/Reconstruction of the Römerberg

1

2

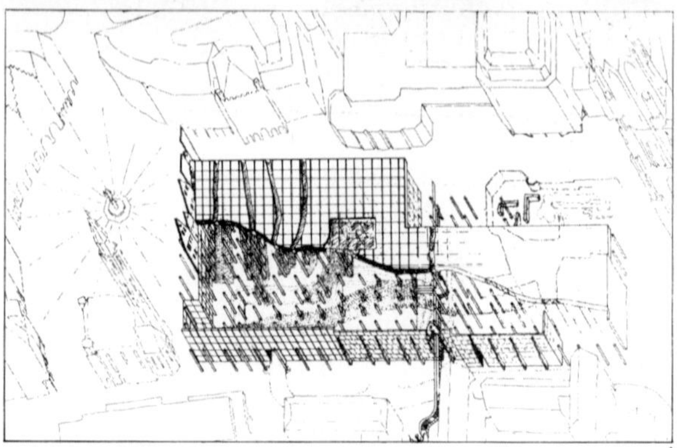

3

La proposta di Natalini vede l'architettura come un processo, non solo in senso tecnologico, ma anche come accadimento spirituale. E, poiché Römerberg è parte della storia culturale di Francoforte, anche il progetto si fa documento di una storia della cultura nel quale le tracce del passato si riflettono e, al tempo stesso, acquistano spessore e diventano esse stesse nuovo messaggio.

Questo progetto è espressione della reazione di uno spirito ricco di sensibilità di fronte a una realtà o a ciò che di essa è rimasto. Esso rispecchia al livello più alto la memoria collettiva della crescita e del mutamento della città di Francoforte.

Non si pone qui il problema delle banali attività di una quotidianità orientata in senso consumistico, bensì quello della qualificazione e dell'autocoscienza della città. Francoforte, come città, si coagula, per così dire, nella sua piazza centrale, nel Römerberg. E, al modo che un Foro romano contiene in sé le tappe più importanti del mondo spirituale e materiale del suo tempo, così nel progetto di Natalini è contenuta anche l'esistenza spirituale di Francoforte, ma addensata in un ambiente poetico, nel quale gli abitanti della città possono ri-identificarsi col luogo. Anche questo, o proprio questo, corrisponde al modo d'intendere l'architettura sociale, che è innalzamento di tempo e di luogo e, con ciò, innalzamento dell'esistenza stessa dell'uomo.

Il contributo formale di Natalini al Römerplatz è fra le più belle "poesie architettoniche" della più recente storia dell'architettura in un mondo che la tecnocrazia ha irrevocabilmente impoverito. Un progetto che dovrebbe farsi occasione di ripensamento e di nuove riflessioni. Pur trattandosi di un progetto presentato fuori concorso, dovrebbero essere ovvii un riconoscimento da parte della giuria e un contributo materiale da parte della città.

O.M. Ungers

Natalini's proposal presents architecture as a process, not just in the technological sense, but also as a spiritual happening. And since Römerberg is part of the cultural history of Frankfurt, this project too becomes a document in the history of a culture which reflects the traces of the past, themselves acquiring deeper significance and becoming a new message.

This design is the expression of the reaction of a spirit richly endowed with great sensibility to a reality or what is left of it. It reflects at the highest level the collective memory of the growth and changes in the city of Frankfurt and its central square.

Here the question of humdrum everyday activities directed towards consumerism does not arise; instead, the concern is with the definition of the city's self-awareness. Frankfurt, as a city, becomes crystallized, so to speak, in its central square, the Römerberg. Just as the Roman forum contains within itself all the most important stages of the material and spiritual world of its time, so Natalini's plan likewise contains the spiritual existence of Frankfurt, but densified into a poetic milieu, within which the city's inhabitants can re-identify with the place itself. This — precisely this, in fact — corresponds to the way in which social architecture should be understood, an elevation of time and space which is at the same time an elevation of man's existence.

Natalini's formal contribution to the Römerplatz is among the most beautiful "architectural poems" in recent architectural history, in a world irrevocably impoverished by technology. A plan that should become an occasion for rethinking and further reflection. Though it has been presented as an unofficial entry, an acknowledgment by the panel of judges and a material contribution by the city would not be inappropriate.

O.M. Ungers

1. Veduta di Francoforte nel 1549.
2. Römerberg: veduta aerea della zona con la copertura provvisoria dei parcheggi.
3. Proposta di progetto.
4. Stratificazioni storiche.

1. View of Frankfurt in 1549.
2. Römerberg: aerial view of the site with the provisional garage roofing.
3. Project proposal.
4. Historical stratifications.

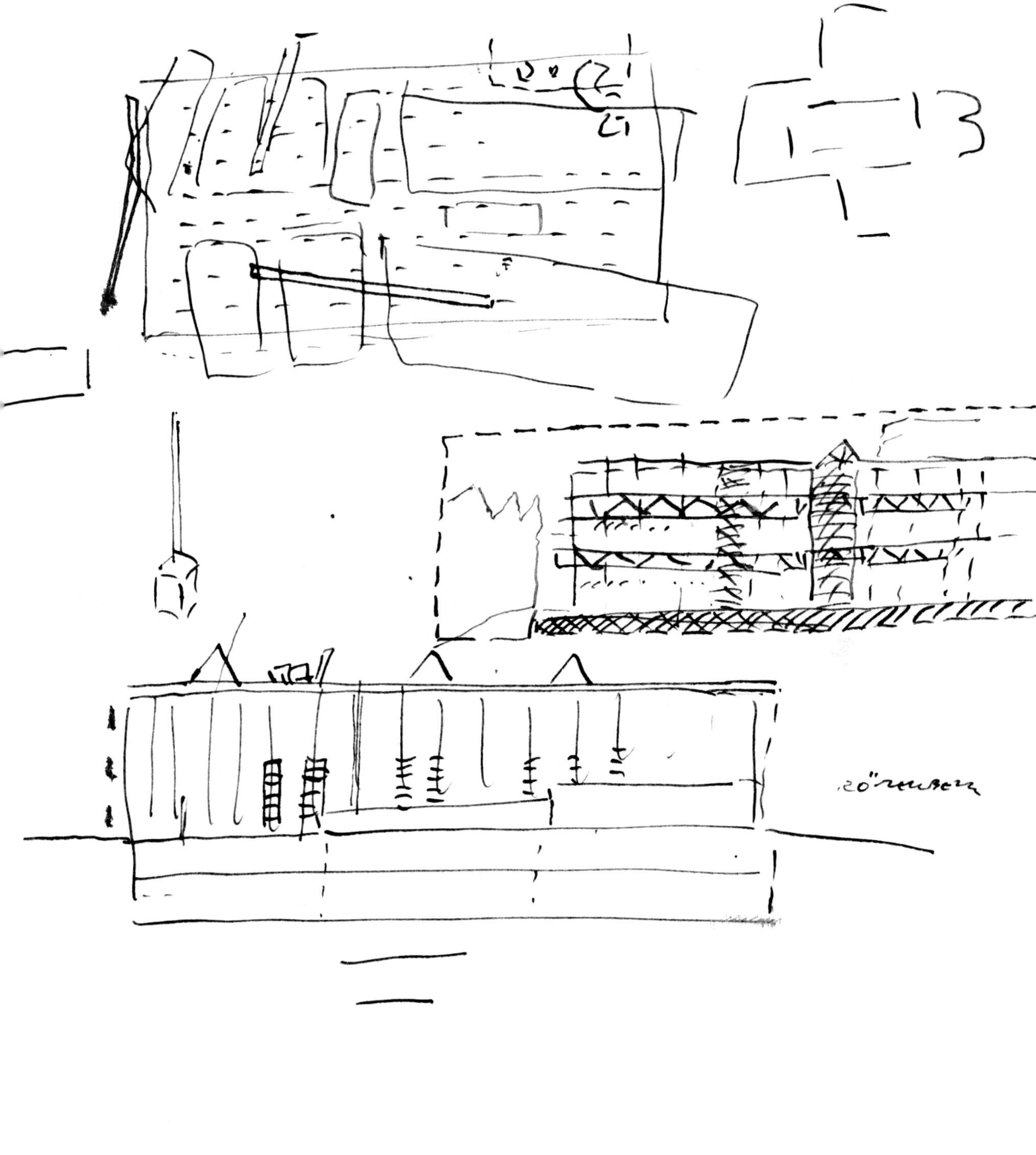

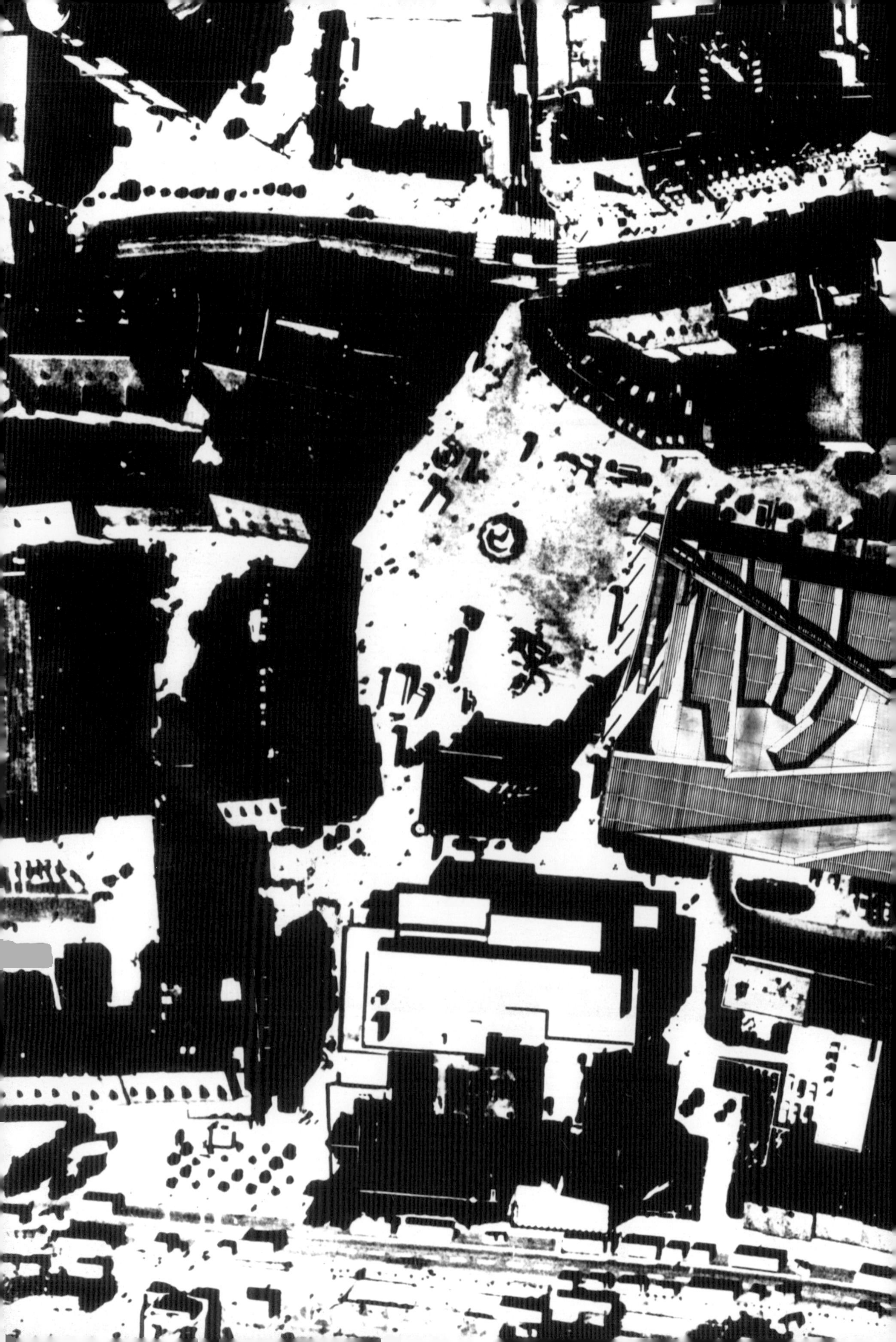

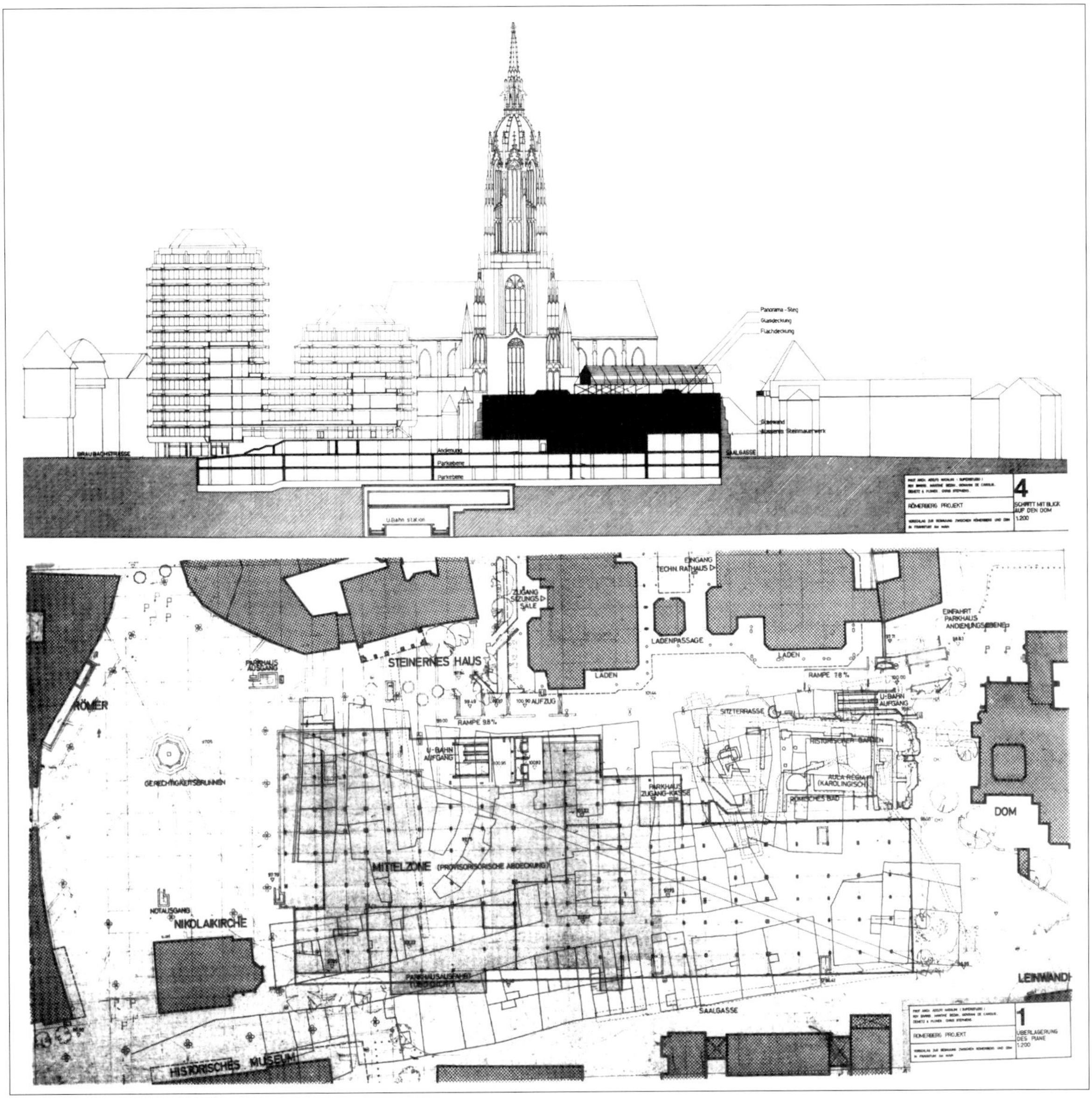
Panorama - Steg
Glasdeckung
Flachdeckung
BRAUBACHSTRASSE
SAALGASSE
U-Bahn station
RÖMERBERG PROJEKT
4
SCHNITT MIT BLICK AUF DEN DOM
1:200
EINGANG
TECHN. RATHAUS
ZUGANG SITZUNGS SÄLE
EINFAHRT PARKHAUS
LADENPASSAGE
LADEN
STEINERNES HAUS
RÖMER
RAMPE 9,8 %
RAMPE 7,8 %
AUFZUG
U-BAHN AUFGANG
SITZTERRASSE
HISTORISCHER GARTEN
AULA REGIA (KAROLINGISCH)
RÖMISCHES BAD
PARKHAUS ZUGANG-KASSE
GERECHTIGKEITSBRUNNEN
DOM
MITTELZONE (PROVISORISCHE ABDECKUNG)
NOTAUSGANG
NIKOLAIKIRCHE
LEINWANDHAUS
SAALGASSE
HISTORISCHES MUSEUM
RÖMERBERG PROJEKT
1
ÜBERLAGERUNG DES PLANE
1:200

BERLINESE

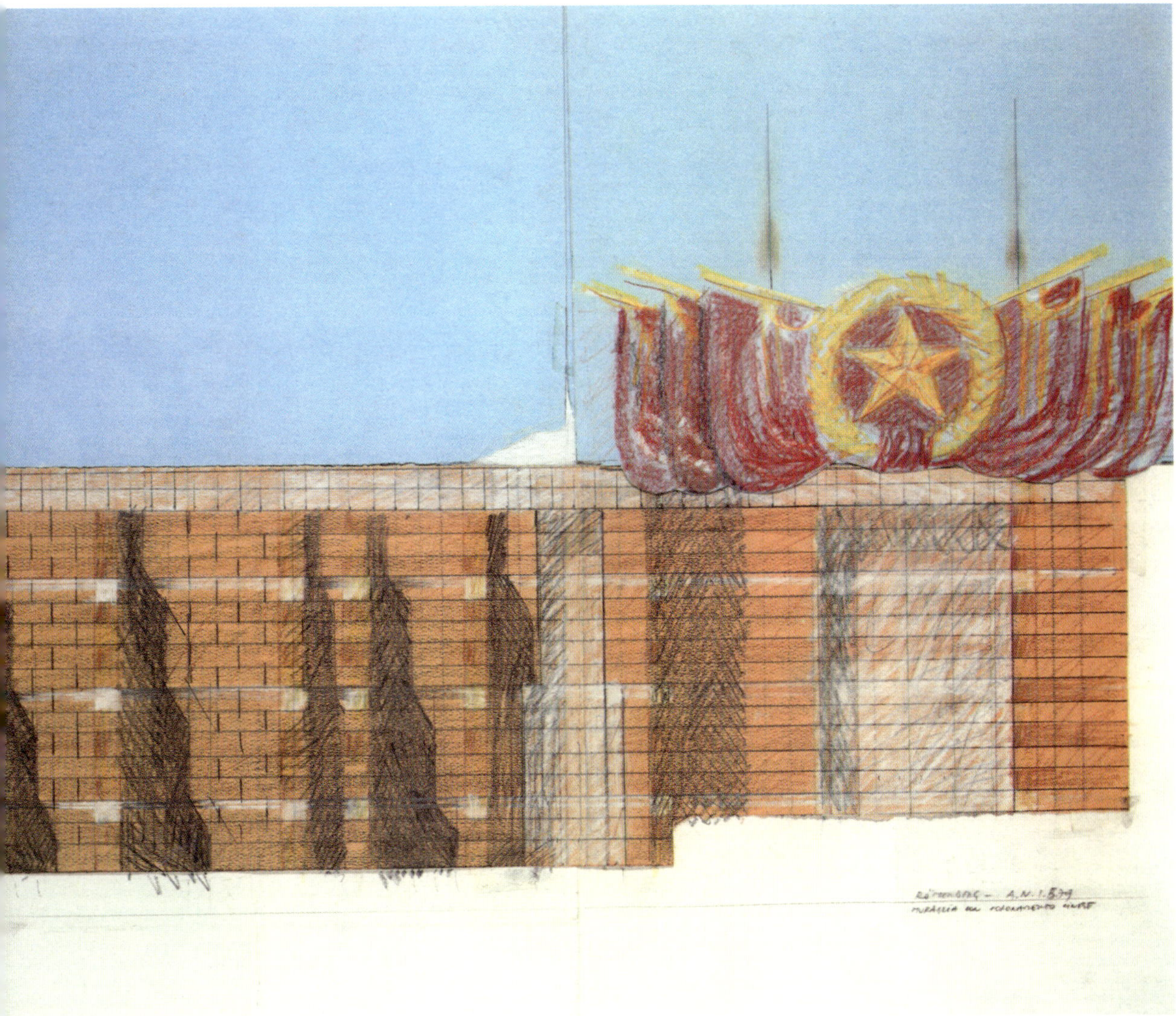

House in Saalgasse, Frankfurt

1980-1989

The house is situated on the corner between Saalgasse and the passage with its adjoining stairs to the central building. It is almost square in plan and divided into two rectangles: the larger one holds five apartments one above the other (or two maisonnettes and an apartment) and the smaller one contains the stairs and the ventilation ducts for the public garage underneath. The ducts have been led to the corner of the facade and are contained inside two cylinders which partially interpenetrate. The two copper-clad cylinders bear elements in the shape of branches and leaves, visible from the stair-well and from the outside.
The homogeneous surfaces of the facades are made from unclad reinforced concrete poured into metal forms.
The two surfaces are interrupted at the corner, leaving visible the shaft-like structures of the ventilation ducts. The grill so created by the metal form-work leads to the crossing of the bronze branches, projecting 90 cm from the facade, that bear the leaves and fruit of oak and lemon. The windows are regular, square openings, with their edges framed in copper. Copper elements cover and emphasize all the edges of the construction.

A tree grows on a corner between two roads: a tree that splits into two or two trees that fuse into one? The branches bear two kinds of leaves and fruit, like in some strange graft.
The double tree is a tree of two cultures: it is the tree of the two cultures (Italian and German, represented by the lemon and the oak of so many poems) that can be seen through the house that stands on the corner. Some branches emerge through windows without glass, others sprout from the concrete of the facade. The geometric grill of the facade and the organic one of the branches are superimposed. The natural is grafted onto and is reassembled with the artificial. The branches which shoot out suggest an ambiguous budding of the architecture. They also suggest vegetable mysteries inside the house...
So the house returns to the archetype of the grass hut (Adam's house in paradise), and recalls the archetype of the tree and of the forest.

The project for the house answers to the need to recover the individuality of the construction as an expression of the different factors that have gone into its creation (Matisse maintained that a good portrait is one that grasps the "diversity" of the sitter).
The streets of the old city, in Frankfurt for example, look like family portraits, with the houses identified by a baptismal name: Judengasse, Ostseite des Römerbergs with the Grosser Engel, Weiland, etc., Fahrgasse with its baroque facades Neue Falkenstein, Zum Wolf, Roter Ochs, the house on the corner with the Schnurgasse Würzburger Eck, or the Goldene Waage with its beam supporting a balance... The house of Goethe's butcher on the corner of Saalgasse with Heiliggeistplàtzchen...

The second project
The design of the house with the branches was not accepted by the local authority, since it was considered excessively hermetic and not modern enough. The new scheme keeps the tree on the corner in the shape of a nearly cylindrical column which contains the ventilation ducts. The bronze grid for the air input is covered by lemon and oak branches, and the leaves (and the bronze gilded fruits) remain untouched by the air flow. The house is a compact volume out of which two longitudinal slices are cut which combine all the windows of the building.
It is constructed of dark red fair-faced concrete blocks, with the floor levels accentuated by subtle bands of glazed mosaics, in black, gold, red, white and green. All the fittings are of bronzed metal.

p. 189
House in Saalgasse,
1st project

p. 190
House in Saalgasse,
oak and lemon trees
from *Quaderni Neri*

p. 191
House in Saalgasse,
tree growth
from *Quaderni Neri*

p. 192
House in Saalgasse,
1st project, elevation

pp. 193-195
*Casa in Saalgasse,
modello azzurro,
modello d'oro
modello verde,
modelli in bronzo*
[House in Saalgasse,
Blue model
Gold model
Green model
Bronze models]
by David Palterer

p. 196
House in Saalgasse,
Goethe's butcher's house

p. 196
House in Saalgasse,
Friederich Overbeck
Italy and Germany

p. 197
House in Saalgasse,
2nd project
(incomplete construction)

Project
Adolfo Natalini;
Collaborating team
Fabrizio Natalini,
Aldo Roda,
PAS Frankfurt am Main.

Photos: Mario Ciampi

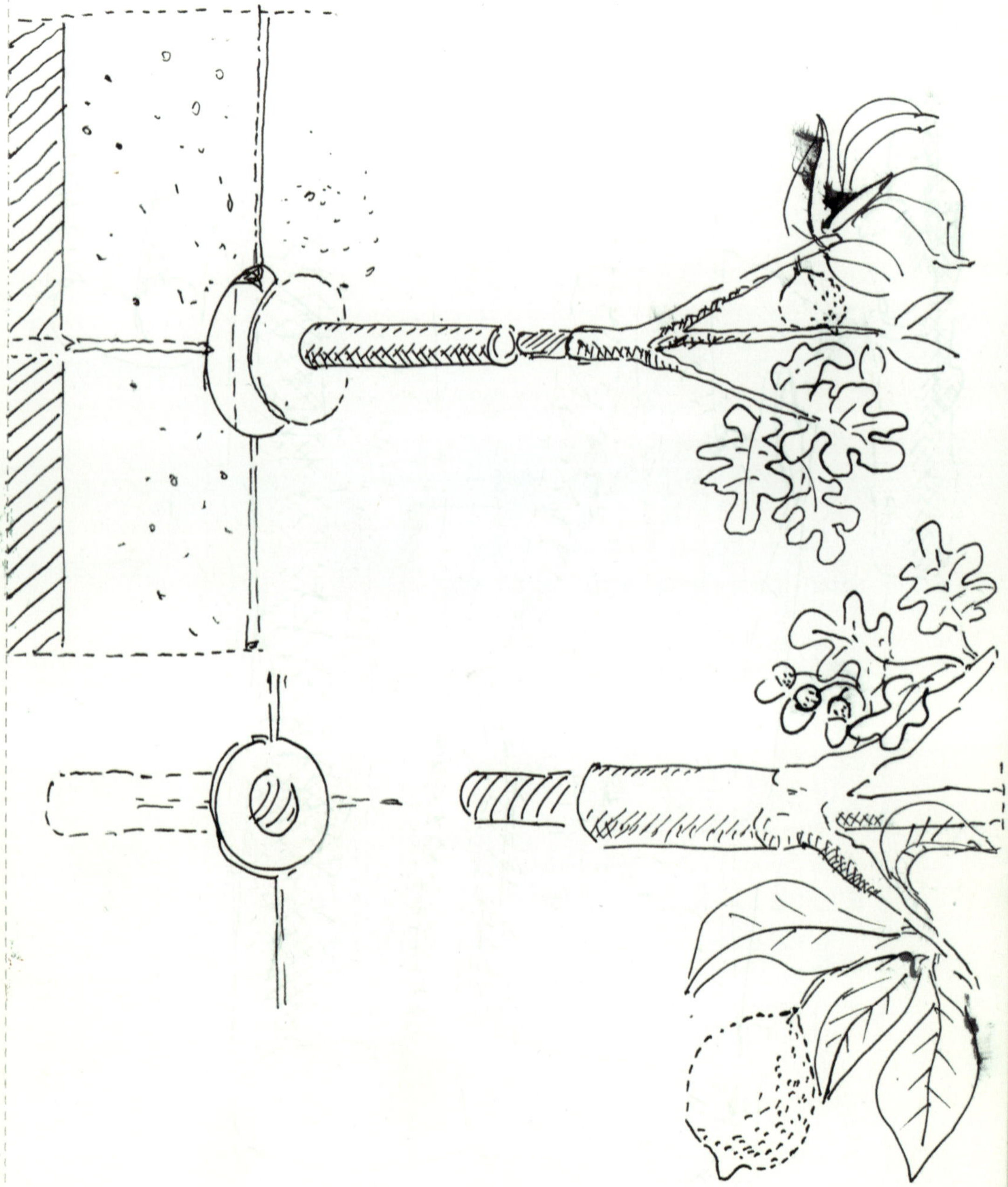

5.1.81

SAALGASSE Nr. 4 "CRESCITA DELL'ALBERO" – 7.2.81

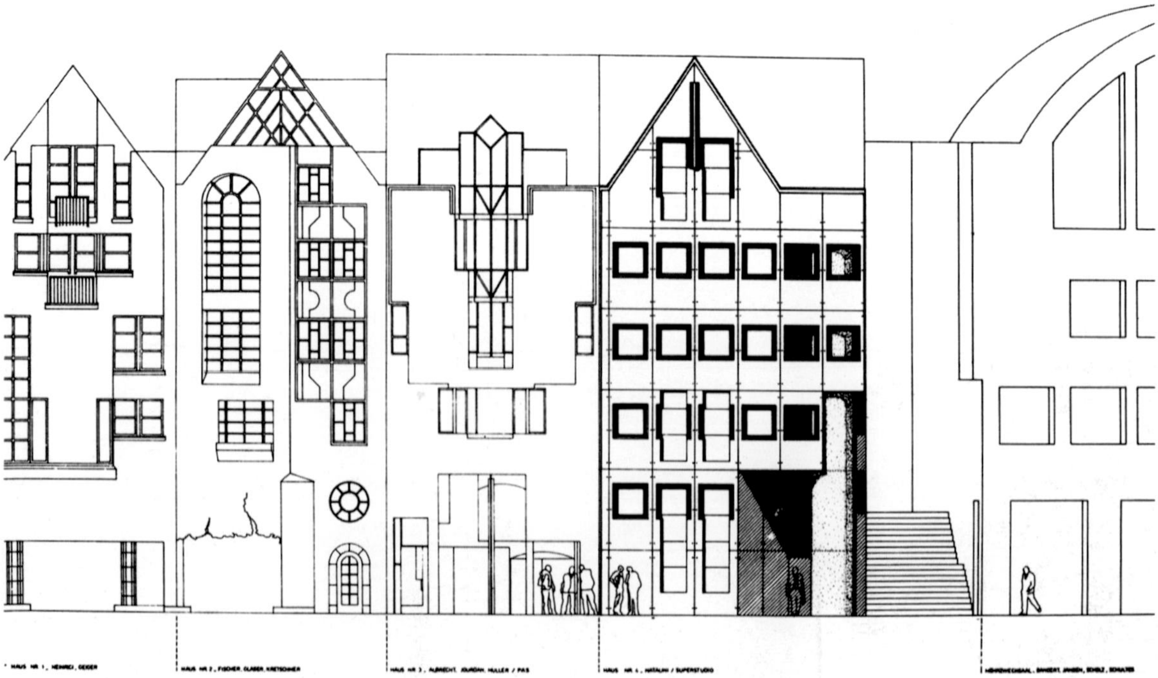
HAUS NR 1, HEINRICI, GEIGER
HAUS NR 2, FISCHER, GLASER, KRETSCHMER
HAUS NR 3, ALBRECHT, JOURDAN, MÜLLER / PAS
HAUS NR 4, NATALINI / SUPERSTUDIO
MEHRZWECKSAAL, BANGERT, JANSEN, SCHOLZ, SCHULTES

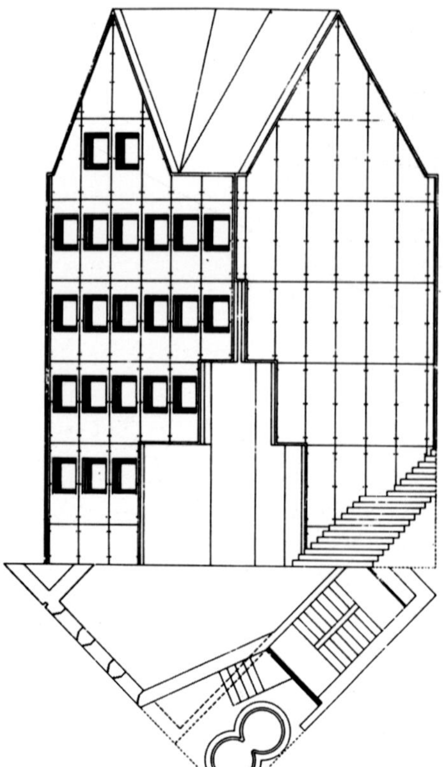

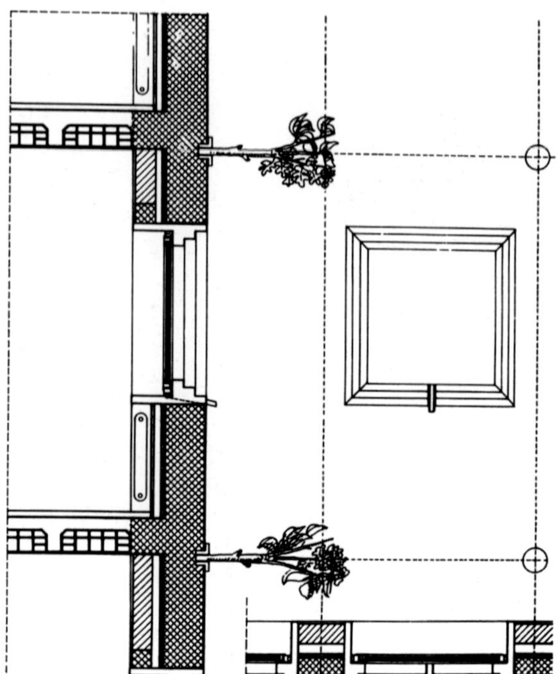

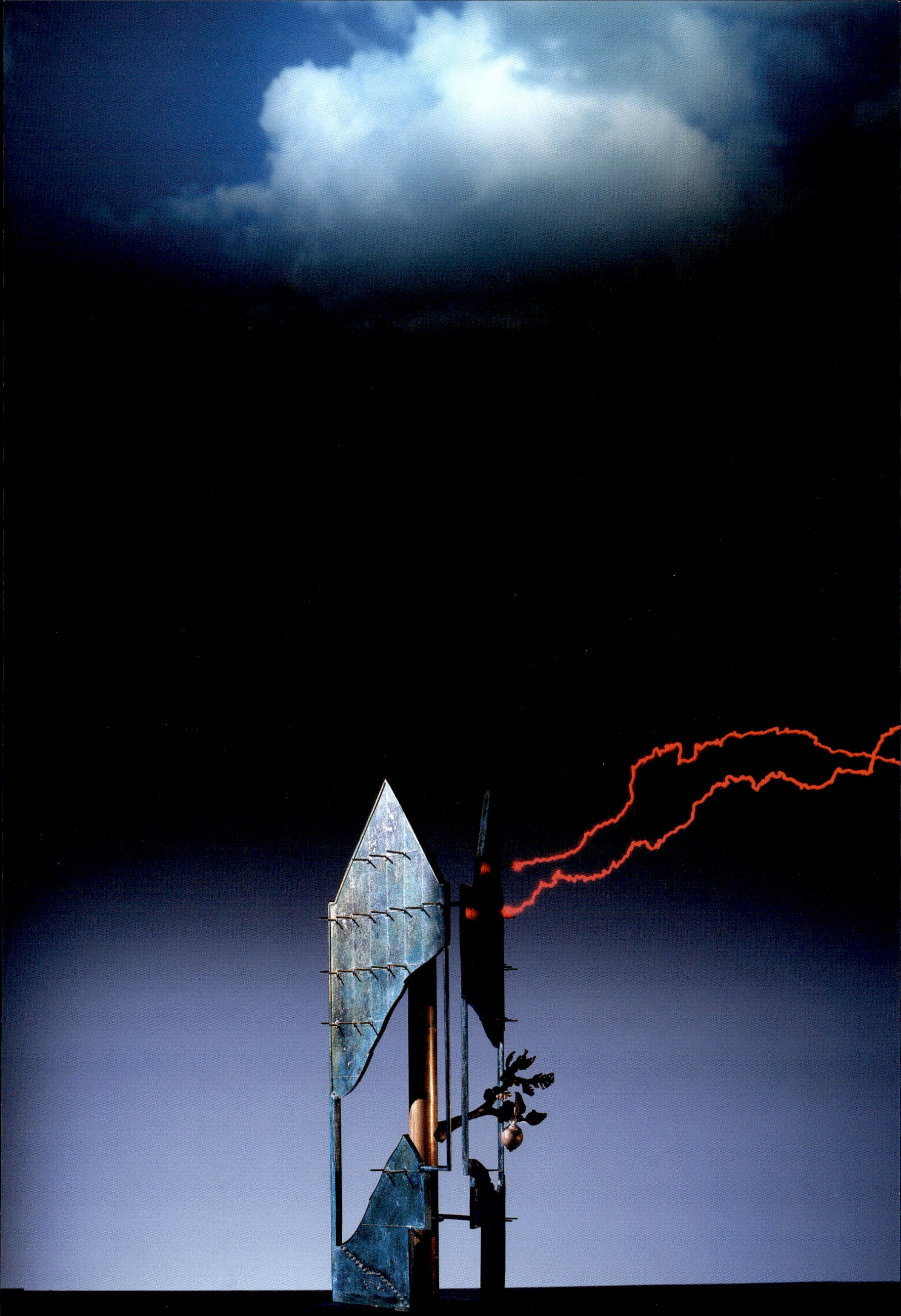

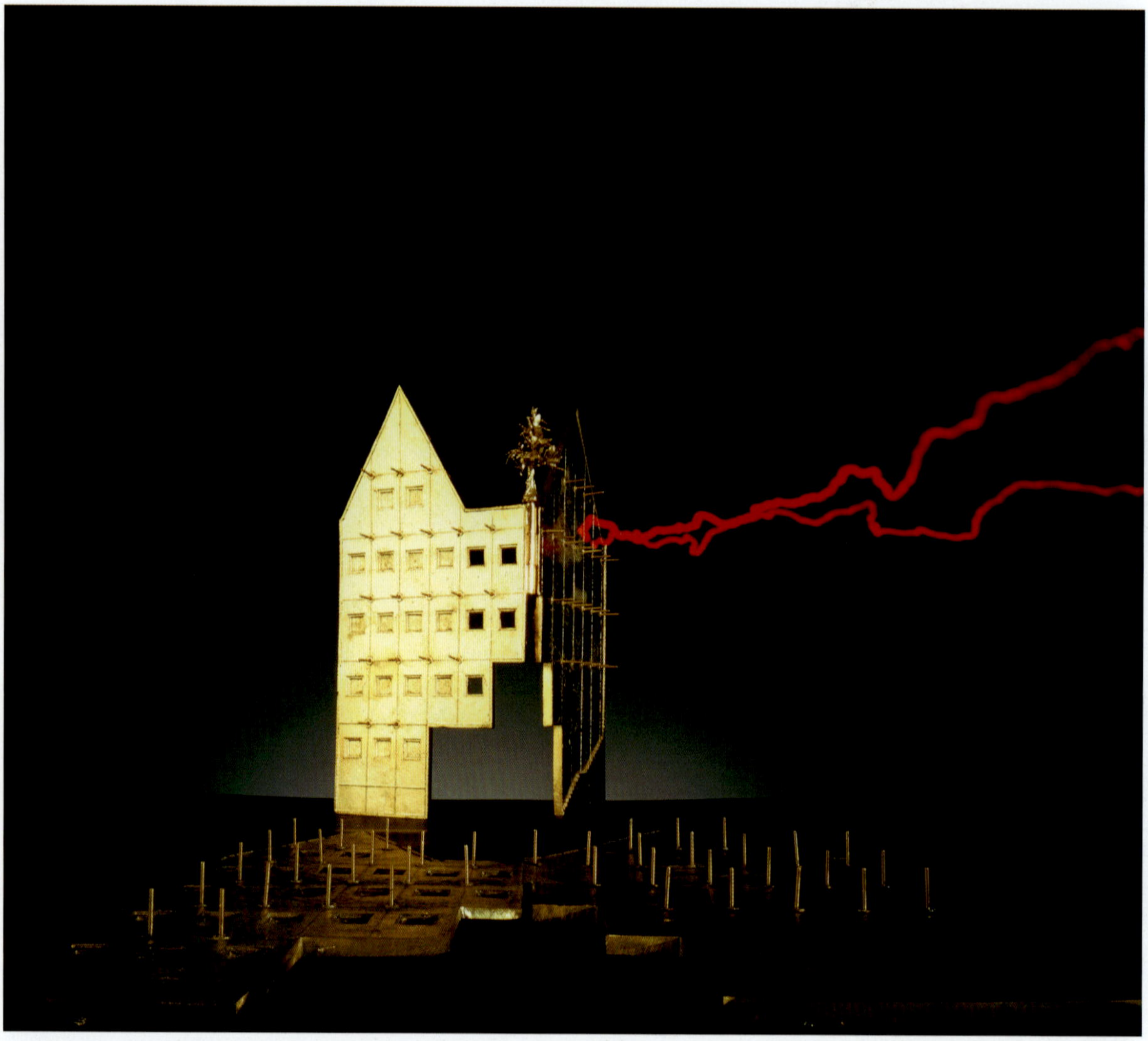

Reconstruction of a city block on the Hofmeisterstrasse in Leipzig

1993-1994

p. 199
Hofmeisterstrasse, view

p. 200
Hofmeisterstrasse, layout

p. 201
Hofmeisterstrasse,
Model by Franco Gizdulich,
photo Mario Ciampi

Project
Adolfo Natalini
with Carla Schorn;
Collaborating team
Marco Magni,
Marco Matteini,
Nazario Scelsi.

Introduction

I have always looked in amazement at a painting by Bernardo Bellotto depicting the ruins of the Kreuzkirche in Dresden. A little man climbs a broken stairway to the top of the tower, which remains standing in the midst of a heap of rubble. It seemed extraordinary to me that the painter who used the *camera obscura* to portray, in all their glory, the cities of Rome, Florence, and Venice, and later Dresden, Vienna and Warsaw, would so carefully make note of ruins and rubble. The painting investigates the city and its architecture, down to every minuscule detail: its bricks and its stones, but also tables in the pile of rubble, placed as they are by the laws of gravity. Meanwhile, the little man climbs the stair, higher and higher, suggesting a resurrection similar to that of the allegorical painting *Inclinata Resurgit*, which depicts Saxony ready to rise again towards the end of the Seven Years War. Later, I saw another painting by Bellotto, *Dresden, the Ruins of the Pirnaische Vorstadt*. Bellotto himself lived in this suburb of Dresden, and his house was also destroyed. A small black figure, seen from behind, similar to the one by Caspar David Friedrich, stands contemplating the ruins: "It seems that men are already accustomed to living with ruins ...".
These paintings came to mind when I was looking at the ruins of the Crystal Palace in Leipzig on a cold sunny day in February. I walked through the centre of the city, where splendid, ancient buildings stood adjacent to gaps left by the ravages of war and to the new buildings, often unsuitable for the context, being built to fill in the gaps. The ruins and the construction projects flanked each other as in a cruel stereoscopic vision. About ten years earlier, I happened to write (regarding the project for the Karmeliterkirche in Frankfurt): "the ruins of the by-now forgotten buildings and projects of paper architecture resemble each other. They are unified in the melancholy of their absence of construction. The dead and the unborn share the same wistful fate of absence. Ivy and brambles, nourished by memory, grow over the ruins. Sometimes large trees put down their roots, and the stones are slowly incorporated into the vegetation. Where there are ruins, memory maintains the presence of the architecture and of the lives that generated it (memory also maintains death and the events of destruction). Projects can have at most the hope of a new life, but they often contain only the memories of other projects, already dead, or of other ruins. In the best cases, projects hold the memories of the vivid presences of other architectures.
Thus ruins and projects are both marked by absence and memory."
This might seem like a nostalgic point of view, and in my country (Italy) nostalgia is always viewed with suspicion. In Germany, a country with a much broader range of sentiments than ours, there are two terms for nostalgia: *Sehnsucht* and *Heimweh*. The first refers to aspiration to something that does not yet exist, while the second refers to a wistful feeling regarding something we would like to return to, for instance our childhood home. Thus nostalgia has this double connotation in the two directions of time: this is how it often feels like I move, like Walter Benjamin's Klee painting, *Angelus Novus*, in which the angel proceeds towards the future while looking back to the past...

The apartment building between Hofmeister and Friedrichstrasse will be preserved. The Hogenforst factory will be eliminated, but the corner building between Liststrasse and Poechestrasse will be maintained and restored to its original appearance. The new buildings will keep the same alignment along the street and the same facade rhythm, and the heights will be in line with the surrounding buildings. From the exterior, the block will appear composed by different buildings, shaped by a single architectural language but with a series of variations. The project provides for four buildings, unified around an elliptical courtyard and by the roof treatment.
One apartment house is situated on Hofmeisterstrass. One of the office buildings is located on Brandenburgerstrasse at the corner of Hans Poeche, and the other, analogous to the first, is situated on Hans Poeche at the corner of Friedrich Liststrasse. There is a second apartment house on Friedrich Liststrasse. The ground floor of all of the buildings will be used for shops or other commercial activities, as well as for accessing the courtyard, which in turn provides access to the various volumes above, consisting of three upper floors and two mansard-level floors.
There is also an underground parking level, with access from Hofmeisterstrasse. If necessary, an additional underground level can be added. The complex features stone cladding in regular courses, with deep joints creating the appearance of large wedge-shaped ashlars above each of the windows. The plaster wall finishes of the apartment houses and the brick cladding of the office buildings terminate with a copper cornice. Further above, the sloped roof of the mansard levels creates a fantastic crenelation effect. Thus the building is clearly divided into three bands: the stone base (at the ground floor), the "piano nobile" in brick and plaster (consisting of three equal floors), and a metallic attic level (two floors within the mansard roofs). While the stone base is the same around the entire block, the upper portions feature a series of variations: towards the corner on Brandenburgerstrasse, the windows yield to a series of glazed metal *Erker*, as if the corner facing the main street became more plastic and extroverted. The words "Hofmeister-Hof erbaut 1996" (a tribute to the location and a reasonable hope) are carved into the upper stones of the largest arched passageway located in the middle of the facade along the street.

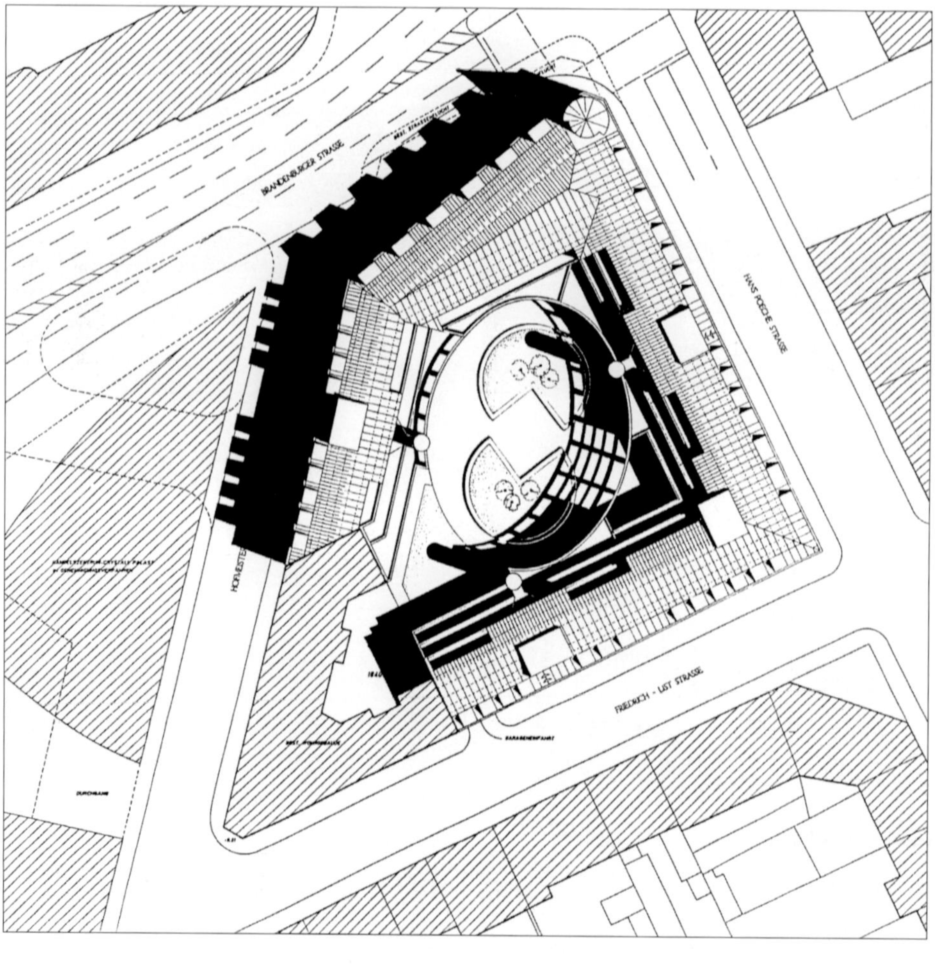
BRANDENBURGER STRASSE
HANS POECHE STRASSE
FRIEDRICH - LIST STRASSE

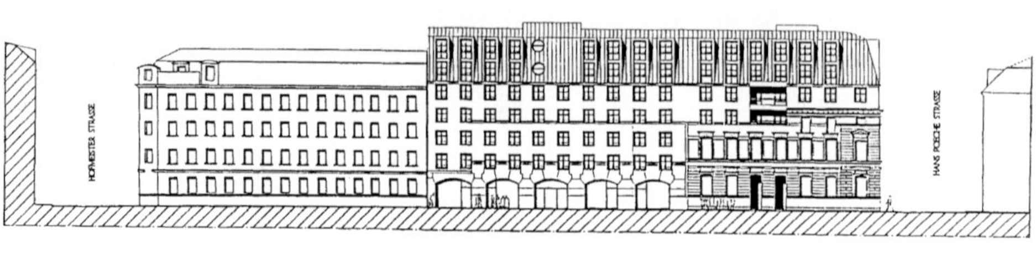
HOFMEISTER STRASSE
HANS POECHE STRASSE

Reconstruction of a city block on Manetstrasse in Leipzig

1993-1994

Site visit: notes from a sketchbook
On a rainy day that made Leipzig's stones darker than ever and its trees and grass even more green... It was not easy to enter the old Dratchemie factory, abandoned as if its occupants had disappeared due to some sinister curse. Inside, a hole in the floor revealed the bowels of the building, the ruins of the foundation, pipes, rubble, like a bomb crater, full of water, and with more water dripping from above. The noise of the dripping... light from above through an old skylight, a metal chair with its legs in the water, as if for a meeting that would never take place.

The old Drachtemie factory is located on the edge of the historic city centre, not far from the town hall. One corner looks onto Dorotheenplatz, a historic square that has been rebuilt with respectable prefabricated buildings.
The project involves a building with a courtyard that opens onto a green landscape facing the kindergarten. The three building volumes are arranged on three sides along the new street alignments proposed by the city administration. The fourth facade follows a curve to enhance visibility towards the interior. This curved facade is interrupted at the centre, where new trees have been added to the existing trees along the green passageway. The interior courtyard has an elongated lenticular form, with two symmetrical openings towards Manetstrasse and Reichelstrasse, in addition to the green passage already mentioned. The buildings looking onto the courtyard are characterised by differing heights and uses.
The volume along Manetstrasse consists of a ground floor for shops and public establishments, and three upper floors, as well as two mansard-level floors, devoted to offices. The two buildings facing the green passageway contain apartments. Each is arranged with four linear units on the three floors, some of which crowned by a mansard roof level. Thus the integration between offices, homes and shops is similar to the integration between public and private spaces, created by means of various passageways. The sequence of street-passageway-courtyard-green passageway goes beyond the division by areas, thereby creating a level of integration that should render the block more interesting and make the entire area more visible. The project proposes to contribute to the configuration of Dorotheenplatz with a cylindrical corner element, a sort of tower, one floor higher with respect to the buildings, which terminates at the top with radial mansard roofing. This element juts slightly forward with respect to the other volumes, in response to the geometry of the square and to establish a distinctive "signal" at the front end of the city block. In particular, the tower presents itself in analogy with the treatment of the (projecting) corners of the other buildings overlooking the square, and also makes reference to the old tower of Pleissenburg. The building is slightly curved along Manetstrasse. The corner on Zimmerstrasse recalls the old industrial building with its regularly spaced windows. Along Zimmerstrasse, however, the facade is more open, with a grid consisting of beams and uprights that continues into the cylindrical element at the corner with Reichelstrasse. On Reichelstrasse the complex is treated in a manner similar to the portion on Manetstrasse. The apartments that curve towards the green passageway are arranged like terraced houses, but with a more domestic treatment, with some of them featuring gabled roofs. Inside the courtyard, the treatment of the facades is made uniform by a regular grid (which almost recalls an industrial building), in contrast to the "domestic" facades of the apartments. The courtyard and the passages are paved in terracotta and stone, with vast green areas bordered by low stone walls with seating. All of the facades are in facebrick, while the base is clad in stone, and the roofs and mansards are in pre-oxidised copper with a blue-green patina.

In a city devastated by war and the brutality of bombs, the aim of the project is to provide a "suitable replacement" that respects the surrounding context. (In short, the architect presented the city block as a work of urban architecture, with a dignified exterior and a pleasant interior, open to the passage of the inhabitants. He listened to the city, trying to learn its language, while at the same time bringing additional vocabulary from other historic European cities: and now he waits for the dialogue to begin...).

p. 203
Reconstruction of a city block on Manetstrasse in Leipzig, courtyard

pp. 204-205
on Dorotheen Platz

p. 206
Layout

p. 207
On Manetstrasse

pp. 208-209
Courtyard seen from green passageway

Project
Adolfo Natalini
with Carla Schorn;
Collaborating team
Adrian Blanchard,
Marco Magni,
Marco Matteini,
Nazario Scelsi;
Client
Seeste Bau GMBH (Leipzig).

Photos: Burg / Schuh

Nr.1

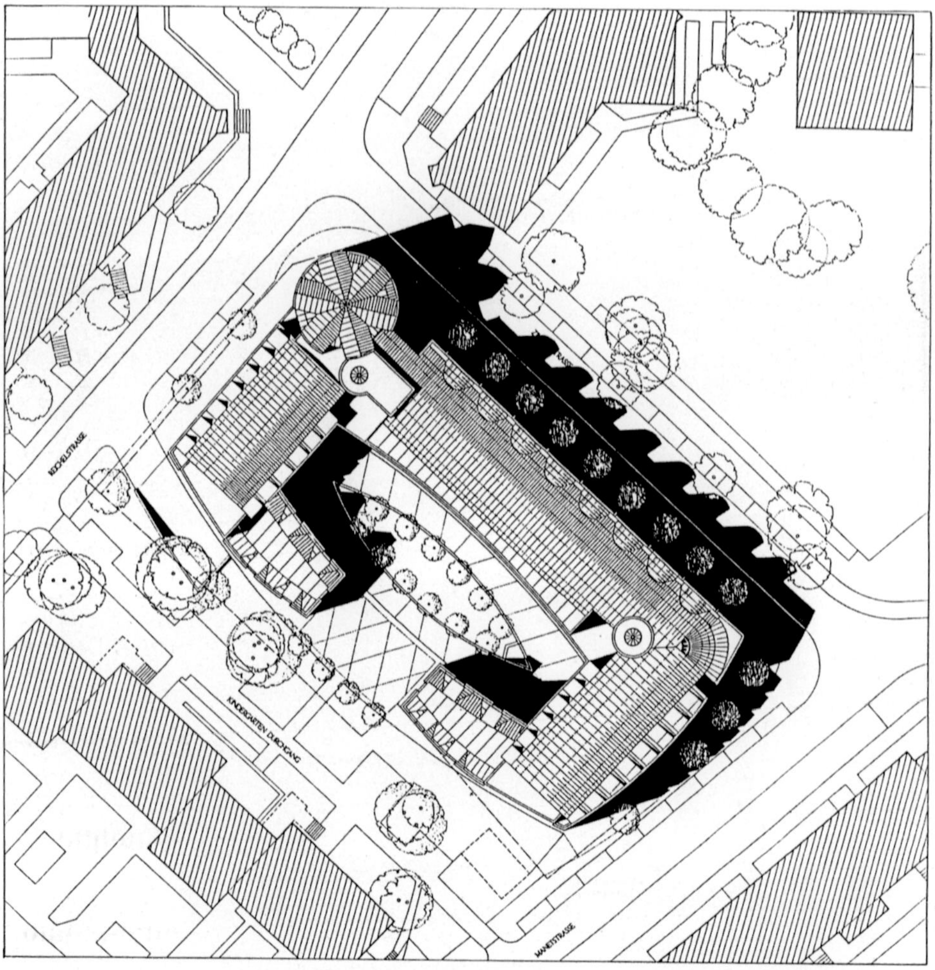

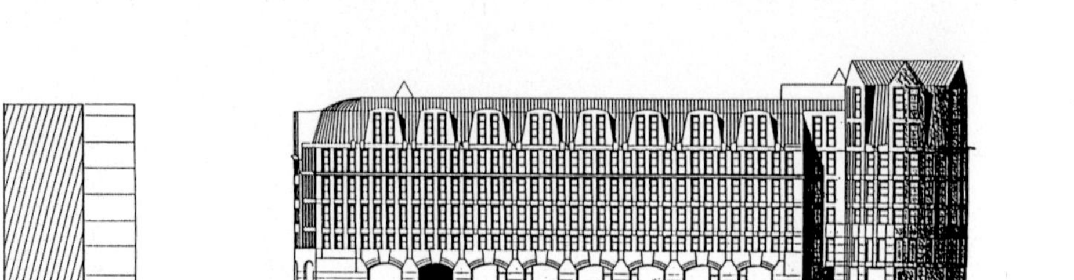

SEESTE
BAU
VERMIETUNG UND VERKAUF
IMMOCONSULT GmbH
Tel.: 0341 /6 96 57 19 - 23
FFB-MD 319

Invitational competition for the Breitestrasse, Berlin

1993

The project tries to satisfy three different requirements: complete the city block between Breitestrasse and the Spree, with special attention to the portion facing Muhlendamm; provide different connotations to the side overlooking the Breitestrasse and the side overlooking the river and the bridge; and finally, create three different buildings: one that is more monumental in character, for the headquarters of the Ministry of Industry, one for commercial and office spaces, and one for housing.

The completion of the city block is achieved by filling in the gaps along its boundaries. The facade on Breitestrasse is tied to the regional and national archives building, echoing its slightly diagonal layout and realigning itself along the street line. The facade along the Spree, on the other hand, resumes the slight diagonal of the pre-existing building and then curves as if pushed back by the water, resulting in a more interesting facade along the river and permitting a view further on, towards the Berliner Dom.
Finally, the block seems to diminish in width towards Muhlendamm, to the point that a portion detaches from itself, taking on a closed regular form: an ellipse whose main axis is parallel to Muhlendamm Brucke. In this way, the volume of the block is interrupted before the bridge, creating an invitation for pedestrians to walk down to the river.
The arched facade overlooking the Spree creates a panoramic terrace, which during warm weather can host the tables of a café-restaurant. The terrace is also accessible by a route through the block from another direction, near where it adjoins to the existing buildings. This creates a network of public passageways which, in addition to providing access to the various parts of the complex, offer views of the river and of the large inner courtyard.
The project consists of three buildings: an L-shaped building for the offices, with the long side along the Breitestrasse, a curved apartment house overlooking the Spree, and a building with an elliptical plan for the Ministry of Industry and Commerce (DIHT), located on the corner between Breitestrasse and Muhlendamm. All of the buildings are seven floors in height. The office building is 18 metres deep, on average, with five-metre deep spaces on each side and a central area occupied by stairs, lifts, services, archives and meeting rooms. The apartment house overlooking the Spree is divided in two, with the smaller volume adjoining the existing building and connected to the larger volume towards the top, by means of a series of loggias. A café and restaurant is located at the ground floor. The upper floors contain apartments in various sizes. The Ministry building is elliptical in plan and contains a central atrium that provides access to the vertical circulation, various passageways, and some meeting rooms.

There is an underground parking garage on two levels, while the land overlooking the Spree is free of structures and will be planted with trees. The interior courtyard will have plants in large containers. All of the buildings are clad with stone in two different shades: darker for the first three floors and lighter for the floors above. The facades of the apartment building and the office building are pierced by windows. The DIHT (Ministry) headquarters presents a composition of very slender vertical and horizontal elements and ample openings. The sixth floor of both the office and apartment buildings is located within the mansard roof, and features large glazed expanses alternated by roofing in blue-green pre-oxidized copper. The same level in the DIHT building is stepped back, with a terrace screened by structures similar to those of the facade. All of the passageways, the courtyard, and the terrace overlooking the Spree are paved in stone in various patterns. There will be a colonnade along the Spree, with a continuous entablature: a sort of screen facing the water, memory of other, nobler, columns situated on the opposite bank of the Spreeinsel.

p. 210
Invitational competition for the Breitestrasse, Berlin, street view

p. 211
Layout

pp. 212-213
View of the Spree

pp. 214-215
View of the Spree, sketch

p. 216
View of the Spree and street, sketch on napkin

Project
Adolfo Natalini;
Collaborating team
Marco Magni,
Marco Matteini,
Nazario Scelsi,
Carla Schorn.

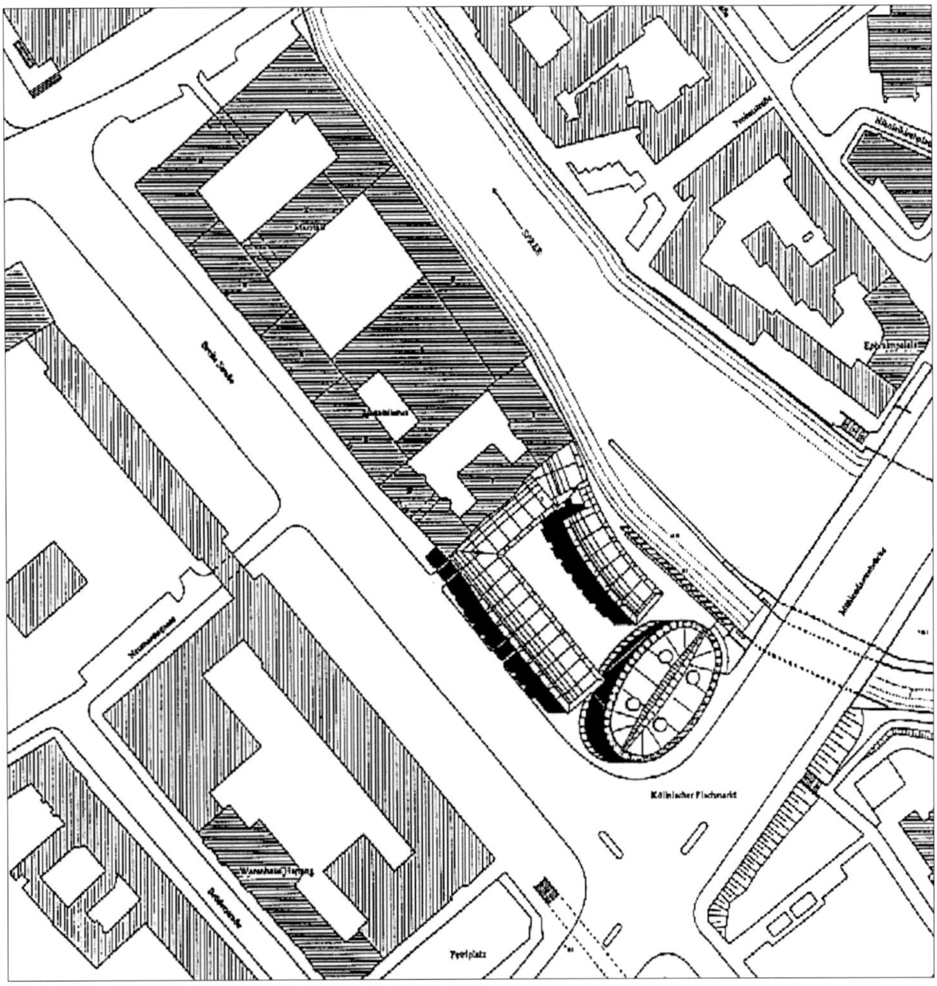
Kölnischer Fischmarkt

Lemmario 4

[Lexicon 4]

—

On previous page:
M. Lodovico Guicciardini, *The Description of the Low Countreys*, Antwerp, 1581

Reconstruction of Waagstraat in Groningen, the Netherlands, historical map

Reconstruction of Waagstraat in Groningen, the Netherlands, sketch, from *Quaderni Cinesi* 1992

Memoria
[Memory]

01. From Zeus's union with Mnemosyne, the nine Muses were born (at least according to Hesiod's *Theogony*), thus all the arts were born from this goddess of Memory, an obscure goddess who has been forgotten.
Oftentimes, remembering is unbearable and history too heavy a burden. In an extraordinary drawing, Füssli depicts *L'artista disperato di fronte alla grandezza delle rovine antiche* [The artist in despair before the greatness of ancient ruins] (a small figure covers his face with his hand before the foot and hand of the colossal statue of Constantine in Campidoglio).
I am obsessed by time and memory and by the traces they leave behind; I would like to be a diviner and practice an architecture of discovering.
If I think of the places I've lived, I see them crowded with things. A reluctant traveler, I found myself in several different places, which were strange at first sight but then became inhabited by the reassuring presence of furniture and objects.
I did not have the good fortune be surrounded by particularly beautiful furniture or objects (nor antiques or well-designed pieces), nor did I live in houses with cellars and attics filled with expensive things in bad taste. Normal homes and normal things surrounded me, and I have banal memories of these, connected to the roundness of a corner, patches of plaster, the roughness of a fabric. Perhaps it if for this reason, in search of a past that I did not have, that I look affectionately upon all creations that are intentionally filled with memory; or perhaps it is only because, unlike Füssli's artist, I look with dismay at the smallness of the present and the uncertainty of the future.
["Alcune note su mobili, oggetti...", 1985]

02. *Memory and Hope*
Each project swings between memory and hope. There is no city that is entirely ancient and no city that is entirely new; the historical city is an extraordinary time machine through which we can travel in both directions.
Designing in these places, where the ancient *cardo maximus* intersects the river, looking sidelong at photos of the ruins of war with medieval towers rising up out of them, can provoke two different reactions in a student. The first is a violent rejection of the historical accumulation, a kind of claustrophobia caused by the city, completely (and repeatedly) built, a desperate desire to leave it (the history and the city) in order to enter the thrilling (and risky) streets of the plan for contrast. The second is an attack of nostalgia for what has been, a type of sentimental attachment to places that lead to a contextual plan with all the risks of mimicry and replication. After all, even Berenson and his people wished for a reconstruction as it was and where it was.
Nostalgia in Italy is always looked upon with suspicion. In Germany, a country far richer in sentimental feelings than ours, there are two words for nostalgia: *Sehnsucht* and *Heimweh*. The first is the hope for something that doesn't yet exist; the other is nostalgia for something to go back to, like one's native home. Thus nostalgia has this double meaning in two directions of time. This is how I often seem to move, like Benjamin's *Angelus Novus*, which moves towards the future with his face turned to the past.
[10.03.96]

Moderno
[Modern]

01. I cannot call myself modern. I cannot call myself modern because modern architecture is an oxymoron, or rather a contradiction in terms since architecture refers to long periods of time (architecture lasts a long time, longer than man's lifespan); modern, instead, deals with short periods of time. The word "modern" derives from the Late Latin *modernus*, arising in the 5th century A.D. from the adverb *modo* which means "just now". Therefore architecture cannot be something "daily fresh" that expires tomorrow like milk and, for this reason, modern architecture does not exist. Architecture exists; something which is created at a certain time but not only for that time. Moreover, every work of architecture, in order to have the possibility of surviving, must have very deep roots. To travel into the future, it must be strongly rooted in the past. Botanists teach that in a tree the foliage section corresponds to the root section; that is, the part below ground is the same as the part above. Similarly for architecture, we need to sink the roots very far into the past in order to hope to extend the branches and leaves equally far into the future.
All avant-garde has had a destructive historical role; the avant-garde serves to destruct a firmly established situation by opening the field to something new that is not necessarily brought to its conclusion by the avant-garde, which usually dies in this suicide attempt, because its destructive work, in the end, also leads to self-destruction. At a certain point, I thought that the time for this kind of cultural guerrilla warfare was over and that a different kind of work was needed, one that is more commonplace and humble: a work that involves building. On the other hand, there is a time to destroy and time to build, as it says in *Ecclesiaste*. There is no doubt that the work of building is far less striking and fascinating than that of destruction.
Have you ever seen something positive on television about building, or in the newspaper, where architecture exists only as a criminal element, as over-construction, destruction of the landscape, an ecomonster? Clearly destruction has a far greater appeal than construction, but this does not mean it has a greater value. If we look at media results, something monstrous will stand out in a way that something normal never will. Everything that is published in current magazines is criminal. It is stuff that has nothing to do with the real world. It is an image of drugged fantasy that has nothing to do with the place, the people, their desires, their hopes. They are things based on an attempt to be different, and it is hard to understand why there is a need to be different, to be modern. A horse, a woman, a tree – are these modern? No, they exist and that's all. There is no need to increase the number of legs on a horse or a woman. They are fine as they are. Architecture is like a bicycle; there is very little to invent. In the last century, only two useful things have been invented in architecture: the elevator and the lavatory. Of the two, the lavatory is more useful, the elevator less so, because it has allowed many people to foolishly create skyscrapers. It's hard to understand why something should stand straight up if it can lie across more comfortably.
["Narrate, uomini, la vostra storia", 2006]

02. *Nuove città e antichi segni* [New Cities and Ancient Signs] wants to reaffirm the need to shape the contemporary city with historical marks. In other words, to draft new stories with ancient words (after all, this is what poets do when they find new uses and

new associations for words that everyone uses).
The two adjectives "new" and "ancient" in the title reopen the age-old debate between ancient and modern, "una coppia occidentale e ambigua" [a western and ambiguous pair], according to Jacques Le Goff's definition in his entry for the *Enciclopedia* Einaudi, 1977.

["Note in margine", in G. Cavallina, *Nuove Città e antichi segni*, Fup, Florence 2006]

03. Etymologically speaking, modern refers only to something that is happening now, at this moment, and modern architecture is the architecture of the present, in a world where change is increasingly rapid (and desired!), therefore an architecture of the fleeting moment... very different from what I think architecture is: an art of time and memory, an art of long periods of time.
Modern architecture aspires to be instant architecture (like instant coffee) but, without going as far as Neapolitan coffee (including the "cuppitiello" [paper cone on the spout] described by Eduardo De Filippo), I prefer coffee brewed in a moka pot).
"Modern architecture" is an oxymoron.
"To every age its art. To every art its freedom" was written in gold letters on the entrance to the pavilion of the Vienna Secession. The age of architecture is a long age where yesterday, today and tomorrow overlap like stones following the laws of gravity.
I seem to be reciting self-evident truths and commonplaces, but I'm not ashamed, since even Cicero in *De oratore* maintained that many truths are contained in "commonplaces" that we use in speeches.
I hope that architecture rediscovers its awareness of long time spans and of need and that it continues to be "local", leaving globalization to goods and men (who are increasingly unhappy).

[26.09.03, from C. Donati's interview, in *Costruire in Laterizio*]

Muzenplein

01. In 1993 I was invited to design the central zone of the De Resident neighborhood planned by Rob Krier in The Hague, 150 meters from the Royal Palace, a dense neighborhood where a group of Dutch and foreign architects had to plan houses towards the center of the city and towers towards the outskirts.
I built two squares, the Muzenplein and the Clioplein (the neighborhood was dedicated to the Muses, the daughters of Mnemosyne, the goddess of memory), the first was a horseshoe and the second was circular, surrounded by buildings. I went to see them one sunny morning in early October. The shadows were still long and they cut the horseshoe like a sundial along the intersecting diagonals of the ground made of slender, different colored bricks. The dark stone lines were a bit sunken; they must become shiny and "fluid" under the rain. The trees were still small, but positioned in the right place, as were the lampposts and benches.
The portico pillars, tapered at the base like the ones in Groningen, seemed whiter than in the designs, but the bricks are much more beautiful and it all works.
The circular square (with a tree in the middle) is modest and secluded. I would have liked to call it my "red O" paraphrasing Shakespeare's "wooden O" referring to the Globe Theatre...

The Muzenplein and Clioplein squares in The Hague, the Netherlands preliminary sketches, 1993

It seems to be faithful to Rob Krier's intentions and to my plans. By now I know how to design houses and courtyards; for town squares I still need some time, but the next one will be even more beautiful, but perhaps it will not have this October morning light or the melancholy suspended between possible happiness and certain fragility (the world is terrorized by a nameless war and I am coming out of a hospital).

[28.10.01, from M. Pisani's interview, in *L'industria delle costruzioni*]

Narrazione/Figurazione
[Narration/Figurative Representation]

01. Many Vitruvian precepts have also been dismissed, such as the need for a triad of "strength, utility, beauty"...
Every project stems from a place (and in turn is able to generate more places).
It is inherently composed of a large quantity of elements and it is up to us from time to time to choose its generating elements.
And it speaks to us through figures, using techniques of effective communication, namely rhetoric.
Many times the Vitruvian triad of *firmitas, utilitas, venustas* was dismantled. In place of architecture, therefore, we have had built objects that, from time to time, were produced by the sole element of *firmitas* or by *utilitas* or *venustas*.
Inert deposits of materials, beings that are incompletely formed or, worse still, blocked in their metamorphoses to become architecture...
Other times, however, in architectural works guaranteed by the effective presence of the triad, if we look closely we can distinguish the presence of a singular element: the narrative one.
Narrative architecture tells its own story in its making. It tells us about those that created it and it tells us about the world that they belong to and that they are expressing.
Today the great narrative architectural works of the past are hard to read as we have lost the key to deciphering them. The complex network of metaphors and allegories through which they spoke to us has become unraveled and broken.
And yet, these continue to speak to us through the motions of wonder (the Pyramids, Bomarzo, Casa dello Zuccari). The façade of Casa dello Zuccari goes beyond expressing the virtues of its creator as a painter, sculptor and architect; the stones, the figurative representations and the symbols weave another, more subtle, story (a tale that is certainly not anomalous compared to a lot of the contemporary production of Mannerism).
The history of narrative architecture unwinds along the so-called architectural works of wonder, fantastic architecture, from Buontalenti to Ammannati, from Gaudí to the expressionists, but also through architects less inclined towards effects and gestures.
Architecture is a language that can communicate according to the rules of excellent communication, namely rhetoric. Architecture tells a story...
but about what?
Certainly not only about its plan (that is, the collection of requests from the commissioning client, a necessary

subject but not enough for architecture's story).
The theme of the architectural work is always the representation of the world and the relationships that connect one to the other.
This attempt at narration is borne out of a desire for figurative representation throughout the design. It stems from architecture's desire to abandon its undeserved statute of scientific discipline, to abandon abstraction in order to re-immerse itself in the world and in things.
For too long, architecture has been seen as a service discipline, as an efficiency-minded response to a series of needs. Architecture does indeed respond to a system of needs but also to a system of desires; it responds to necessity, but also to dreams and aspirations. Architecture responds to need, but it also anticipates it. It responds to primary needs (shelter, protection) but also to more subtle needs that find their expression through it.
In this way it abandons the guaranteed world of scientism and technicism, in which it seems that the problems are properly posed and that their solution is reserved for architecture through the proper application of a system of laws and rules, in order to face a more complex and real world in which it is up to architecture to redefine and reformulate the problems.
The need to figuratively represent architecture leads to walking a difficult road where different elements merge and mingle through the difficult road of metamorphosis.
It is the road of poets where things express more than just what they are; they join together to create other things through an attempt to stage the ever-changing comedy or tragedy of existence.
In the architecture of the past, figurativeness was expressed through the correspondence to canons and systems. The architectural machine was brought back to a collection of rules and fantastical exceptions. Figurativeness was also entrusted to sculptural and pictorial elements and to elements which we incorrectly call decorations. Sculptures and paintings were not superimposed on architecture, but were an integral part of its narrative plan.
This figurativeness was removed from this century's architecture, which attempted a purist path, a path of abstraction similar to other arts; architecture was reduced to a bundle of nerves and bones, fascinating perhaps, but in that same morbid fascination for an anatomical discovery or Zumbo's wax sculptures.

[From a report at the conference *Virtuosi Decori*, Verona, 8 May 1987]

02. The messages from an architecture that speaks will be the story of those relationships that connect the designer to the world around him, the story of the lives that created the work and something from those lives that will continue to make it live. They will be stories of daily acts of heroism, of small conquests, of fears and hopes. They will be small promises for eternity, or at least for survival. Allegory and metaphor are just a few of the rhetorical mechanisms that make the story more effective.
On the other hand, "In principio erat verbum"...

[08.92, from an interview by di P. Morgera, "20 domande... a Adolfo Natalini", in *Archi & Colonne*]

Het Eiland in Zwolle, the Netherlands, 1996-2001, Ground and first floor layouts

Normale
[Normal]

01. "Normal: conforming to the customary and to generality, regular, usual, common... from Latin *normalis*, perpendicular, derived from *norma, rule, square*."

[Translator's translation - G. Devoto - G.C. Oli, *Nuovo vocabolario illustrato della lingua italiana*, Milan 1992]

-

"Normal: adj. Conforming to the rule, the norm, the law, the custom, regular, ordinary, usual, solid. Synonyms: common, natural."

[Translator's translation - A. Gabrielli, *Dizionario dei sinonimi*, Mondadori, Milan 1971]

-

"The line between psychic normality and abnormality cannot be defined scientifically... it has only a conventional value."

[Translator's translation. Source not found - S. Freud, *Breve compendio di psicanalisi*, Boringhieri, Turin 1977]

02. *Normal Architecture*
The title of this lesson could have been more inviting (interesting, scintillating), such as *Towards a Normal Architecture* or *In Search of Normality* or *I Would Like a Normal Architecture*. Or even *Normal and Abnormal*, with a pair of opposing terms, but I do not wish to talk about what is abnormal and I would like to focus on the need and value of normality in architecture.

-

Normal signifies something positioned correctly, in the proper way, at right angles with something else. Something that is normal is in the right place in the world. If being on the straight path means walking the right way, being normal means being in the right position. For inhabitants of the old city, the daily experience of the home, the road and the town square is normal, reassuring, with no surprises or shocks. We pass through here without our attention being aroused. It's a world we are used to, a world we love without realizing it. In a certain sense we have been shaped by this world without having built it ourselves. The structures of the homes and the city have shaped our cognitive structures, the mental maps which allows us to find our direction in the world.
Every day we move about through the same things. We have made these things that surround us habitual; we almost don't see them anymore. We know this is how they are and that's enough for us. Their permanence and the habit that is created in us make us suspect the presence of a norm, a rule. If this is how things are and if they stay this way, there must be a law, a necessity.

-

"Etymologically, the Latin norm is a square: something that doesn't lean to the right or the left. But this meaning was soon replaced by what it should be. In the classic sense, the normal state will indicate the usual state and at the same time the ideal state." [Translator's translation]

[C. Descamps in the entry "normale/anormale", in *Enciclopedia*, Vol.9, Einaudi, Turin 1980]

-

"Utopia is a logic, a closed system: Plato, Campanella, More or Cabet hate time, innovation, abnormality." (id.) [Translator's translation]

-

"For Nietzsche history is divided in two: on one side, the multitude of those who repeat the normalized models;

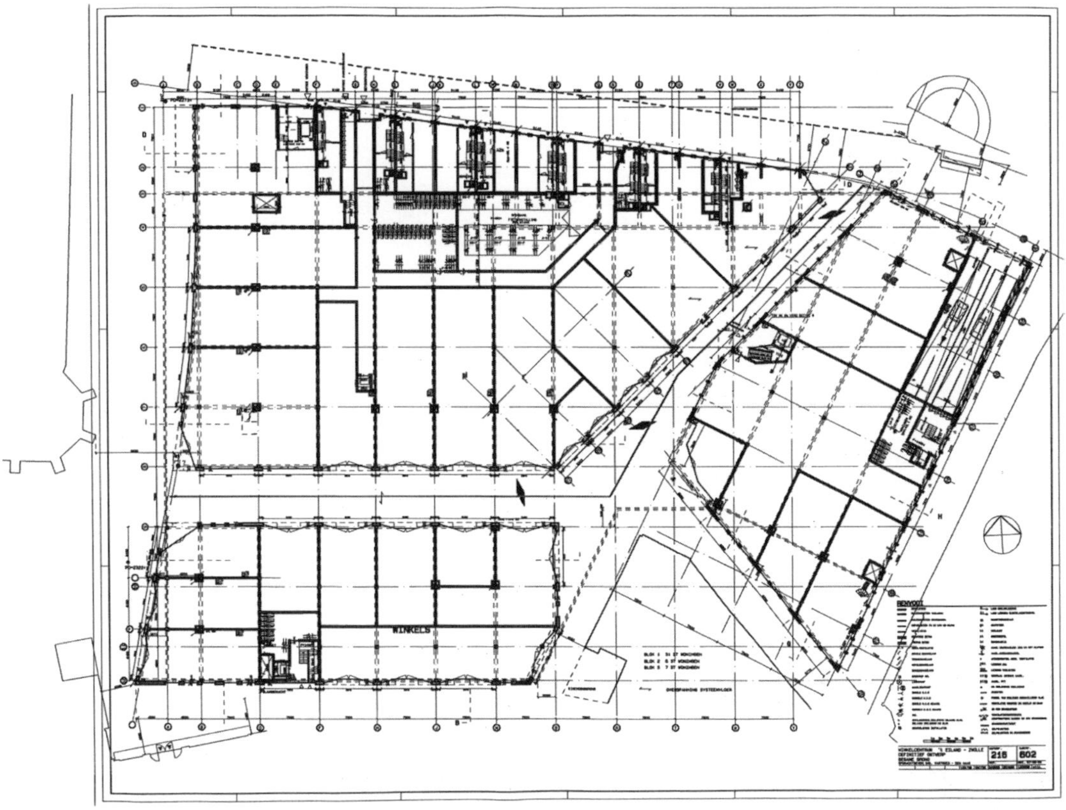
WINKELS
216
602

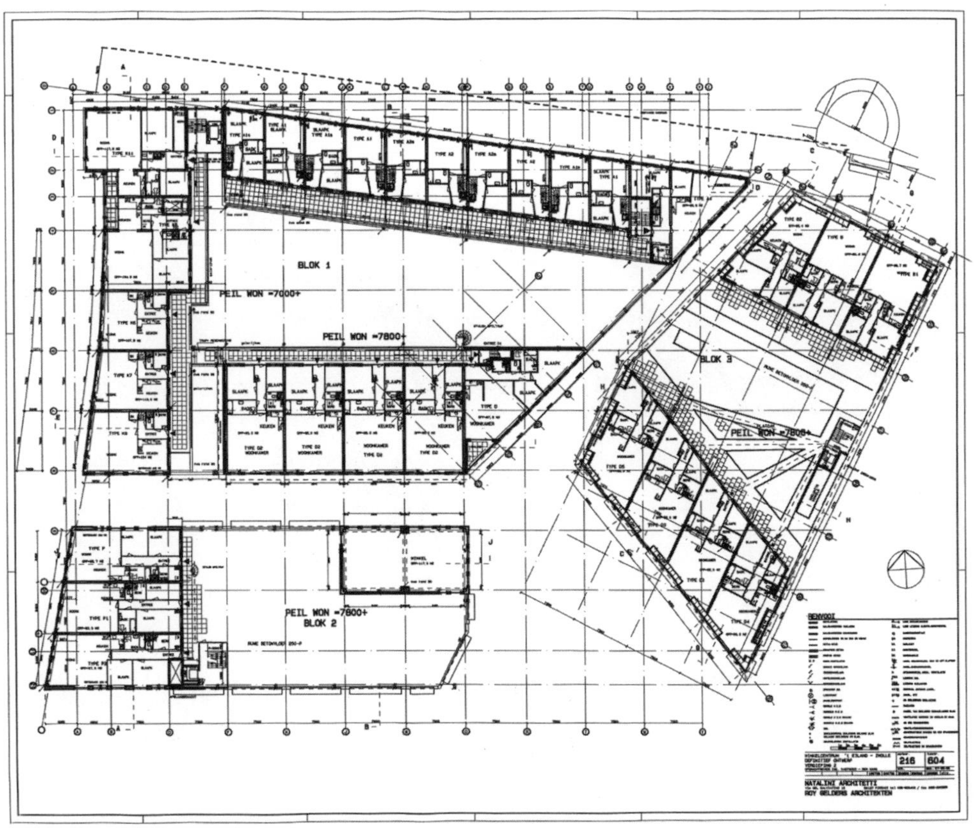
BLOK 1
PEIL WON =7000+
PEIL WON =7800+
BLOK 3
PEIL WON =7800+
BLOK 2
216
604
NATALINI ARCHITETTI

11.11.96

on the other, the individuals, the inventors, those who provide norms. Here morality, religion; there art." (id.) [Translator's translation]

-

That which exists, that which lasts over time, affirms with its immutable presence a need, a norm. It refers to a law, a custom. It speaks of the many (present or past) who conceived it, built it, lived it, loved it.
By existing, it justifies itself; it authorizes itself to exist. Its endurance over time, having survived changes, attests to its necessity, its suitability to places, people and history.
I strive to define a normality in architecture and the city.
I search all over for a landscape to describe.
And it is this sought-after normality that makes it elusive. Having nothing unique, it doesn't require or aid the description. Not standing out from the rest, it remains in the background, silent. Therefore I will describe the impossibility of a description and look hard for adjectives for it: regular, uniform, customary, similar to others, usual, immobile over time, devoid of violent changes.
I try to look, in an old photo (postcard) for instance, at an almost straight road, with houses on either side. The houses respect the road's alignment. They are slightly different heights, with the eaves in a bit of a wavy line. The height is appropriate to the street section: not too high or too low. The sun and the shadows do their jobs. The eaves provide a bit of shelter from the rain and the road is slightly curved to combat the wind. In other words, the houses protect the street and the passerby.
Each house has its own identity, with small variations in the façades, details and colors. But they all respect a rule of etiquette; they seem to belong to one family. Overhanging eaves, cornices and balconies cast shadows on the façades so as to create plastic movement, but without overdoing it. With just the small curve of the road and the variety in the façades, the scene becomes animated.
It is a road with short perspectives. The façades appear slightly foreshortened, thereby emphasizing their individuality in the uniformity.
Every so often there is a small gap between the houses: an entrance to a garage or secret garden, the foliage of a tree appears.
The houses are three or four floors, sufficiently high to feel like a city, but able to keep their feet on the ground, to anchor the dimensions to the ground, to maintain the relationship with the land of their inhabitants.
A medieval street, in a historical city in Italy.
It is a narrow street, with high houses huddled together to create a curtain dotted with uneven windows.
The fronts are narrow, the heights different.
The doors of the houses and shops open up onto the street. A few doorways lead to a small inner courtyard. It was a road made for living and working, where the activity started from within and extended to the street, even if this street was narrow and winding. The street fronts seemed closed, yet there was a continuous exchange between inside and outside, with chairs on the street, with inhabitants outside chatting or working.
The craftsmen moved their work to the street and the shops opened stands on the street. There were pedestrians, a few horses, carts, a few wagons or carriages.
A nineteenth-century road in the center of an Italian city. Large residential buildings. Even windows, simple rhythms, considerable heights (5-6 floors), cornices, overhangs (terraces), mechanically repeated decorations. An idea of dignity and respectability. Entrances which were large but without revealing the interiors. The buildings take the old building model (ground floor, main floor, attic), adapting it to the demands of bourgeois society.
Even the workers' houses conform to this model.
A nineteenth- and twentieth-century street in the outskirts of town.
On the street, there are houses and villas in a row. Some are set back from the street. There are a few gardens. Railings, low walls, symmetrical palms, a few decorative or fruit trees rising from behind the fences.
But if it's possible to describe the stereotypes of normality through the centuries, it is no longer possible in contemporary times. There is a catalog of types, but the catalog has become an immense catalog of exceptions and differences, as if the only rule was the lack of rules. And this is the case despite regulations and plans and rules; rather, it is as if the regulations aroused, created the exception.

Nostalgia

01. We display a certain nostalgia for a world made of solid walls, for a world of materials that say what they are and declare their desire to endure. Even if we know that all of this will not be made for eternity, it somehow, through the image, aspires to eternity. This is all tied to nostalgia. Having worked for fifteen years in Germany and for fifteen years in the Netherlands, I learned something from these two languages. In German, as well as in Dutch, there are two words for nostalgia: *Heimweh* and *Sehnsucht*. *Heimweh* is the nostalgia to return home, nostalgia as we use it, from the Greek for homecoming and pain. The other word that denotes nostalgia, *Sehnsucht*, is a nostalgia for something that one is missing. This is the nostalgia that made the Dutch build New York, which they called New Amsterdam. The Dutch colonies that arrived in the New World constructed a new city, their city. This was not a desire to return home, rather, it was a desire to stay in a new world, to be modern. It was the hope for something that they hadn't yet seen. In a certain sense, it's a kind of nostalgia for the future. Perhaps this is what inspires the buildings constructed by those who are trying to create normal architecture.

Olanda
[Holland]

01. *Dutch Paintings*
Holland is a country of low, flat lands largely below sea level, and often intimately mixed with waters and a frayed network of canals and ditches.
Moses had miraculously opened the Red Sea: the Dutch, without resorting to miracles, closed off the seas around them and converted them into fields and cities.
The Dutch landscape seen from the plane appears largely artificial: a vast work of art where the marks of project designs far outweigh those of nature.
The outlines of the water, lattices of fields, extensive greenhouse areas (which light up at night, transforming the plain into a crystal), traces of ancient cities, road

Het Eiland in Zwolle, the Netherlands, 1996-2001, sketches with the Casa del Gallo Rosso (Rohe Hen)

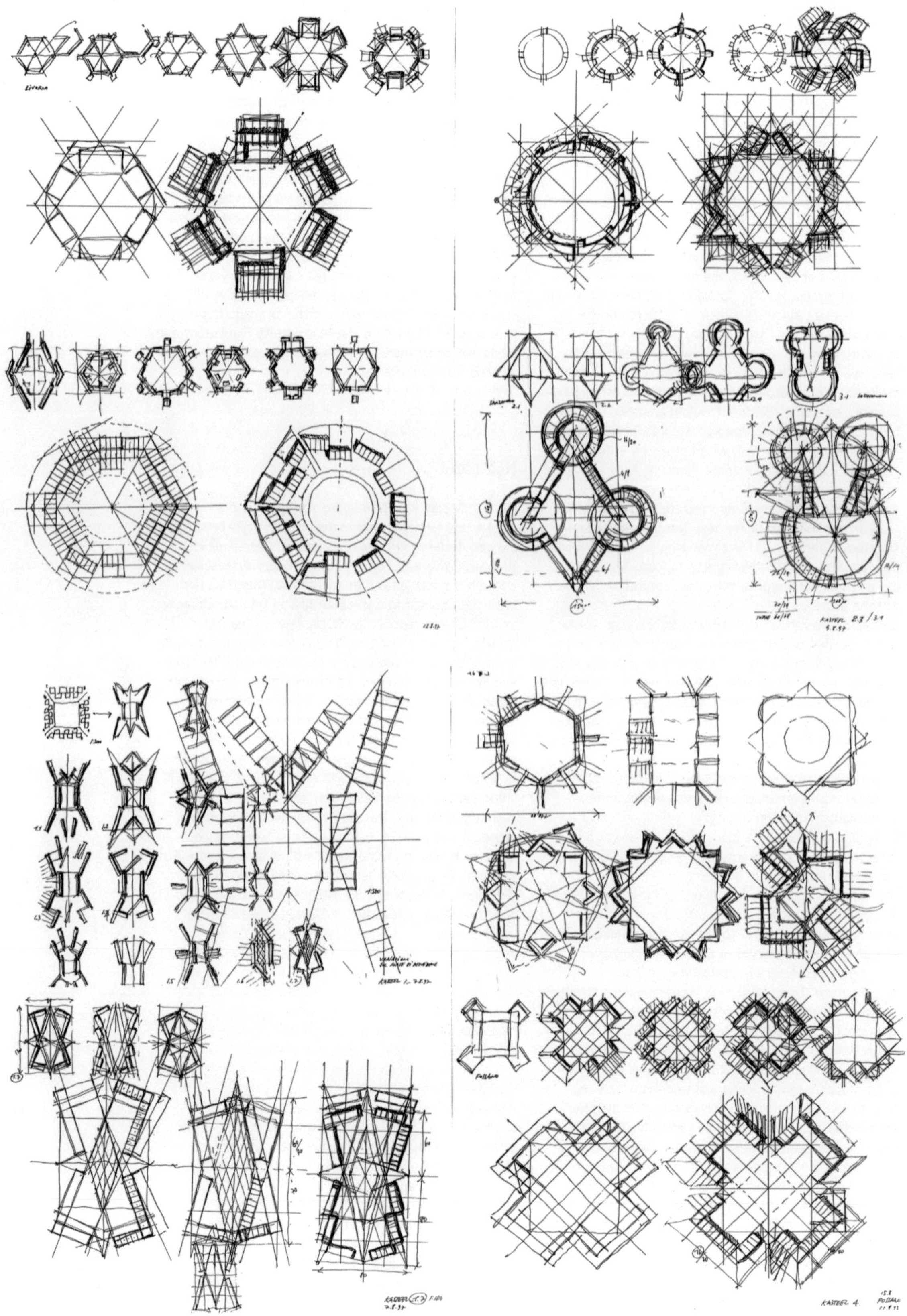

networks and new urbanization form a fantastic weave, like a large scale model of a project in the developing phase. Throughout the months as the plane landed, I could not help but notice the changes with amazement. Then when I got to the ground, I was able to contemplate the Netherlands through the paintings I love: the lady with the dog, in Groningen, the *View of Delft* by Vermeer in The Hague, the interior of St. Odulphuskerk of Saenredam, the small portrait of Rembrandt's mother, the many paintings of little known local masters all the way down to the bedroom of Van Gogh, the Mondrian landscapes, and the self-portraits and landscapes of Ackerman to the black and whites of Wessel Johannes Huisman. All were small paintings hung to show us closely the daily reality. Without being bold, the paintings were close to the truth and without the trappings of realism.

Of Holland I would like to remember the landscapes seen from the airplane, extraordinary elements woven from water and land, with bright lines drawn on green fields dotted with houses, slabs as bright as crystals at night (large greenhouses) where architecture appears always new to me with every transition (so large as to be recognized from the above).

I would like to remember all the low horizons and endless views from my travels by train from Amsterdam to the north (Groningen), south (Maastricht) and east (Eindhoven).

I would like to remember the water, those lazy canals, the fast and endless gray rivers marked by the trails of long and silent boats, and the sea of Scheveningen behind the windy dunes, infiltrating the fields like thin veins. The water was of varying shapes and regular lattice, and later deformed, then snagged. Ponds, pools and marshes were in an endless maze, and large expanses of water were harnessed by dams and embankments in their attempt to blend with the sea. In one frosty year, the whole Netherlands turned into a solid state, the water just disappeared under ice and snow...

I would like to remember Holland as in the poetry of Mario Luzi, numerous travelogues, and paintings (starting with Vermeer and Saenredam all the way to Huisman) and the museums, streets, houses, people, food and language.

[A. Natalini, in *Album Olandese*, Aion, Florence 2003]

02. *The Netherlands: a challenge or an escape? What kind of world exists for you in this country and how much has your life and the organization of your studio changed?*

It is neither a challenge nor an escape: they are simply opportunities and necessities. I looked for architectural opportunities in faraway places, considering I couldn't find any in my own country. After about ten years of working in Germany, in 1991 I was invited to a competition in the Netherlands in Groningen. I won the competition and have since started my relationship with this country.

I participated in many competitions, won several and almost always managed to build projects in reasonable time, five or six years, a timeframe which in Italy seems impossible.

I worked in historic town centres (Groningen, Maastricht, The Hague, Den Bosch, Zwolle, Helmond) but also on new reclaimed lands (as in the middle of a lake at Haverleij). Each and every time I was amazed by the wisdom of laws and regulations for the professional organization of the projects and efficiency of the construction sites, but especially by the "visions" from which transformations originate.

It seemed to me that the Dutch, inhabitants of "the Netherlands," always observed their country from above, pushing their gaze very far. The transformations of the projects were always grand and the waters were transformed into lands developed and inhabited, transforming the historic centres. The great rationality of the design of the area is joined to an innovative urban design and the architecture style of lunatic modernity. But the Netherlands is a country of great tolerance, so it knew how to receive my work, which together with that of Rob Krier and Charles Vandenhove, is now labelled as "new traditionalism" or "romantic architecture". The Dutch continue to wonder how it is possible that Natalini, founder of the legendary Superstudio, an innovative avant-garde group of the 1960s and 1970s, and who had among his pupils Rem Koolhaas, could bring forward an architecture style "that seems to have always been." The Dutch, for which the avant-garde is a permanent condition, looked at my creations with certain embarrassment. They recorded my success with the people, and they listened perplexedly to my lectures and remained politely silent. Some racked their brains to understand the reasons for my change of style while Martin van Schaik, Werner van den Belt and Hans Ibelings (the most famous of the young critics, and author of the bestseller *Supermodernism*) tried to write books on this subject.

In 1994 Corinne Schrauwen, a young Dutch architect who had worked for Natalini Architetti in Florence for some years, returned to Amsterdam and opened a studio there to carry out our projects. I usually go to the Netherlands in the last week of the month, travelling around the country (which is not as small as it seems!) on those "yellow trains in continuous movement between houses, grass and canals", as Mario Luzi describes in his poetry.

[26.09.03, from an interview by C. Donati, in *Costruire in Laterizio*]

03. *The Dutch Sketchbooks*

From 1979 I have worked in historic cities in Italy, Germany and the Netherlands with projects founded on the identity of the place. I studied the traces engraved in my memory and my visits were more emotional rather than scientific; I analysed the different geographical, historical, and human dimensions, and was aware of the uniqueness and diversity of each place. Because the architecture must be rooted in the places themselves, I needed each building to be different, but appropriate. In 1991, with the project for the reconstruction of Waagstraat in Groningen, I started my exploration of the Netherlands, a country where the radical renewal in architecture (the *Supermodernism* described by Hans Ibelings) had completely erased any identity. In this exploration I had illustrious predecessors: Lodovico Guicciardini in 1567 published in Antwerp *The description of all the Netherlands*, Edmondo De Amicis in 1914 wrote, *A sentimental-literary guide of the Netherlands*, and John Fanelli in 1968 wrote, *Modern Architecture in the Netherlands from 1900 to 1940*.

With projects for Groningen, and later in The Hague, Zwolle, Helmond, Den Bosch, Roermond and many other cities, I started the trend defined as *Traditionalism or Un-modern Contemporary Architecture*. If in the 1980s the movement for the reconstruction of European cities and critical regionalism had put context behind the projects, afterwards other lines of research occupied the media scene. A distinction between an architecture

Haverleij Castle in Den Bosch, the Netherlands 1997-2001, sketches, from castles to houses

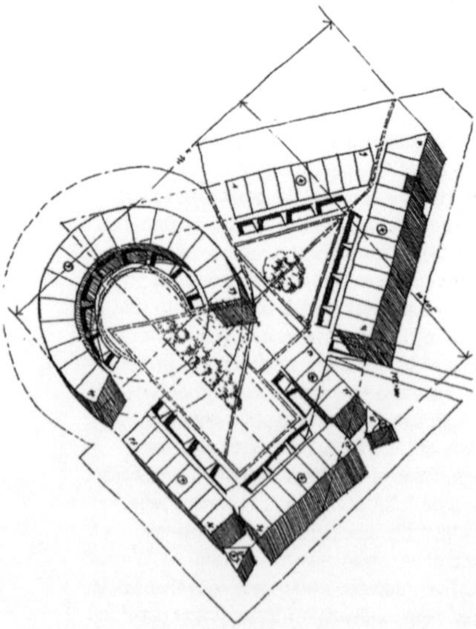

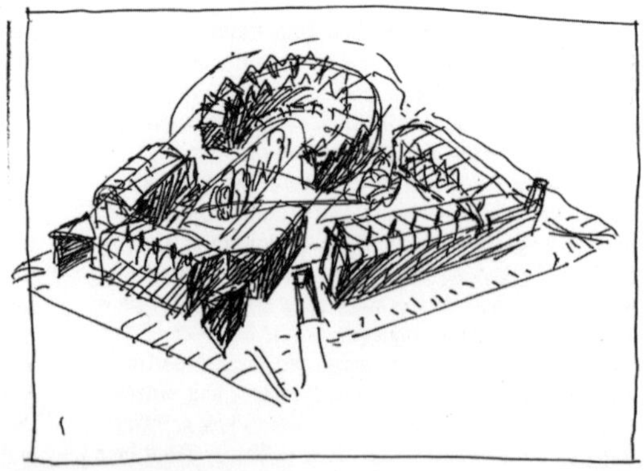

built for the human environment and that used to communicate between the real world and the virtual one (paper or digital) must be made. In the latter abstract languages of context prevail, based on fictitious values of novelty and diversity. Contemporary conservatism is an alternative to globalization and the displacement of space and time. Every project rests on lands that are accumulations of traces, ruins and other projects. As in every living thing there is DNA constructed in the past, but that can change flexibly foreshadowing future developments. Attention to context, sympathy with the places, along with the techniques of reading and analysis, enable us to understand what the place is and perhaps even tell us "What it wants to be"... But between this and the summary of the project, there's a logical leap to be taken, a *lapsus*. The program, constraints, needs, and desires, play a role in the transformation of the site and construction of the project.
We try to superimpose new evidence to existing ones, aiming at continuity. We tried to pass on the legacy that has been entrusted, bearing in mind the parable of the talents. In a sense, we seek the eternal in the new.

[A. Natalini, in *Identità dell'architettura italiana*, Diabasis, Parma 2013]

Punto di vista
[Point of view]

01. Adolfo Natalini enjoys a paradoxical popularity, in the Netherlands perhaps even more so than elsewhere. In a country where radical change in architecture has long been held in high esteem – how could it be otherwise with Rem Koolhaas as guru and role model for generations of architects – Natalini is still highly regarded as the founder of Superstudio and action hero of 1960s radicalism. It was Koolhaas who, while studying at the AA School of Architecture in London (from 1968 to 1972), invited Natalini to come and teach there. (It is not clear whether this should be seen as a telling example of exceptional boldness, or merely as typical of that period of democratization when students called the tune).
Yet Natalini is also one of the leading representatives of a contemporary traditionalism that has been causing quite a stir in the Netherlands of late, despite or thanks to the supermodernism for which the country became internationally famous during the same period. Natalini's recent umnodern architecture has made him especially popular with that majority of people who are unable or unwilling to call themselves architectural experts. And thus also with property developers, who are guided by the commercially understandable argument that it makes sense to build what the market wants. At first glance, there appears to be a world of difference between the "early" Natalini, founding father of Superstudio, and today's Natalini, the name behind Natalini Architetti. That difference is in fact considerably smaller- than his schizophrenic popularity in the Netherlands presupposes, and also smaller than the external differences between the Superstudio designs and the buildings might in first instance lead one to surmise. To begin with, Natalini is still one and the same person, whose views on many things have not changed fundamentally. Moreover, in retrospect the early work can be seen to contain numerous indications of the direction in which he has developed, such as the *Catalogue of Villas* (1968-1969), which proclaim an approach to typology that seems to be just as valid today. Intellectually speaking, too, the difference between his work then and now is slight.
As Pier-Luigi Nicolin rightly remarked, Natalini has remained an extremist. The only difference is that it is perhaps no longer so easy to recognize the radicalism in his work. One reason for this is that the early "inbuilt" Superstudio projects have stood the test of time so well that they have secured a place in the history books and have recently started to cause a *furore* all over again. They have certainly lost none of their conceptual and visual eloquence and they still speak to younger generations. Natalini is one of the many architects who are destined to be confronted with their early work for years to come. This is in part due to a mechanism in architectural criticism and history whereby everything is constantly repeated and everything and everybody is destined to be compared with their earlier selves. Accordingly, early work by an architect is almost by definition considered more important than late work. And it is almost impossible for the work of Natalini Architetti to emerge completely from the shadow of the early Superstudio designs. Another reason why people sometimes view the recent work with something like incomprehension, has to do with the subversion of everything having to do with tradition and modernization. That subversion was indeed accomplished in the period when Natalini was still operating under the Superstudio flag. Once upon a time, architects had to break free from the dominant tradition in order to be able to modernize. In the course of the twentieth century; however, modernization became the norm and consequently the new tradition. The few architects who do not conform to this dominant tradition like Natalini, are inevitably treated with incomprehension.
The awarding of Natalini's first Dutch commission in 1991 had a lot to do with his early work. It hadn't yet fully dawned on the client, Maarten Schmitt of Groningen City Council, that Natalini's architecture had evolved since the late 1970s and now looked quite different from the work of his Superstudio days. On the strength of this misapprehension, Natalini was invited to take part in a limited entry competition for a project directly behind the neoclassical town hall. The choice of which project would be built was decided in a referendum by the citizens of Groningen. The outcome of that vote was overwhelmingly in Natalini's favour (83.6%). This project was the first of many Dutch commissions, so that Natalini's work is no longer an exotic incident but an integral part of the Dutch architectural panorama. The score to date (2003) is six completed projects and a similar number under construction. Apart from the shops and dwellings in Groningen, the other completed works are: housing in the mixed-use De Resident development in The Hague downtown; apartments, a cinema and municipal facilities in the centre of Helmond (Boscotondo); shops and dwellings in the centre of Zwolle (Het Eiland); an office building on the outskirts of Roemond and housing (Zwaenestede castle) in the Haverleij park next to 's-Hertogenbosch...
In all these projects, Natalini's signature is immediately recognizable.
The architecture is in every instance abstract. Insofar as the works contain identifiable traditional forms, they have been reduced to their geometrical fundamentals. The flat facades of brick, with natural stone and concrete accents, are interrupted only by the regular pattern of window openings. Sloping roofs (where they exist) likewise appear

Haverleij Castle
in Den Bosch,
the Netherlands
1997-2001, sketches,
from castles to houses,
from *Quaderni Neri*

Haverleij Castle
in Den Bosch,
the Netherlands
1997-2001, sketches,
from castles to houses,
from *Quaderni Neri*

as large planes, usually of copper or zinc. The carefully designed detail is always at the service of the building as a whole and is frequently cull but invisible, as if all the parts connect smoothly of their own accord. This all adds up to an abstract architecture that is miraculously light and ephemeral, no matter how heavy the materials from which it is made. The abstraction relates not only to form and materiality but also to the way Natalini inserts his project into the context. What he makes is, in my-Dutch-eyes, never typical Dutch architecture, let alone typical Roermond or typical Groningen architecture.
The projects eschew mimicry: It is patently obvious that what concerns Natalini is not the letter but the spirit: rather, the interpretation of the context. In this he differs from those architects who take context and history as a literal starting point. His approach to typology is likewise characterized by abstraction. Natalini does not seem to be searching for an archetypical simplicity (which in architecture inevitably leads to dry-as-dust academism), but for simplicity as such. In this context, the anthropological studies Superstudio carried out in the 1970s at the University of Florence into simple implements, self driven processes of change and extra-urban material cultures are relevant. These studies are an important link with the current architecture of Natalini. After he, along with the other members of Superstudio, had analysed products and processes that lack a conscious act of designing, Natalini began to apply comparable logic to his own work.
Of course, no architect can ever avoid the act of designing, but in his architecture Natalini continually circles around the naturalness attributed to the non-designed artifact. In his case this leads not to architecture that looks as if it has always been there, but to architecture that looks as if it might always have been there. It is a crucial difference. In the first approach architecture would not have advanced much further. Eternally imprisoned an endless reiteration, it would have ground to a halt. In the second approach, that of Natalini, architecture remains constantly in motion, like an electron moving around the nucleus of an atom, in a ceaseless attempt to get closer to the nucleus of architecture. And just as its electrical charge keeps the electron at a distance from the nucleus, so the tragedy and beauty of architecture is that it can never coincide with its nucleus. But as his work in the Netherlands and elsewhere demonstrates, Natalini succeeds in coming very close indeed.

-

Hans Ibelings is an architectural critic. He lives and works in Amsterdam. He wrote *Supermodernism* and a book on contemporary traditionalism in the Netherlands.
[H. Ibelings, "Un punto di vista olandese sulle architetture olandesi di Adolfo Natalini" in A. Natalini, *Adolfo Natalini. Album olandese*, Aion, Florence 2003]

Originalità/Originarietà
[Originality/Origination]

01. *"Often novelty is only an inadvertence, and to forget in a world with so little knowledge is criminal." These words may also be a testimony to the distrust that you have for technology, when during class at the University you told us of how an artisan's technique transforms and uses the materials in the building: now, after big construction sites and prefabrication what has changed?*
My distrust of novelty continues to exist. Before, I spoke of an interest in origination and an absolute disregard for originality. With technology I am beginning to have less and less distrust as I took hold of it. But I do try not to get carried away by the enthusiasm for techniques: techniques are a means, not the end in architecture. In my work I use traditional techniques and more sophisticated techniques concurrently, simple materials and older ones and still others, though not many, more complex and modern. The problem is always to get the most with the least effort and put everything in their rightful place.
[25.10.97, interview by E. A. Gonzo and Vicari, in *Costruire in Laterizio*]

02. *Do you also feel that the architecture is providing chaos, in short, that this race toward the unusual and surprising is producing only those who in a recent conference organized in Rome by Antonino Terranova, were defined as metropolitan monsters?*
Yet while monsters were conjured to frighten children today, they seem to be appreciated or at least tell us that we must get used to living with them and are often referred to as wonders.
The unknown and awe are not new values at all, like Marino once already sang: "The scope of the Poet is to marvel [...] those who can't let people stupefied, they'd better change their job (go and groom horses)" and Metastasio once warned: "Those who ascend too quickly, are destined to come down at precipitous velocity."
It seems that novelty is the only value and architecture should always impress, but remember that "stupefy" and "stupid" have the same root word.
The world of architecture seems pervaded by a longing for renewal, as if the ascertained impossibility of changing the world (no more practical than utopia) sparked the need to change architecture. Typological, morphological and technological experiments succeed one another and are summed up together.
As in all experiments, failures outnumber successes ("trial and error" was the motto of the Accademia del Cimento, and design advanced with "trial and error"). So instead of solid, useful, beautiful buildings, which coexist with the rest of the world, we have buildings that are exceptionally strong or exceptionally useful or exceptionally beautiful but never the three things together and that always differentiates them from the rest of the world. Even in accepting the partiality of the result, we have to ask ourselves the reasons for this exceptional nature: were they really needed? I know that architecture was born more from desire than from a need (and that no dream is bigger than the man who dreamt it) but I do not think we are rich enough to be able to afford this waste of material and mental resources. Architecture as in the other arts, constantly questions itself, but it cannot forget its status of necessity. Experimentation and research are justified only by the formation of new needs. Besides, the world is already wonderful enough as not to need monsters...
[28.10.01, interview of M. Pisani in *L'industria delle costruzioni*]

03. Pierluigi Nicolin, the director of *Lotus*, argued that Natalini is as always, excessive, whether as an avant-garde or as a traditionalist. Maybe he was right: this resorting to the extremes is part of a teaching attitude. I may not have understood anything about the

Ijsselkade urban addition in Doesburg, the Netherlands, 1999-2006, Recovery plan

Ijsselkade urban addition in Doesburg, the Netherlands, 1999-2006, Historical map

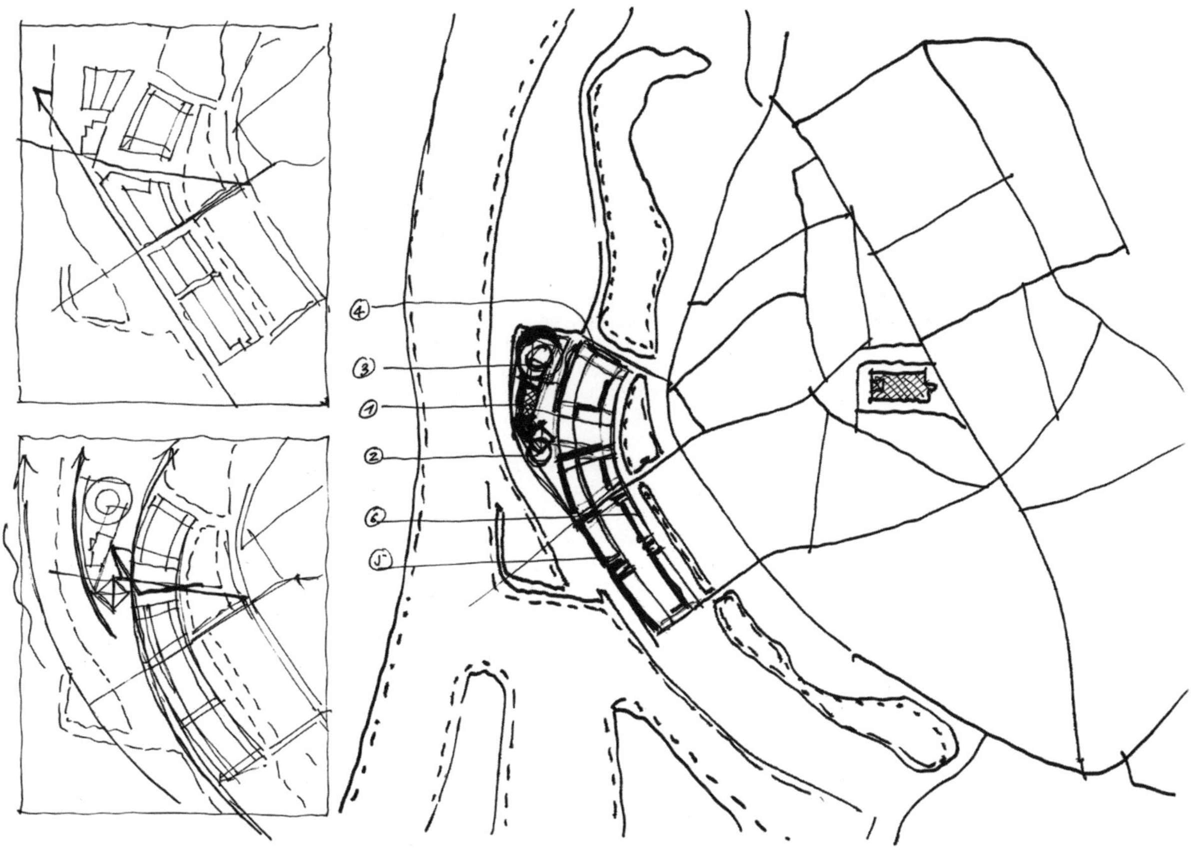

DOESBURG

University, but I was a teacher for 40 years and using *demonstratio per absurdum* tools of rhetoric is a way of making myself understood. If you bring something to the extreme it becomes much more comprehensible. The great communicators, the stand-up comedians use these systems: Ferrara, Sgarbi, or further down in time, Marinetti. It brings the discussion to its extreme consequences which often border on the absurd, in order to make concepts understood. As Corbellini said about the fact that what I say does not have absolute validity or holds true in every place, there are situations where you new and more experimental approaches, and others need more realistic and traditional methods. Certainly no one ever said that in building an airport or an interspatial communication system, one should use an existing form, a stable, a carrier pigeon, or the wireless phone. What I am saying is that after all, there are not so many new architectural needs. In most cases we are required to build shelters, homes, schools, health centres or the last resting places for people who have not changed in their structures and fundamental motivations. So there isn't this great need for innovation. About 50 or 60 years ago, Giedion noted that the only inventions of the 20th century that have influenced architecture were the elevator and the water closet.

We all agree with the usefulness of the water closet because it allowed collective housing; we have doubts about the usefulness of the elevator because the elevator is what led to September 11 (if there were no skyscrapers no one would have thought of blowing them up). The elevator allows skyscrapers, which are a total stupidity. In the same way, concrete allowed the most infamous of designers the most tremendous things, which if they had been built of stone would crumble. The protruding balcony, the crooked wall is wrong. The 40-metre projecting roof shelter would not have been possible using normal material. The British protectorate of Jerusalem did not make a plan for the city but gave only one rule, that all buildings in the historic centre should be made with the "Jerusalem Stone," large blocks of local stone.

Many of the discoveries of the new technology have led to an improper use; the same thing can be said of gunpowder and weapons. Things in themselves are neither good nor bad but knowing that man is basically evil, the more weapons you give him, the worse he becomes. Man should not have been on this Earth, he was created to disappear long before; and then thanks to the invention of culture, he remained on Earth even when his cycle should have ended. The Earth was made for others, the cockroach, mouse, these little animals that are smart, which are doing well and don't annoy anyone. Because of culture, man remained even if he should not have and has transformed the world into his own image and likeness. In ecology the animal adapts to the environment, and it is not the animal that changes the function of the environment for its own purposes. Man is by nature anti-ecological. If we accept the fact that man exists, we cannot attempt any ecological actions. Incidentally it must be remembered that ecology was invented in Usa to distract students from demonstrations against the invasion of Cambodia. Most of the tasks that are given to architects could be solved using very elementary technology and formal

View of Delft,
J. Vermeer, oil on canvas,
1660-1661 circa

Doesburg,
a book on the city

characteristics, which have already been experimented on. The so-called architecture without architects is an architecture that has never done great damage. Today we have faculties where biotechnology or the like are taught; they are all systems to correct the nonsense of contemporary architecture. As long as houses were built properly, put in the right places, with small windows and thick walls, there was absolutely no need for insulation, heating and so on. The moment they said they could build glasshouses, because anyway there were methods that could heat them, disasters began to happen. Now they continue to build ridiculous glass boxes that have an immeasurable cost and if you make crazy things like that – think about the amount of energy and water needed to produce aluminium and glass – it's as if one went around naked and to withstand the cold brings with him hot water bags and radiators. Architecture is simpler than what we believe it is. It has become complicated because now it is a specialized discipline and is divided into many parts. We have lost the global vision of the problem since we have become specialists, people who know more and more about fewer things, ending up in knowing everything about nothing.

[16.04.08, round table in Ferrara with Ravalli A. and G. Corbellini]

Pietre
[Stone]

01. I was born in Pistoia, a windswept, stony city with some extraordinary stone buildings, like the two-tone striped façade of San Giovanni, the pulpit by Giovanni Pisano, Marino's horsemen...
I was first a painter, later an architect in the Avant-Garde movement with Superstudio.
At the time of my passage between utopia and reality, I wrote in my book *Figures of stone* (Electa, Milan 1984): "Architecture is a lapse between pencil and stone. Too often they call architecture what comes off the tip of the pencil. Too often they call architecture what is merely a jumble of stones, brick, wood, concrete, iron and glass. Sometimes the soft tip of the pencil imitates the hardness of the stone, and attempts to freeze the speed of the drawing in the unalterable and exemplary destiny of the stone. This constant oscillation (and error) between pencil and stone reveals how every lapse, every unresolved tension between project and reality, is the repressed desire (and fear) of letting the pencil's stroke become the final, permanent reality of the stone.
The construction, made of stone (curious that the Latin work for stone is *lapis*, which is also the Italian word for pencil) is what is missing here, and noticeable for its absence when perhaps, once built and finished, it could fill the gap and cure us of these continuous lapses."
Stone has accompanied architecture through the centuries in its laborious struggle to rise out of the earth, as a monolith, a column, a lintel, a figured element, or as a section or slab in the walls or floors. Detached from the wall of the quarry, cut and shaped by the hands of men, stone acquires the permanence and solemnity of a gravestone. "Laying stone on stone" has always been a synonym for building.
On evening, at Stonehenge, I felt as if I had been buried in the cloister of the teeth of the earth, and the teeth were made of stone. Two other times I have felt the irresistible force of stone in a similar way: before the gigantic rusticated wings of Palazzo Pitti and the

light entablatures of Palazzo Rucellai.
I began to build quite late in life (1979-84). My first building was that of Alzate Brianza on the road between Como and Bergamo. Now the laborious process is finally complete and I would like it to be remembered (as Palladio was for his Basilica) for "the material that is all living stone and very hard" and for the stones that were "shaped and held together with great diligence."
In Florence, I built the Teatro della Compagnia (1984-86), a hidden architecture near the Duomo, and also near the place where (with *Euridice*) the history of Italian theater began. My theater was a sort of palace courtyard, a small meditation on the history of the theater.
According to Thesaurus, the commentator of Aristotle, architecture is a metaphor of stone.
Vasari in his *Lives* wrote of stone: "Truly, more than good stone and well-tempered iron, what matters are the art, the intelligence and the judgment of those who work with them... To achieve all the perfection and beauty of the things we so greatly praise, with the extremes of admiration that is given to the things that are so judged by those who understand them, it is necessary to apply oneself with great industry to make them perfect and beautiful, indeed to make them extremely perfect and extremely beautiful." The theater also grew out of my travels in my city: the extraordinary façade of Palazzo Antinori, seen by night at the end of via Tornabuoni, where it appears like a graffito on stone. Fine lines mark it as if to prove theorems of hard beauty.
On other nights I have gazed at length on the façade of Palazzo Rucellai by my great favorite Alberti. The sharply delineated courses between the floors with their orderly entablature, the cornices, the design of the rustication: everything is flattened. The back of the benches lining the front, in *opus reticulatum,* seem to have come from one of Magritte's paintings (one of the many in which a passerby is turned to stone) or the portrait of the Marquis De Sade by Man Ray.
In those same years I designed several rearrangements of public spaces, attempting to avoid the ambiguous discipline of urban decor. I built the plaza and the new fountain at Palazzuolo sul Senio (a town in the province of Florence), 1984-86:
"For more than ten years I spent a few days every summer in a mountain valley on the border between Tuscany and Romagna, living in an ancient cluster of stone cottages known as Il Fornello. We used to go down from the valley from time to time, to visit the town, which was called Palazzuolo sul Senio, because it lies on a river of that name. Two other rivers, the Visano and the Salecchio flow into the Senio near the center of the town. I thought of some small designs to make on the pavement, as a sort of indicator of the way, and I thought of replacing the grotto with a stone fountain, which would bear three bronze figures of rivers and pilgrims who slaked their thirst at its waters. And the rivers and stones returned in that way right to the center of the town."
In 1988 I presented these three works to the Marble Architecture Awards jury here in Carrara. Alzate won the prize in the architecture section, the theater came in first in the interiors section...
In the '80s, I had the opportunity to learn a great deal about marble and stone, working for an extraordinary company of this area, called Up & Up, one of the first in Italy to focus on design in marble. I had the good fortune to meet Voltero Tonlorenzi (inventor of processes) and Baldini, and to work in their workshop with Sottsass, Castiglioni and Aldo Rossi.

Buitenop and the Natalinitoren offices in Roermond, the Netherlands, tower-bearer, from *Quaderni Neri*, 1999

Buitenop and the Natalinitoren offices in Roermond, the Netherlands, Caryatids and towers, from *Quaderni Neri*, 1999

I designed objects, tables, floors...
From all of them, in the workshop and in the quarries, I learned a great deal about marble, which until then I had always viewed as the material of legends.
I had even written:
"When I was a boy and lived in the Versilia district, I observed the snowline on the Apuana mountains: for years I waited for the snow to melt, until finally I discovered that it was white marble. Later, I lived in Pistoia, and on the outside of San Giovanni Fuoricivitas, alternate stripes of white and green marble marked for me what was a fantastic geology: that discontinuity harbored the beasts of the Apocalypse. The first time I entered the cathedral in Siena, I couldn't take my eyes off the floor to look at the pillars and vaults. I was hypnotized like a chicken by the white chalk line drawn on the ground, and continued to run my eyes from one square to the next and then, walking, I half-closed my eyes so as to "see it" with my feet. Another time, in the cathedral in Florence, peering through the railing of the Cupola, I was bewitched by the vertiginous plunge of the well shaft created by the floor designed in the perspective of the octagon. One of my favorite places, however, is the Baptistery, with its intricate, changeable floor, much like a kaleidoscope. Of the old country houses I have lived in, I remember every little unevenness in the floors: certain bricks that grew more wobbly or chipped with the passage of time and that guided my steps year after year... this fascination of mine for floors perhaps is the reason behind my obsession with time and memory (and the traces they leave on places): it is on the earth (natural or artificial as it may be) that the animal leaves its imprint... the floors I love most tell stories. In them, the materials, designs and colors mingle like the threads of a tapestry woven by three benevolent sisters. While waiting in an empty room, or seated on the corner of a table, the eye follows the floor, abstracted by the rhythm of the patterns and colors: playing against an invisible adversary who moves his pieces on an infinite chessboard, making up the rules as he goes along. With other figured floors, following the deceptive lines drawn in perspective or in axonometry, the spaces suddenly tilt: the convexity of the trihedron becomes a protuberance, up becomes down, inside out. The domestic cosmonaut grasps hold of the umbilical cord of memory and slowly finds the road that leads back home. Once I drew a marble table with the sun and the moon. Maybe some evening, after dinner, the crescent moon will gaze in at my window and see itself...
I have designed many pieces of furniture in marble: the tables were small pieces of architecture, like the *Antiquaria* table: "I've always thought that one should never make crystal tables, because a transparent surface only serves to show the base that serves to hold up the transparent plane that serves to show the base that... Then, after working for years on marble tables whose architectural beauty, in my intention, was supposed to enable one to forget the bases, I began to work again on bases that had a great deal of architecture in them and that were always columns or pillars. So in the end I chose two different styles from the vast catalogue I had put together (even more dizzying than the samples of marble with which I surround myself: one was a grooved column and the other was a T-shaped pillar. On top of them I set a crystal tabletop because even designers, as they grow older, can change their minds."
In Florence, I built the museum of the Opificio delle Pietre Dure, where among the many other marvels,

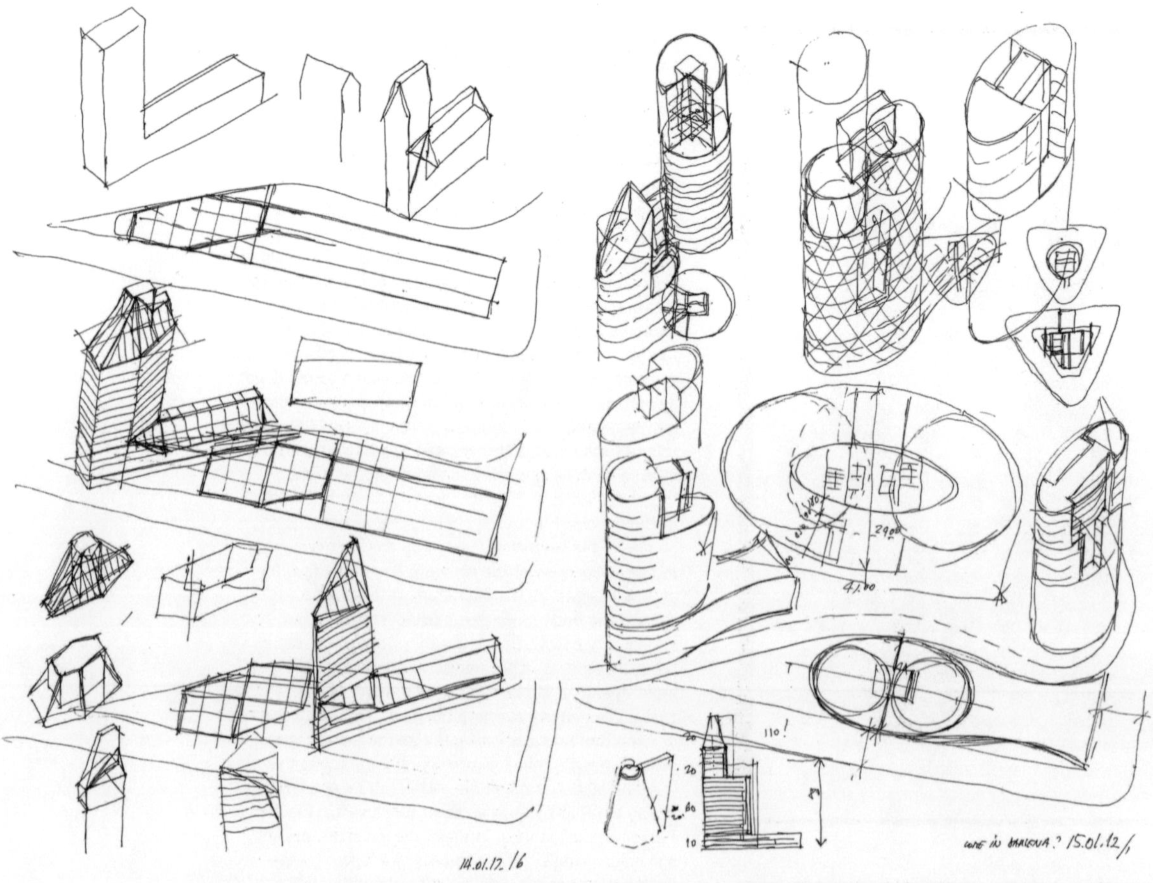

there is a design of architecture in an inlay of semi-precious stones by Zocchi. It is a figure of stone that seem to exemplify in real life the metaphor that gave the title to my book (*Figures of stone*):
"The museum contains a phantasmagorical, magical collection of stone inlays", as Annamaria Giusti writes, "It is the ideal meeting place for the intersection of nature, art and science."
The semi-precious stones are made precious by the art of the craftsmen, just as all stone are made precious by the skillful work of men.
In Tuscany, in the days of the Lorraine Duchy, it was considered lucky to find these stones but, more in general, we can say that the cities where quarries coexist with the constructions where they are used can be considered lucky. Von Humboldt calls them "the most beautiful cities in the world."
In 1991 I initiated the activity of Natalini Architetti with Fabrizio Natalini (same last name but not a relative, as we write in our résumé) in the studio at Salviatino in Florence, building structures and parts of cities in Italy and the Netherlands, trying to concentrate our activity in these two countries: I have always tried to make my architecture contextual, attentive to the place and capable of speaking a local language as my one attempt to give globalization some uniformity.
Whenever we built something, we tried to find the principle that made it livable, even when there might not seem to be any. We extended our study to the dimensions of space and time. We tried to learn what was there and what had been there, and imaging a pleasing future for the inhabitant and visitors. We searched the city, trying to recreate the effects even where there were none, as in certain parts of the Netherlands that had just be reclaimed from the waters, or certain outlying sections of Italian cities which were no longer country and not quite city, or in discontinued industrial zones. We applied simple rules of composition, based on rational principles of order. On the disciplinary body of architecture and urban design, we superimposed only the essential innovations required by the latest building techniques (but only when they were more appropriate than the ancient ones) and by the new models of social or residential aggregation.
Materials played a more and more important role in this work, enabling the new buildings to fit into the historical fabric of the city centers, or to recreate an urban effect.
We always preferred natural materials, capable of lasting in time, like terracotta and stone.
We have given stone the most representative part in our constructions, even the residential ones, a little like what Biagio Rossetti taught in Ferrara. Stone also serves to create the decoration of the buildings, alternating with the other materials, marking the nodal and focal points. They are decorations in the real, ancient sense of *decus*, dignified, appropriate. Not a mere decoration but a necessary accentuation of parts and buildings.
Once again recalling the words of my extraordinary professor of Mineralogy, Professor Rodolico, I have tried to use local stone: thus in northern Italy I relied on granite or gneiss, in Tuscany on sandstone, travertine or other types of marble, in Frankfurt on *roter buntstein* in the Netherlands on h*arte steen,* and so on, although I have also occasionally used Italian stone elsewhere on account of its exceptional quality. If our buildings seem nostalgic it is not nostalgia for the past, or even nostalgia for the future. They are buildings and parts of cities designed for a long life, capable of taking us smoothly from the past into the future. They are buildings meant to be scenes of everyday life, in the construction of places where human beings can feel at home or, as Heidegger puts it "pacified on the earth under the sky." Now we can call this architecture an architecture of resistance.
Thesaurus, commenting Aristotle, calls architecture a metaphor of stone. It seems to me that my work in these thirty years has been a passage from the metaphor to the reality.
With *Eupalino* by Valéry we can dream of architecture that sings and the stones are its highest notes. In these thirty years I have learned from my materials, confirming the Latin saying *Ligna atque lapides te docebunt quod a magistris disceri non possis* [Trees and stones will teach you what you cannot learn from masters], and for this I am grateful to the stones and their companions.

[31.05.08, *Lectio magistralis* on the occasion of his receipt of the career award at Carrara Marmotec]

Polo universitario a Novoli
[University Campus in Novoli]

01. In 1993 I started the project for the University Centre in Novoli, Florence, within the frame work of a guide blue print by Léon Krier.
The seven buildings have classrooms of all sizes, the faculties, offices, students' hub and a big library aligned on an arcade walkway looking out onto a square.
These are like buildings with the basement and arcades in stone, the upper part in red plaster and at the top loggias and copper plated roofs.

Polo universitario a Siena
[University Campus in Siena]

01. The second project is different since the city, Siena, is different, an extraordinary historic city where, within the city walls, I was asked to restructure an old paediatric hospital built in the '50s by the civil engineers. It was a huge building, absolutely inappropriate for Siena, to be transformed into a seat for a university faculty.
To my mind, it was impossible to transform it into a university faculty. The building was ugly so I proposed and obtained its demolition and substitution with another building. Then as the project progressed, the building grew: at the start it was supposed to contain a faculty of about 10,000 sq. m and in a second phase, it became 20,000 sq. m.
So we had to build a big part of the building underground and then we tried to lay it out in a way as to break this big mass. The building is divided into three parts: a rectilinear part containing the departments and the professors' studios, a central part with the classrooms and the amphitheatres and a curved part containing a big five-floor library. The three parts open out downwards in order to have viewpoints, the courtyards looking out over the splendid panorama of the Sienese countryside. Towards the city, the building is rooted to a huge wall located on the road: there was once a historic wall which we had to partly demolish. The wall had been built in different periods, between the 14th and 19th centuries.
So we kept a 14th century fragment and the rest was

Buitenop and the Natalinitoren offices in Roermond, the Netherlands, sketches for the second tower, 2012

Buitenop and the Natalinitoren offices in Roermond, the Netherlands 1999-2010, the second tower (project) and la Natalinitoren

replaced with a perforated wall, in order to create a respect zone, a stop-over zone for the students, since the road is very narrow and rather busy.
The building is not so visible from the outside and aspires to create a layout that resembles that of the Sienese wall confines. In these pictures one can guess in some way, the geometry of the structure of the building of various floors, while this is the view from outside the city and the way in which it fits into the landscape, as in a dialogue. It is huge, since it is the building of an institution, a part of the university, and a real estate of 20,000 sq. m and interacts with the other big structures of the convents and scientific institutions. There is a series of interspaces between the road and the building, consisting of passages of small unroofed courtyards. The building is massive, solidly rooted on the ground, since the buildings in brick have to keep their feet well planted on the ground! It is made up of classic, robust materials, able to resist to the passing of time, it is a building of brick and travertine even if (of course), it has a reinforced concrete structure. The photos I am handing out are part of two different photo features: on one part there are professional architecture photos, that is, in which the building is empty and standing in the light. The others are reportages to verify how the building is used.
The architects build a sort of fixed stage for the tragedies and comedies of daily life, then the building is modified by its users. The building is not so much what the architect designed but that which it will become according to use and interpretation of others. Here is one of these open courtyards going towards the valley, where of course the photographer framed the architecture from downstream towards the building to show it, even if this is of no importance to the students or those inside it, since the fundamental thing for them is instead, to have the windows from which to contemplate the valley. In this photo, which is part of this reportage with the students, there are not many people, but the building seems as if it has been there for many years, that is, it does not have that invasive aspect of a new building in a historic context.
["Narrate, uomini, la nostra storia", 2006]

02. In 1995 the University of Siena asked us to restructure a hospital of the '50s in Porta Tufi to host the seat of two faculties: we proposed to demolish and replace it with a building that is more suitable to the place and designated use.
What we built is laid out in three bodies, open like the fingers of a hand, towards the Sienese valleys, arranged on the slope towards the wall and attached to a big perforated wall on the road leading from Porta Tufi going towards Piazza del Campo.
The building has great brick walls perforated with windows of various forms and dimensions framed and divided by travertine elements. From the road, the building looks compact, but towards the valley three triangular courtyards open out and on the sloped roofs one discovers terraces with grass lawns and loggias.
From a distance you can also see the green copper roof (the classrooms' gallery) that set a discussion among the Sienese. At the start of 2001 the students and professors started to use the building and now it seems as if it had always been there.
These are some of the projects on which I worked with Fabrizio Natalini and the studio of Natalini Architetti in Salviatino, Florence and with Corinne Schrauwen in the Amsterdam studio. We have worked on many others, and continue to do so.

Paleiskwartier,
Den Bosch, the Netherlands,
2002-2012, project

Regarding our buildings I try to forget the difficulties, the bureaucratic impediments, renunciations and daily tragedies to concentrate only on the images of the sun, rain, grass, waters, red and yellow bricks, white and grey stones, green and silvery roofs.
Perhaps because we have a desperate need for normality.
[28.10.01, excerpt of the interview of M. Pisani, in *L'industria delle costruzioni*]

Porta Reno

01. *Porta Reno*
I returned to Porta Reno to compare the finally completed and inhabited building with my ideas and projects from 1989. I would have liked to see it under a clear blue sky or perhaps in the fog, but the weather was uncertain and the sky, a grey-blue colour with a few slices of cold sunlight. The city centre was already decorated with Christmas lights, so the building looked as if it were crowned with garlands and baubles when I tried to take a photo from the base of the tower to compare it with the corner view and the Ferrara cyclist I had sketched rapidly with coloured pencils ten years before.
On the small corner piazza, there are three buildings, two in brick and one in stone. The stone building seems like a small tower: it is topped with three cylindrical columns, and opens up with wide archways at ground level. The corner looks like many traditional places in Ferrara... but here, it is not set at a crossroads, the arches do not lead to a green shaded courtyard, and the tower is not part of a castle... It is as if Ferrarese "words" had come together in the midst of an interrupted conversation. Corner, arch, tower, but also pilaster, string course, keystone, portico, visual words made solid by centuries of work that have been arranged in a small fragment of the city to heal a wound and protect collective memory from a traumatic event (war destruction) and absence.
It is if the buildings were arranged around a missing element: the corner between corso Porta Reno and via Ragno.
The building contains the red of terracotta and the white and rose colours of the stone. It bears the colours of the city, of its dreams and heraldry.
It is a dense building, set firmly on the ground and its bases, as if compressing what lies beneath: medieval remains, ancient wooden houses...
However, it is precisely from these historic layers that the building draws its strength through invisible roots. If this building had been finished earlier, (in 1993-94) perhaps my story would have been different, because at the beginning of the 1990s, together with the Teatro di Rimini, it would have expressed a possible logical direction for architecture within a solid tradition.
However, the building construction was delayed (tied up with the red tape of bureaucracy and superintendence and the economic disasters caused by delays) and so, the opportunity was missed. Now it exists under this grey sky on the first of December 1999, to close the decade on a melancholy note.
This is not a fin de siècle piece of architecture, but simply a belated tribute to a very beautiful city (Ferrara) with the heartfelt hope it achieves its possible transformations.
[01.12.99]

Postmodern

01. *What are your thoughts on Post-modern design?*
In my long journey to move closer to architecture, I have not yet reached modern design. What I create is an architecture that recognises and uses certain archetypes from the past. It has a lot in common with traditional popular architecture (I am strongly Strapaese!) [Strongly attached to regional identity] but it does not manage to apply certain products of modern architecture that continue to remain foreign to me. My lack of familiarity with technology and my non-affinity with the modern in its attempt to live "here and now", do not allow me to accept the short-lived nature of its ideas and architecture. For the same reason I am tempted to maintain a certain distance from a label like Post-modern: I prefer the Post-antique invented by my distinguished university professor, Quaroni. I like antique more than modern. I am wary of the buzzwords on everybody's lips, like fashion ideology; I am not drawn to current ideas that are madly successful and which, for that very reason, are quickly worn out. I do not accept the "fashion system" applied to architecture and am very suspicious of anything that is interpreted as a trend and that is easily outmoded. I was very happy with the expression used by Portoghesi: "end of prohibition." It was a great liberation from the concept of modern as the only source, but I do not feel like subscribing to another type of trend that, while being more inclusive and eclectic, still considers itself as a precise source of reference. I feel that the only rules are those that apply to cohesion with a sense of place and knowledge of construction. I find the buildings and entire works of Buontalenti, Scarpa e Ridolfi more interesting than accepting a more or less pre-determined reference package.

[02.05.86, from the interview with Adolfo Natalini by M. Pisani.]

Riparazione urbana
[Urban restoration]

01. *Urban restoration*
Rare are the cities that have been built according to a single project and within a limited time period. Even more rare, are cities that have been abandoned, frozen in time because of some catastrophe or that have crumbled to dust. Almost every city has been built and rebuilt gradually, in an ongoing process that made small changes acceptable and gave the possibility of correcting any errors. Certain exceptional events (wars and natural catastrophies) have brought dramatic changes, and just as dramatic have been the rapid transformations due to insufficient time and a lack of careful consideration concerning these changes and their effects. For this reason, at the end of the 1970s, discussion began, published in the architectural review, *Lotus*, concerning urban restoration in a movement for the reconstruction of European cities. The restoration was aimed at repairing urban traces and layouts, and mending the damaged networks of the sense of the city. It was hoped to re-establish the *urbs* and *civitas*; it was directed at bringing back the art of city building, eclipsed for a long time by short-sighted but generous urban planning and daring but selfish architecture. The means were varied: from the replanning of urban layouts to manuals for recovering traditional construction techniques, grafting onto this corpus of permanent elements, the innovations required by new needs and desires and available through new technologies. Not so much a reconstruction, but more of an evocation. From this perspective, the projects will be, first of all, a fitting compensation for any damage suffered by the city, and in the more fortunate cases, a contribution to its beauty. In any case, (as Louis Kahn stated) they will be a gift to architecture.

[From the introduction of a book of projects for a new reconstruction of the Ponte Vecchio area on the banks of the Arno, 1996]

Riviste
[Magazines]

01. *One only has to browse through an architectural magazine to discover that the star system has focussed on a battle against harmony, order, beauty and practicality to propose works that feature chaos, disorder, and ambiguity, a laconic minimalism, or affected and ridiculous expressionism. It really does seem that light years have passed since the laying down of key principles on which architecture was based until recently. What is the reason and how did that happen? Are designers responsible and in what way?*
Architectural magazines belong to various categories: technical publications (that deal with specialist subjects concerning buildings, materials and building techniques), trend magazines (that feature theories and that have almost disappeared), illustrated magazines (that only publish images of exceptional and "monstrous" architecture in the hope that from the many experiments, something good will emerge). Illustrated magazines are always hunting for something new, because that is the only aspect that, journalistically speaking, makes news. So, they publish the latest designs by famous architects and buildings that are outside the norm. In this way, information and discussions on architecture become little more than social or gossip column news... However, we cannot put all the blame on illustrated magazines for this surprising (and depressing) panorama: many architects direct their research towards chaos, disorder, and ambiguity (as noted by my interviewer) taking a similar route to the majority of visual arts. Architects are no longer satisfied with their role as "masons who studied Latin", so they assume the role of philosopher, scientist, and artist, each time producing works that force the limits of construction to become manifestos, scientific experiments or sculptures. But, (as Palladio sustained) an architect is an amateur, and wants to absorb the whole world in order to understand it. In its race for something new, end of century architecture has been subject to impossible acceleration.
Now is the moment to reconsider the long timescales in architecture and reinstate the principle of necessity.

[28.10.01, from the interview by M. Pisani, in *L'industria delle costruzioni*]

Paleiskwartier,
Den Bosch,
the Netherlands,
2002-2012, variation

Tempo
[Time]

01. *Invincible architecture*
In the Chinese rock-paper-scissors hand game, the trump card is stone, but stone crushes scissors and scissors beat paper.
Towards the mid-18th century Schopenhauer wrote: "The new is rarely good because the good remains new only for a short time."
And towards the mid-20th century Raymund Erith wrote: "Modernism is too restrictive since it is completely subjected to tradition while attempting to avoid it. From my standpoint the only alternative is an architecture that does not reject tradition."
Leaving to the modernists the difficult task of defending their architecture, the resistant stone architecture has no intention of avoiding the scuffle.
Architecture by nature is used to battles. Architecture is not platonic, but consists of local realities, differences, desires and errors. Architecture builds up by defying the world's catastrophes, hurricanes, and earthquakes. It challenges the disasters of time (ageing, forgetfulness and loss of sense). It challenges the disasters of the individual (self-assertiveness, competition and the desire to survive), and that of matter (collapse, cave in, decay). There are so many possible catastrophes that may provoke ignorance, inattentiveness, and errors, that the architect tries to avoid the evitable mistakes by turning to collective memory, common knowledge, warning signs, and shared experiences.

02. *Why we cannot call ourselves modern*
"The term *modern* comes from the Latin root word *modo* (adv.) = now, at this moment." Etymologically, modern is what occurs now, at this moment. Modern architecture is one of the present, in a world where change is always faster. Therefore, architecture of the fleeting moment is thus very distant from what architecture should be: the art of time and memories and of duration. "Modern architecture" is thus an oxymoron.
An architect cannot be modern: architecture simply is (as Louis Isadore Kahn said).
The stories of architecture, but especially the chronicles of architecture reported in magazines, present to us a series of overwhelming buildings because of their novelty, as if they make history (or news) only through originality and diversity...
We are pushed to extreme experimentations as if we were bored with the world of constructions that are well made, comfortable and nice... And this would be comprehensible for a long-lived and industrious architect like Michelucci who, after experimenting on rationalism and regionalism, felt a different need and became an expressionist.
In short, perhaps after 30 years of brick houses an architect may feel the need to make one of meta...
The story of the three little pigs is about these three that in deciding to each build its own home, had to build three houses instead of uniting, cooperating and turning to a good architect. The first made one of straw, the second of wood and the third (the more serious and least creative) of brick.
On what basis does forced experimentation and diversification arise? Why did the three little pigs, offspring of the same mother and with the same plan (to build a safe shelter), build three different types of houses? We could respond by saying that they have three different personalities (the first two are more extrovert and optimistic, and the third, more reflexive) or that they did not cater to a need but to a desire.
Architecture in fact, is governed by need and desire.
It is desire that pushes us along the path of diversity.
In his treatise, Vitruvius wrote that architecture should respond to the need for *firmitas*, *utilitas*, and *venustas*, which means (also for those who do not know Latin) that it has to be built in such a way so as to be resistant, economic, functional, and lastly, beautiful.
Vitruvius does not say in what way these diverse needs can be combined, nor did the succeeding biographers do so. In more recent times, in constructing almost always within an already built-up environment, we have to respond to a fourth need, that of *propinquitas*, in order to fit into the context.
The architectures that respond in a balanced way to this fourth need are not bizarre, anomalous or exceptional architectures. They constitute the civilised and dignified environment we live in, but being extraordinary or harbingers of novelty, are rarely highlighted in architectural books and magazines. Especially the latter respond to a journalistic vision, and tend to prefer exceptions and not the rule, according to the principle by which a dog that bites a man does not make news, while a man who bites a dog does.
So magazines publish the architectures that make up the image of the architect and not those built by architects for their commissioners.
Various works are published, almost as if diversity is a value.
The newspapers today are full of news that seem extraordinary or interesting then and there, but which lose all interest in just a few days. Another thing altogether is the fate of a good book or a poem: the interest it arouses remains or grows with time.
Novelty makes news and captures our interest but only for a short time. The image that brings novelties would be valuable if time was short. If our lives were to last just one or a few days (as for certain insects), certainly every novelty would have an absolute value. But we work on lives that are quite long, and even never long enough ("vita brevis, ars longa" [life is short, art lasts forever]). The architects should have much longer lives to be able to learn and experiment.
What value is given to difference, originality?
It is of value in the short term ("it's news"), but could also be valuable in the long term when it is able to open new research paths.
Often, novelty is an experiment, an attempt to open new roads starting from the consideration that our life changes, that the world around us changes, and that we have other morphological and technological possibilities. Experimentation is necessary if we have to respond to new needs.
But new needs are few.
We could start an analogous discussion on windows.
The openings of houses were limited in size by the resistance of the architrave and availability of glass.
The openings and windows became bigger and bigger...
But their increased size certainly did not enhance better livability in the house, or in the toilets, the bedrooms or in the kitchen...
Maybe only the living room could improve with bigger windows, provided there is a nice panorama to see.
If it had a fantastic view because the house is in the countryside, one usually views it outdoors and when

Paleiskwartier,
Den Bosch,
the Netherlands,
2002-2012

the indoors tried to find shelter and protection not only from the climate, but also from the big open spaces.
If the window in the house is big it is relatively of little use, and would not even be so useful in the work place (office, school etc.). Transparency would be necessary only for those who are forced to stay home due to illness or disability. In the high rise homes (above the fifth or sixth floor) the user is completely dependent on the mechanical transportation systems.
The space needed increases as the height increases, reducing the service space on every floor.
There is a prevalent idea of height as a sign of one's *status*: the stars climbing ever higher (possibly to the top of the world) signify shining.
Height augments dependency and danger, but high-rise buildings multiply the value of the plot... and increases living density and, therefore, the profits. But this increase, from a certain limit onwards, is controversial.
The need to grow in height remains in those places where there is no more land, as in Montecarlo and Hong Kong, real urban monstrosities.
For thousands of years, regardless of the floor plan, the walls were straight, that is, perpendicular to the ground ("plumb line").
Nowadays, on one hand all are busy straightening out the leaning tower of Pisa (or preventing its collapse). On the other, numberless architects are committed to make leaning walls ("no plumb").
But the floorings continue to be horizontal and, therefore, the relationship with a no-plumb wall is extremely problematic. The leaning wall, as every imminent catastrophe, challenges gravity, an effort to bring static nature to the extreme limits.
Competitive originality arises from a suicidal drive. Perhaps the human race self-regulates itself through new diseases, the traffic or contemporary architecture. Also in the production of great architects we find historic turning points marked by novelties as in Picasso or Le Corbusier.
From the harmonic buildings of the 1930s, Le Corbusier moved on to brutal material constructions of those years with the Tourette or l'Unité d'Habitation, to then reach the irrational sculptural turning point of Ronchamp (Ronchamp as the betrayal of the modern).
Perhaps we need a change for a biological or mental survival, somewhat like biodiversity or the natural selection of evolution (for biologists, the mutant genes are said to be "sportive").
Man has survived his biological fate through culture, to then worry about ecological equilibrium which he himself disrupted by remaining on the stage when his role had already ended.
Diversity is thus a means to guarantee survival or the improvement of architecture. But we don't see why architecture has to feel this need for renewal.
Is what we do new and better than what we have done till now? Or rather: is it more suitable to the new needs and desires?
Architecture, through the renewal achieved by novelty, seeks to defeat time and thus, death.
If tending towards diversity responds to the need to forestall decay and death, I don't see why we shouldn't pursue the path of repetition.
Architecture is an art of duration.
Architecture is an art of resistance not only against the climate and catastrophes but also against time.
This guarantee of duration is based mostly on experience. We return, that is, to an idea of typological, morphological permanence. In the time in which we are immersed, every action has roots, motivations, codes in the past, or that occurs in the present, aimed at having an effect in the future. Our outlook in the past can go far beyond: it is a consolatory vision.
Our view in the present is difficult since the present is a separation point between two convergent classes of the past and the future, and, therefore, has no dimension and is always in movement.
It is even more difficult to look to the future since it is based only on hope, and encounters the anguish of our demise or of the unknown. The outlook on the past is based only on memory, on the nostalgia of a return.
Through constructions the architect tries to ensure a survival through remembrance of himself implied in the construction.
To establish relationships with others (and with the times) its seems logical to use the elements of experience or those built on a "reasonable experience," rather than those new ones of which we know nothing and could cause catastrophes.
To abandon originality in favour of originations signifies admitting the limitations of our experience, the time limits of the act, and accepting the fact that we are on this earth only to say a few words.

Ijsselkade urban addition in Doesburg, the Netherlands, 1999-2006, sketch, houses on the river

Ijsselkade urban addition in Doesburg, the Netherlands, 1999-2006, view of the river

Ijsselkade urban addition in Doesburg, the Netherlands, 1999-2006, sketch, the square

Terra
[Earth]

01. Like a big tree that digs its roots deep below the ground and raises its branches to the skies, architecture lies beneath the earth, on the soil and under the sky.
It lies below the soil, seeking a solid base on which to rest, and in the basement sets the storage for machinery and installations, and sources of energy. Underground it stores memories (in the archives) and objects (in the storage rooms).
The architect pushes his foundations inside the earth in search of the solid rock on which to build. "All is built on sand and nothing on stone, but we have to build on the sand as if it were stone." This is what Borges wrote, in one of his ambiguous fables. We seek the stone ("Tu es Petrus et super hanc petram aedificabo Ecclesiam meam" [You are Peter and upon this rock I will build my church]), as the secure foundation or else we entrust safety to a terrain that is made solid by a forest of poles. We build on a stone-solid forest... In the diversity of foundation techniques, lying on the earth, stuck into the soil, and digging its roots into the earth, architecture declares its physical relationship with mother earth.
Architecture resembles agriculture in its rapport with the soil. Just as the farmer cultivates the earth so that it yields fruits, likewise the architect cultivates the earth so that architecture can rise...
Architecture is a non-migratory activity, like that of farmers, and not of nomads, hunters and scavengers...
A great part of the new architecture is produced by the new nomads in transit towards the non-places, or by scavengers who, from the debris and wastes, extract unfinished and incomprehensible remains to be assembled into improbable *Merzbau*, or by untiring hunters chasing monsters, phantasmagoric animals, and mutants, rejoicing only in the killing of every residue of beauty, humanity, memory...

Ijsselkade urban
addition in Doesburg,
the Netherlands,
water colour, 2001

We seek a capacity to support a burden and endeavours, to then set architecture on the shoulders of the earth...
["L'architettura sta sulla terra", 2005]

02. *Hypogeal architecture*
There is a particular charm in hypogeal architecture, which consists not only in the mystery of cellars and basements, but in the sense of protection (refuge, bunker), a hiding place (where they will never find me), conquered spaces ("taken from something") in the bowels of the earth, cellars for wine, and cisterns for water...
The Salviatino cellar
It is a rectangular facility about 3.50 m underground having at its centre stocky pilasters in brick with a square base of 56x56 cm with base and capitals (*pulvino* or concrete saddles) in stone, a double series of depressed cross-vaults and four air-flow grill spouts on the outside from which light is drawn. Aeration is ensured by the four air vents (two on the long side, two on the opposite side) that open out on the roof. An internal drain channel system and small grooves under the floor keep the room dry. At the center of the square floor frames in stone there are grills with underlying storage pots. The temperature is more or less constant: 17° in winter, 18° in summer.
The entrance is a big, tiered ramp in stone. The cold air underground is arranged along the ramp like a lake and millworks allow an exchange with warm air above... which then rises and in the summer flows out from the skylight under the roof. Only in the hotter days is this movement helped with rotors (diffusers). This is an effective elementary passive air-conditioning system that ensures a temperature of about 24° in the big room of the studio with an outdoor temperature of 34°. But the attractiveness of the cellar does not only lie in its being a perfect bioclimatic machine, but in the beauty of its interior and wise construction, achieved by the ability of bricklaying masters who are able to cut the bricks into cross-vault ribs with mosaic hammers as they did 400 years ago. These were like those once laid in the vaults. Credit also goes to those who sculpted brackets and capitals designated to darkness (and cobwebs) of the cellars, and lit up only now and then by a lantern, so that everything, even the darkest corners, could be in a state-of-the-art condition.
And here, it was not even like in the sculptures hidden in the lofty pinnacles of cathedrals "Ad maiorem Dei gloriam" [To God's greater glory]...
Architecture has a physical and spiritual relationship with the earth. The "Bluth und Erde," soil and blood is not only an imperative of nationalism, nor is Heidegger's *genius loci* diffused by Norberg-Schulz.
["L'architettura sta sulla terra", 2005]

Ijsselkade urban addition in Doesburg, the Netherlands, 1999-2006, view towards the city

Il quaderno olandese

[Dutch sketchbook]

—

Reconstruction of Waagstraat in Groningen

1991-1996

In March 1991 the authorities of Groningen invited Adolfo Natalini to take part in a competition for the reconstruction of Waagstraat, a central area of the city between the fish market square and the main market square. The subject of the competition was the reorganization of the entire market square and the design of the Waagstraat area, taking into account the demolition of the Council office building and the conservation of the small Goudkantoor building (the gold exchange). The latter had been rebuilt after the destruction of the last world war, which had erased the other two blocks.
The competition project included the reconstruction of two blocks situated between Guldenstraat, Waagstraat and the back of the Town Hall, as well as the addition of a third block to the north, slightly indented in order to follow the movement of the square, with a passageway crossing through it which was to constitute the continuation of Waagstraat. The first block was assigned to housing, the second to social and cultural functions and the third to offices (an extension of the Town Halt). On the basis of the opinion expressed by two panels of judges and a referendum (in which Natalini obtained 83.6% of the votes) the council administration unanimously chose Natalini's design. After some modifications introduced in 1992 it was put into force, and lead to the creation of a rich urban fabric composed of blocks and squares. The residential block is formed by a base level taken up with double height shops, above which we have the entrance court to the two parallel residential bodies, with flats in the heads and twelve two-storey houses with mansards in the long wings.
The building for social and cultural functions is connected to the Goudkantoor by a metal structure loggia, with tall ramified columns supporting a transparent roof. This links Waagstraat with the small square behind the Council offices which has became the center of the new urban sector. The restaurant planned in the Goudkantoor and a new coffee house appear below the loggia.
On the ground floor of the office building there is a cylindrical structure containing the stairs situated in the passageway. The offices are distributed by double corridors and around the hollow stairway cylinder there are spacious waiting and meeting areas. The east and west heads of the building were designed as small towers to house the meeting rooms, and on the top floor we find the restaurant and nursery. The towers have stone facing and so they differ from the remaining buildings which are in fired brick, with some details in stone.

Comment on the Dutch projects. I would have liked to reach the Netherlands by sea, following the merchant routes of the Dutch Golden Age... I would have liked to see the low lands rise out of the sea, and explore the view of the bridges, the warehouses, and the docks... Then perhaps enter the city along the canals, patiently waiting at the locks and drawbridges.
At that time, the houses would have seemed so tall and the churches appeared to soar... However, I have always arrived in the Netherlands by air, each time trying to distinguish the limit between land and sea, between the original terra firma and the man-made terrain... Each time I reflected on how the Dutch have managed to change their geography, modifying land and sea, and that perhaps they were also able to change history as well... But if the first changes have been a necessity, the second is not... If the past continues to manage to generate the future, why reinvent it? Or forget it?

Architectural project
Adolfo Natalini /
Natalini Architetti (Florence)
with Corinne Schrauwen
Architectenburo
(Amsterdam);
Structural project
Ingenieursbureau Grabowsky
& Poort b.v. Groningen
Blaauw & Partners;
Installation design
Technical Management
Consulting Engineers b.v.
(Groningen);
Project manager
Architektenbureau Cor
Kalfsbeek b.v. (Borger);
Construction company
BAM (Groningen);
Client
Groningen Public
administration
and (MBO
and Nationale Nederlandse),
ING Vastgoed.

First prize in an international invitational competition, 1991.

Preliminary project, 1991-92;
Final project, 1993-94;
Working plan, 1994-95.

In collaboration with
Cor Kalfsbeek, Borger;
Construction, 1995-96.

De Zeven Pyramides,
Prize, 1998 (NL).

Photos: Mario Ciampi

Cottonfield
BC

HOUSE
OF CARLI GRY
Jackpot
by Carli Gry
Cottonfield
BY CARLI GRY

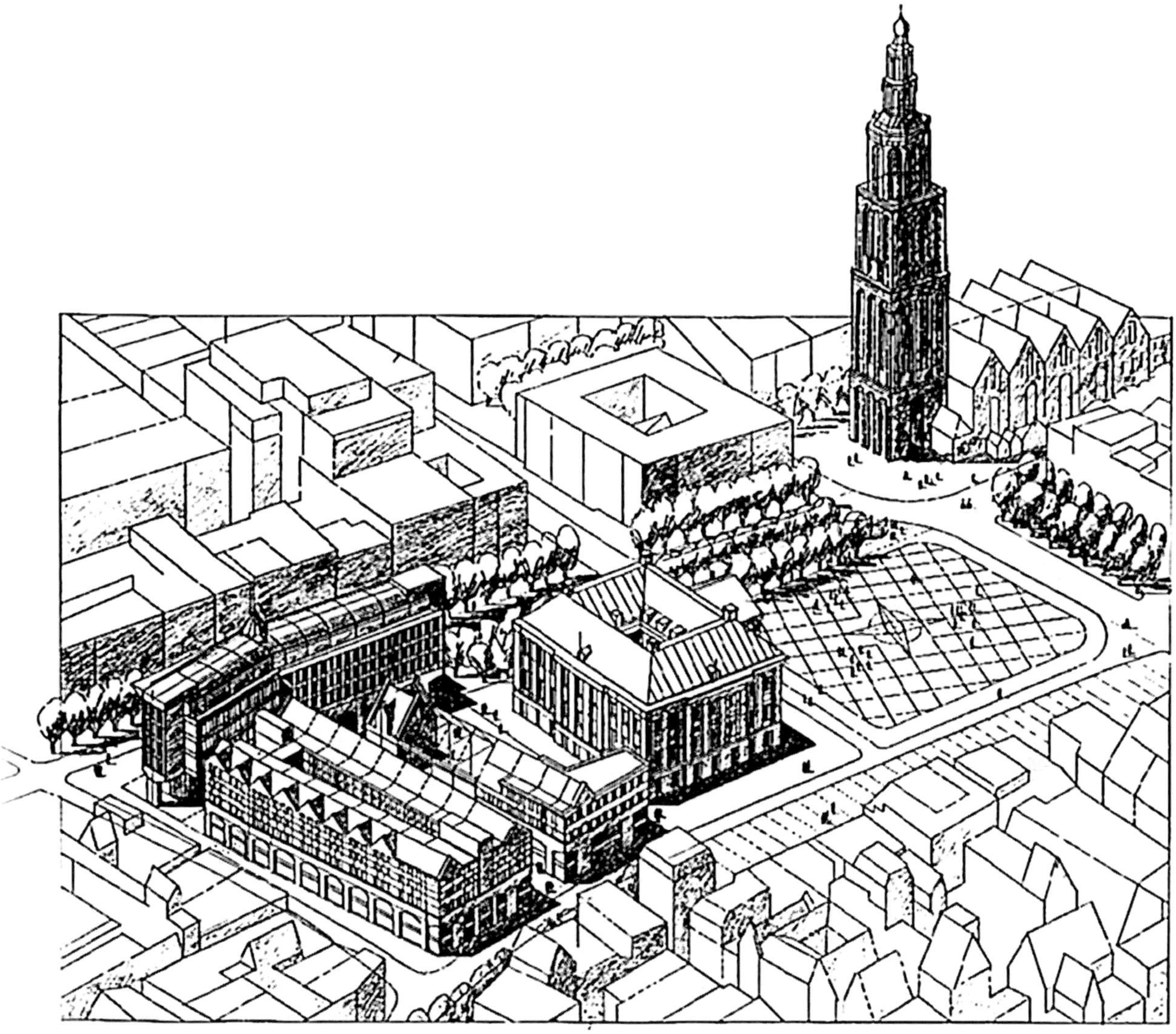

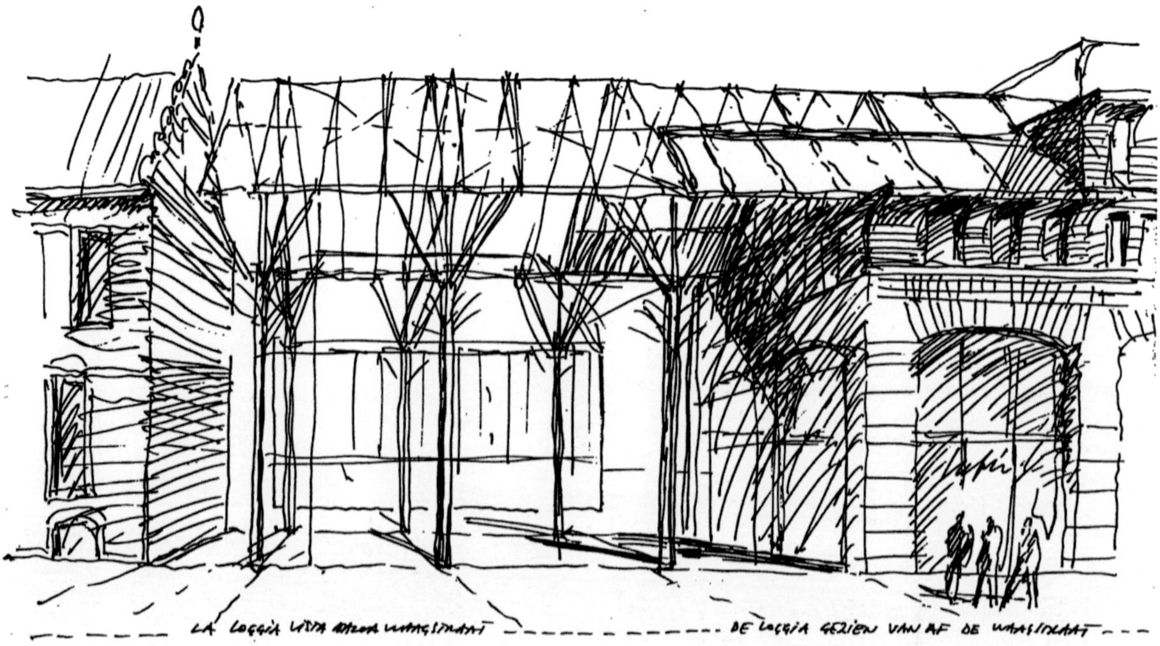
LA LOGGIA VISTA DALLA WAASSTRAAT
DE LOGGIA GEZIEN VANAF DE WAASSTRAAT

WAASSTRAAT KANTORENBLOK . NOORD/PASSAGE
3.93

FUJI FIL
SUPER PHOTO
Waagplein

SU RCLUB

TAXI
uitgezonderd
ecco
SALE

AN, 8.91

Musenplein Square and Clioplein Square in The Hague

1993-2000

In 1993 Studio Natalini was called to design a part of the De Resident (a central district of The Hague. destroyed by the events of the war), in accordance with the plan drawn up by Rob Krier. The block stands on the south-east edge of the old centre of the town. Its trapezoid form, delimited by multifaceted streets, was generated by a canal. It is situated on the border between the old part of the city, with its measured spaces (the Parliament is not very faraway), and the great buildings of the new city, and it is brushed to the south by the axe on which the plans for the new urban centre are aligned. Natalini was assigned the horseshoe-shaped Munzenplein (the square of fhe Muses), with an adjacent small hexagonal square and a round courtyard (Clioplein). It was as if the squares were dug into a dense block of residences, ranging from seven to thirteen storeys high. The design adhered to Kier's plan, which foresaw an extremely articulated city image in which the various typologies, from low houses to skyscrapers, were intertwined, mixing their different languages. Given the complex nature of the situation, embellishments and variations in the building units were discarded. Instead the plasticity of the whole was underlined with a simple and uniform treatment. The idea was that of a series of buildings unified by the facades facing the public space, subdivided according to the traditional distribution between base level, "piano nobile" (or intermediate floor) and attic floor. The differentiation between the three zones was obtained by a double height portico at the base level, and a series of recessions in the Attic floor.

At the point in which the Muzenplein ends against the hexagon and intersects with the new street, the tall houses continue the typology of the façades with a series of variations and a different roofing treatment. The texture of the façades is slightly three-dimensional, with a system of beams and strips in fired brick, underlined by white concrete elements at the intersections, while the empty spaces are occupied by perforations or loggias. The portico is supported by white concrete truncated cone pillars which end with capitals. The latter connect the arches to the fire brick framework. The façade is modulated following the rhythm of the city building fronts: a regular sequence of large windows, usually organized in groups of three. Horizontal bands of galleries run along the facades facing Clioplein, alternated with bands of windows, within a uniform grid. The facades on the internal courtyards appear more domestic and irregular due to the presence of stairs, balconies and galleries. All the building fronts are in fired brick with stamped concrete components and drawn fired brick elements made to design. The pillars of the portico are in face concrete, the tower ones have stone faring, while the roofing is in greeny blue pre-oxidized copper. The cladding of some of the brickwork on the top floors and below the porticoes is in the same material. The casing is in white-painted wood. The paving of the square is designed by lines generated by the architectural work, the course and the flow of the waters. The porticoes and external paths are paved with stone, while the other zones are in fired brick with a herring-bone pattern.

Architectural project
Adolfo Natalini /
Natalini Architetti (Florence)
with Corinne Schrauwen
Architectenburo
(Amsterdam);
Structural project
Arcadis (The Hague);
Installation design
BAM-TBI (The Hague);
Project manager
Arcadis (The Hague);
Construction company
BAM-TBI (The Hague);
Client
MAB BV (The Hague).

Preliminary project, 1993-94;
Final project, 1995;
Working plan, 1995-96;
Beginning of construction,
1996-2001.

Photos: Pietro Savorelli

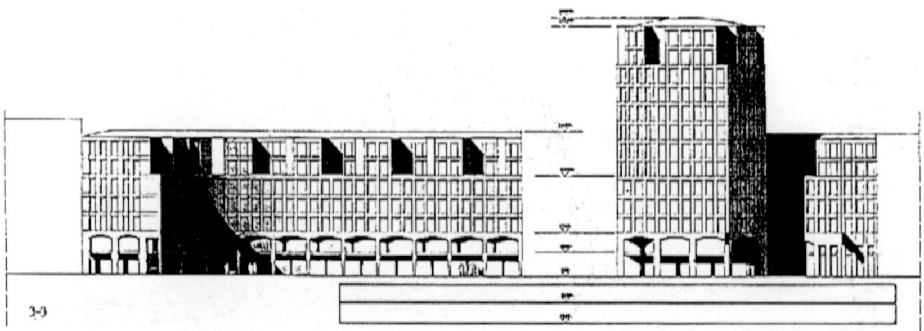
3-3

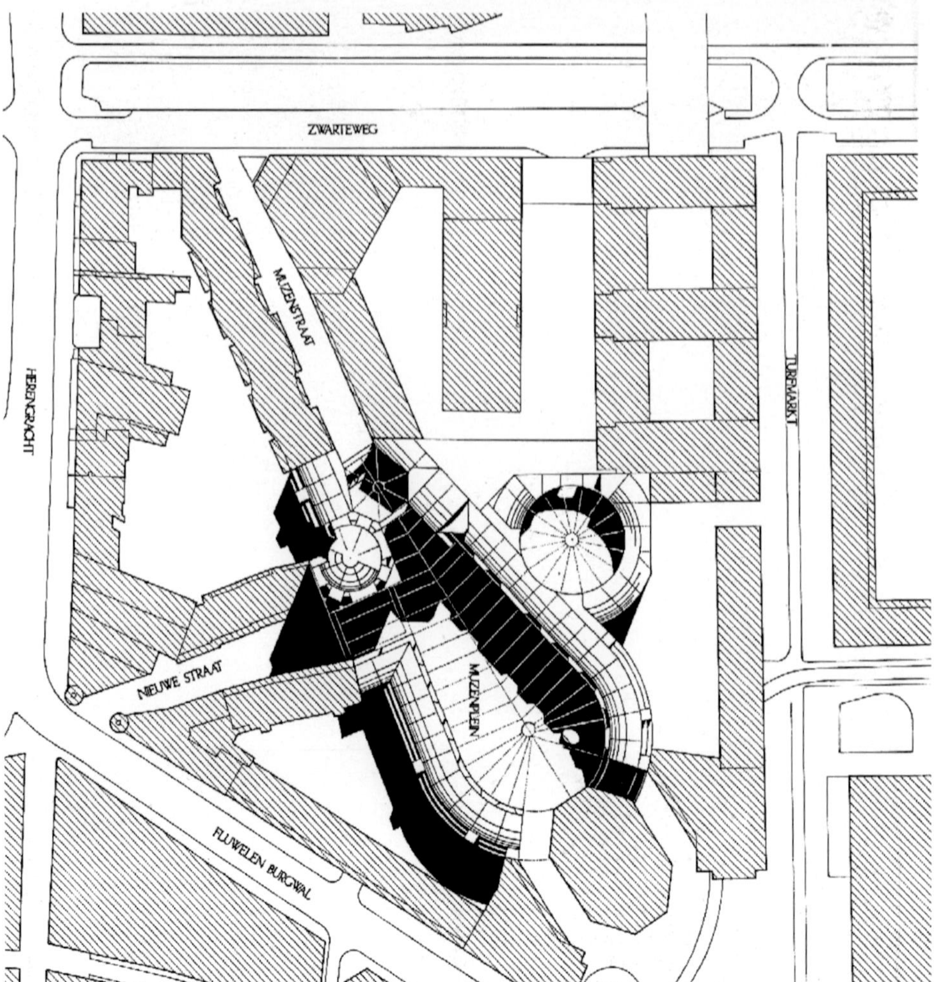
ZWARTEWEG
MUZENSTRAAT
HERENGRACHT
TURFMARKT
NIEUWE STRAAT
MUZENPLEIN
FLUWELEN BURGWAL

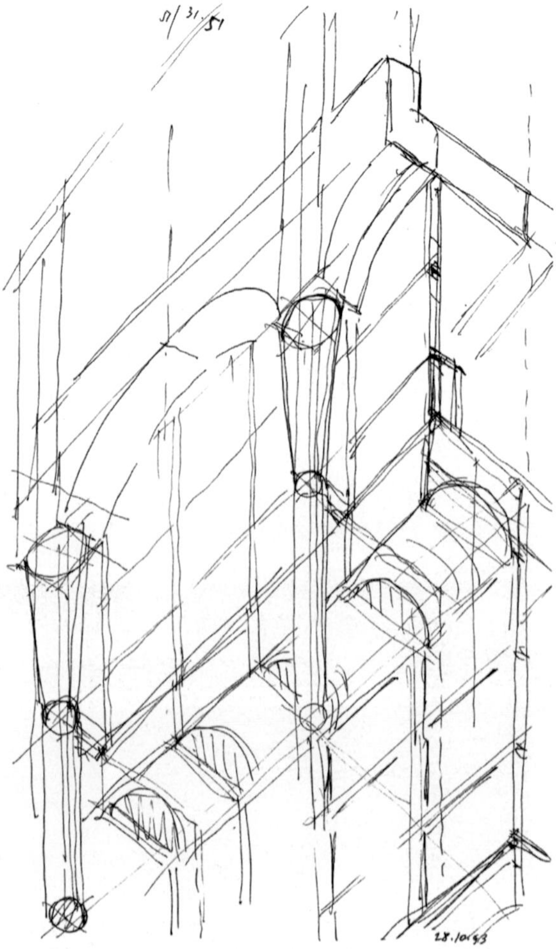
28.10.93

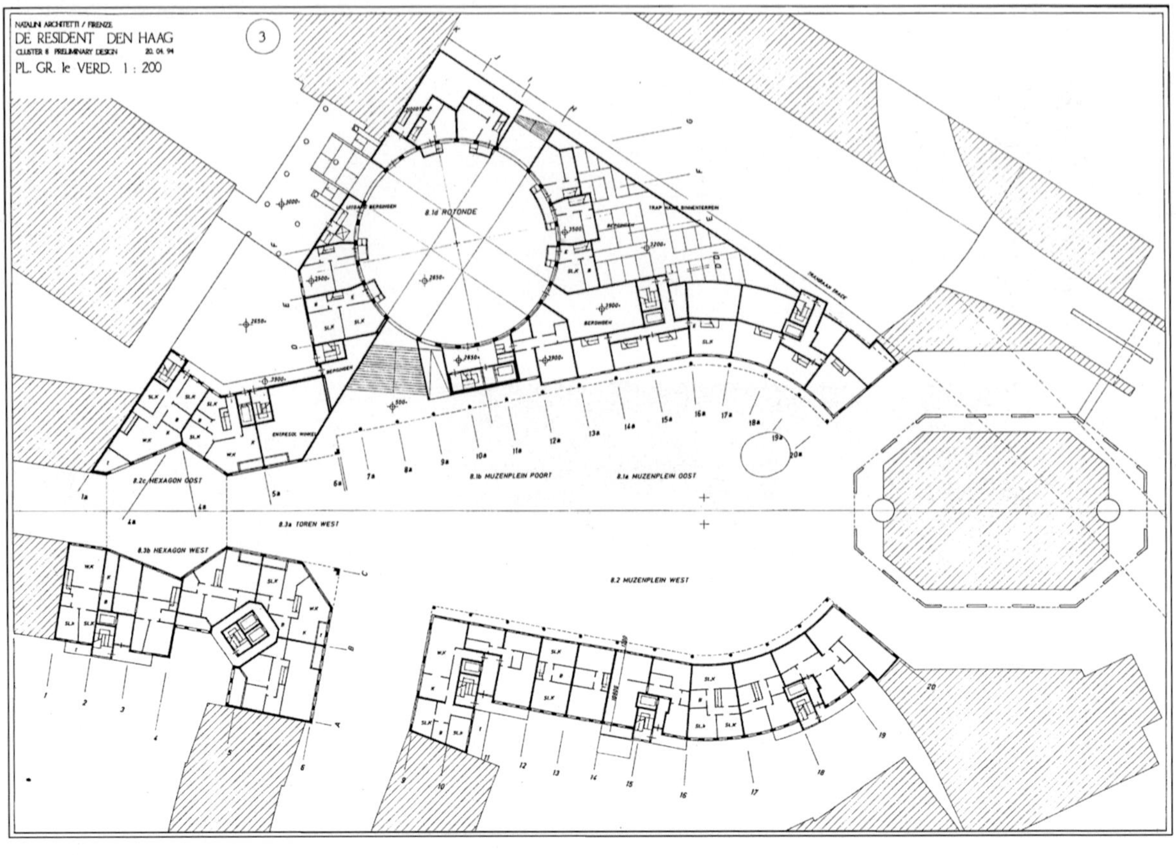
NATALINI ARCHITETTI / FIRENZE
DE RESIDENT DEN HAAG
CLUSTER 8 PRELIMINARY DESIGN 20. 04. 94
PL. GR. le VERD. 1 : 200
3
8.1d ROTONDE
8.2c HEXAGON OOST
8.3a TOREN WEST
8.3b HEXAGON WEST
8.1b MUZENPLEIN POORT
8.1a MUZENPLEIN OOST
8.2 MUZENPLEIN WEST

Frisia
Makelaars
070
342 01 01

Boscotondo in Helmond

1995-2001

The Boscotondo complex, composed of residences and public buildings, was built following an international competition regarding an industrial area no longer in use (Begemann area), south-west of Helmond Castle. The land on which the Begemann industries stood is a large trapezium of about three hectares, and the only surviving memory of the old occupants of the area is a villa on the south-west corner; surrounded by a beautiful tree plantation. The design is an attempt to bring nature back into this area, reinstating, where possible, the pleasant appearance it had before it became an industrial zone. A circular clearing with a diameter of about 120 meters is created in the centre of the area with a thicket in the middle (Boscotondo). The residences, divided into three bodies, are arranged in a ring around the clearing. The ring is broken on the north-east corner where, in accordance with the directives of the Hasterplan. the public buildings are placed. Other residences are positioned along the canal, leaving a large triangular green area on the south-east corner, as the ideal continuation of the greenery around the castle. A bike path crosses the area. The public buildings are positioned at the corner between Kanaaldijk and the Traverse and they look onto a small open square which penetrates with one corner into the thicket. This is an attempt to find a mix between the small paved square populated by Roberto Barni's sculptures and the Boscotondo. Visitors to the Council offices enter the double height hall through an entrance rotunda. The areas for the office workers are on the floor above, and on the next floor again we have the Council board room, which is split-level with an elliptical plan, and the committee and Council group rooms. The space of the hall forms a kind of corner tower. On the ground floor the Bioskoop has a coffee house which looks onto the canal (which can be extended towards the square), a large double height hall and five cinema halls.
The hall has a large curved glass wall which leads to the entrance rotunda of the museum. This structure, with a truncated roof, contains the ticket office, the bookshop and the toilets, and from here we enter the exhibition rooms of the city museum. Even though the public buildings are integrated in an articulated complex, each one has its own identity. The materials used are stone on the ground floor and brick with stamped concrete elements on the upper floors.
The large glass walls of the hall, the Bioskoop and the office entrance rotunda have a metal structure. All the roofing is in green copper. The residences have a raised ground floor with grass slope pathways, and they are divided into five blocks with various flat typologies and different orientations. Even though a certain homogeneity has been maintained in terms of the linguistics and materials, there was an attempt to characterize the different blocks with a series of variations. The external walls are in face brick with stamped concrete elements; some parts such as the balconies, the galleries and the loggias are in stone.

Project
Natalini Architetti (Florence) with Corinne Schrauwen Architectenburo (Amsterdam);
Collaborating team
Nazario Scelsi,
Marco Magni,
Adrian Blanchard,
Damiano Pica,
Giovanna Potestà,
Stefano Tozzi (Florence),
Jaëla van Tijn,
Philip Breedveld,
Jos Roodbol,
Flavia Bindo (Amsterdam);
Structural project
Tielemans Bouwwithstructie (Eindhoven);
Electrical installation design
Ingenieursbureau Nelissen (Eindhoven);
Project management
De Bever Architekten (Eindhoven);
Construction company
Hurks Bouw & Vastgoed (Eindhoven);
Client
Helmond Municipal Administration and Hurks Bouw & Vastgoed, Eindhoven,
Pathé Cinemas, Vitalis Zorggroep.

First prize in an international invitational competition, 1995.

Preliminary project, 1997;
Final residential project, 1997;
Final public building project, 1998;
Beginning of construction, 1998;
End of construction with artwork installation, 2001.

Photos: Pietro Savorelli

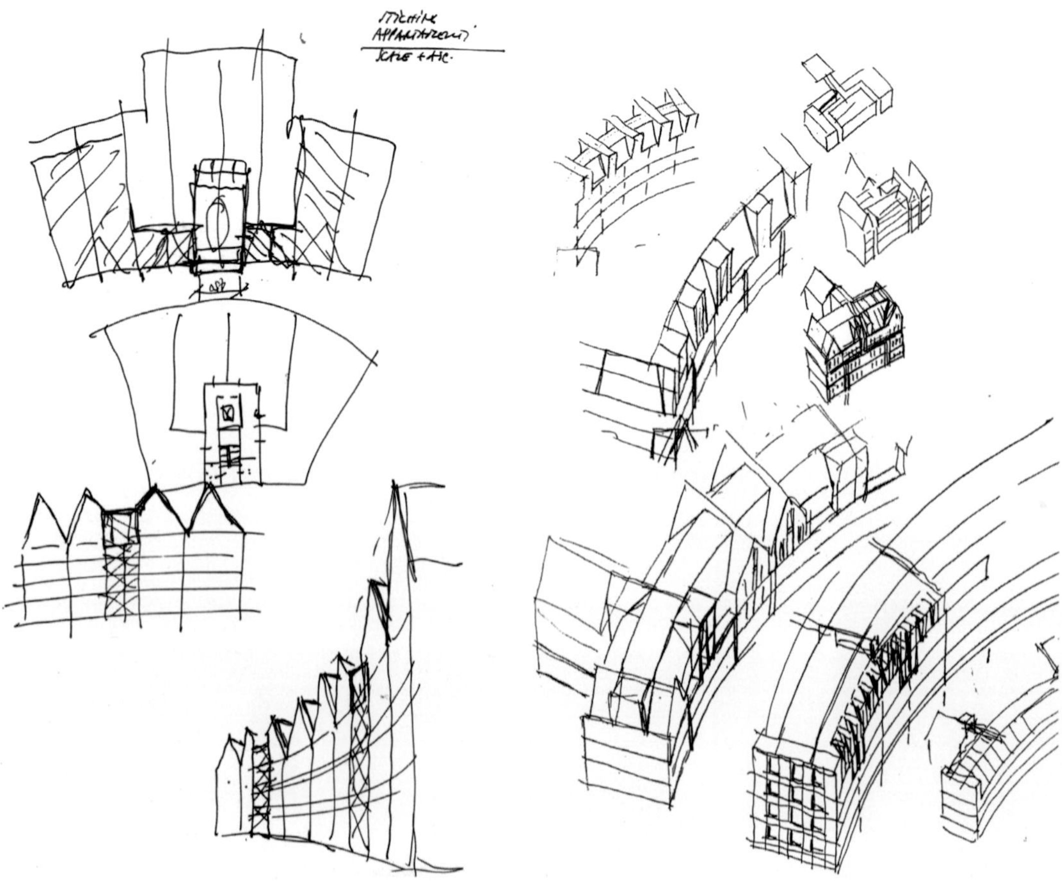

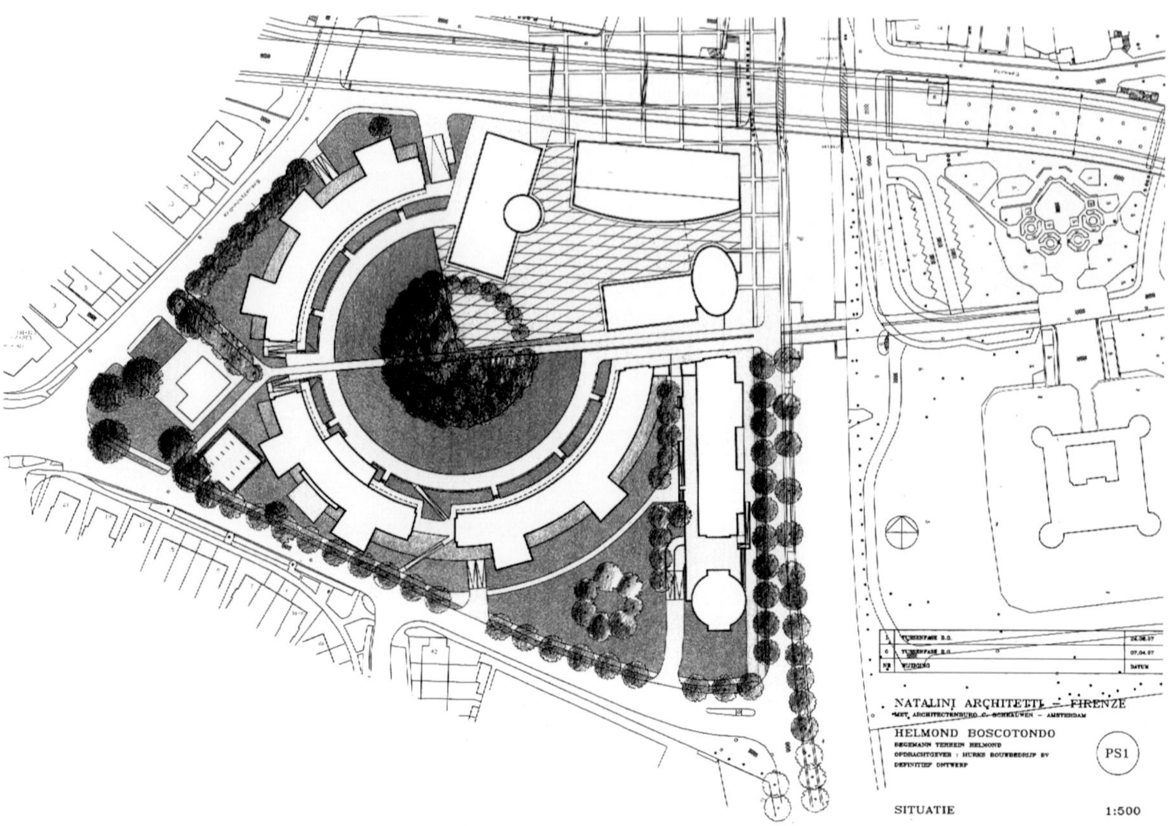
TUSSENFASE D.O. 24.06.97
TUSSENFASE D.O. 07.04.97
NR WIJZIGING DATUM
NATALINI ARCHITETTI – FIRENZE
MET ARCHITECTENBURO C. SCHRAUWEN – AMSTERDAM
HELMOND BOSCOTONDO
BEGEMANN TERREIN HELMOND
OPDRACHTGEVER : HURKS BOUWBEDRIJF BV
DEFINITIEF ONTWERP
PS1
SITUATIE
1:500

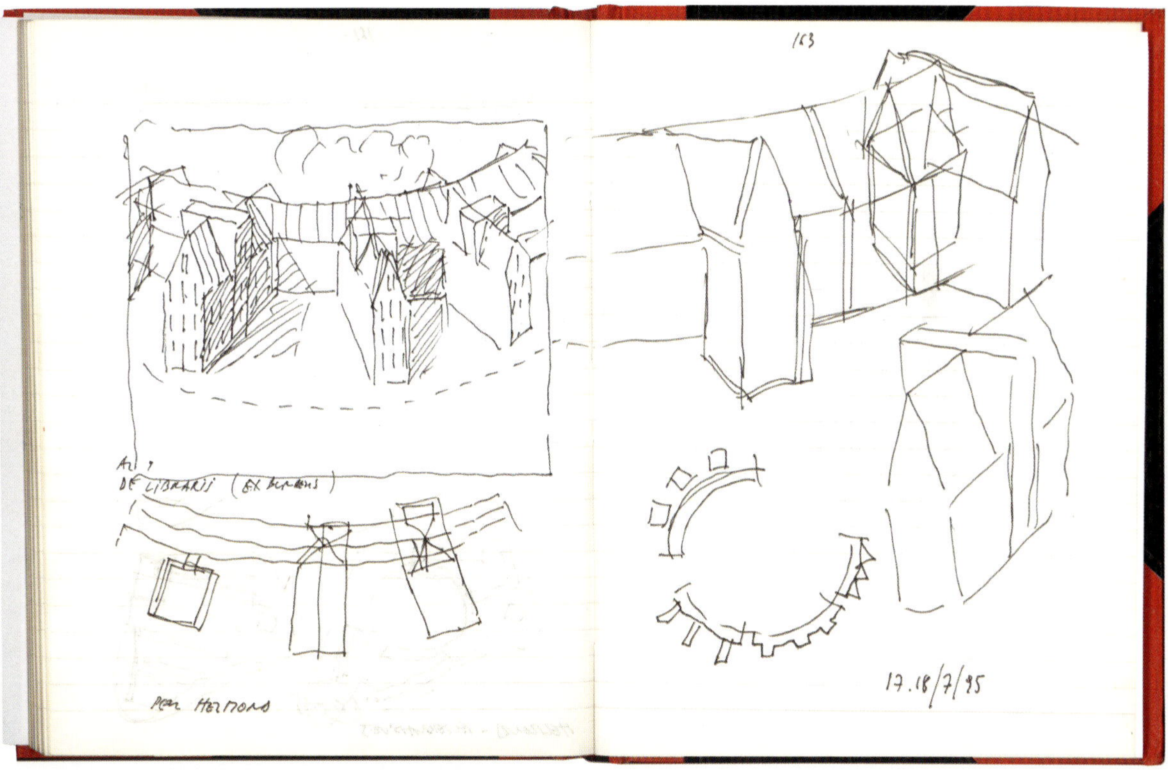
17.18/7/95

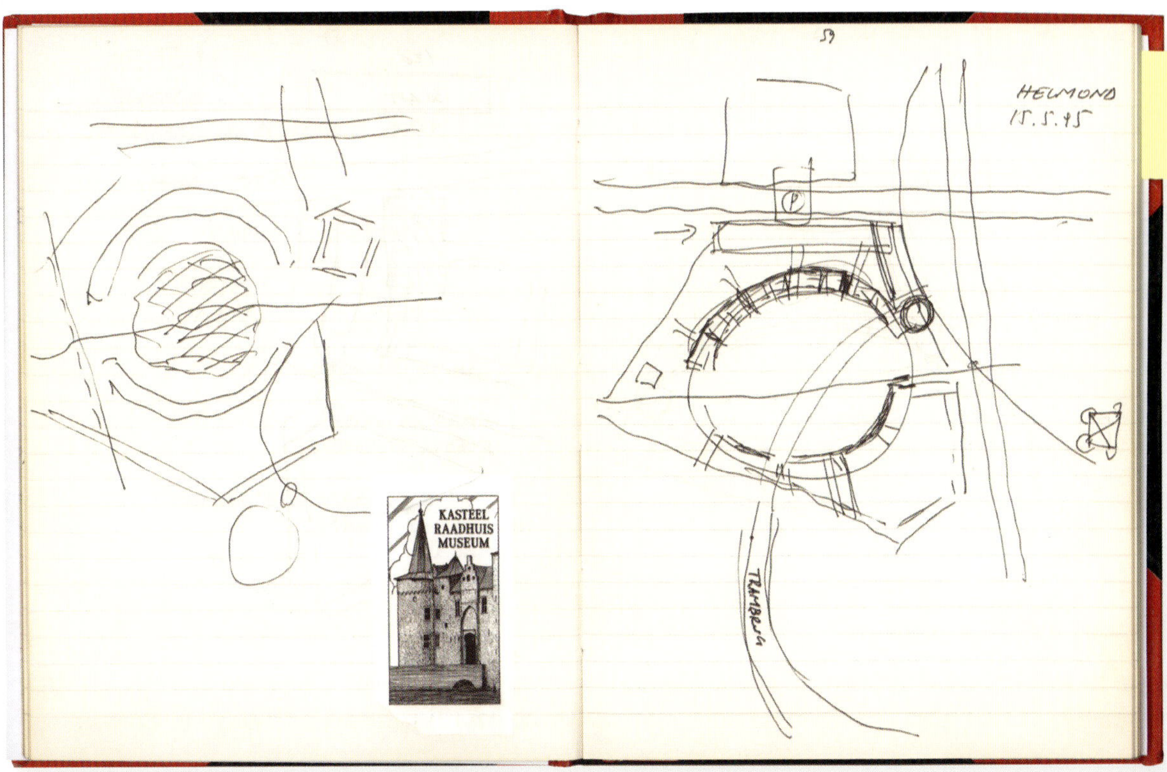
HELMOND
15.5.95
KASTEEL
RAADHUIS
MUSEUM

Het Eiland in Zwolle

1996-2001

Project
Natalini Architetti
with Roy Gelders;
Client
ING Vastgoed (The Hague).

Photos: Pietro Savorelli

Zwolle is a town on the meanders of the Ijssel; the quarter of the island (Het Eiland) has been destroyed at the end of the sixties. It was a working-class neighborood, poor but pleasant, inhabited by merchants, street vendors, street musicians, and knife grinders with several small factories and warehouses, similar to the Jourdaan in Amsterdam. The neighborood was situated between the big church of Broederen, the town walls on the canal (thorbeckegracht) and the old course of the river Aa, next to the old town centre, where in the meanwhile several shopping centers have been built.
Roy Gelder's project of 1994 included the reconstruction of a group of commercial areas and residences, but the Superintendent and the "Friends of the town" refused this project and asked Natalini to draw up a new project, which had to be closer to the characteristics of the old town centre.
A new project was developed between 1996 and 1998. This project intended to reconstruct the historical street network with little improvements in order to enlarge the sight of historical elements like the Pelsen Tower and the church.
The complex included three blocks with different characteristics, shops (on the ground and first floors) with residences located above (with one or two floors) around the roof gardens. The frontage on the canal side consisted of a sequence of one-floor houses, which ended with a protruding house on shelves (also called the medieval house). This takes up the motif of the guard crossing of the town walls that are interrupted in correspondence of the church. It was a pedestrian precinct, cars and bikes had to be parked in a big underground car park. The irregular streets, the variations of the profiles and the different architectures created an effect of complexity similar to the historical town. Irregular elements stressed some nodal points of the routes.
The project took under scrutiny the reconstruction of a historical building, the Red Cock (de Roo Haen) with sculptures of Philip Pingboons, but this idea was subsequently dropped and it became instead the inspiration for new houses. Works begun on 10th November 1999 and the first shops opened on 15th November 2001. The first reactions of Zwolle's inhabitants about the reconstruction have been of enthusiasm. On the occasion of its official inauguration the town published a book that illustrates the quarter's history – and the stories of its last inhabitants between 1935 and 1965 with a collection of interviews. A project of "urban reparation", based more on evocation than on reconstruction, has given back a lost part to the old town centre... A section of old town centre that had vanished has recovered a new charm.

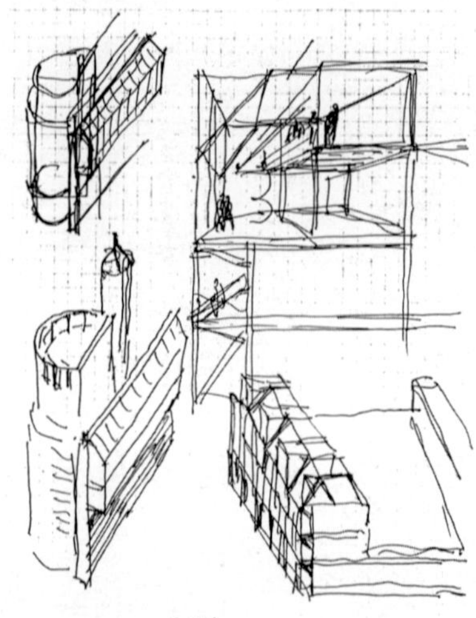

11.11.96

Eiland

SIEBEL
SIEB
SIEBEL
BUINING

1
2
3
4
ZWOLLE
10.9.98

PERRY
PERRY
ZONE
WAANDERS
WAANDERS

WAANDERS
boekverkopers
WAANDERS
boekverkopers
WAANDERS
WAANDERS
WAANDERS

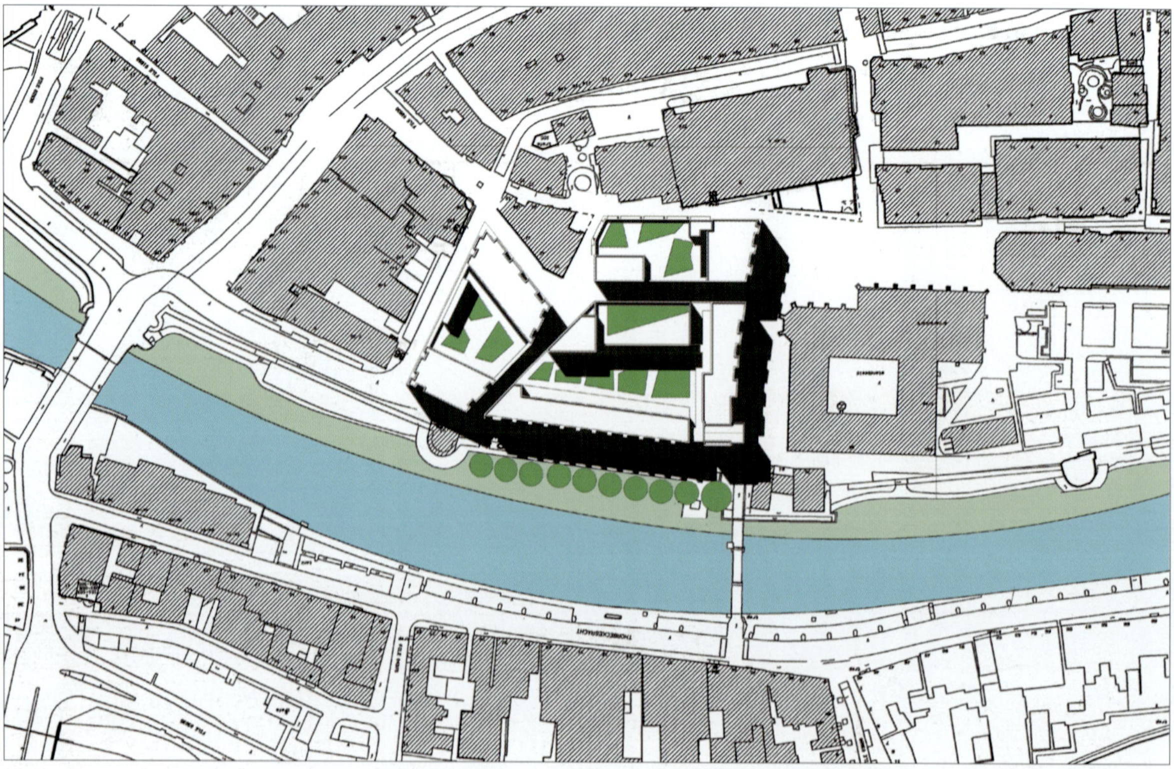

Haverleij Castle in Den Bosch

1997-2001

North-west of 's-Hertogenbosch, between the villages of Engelen and Bokhoven, where the river Maas (Meuse) forms a great bend and a canal joins it to the Dieze, stands Haverleij, a flat green land of about 200 hectares, rescued from the waters and protected by a bank. The plan for Haverleij, drawn up by Sjoerd Soeters and a group of landscape designers, invented a new landscape with bars of wood-land, chessboard arrangements of trees, green circles and triangles, a mixture between natural and artificial. The plan foresaw a large 27 hole golf course, a woodland area, a nature reserve and about 1000 houses, 600 of which united in a village on the lock and the others divided into groups of 60, named "walled villages', positioned at the intersections of a regular grid superimposed on the new landscape. During a seminar to which I had been invited, along with some other architects, I said that I was against the plan (in my opinion too artificial) and I proposed building a road which would connect the two existing villages and suggested to place groups of houses there, superimposing and naturally integrating the greenery, the road and the building complex. My proposal was turned down, however to my surprise I was asked to design a "walled village" inside a small lake (walled village no. 9, known as *swan lake*). I had started working on the "walled village" which the plan took as the ideal model for the groups of houses; I had considered it as a fantastic machine and as a metaphor of the separation between an external reality (chaos) and an internal one (cosmos). I had started to consider the first natural shelters and then the increasingly more complex constructions where the combination of cosmology, geometry and balistics, through Francesco di Giorgio Martini' s work, had arrived at the great star figures of Vauban and (in the Netherlands) of Menno Van Cochoorn. Walled villages no longer have strategic purposes, but purely seductive ones and the walls (see what has happened in Lucca or Ferrara) protect the quality of the city and life... I transformed the diagrams of walled villages and fortifications into a mixtilinear sketch where a gate and a demilune, a semicircular bastion and watts with corner towers were organized. I imagined that the houses had leant against the fortifications and that they had gradually conquered and replaced them.
So in the end there was an enchanted enclosure with water outside and a court-garden inside. The houses are made with bricks of different colors: darker in the parts in contact with the water, redder in the upper parts. The houses at the gates and towers are in stone, with some walls with zinc facing, like all the roofing.

Project
Natalini Architetti (Florence) with Corinne Schrauwen Architectenburo (Amsterdam);
Collaborating team
Nazario Scelsi,
Adrian Blanchard,
Damiano Pica (Florence),
Jaëla van Tijn,
Flavia Bindo (Amsterdam);
Structural project
Raadgevend Ingenieursburo Van Nunen (Rosmalen);
Installation design
N.V.T.;
Construction company
Hurks;
Client
Bouwfonds Woningbouw BV (Eindhoven).

Preliminary project, 1998;
Final project, 1999;
Working plan, 2000;
Construction, 2001-02.

Photos: Pietro Savorelli

16.8

19.8.97

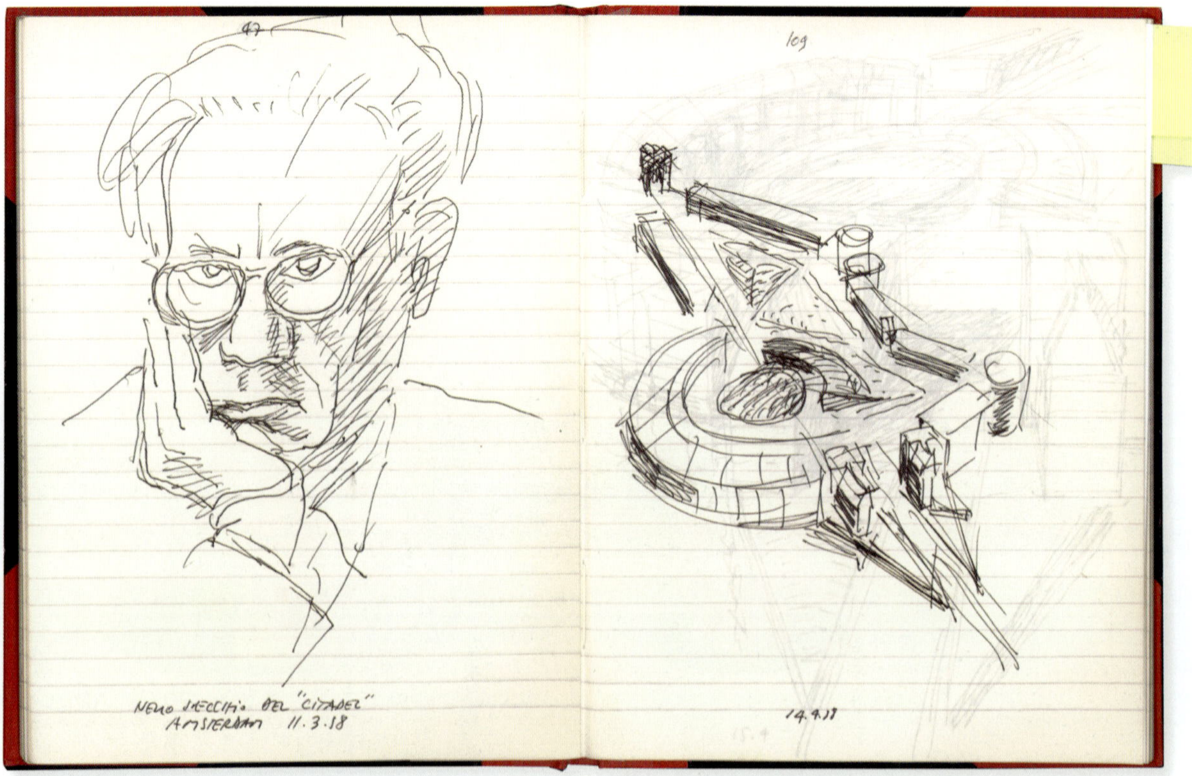

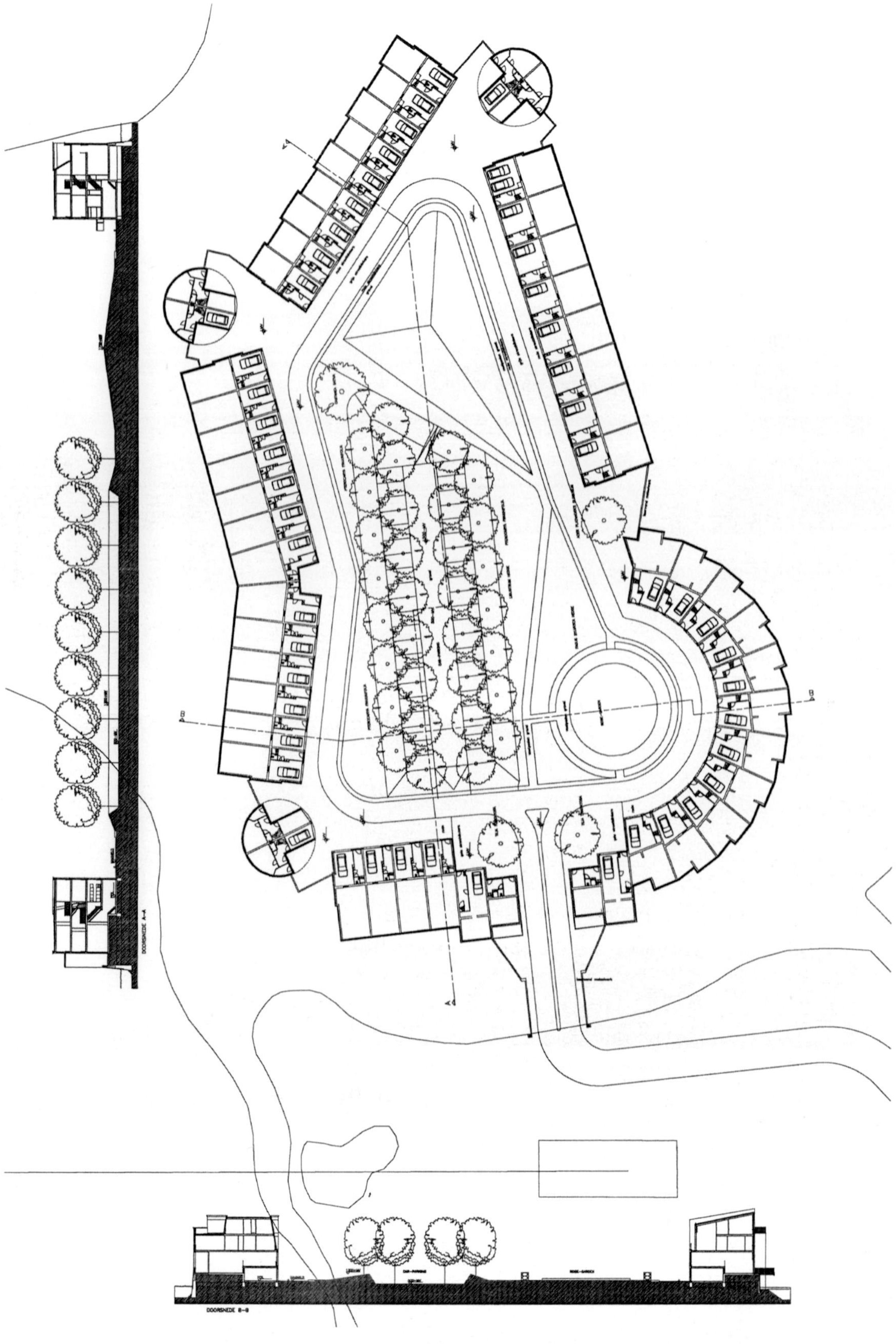

Ijsselkade urban extension in Doesburg

1999-2006

Doesburg is an historic Dutch town on the Jissel river, which once was surrounded by fortifications. The city has regained the prospect on the river thank to this project, which has won an open competition.
Those who approach the river from the centre of Doesburg, on the other side of the tree-line following the bank of the new canal, can see a regular row of houses with pointed roofs. The row is not continuous, but is interrupted and allows the sight on the river for those who come from Veerpoortstraat. More north the row is interrupted by a new square with trees. So one's eyes are turned towards the river, which for a long time has been separated from the town by the factories and the warehouses along its bank. Following the canal northwards the visitor will find a new bridge leading to the tree square, a trapezoidal space lengthened towards the river, with long sides made of two groups of symmetrical houses. A building is situated on the left side towards the river. This building is higher than the others and has a shape reminding of a slender ship. The embankment, which has been projected by the landscape architects of Okra, is composed of a long avenue partly with trees, with a large flight of steps going down towards the river bank at the level of the exposed perspective of Veerpoortstraat and of a passage on the bank. The embankment is about 400 in long and will be the preferred place of the town to regain the river. There will be situated a series of pleasant activities, passages, places for breaks and observation of the river and of its life, places for fishing and boating. An orthogonal square of the river divides the project in two islands: the island south is divided in three parts by an orthogonal passage toward the river and by another passage on the axis of Veerpoortstraat. The island north is divides by a smaller street parallel to the river, ending with the square. As a result there are five blocks, three south and two north with gardens and courts. The fifth block will be taken by a Hotel, with a Grancafe-restaurant and a terrace on the square. The various blocks have therefore a different composition on the street side and a different image on the square side. We have tried to produce a maximum of variety through the urban design taking advantage of the curve and inclination of the fronts and their interruption, with the insertion of different typologies. The front on the river gives the image of a town border, similar to a fortification with a barrage with towers and gates. But this fortified aspect is actually made of house facades, exposed on the river with loggias and windows with different orientations in order to allow the best sight. The front towards the town is calmer and more homelike with a series of lower houses with pointed roofs. The tower on the dam has a tapered shape on the plan, like a boat, and its major height characterizes it as a Landmark on the river. The block on the corner must be defined more accurately on the base of the hotel managers programs, but its shape and the division in three parts has already been fixed. One part will be lower and public with a terrace on the roof which is enlarged and allows a better point of view on the river. Finally a plastic element (similar to a lighthouse) can be placed on the terrace. This will allow to go up to the terrace from the lower level of the square and to come down from the upper level of the clam. It could be a work of art such as a luminous sculpture or a ray of light.

Project
Natalini Architetti (Florence) with Corinne Schrauwen Architectenburo (Amsterdam) (Selected for the Gelderse Prijs 2006);
Collaborating team
Nazario Scelsi, Adrian Blanchard, Damiano Pica (Florence), Jaëla van Tijn, Flavia Bindo (Amsterdam);
Town planning
Teun Koohlaas Architecten (Almere);
Landscaping project
Okra Landscapsarchitecten (Utrecht) (Betonprijs 2001 prize for public space);
Structural project
Corsmit Raadgevend Ingenieursbureau BV (Rijswijk);
Installation design
Cauberg-Huygen Raadgevend Ingenieurs (Zwolle);
Construction company
Moes Bouwbedrijf Ost BV (Zwolle);
Client
Doesburg Municipal Administration and Johan Matser Projectonwikkeling (Hilversum).

First prize in an international invitational competition, 1998.

Preliminary project, 1998-99;
Final project, 2000-01;
Working plan, 2001-02;
Construction, 2003-05;
End of construction with artwork installation, 2006.

Photos: Raoul Suermondt

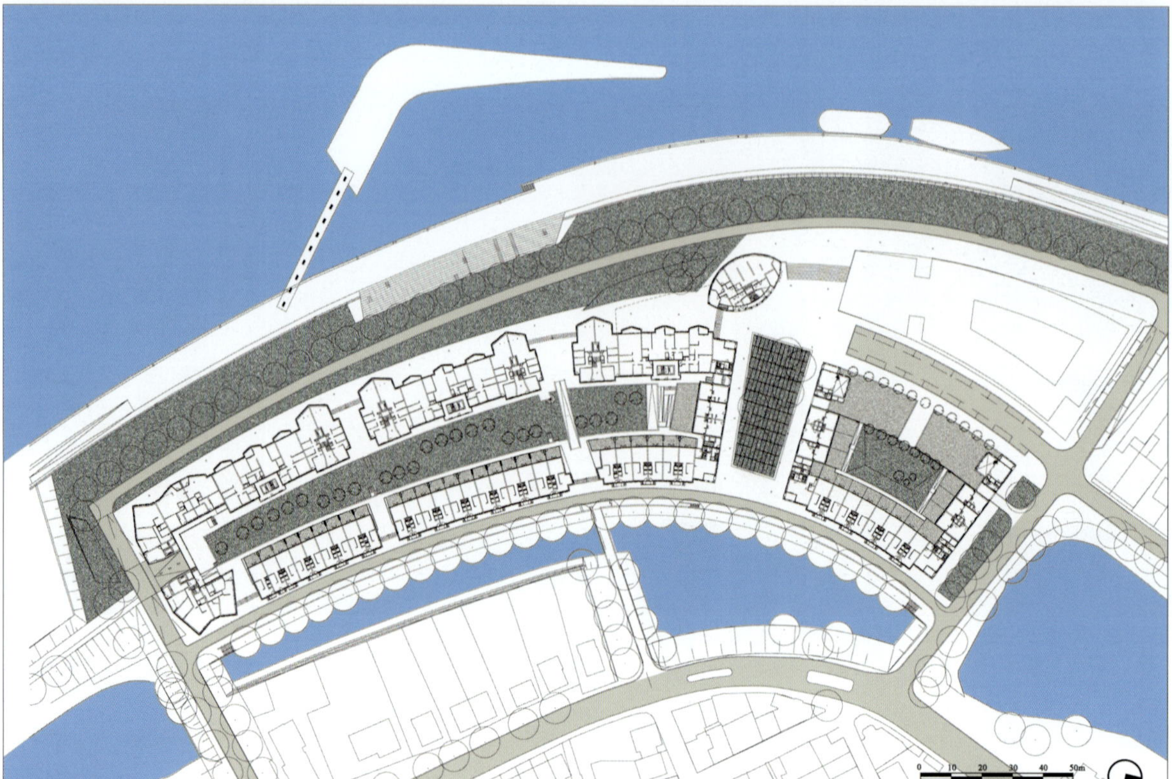
0 10 20 30 40 50m
N

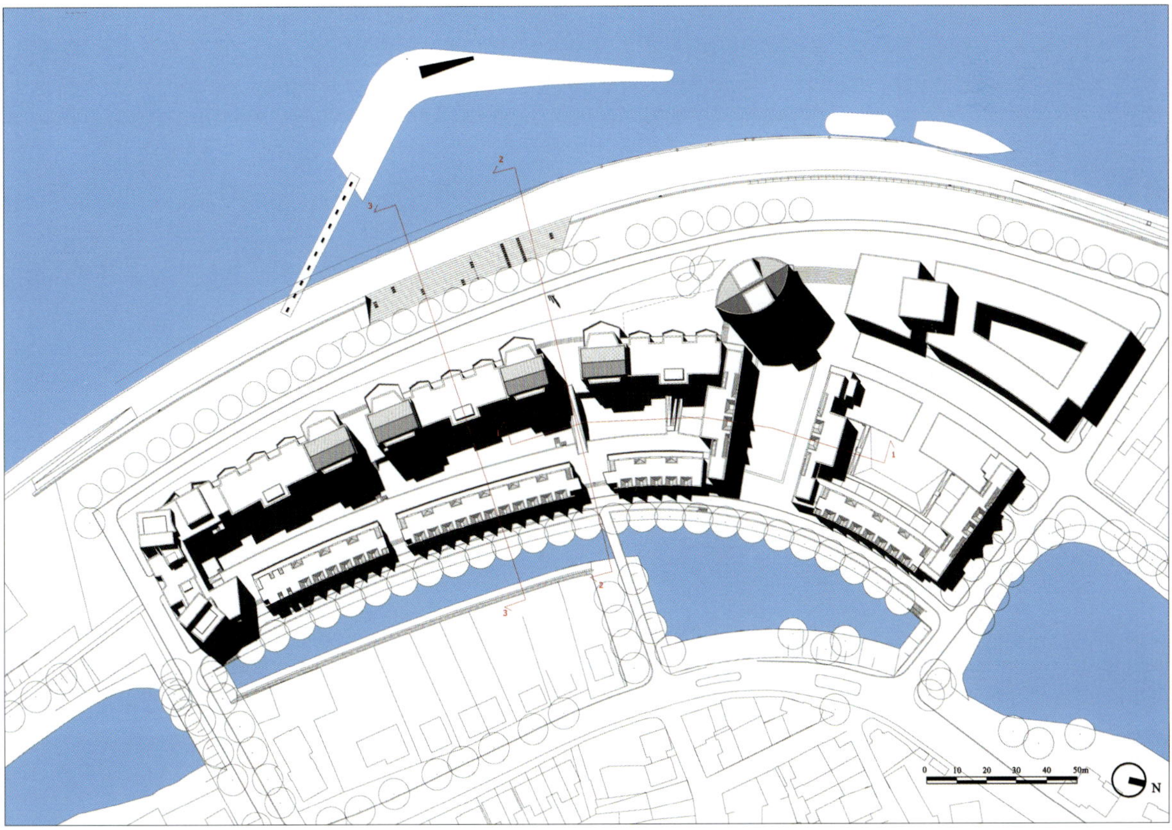
0 10 20 30 40 50m
N

RIPENSANDO IJSSELKADE A DOESBURG GRACHTWONINGEN

07.05

CASE SUL

Buitenop and the Natalinitoren offices

1999-2010

Roermond is on the Roer, where it joins the left shore of the Meuse.
The historical town still preserves its visible profile within the outlines of the walls and the gates. Anyone who arrives in Roermond from the west can see the town's delicate profile with the tower of the cathedral (Sint Christoffel) and the twin spires of the Munsterkerk.
At present the approach to the town across the Maasburg is faster (Hornerweg), and since 1992 the town's profile has been changed by a group of new buildings (Maasover, Tower of Oranjerie, the SIB Bank). On the other hand it is difficult to stop before the bridge in order to observe the ancient skyline of the town: we only can do it with the eyes of fantasy and with historical memory, comparing the old skyline with the new one...
But each town is a living organism in evolution and changes are inevitable: we only have to avoid that the new landscapes make us miss the old ones. This is certainly a difficult task for the town planner and for the architect: things that exist for long times are part of us and of the collective memory and new things are always seen as a traumatic removal of the memory. Existing things have the legitimation of long times, new things have still too short times...
A triangular plot of land, like a sort of peak of the town between the two rivers is situated where the Roer and the Meuse meet. The plot of land is bordered by the Roer (and by the Looskade) on the west, by the Buitenop on the east and by the bank of the Maasburg on the north. The land keeps thus a visible connection with the historical town, even if it has been "lowered" by the superstructure of the road bridge.
On the base of the bridge a little tower for offices has been planned. The tower has a mixtilinear plan with an elliptical base and two cylinders placed side by side with less a polygonal part on the superior floors. The two cylinders end with two cusps.
The tower is made of bricks, with a regular structure of apertures; the cusps and the central part are covered with metal (pre-oxidized copper or zinc).
The position of the tower has been carefully studied in order not to interfere with the tower of the cathedral, and this way we have tried to answer the prescriptions of the "Atlas Voor Ruimtelijke Kwaliteitszorg". The tower attaches the profile of the town to the Roer. It tries to balance the new high buildings that were raised south of the cathedral and guarantees to the tower of Sint Christoffel its rule of central element, visual fulcrum of the new skyline. In accordance with the profile and the materials of the tower a new building of the Square Gebouw has been studied in order to complete the town planning scheme of the area in a harmonious way. The slight bending of the front of this building takes up the bending of the "Centrum Poor Arbeid en Inkomen" (CAI) and of the tower with the intention to increase the sensation of fluidity of the whole, as if the water of the rivers had sculpted the buildings.

OFFICE BUILDING (BUITENOP III) IN ROERMOND, 1999-2002

Project
Natalini Architetti (Florence) with Corinne Schrauwen Architectenburo (Amsterdam);
Structural project
VSM Engineering (Heythuysen);
Installation design
Utiwith & Dynatherm BV (Eindhoven);
Project management
Van Sambeek BV (Eindhoven);
Construction company
Aannemersbedrijf Luois Scheepers (Roermond);
Client
Buitenop BV Roermond.

Preliminary project, 2000-01; Final project and working plan, 2001-02; Construction, 2002.

Photos: Pietro Savorelli

OFFICE TOWER (NATALINITOREN) IN ROERMOND, 1999-2010

Project
Natalini Architetti (Florence) with Corinne Schrauwen Architectenburo (Amsterdam), Abken Schrauwen, Architecten Ijsselstein;
Structural project
VSM Engineering (Heythuysen);
Installation design
Utiwith Installatieadvies (Eindhoven);
Project management
M.J.A. Van Sambeek (Leende);
Construction company
Luois Scheepers (Roermond);
Client
Buitenop BV Roermond, Van Pol Beheer (Roermond).

Preliminary project, 2001-08; Final project and working plan, 2008-09; Construction, 2009-10.

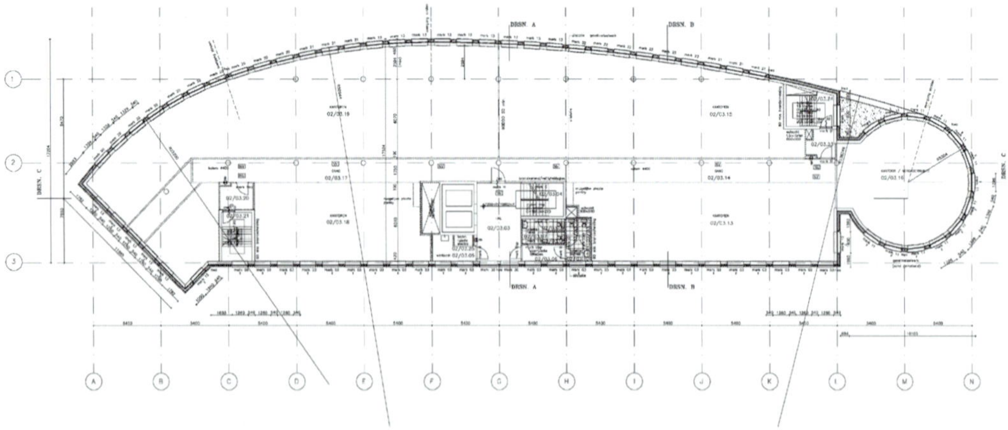

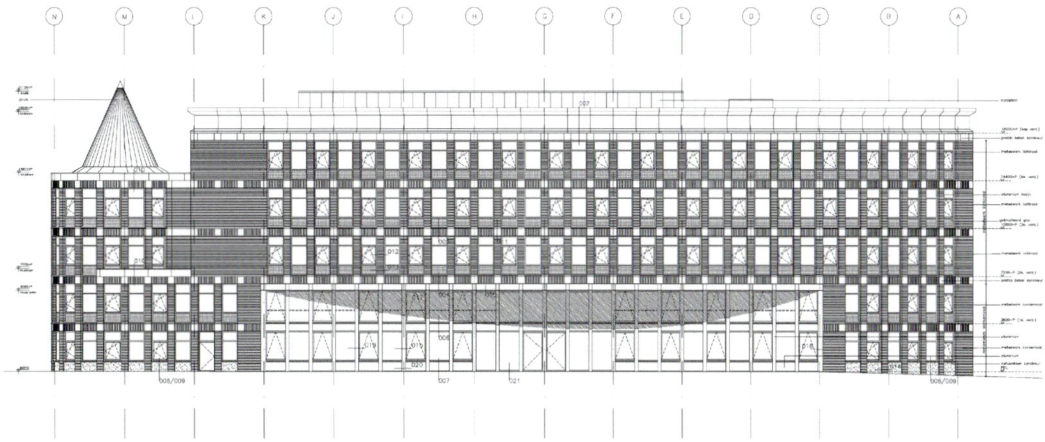

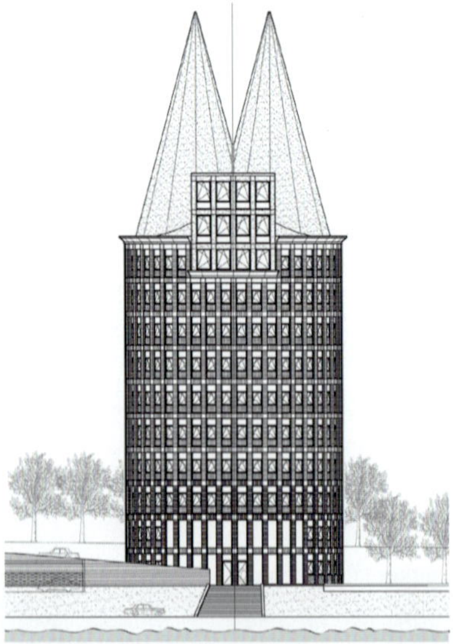

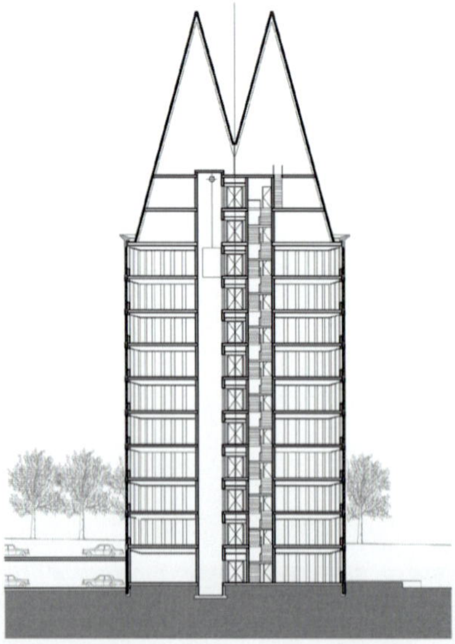

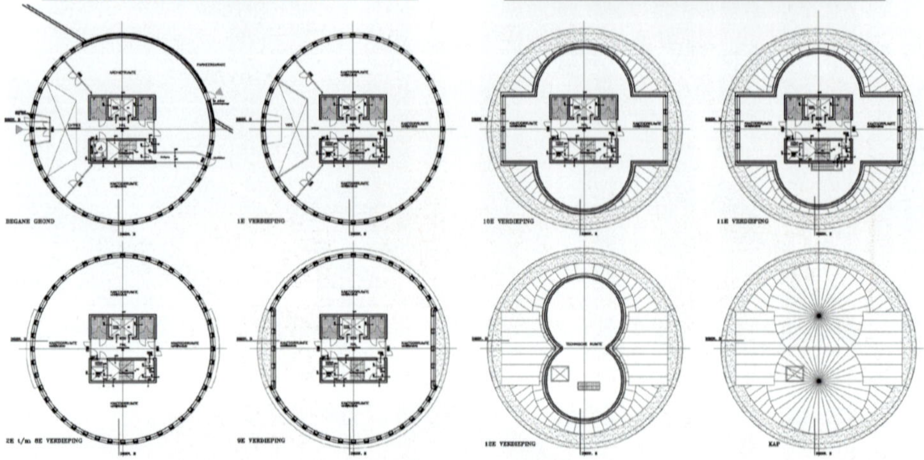
BEGANE GROND
1E VERDIEPING
10E VERDIEPING
11E VERDIEPING
2E t/m 8E VERDIEPING
9E VERDIEPING
12E VERDIEPING
KAP

K

Adolfo Natalini - *Quaderni olandesi*

Natalini has lived in Florence since he was a student, more often in his studio than at home, but he has never moved away. He travels of course, and often, as he is curious by nature. But his architecture has found an adopted country in the Netherlands. Adolfo Natalini has explored landscapes, towns, palaces, so that now he feels akin to Ludovico Guicciardini, who had the same attraction for this country five centuries ago, and who left such detailed descriptions. But here, on the contrary, I feel that it is the Netherlands that was captivated by Natalini's architecture. Initially, like and with others, he had to deal with the demolition of modernity. A modernity that wanted to dictate the rules, and already for this reason, a radical revolution was necessary. A classical patricide, that recognises the parental role, and at the same time, the need to advance further, relegating it to history. To then reconquer an architecture that Natalini himself likes to define as "normal", rather than "traditional": in other words, what comes from the past, from our ancestors, our heritage, that can be translated into any era.
With Natalini's work as well, Dutch architectural culture seems to have followed the same route. While the amazing and surprising provocations of Superstudio travel in exhibitions and are displayed in museums all over the world, they have now become legendary objects, like every other thing that the cult of heritage and our era transforms in mnemonic trace. "Normal" architecture provides everyday living space and lives its untroubled existence in the Netherlands and elsewhere. The "radical" architecture of forty years ago is already a monument to itself.

[by F. Ventura at Spazio A, Florence 24.10.2014]

Appendices

La scuola di Pistoia. Natura e oggetto, Museo di Arte Contemporanea e del Novecento, Monsummano Terme 2010

Superstudio. Storie con Figure 1966-1973, Quaderni Bianchi, 1979

Superstudio & Radicals, Japan Interior Inc., Tokyo 1982

A. Natalini, L. Netti, A. Poli, C. Toraldo di Francia, *Extra-urban material culture*, Alinea, Florence 1979

Figures of stone, Electa, Milan 1984

Adolfo Natalini. Architetture raccontate, Electa, Milan 1989

Adolfo Natalini architettore, Fondazione Centro Ragghianti, Lucca 2002

Adolfo Natalini, Album Olandese, Aión Edizioni, Florence 2004

Adolfo Natalini - Curriculum Vitae

—

Adolfo Natalini (Pistoia,1941). After his experience as a painter, Natalini graduated in architecture in Florence in 1966 and founded Superstudio (with Cristiano Toraldo di Francia, Gian Piero Frassinelli, Roberto and Alessandro Magris and Alessandro Poli). The group was the initiator of the so-called *Radical Architecture*, one of the most important avant-garde movements of the 1960s and 1970s.

Superstudio projects appeared in publications and international exhibitions and works are included in Museum of Modern Art in New York, the Israel Museum in Jerusalem, the Deutsches Architekturtmuseum in Frankfurt am Main, the Centre Pompidou in Paris, and the Maxxi in Rome. Publications include: *Superstudio 1966-82 – Stories, Figures, Architecture*, (Electa, Florence 1982), *Superstudio & Radicals*, (Japan Interior Inc., Tokyo 1982), *Superstudio Life without objects* (Skira, Milan 2003) *Superstudio* (Laterza, Bari 2010), *Superstudio-The Secret Life of the Continuous Monument* (Biennale, Venice 2014), *Superstudio- Storie con Figure* 1966-78 (Quodlibet, Rome 2015).

In 1979, Natalini set up his own practice, focussing on projects for historical city centres in Italy and Europe, researching the traces of time on objects and places, and proposing a reconciliation between collective and personal memory. His works include: projects for Römerberg in Frankfurt and for the Wailing Wall in Jerusalem, bank headquarters in Alzate Brianza, a computer centre In Zola Predosa, a house in Saalgasse, Frankfurt, and the Teatro della Compagnia in Florence

His published works include: *Figures of stone* (Electa, Milan 1984), *Adolfo Natalini - Architetture raccontate* (Electa, Milan 1989), *Il Teatro della Compagnia* (Anfione Zeto 1989).

In 1991, with Fabrizio Natalini, he opened his firm, Natalini Architetti, in via del Salviatino. Fabrizio Natalini, (Florence 1953) graduated in architecture in 1980, and worked with Superstudio from 1971 and with Adolfo Natalini from 1980 on projects and competitions for historic cities in Italy and abroad. In 1994, they began collaboration with Architectenburo Corinne Schrauwen (Amsterdam) and from 2008, with Abken Schrauwen Architecten (Ijsselstein). Their work includes: the Waagstraat area in Groningen, the Opificio delle Pietre Dure in Florence, the Dorotheenhof on Manetstrasse in Leipzig, the Muzenplein in The Hague, Campi Bisenzio, the University Campus in Novoli, Florence, the Boscotondo in Helmond, the University Campus in Porta Tufi, Siena, the Het Eiland in Zwolle, Haverleij in Den Bosch, the Museo dell'Opera del Duomo and the Nuovi Uffizi Museum in Florence.

Their published works include: *Il Museo dell'Opificio a Firenze* (Sillabe, Livorno 1995), V. Savi, *Natalini Architetti – Nuove architetture raccontate* (Electa, Milan 1996), *De Waagstraat* (Groningen 1996), *Temporanea Occupazione* (Alinea, Florence 2000), *Un edificio senese. Le nuove Facoltà di giurisprudenza e scienze politiche* (Gli Ori, Pistoia 2002), *Adolfo Natalini Architettore* (Fondazione Ragghianti, Lucca 2002), *Adolfo Natalini Disegni 1976-2001* (Motta, Milan 2002), *Adolfo Natalini Album Olandese* (Aion, Florence 2003), *Natalini Architetti* (in *Costruire in Laterizio*, no. 97, 2004), *Adolfo Natalini Quaderni Olandesi* (Aion Edizioni, Florence 2005), *Adolfo Natalini Shadow Line* (Lettera 22, Syracuse 2013).

Adolfo Natalini was full professor of architectural design at the Florence Faculty of Architecture.
He is a member of the Order of Architects of Florence, and an honorary member of the Bund Deutscher Architekten, an Honorary Fellow American Institute of Architects, an academic of the Accademia delle Arti del Disegno of Florence, the Accademia di Belle Arti of Carrara, and the Accademia di San Luca.

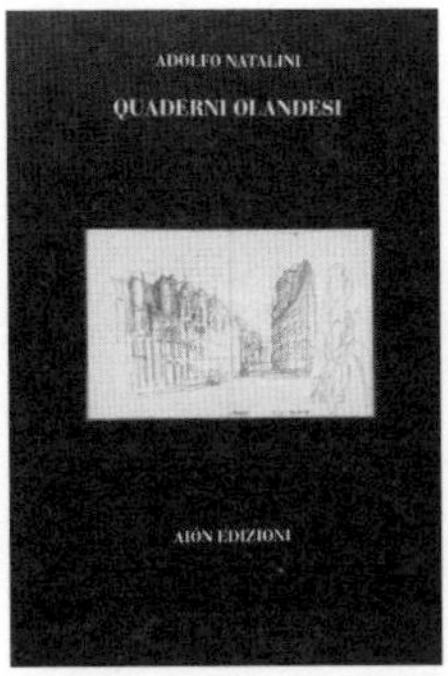

Adolfo Natalini, Quaderni Olandesi, Aión, Florence 2005

Unmodern Architecture, NAI Publishers, 2004

Centro Annonario in Pistoia (IT), 1982-1987

Teatro della Compagnia, Florence (IT), 1984-1987

Teatro A. Galli and piazza Malatesta, Rimini (IT), 1985-2000

Piazza in Palazzuolo sul Senio, Florence (IT), 1984-1986

Sports Centre in Gorle, Bergamo (IT), 1986-1992

Shopping Centre in Gavinana, Florence (IT), 1988

Competition project for piazza Matteotti in Siena (IT), 1988

Competition project for the Italian Pavilion in Venice (IT), 1988

Historical city centre building in Ferrara (IT), 1989-2000

Museo dell'Opificio delle Pietre Dure in Florence (IT), 1992-1995

Former Ginori works redevelopment project in Doccia, Sesto Fiorentino, Florence (IT), 1992-1994

Works

—

SUPERSTUDIO RESEARCH, PROJECTS AND CONSTRUCTIONS, SELECTION 1966-1978

* research

* *Journey to the Realm of Reason*, Catalogue 1966-69

Competition project for the Fortezza da Basso, Florence (IT), 1967

Project for a holiday village, Tropea (IT), 1968

Competition project for a nursery school, La Spezia (IT), 1968

Project for a building complex, Piombino, Livorno (IT), 1968

* *Histograms of Architecture*, Catalogue 1968-69

* *A Catalogue of Villas*, 1968-69

Competition project for the Italian Pavilion, Osaka (JP), 1969

Industrial plant, Pistoia (IT), 1969-71

Competition project, Trigon 79, Graz (AT), first prize, 1969

* *The Continuous Monument*, 1969

Misura series, 1969-71

Misura for Abet Laminati, 1969

Bank branch office, Florence (IT), 1969-70

Isidori house, Florence (IT), 1969-72

Competition project for an urban park, Modena (IT), 1970

Project for the State Archives, Florence (IT), 1970

Prefabricated building for a bank, Donoratico, Livorno (IT), 1970-71

Train projects for Breda Ferroviarie, 1970

Research for air terminal interior design/furnishing, 1970

Two competition projects for air terminals, S. Eufemia Lamezia and Genoa (IT), with Archizoom Associati, 1970

* *Interplanetary Architecture*, 1971

* *Twelve Ideal Cities*, 1971

* *Supersuperface*, 1971

Competition project for Florence University (IT), 1971

Competition project, Trigon 71, Graz (AT), 1971

Competition project for the Modena cemetery (IT), 1971

Train for Circumvesuviana Railway, Naples (IT), 1970-71

* *Fundamental Acts (Life, Education, Ceremony, Love, Death)*, 21 March 1971-20 March 1973

Competition project for the Roman amphitheatre in Cagliari. Research on industrial components for building construction. Research on interior design/ furnishing for public buildings, 1972

Bank branch office, Florence (IT), 1972

Filmed research on living space, 1973

Research on integrated furnishing systems with Anonima Castelli research department, 1973

Competition project for the Urbino cemetery, (IT), 1973

Research on integrated furnishing systems, 1974

* Research on extra-urban material culture, 1974

* Research on practical everyday objects, 1975

Research on fitted wall units, 1975

Volpini house, Urbino (IT), 1975

* Bahnhof Apotheke Krause, Luebbecke Wstf (DE), 1976-78

Competition project for a school, Florence (IT), 1977

* *Memory Instead*, Adolfo Natalini, 1977

Plans for economic social housing, Barberino Val D'Elsa, Florence (IT), 1977

Edificio per unità artigianali per abitazioni, Panzano, Florence (IT), 1977

Branch 2 of the Banca Toscana, Florence (IT), 1977-79

Residential complex with 24 apartments, Vico d'Elsa, Florence (IT), 1978

* *Lot's wife and Zeno's conscience*, Venice Biennale, Venice (IT), 1978

ADOLFO NATALINI SELECTED WORKS 1978-1991

* completed works

* Bank head office in Alzate Brianza, Como (IT), 1978-83

Proposal for the reconstruction of Römerberg, Frankfurt (DE), 1979

* Computer centre, Zola Predosa, Bologna (IT), 1979-81

* House in Saalgasse, Frankfurt (DE), 1980-88

Competition project for the Prehistoric and Archaeological Museum in the Karmeliterkirche, Frankfurt (DE), 1980

Proposal for the reconstruction of the Wailing Wall, Jerusalem (IL), 1980-82

Project for the Secretariat in Owerri, Imo, (NG), 1981

Competition project for the restoration and use of the Castello di Piombino, Livorno (IT), 1981

* Projects for underground car parks, Florence (Piazza dell'Indipendenza, Piazza Ghiberti, Piazza Tasso) (IT), 1982-87

* Centro Annonario in Pistoia (IT), 1982-87

* Piazza Alpi, Palazzuolo sul Senio, Florence (IT), 1984-86

* Reorganisation of the archaeological zone, Piazza Grandi, Fidenza, Parma (IT), 1986

* Teatro della Compagnia, Florence (IT), 1984-87

Teatro A. Galli and Piazza Malatesta, Rimini (IT), 1985

* Sports Centre, Gorle, Bergamo (IT), 1st stage - gymnasium, 1986-92

Competition project for le Murate, Florence (IT), 1988 (selected for 2nd stage)

Invitational competition for Piazza Matteotti/La Lizza, Siena (IT), 1988

Invitational competition for the Italian Pavilion, Venice, (IT), 1988

* Completion of the Monumental Cemetery in Antella, Florence (IT), 1988-2008

* Casa Serena, Leffe, Bergamo (IT), 1988-94

Urban block project, Palazzo Da Porto Festa del Palladio, Vicenza (IT), 1989

Renovation project for the former commodity exchange building, Ferrara (IT), 1989

Historical city centre building in Ferrara (IT), 1989-2000

Former industrial area, Parma (IT), 1989

Former industrial area, Como (IT), 1990-96

Hotel Radda, Radda in Chianti, Siena (IT), 1990-96

Reorganisation of Piazza di S. Giovanni Valdarno, Arezzo (IT), Competition 1st prize, 1991

Invitational competition for the de' Medici stables, Poggio a Caiano, Prato (IT), 1991

Invitational competition for the Leonardo da Vinci canal port, Cesenatico, Forlì-Cesena (IT), 1991

NATALINI ARCHITETTI SELECTED WORKS 1991-2012

* completed works

* International invitational competition for the reconstruction of part of the historical city centre, Groningen (NL), 1st prize, 1991-96

* Library for the Museum of the History of Science, Florence (IT), 1991- 97

* Piazza Alpi, Palazzuolo sul Senio, Florence (IT), 1991-94

Residential complex on former Sime site, Florence (IT), 1993-2007

Shopping centre in Campi Bisenzio, Florence (IT), 1993-1997

Competition project for the Contemporary Art Gallery in Leipzig (DE), 1994

Shopping centre in Dogana (Republic of San Marino), 1995-2000

Redevelopment project for former industrial area in Forlì (IT), 1996-

Redevelopment project for former industrial area in Forlì (IT), 1996-

Building in via Dei Vanga, Bolzano (IT), 1996-2005

Teatro Politeama in Poggibonsi, Siena (IT), 1977-2004

* Museo dell'Opificio delle Pietre Dure, Florence (IT), 1992-95

Project for former Ginori plant in Doccia (in collaboration), 1992-94

* Project for Villa La Quiete for the University of Florence (IT), 1992-97

* Former Sime site, residential complex, Florence (IT), 1993-2007

* City block in historical city centre, Leipzig (DE), 1993-96

* Project for the Muzenplein buildings in the historical city centre of The Hague(NL), 1993-2000

* Shopping centre, Campi Bisenzio, Florence (IT), 1993-97

* University Campus, Novoli, Florence (IT), 1994-2003

International invitational competition (1st stage) for reconstruction of area between the market and the Meuse, Maastricht (NL), selected for the 2nd stage, 1994

Invitational competition for the Contemporary Art Gallery, Leipzig (DE), 1994

* Shopping centre, Dogana, Republic of San Marino (IT), 1995-2000

* University Campus, Porta Tufi, Siena (IT), 1995-2000

* L'Anello di Val Marina, residential complex, Calenzano, Florence (IT), 1995-2009

* Boscotondo, Helmond (NL), 1st prize, 1996-2000

Competition project for the Prado Museum, Madrid (ES), 1995

* Project for a former industrial area, Forlì (IT), 1996-

Project for the Museo di Palazzo Vecchio, Florence (IT), 1996- 97

* Building in via dei Vanga, Bolzano (IT), 1996-2005

* Het Heiland-Shopping centre and residential complex, Zwolle (NL), 1996-2001

* Residential complex Haverleij, Den Bosch (NL), 1977-2001

* Teatro Politeama, Poggibonsi, Siena (IT), 1st prize, 1977-2004

* Sala del Pellegrino in the Santuario di Montenero, Livorno (IT), 1st prize, 1997-2000

* Residential complex in former Stianti factory, San Casciano, Florence (IT), 1998-2008

* Shopping centre Empoli, Florence (IT), 1998-2007

* Uffizi Museum, Florence (IT), 1998-2004

* Museum staging, Palazzo Bonacossi, Ferrara (IT), 1998-2000

* Completion of the Monumental Cemetery in Antella, Florence (IT), 1998-2009

* Residential complex Ijsselkade, Doesburg (NL), 1998-2005

* Chapel of S. Manetto all'Antella, Florence (IT), 1998-2000

Invitational competition for a parish building complex, Perugia (IT), 1998

* Underground car park, Sant'Ambrogio, Florence (IT), 1998-2005

* Dock redevelopment project, Ferrara (IT), 1999-2009

* Office block and tower for Buitenop, Roermond (NL), 1999-2010

* Abdijcomplex Cultural Centre, Thorn (NL), 1999-2001

* Multi-purpose building, Uden (NL), 1999-2005

* Hotel, San Bartolo a Cintoia, Florence (IT), 2000-2006

* Residential complex, Orsi Mangelli area, Forlì (IT), 2000-

Forlì Police headquarters, Orsi Mangelli area, Forlì (IT), 2000-

* Shopping centre in former Longinotti industrial area, Florence (IT), 2000-2005

International invitational competition University of Bologna, Navile (IT), 2000

International invitational competition University of Bologna, Bertalia (IT), 2001

* Police headquarters and Prefecture in Pistoia (IT), 2001-2014

Guideline project for the station and Forum Boarium, Fidenza, Parma (IT), 2001-2010

Guideline project for piazza Luogo Pio, Livorno (IT), 2001-2006

International invitational competition for the Nuovo Museo dell'Opera di S. Maria del Fiore, Florence (IT), 2001

Guideline project Drentepark, Amsterdam (NL), 2001

* International invitational competition for the Paleiskwartier, Den Bosch (NL), 1st prize, 2002-2012

* Restoration of Castello dei Pio, Carpi, 2002-2008

* Sala Civica, Sesto Fiorentino, Florence (IT), 2002-2014

Guideline project Stadswerven, Dordrecht (NL), 2002

Guideline project for Achter de Lange Stallen, Breda (NL), 2002

International invitational competition for the high velocity station, Florence (IT), 2002

* Staging of the Museo Galileo, Florence (IT), 2003-2010

Project for the Chiesa del Sacro Cuore, Pompei, Naples (IT) 2003

* New school building, Fidenza, Parma (IT), 2003-

* Workplan, Nuovi Uffizi, Florence (IT) (con S.IN.TER. s.r.l.), 2003-

Competition project for Europaweg, Helmond (NL), 2008

Competition project for Fontana Park, Hoorn (NL), 2008

* University Campus, Vicenza (IT), 2004-2009

* Guideline project for Saint Gobain complex, Porta a Mare, Pisa (IT), 2004-

* Guideline project for viale Europa, Cesena (IT), 2004-

Europapark residential complex, Almere (NL), 2005

Restructuration of the Palazzo de' Rossi, Pistoia (IT), 2005-2012

* Princenlant, Boxtel (NL), 2005

* Competition project for Henan Publishing Co., Zhengzhou (CN), 1st prize, 2005-

Competition project for Hotel, Dousberg (NL), 2005

Competition project for De Brouwerij, Hengelo (NL), 2005

* Natalinitoren Roermond, (NL), 2005-2012

Guideline project for Piazza del Mercato, Bastia Umbra, Perugia (IT), 2006

Competition project: Città di Pietra – Bari, Stone Lion award at the Venice Biennale, Venice (IT), 2006

Competition project for the Parco di Levante, Cesenatico, Forlì-Cesena (IT), 2006

* Nuovo Museo dell'Opera di Santa Maria del Fiore, Florence (IT), 2007-

Competition project for a church in Castel di Lama, Ascoli Piceno (IT), 2007

Competition project for Oostdijk, Rotterdam (NL), 1st prize, 2007-

* Corte Italia, Yerevan (AM), 2007-2010

Competition project for the new city centre, Ede (NL), 2007

* Piazza della Stazione, Fidenza, Parma (IT), 2007-2012

Competition project for the Parco della Musica, Florence (IT), 2007

Competition project for the Egyptian Museum, Turin (IT), 2007

* Competition project for the Teatro San Carlo, Naples (IT), 1st prize, 2008-2010

Competition project for the Museo di Brera, Milan (IT), 2008

Competition project for the Museo degli Innocenti, Florence (IT), 2008

Competition project for the Istituto Agrario, Siena (IT), 1st prize, 2008-

Competition project, Berg op Zoom (NL), 1st prize, 2008

Project for Corte Italia, Roustaveli Avenue, Tbilisi (GE), 2009

* Redevelopment of the former flower market, Pescia, Pistoia (IT), 2009-

* Hotel San Lorenzo, Bergamo (IT), 2009-2012

* Retail Park "I Gigli", Campi Bisenzio shopping centre, Florence (IT), 2009-2012

Competition project for the new Sant'Agostino museum complex, Modena (IT), 2010

Competition project for the Città dell'Arte e della Musica, Lecce (IT), 2010

Competition project for a new church, Montespaccato, Rome (IT), 2010

* Competition project for the Scoglio della Regina, Livorno (IT), 1st prize, 2011-2012

Competition project for the Burg-Mediatheck, Halle (DE), 2011

* New Casa Toscana del Cinema, Florence (IT), 2011-

* Competition project for the People Mover, Pisa (IT), 1st prize, 2011-

* Competition project for the Museo Civico, Prato (IT), 1st prize, 2012-

Bibliography

—

SUPERSTUDIO – ADOLFO NATALINI – NATALINI ARCHITETTI SELECTION 1969-2014

* monographies

"Tre architetture nascoste", in *Domus*, no. 473, 1969

Casa Vogue, no. 2, 1969

"Design d'invenzione e design d'evasione", in *Domus*, no. 476, 1969

Catalogue "The Continuous Monument", in *Trigon*, no. 69, 1969

"Viaggio nelle Regioni della Ragione", in *Domus*, no. 479, 1969

Casa Vogue, no. 3, 1969

"Il Monumento continuo", in *Domus*, no. 481, 1969

Necropoli, no. 6/7, 1970

* Special issue: "Superstudio/Design", in *Japan Interior Design*, no. 138, 1970

Special section: "The Continuous Monument", in *Japan Interior Design*, no. 140, 1970

Special issue: "Conceptual architecture", in *Design Quarterly*, nos. 78/79 1970

Special section: "The Single Design", in *Japan Interior Design*, no. 144, 1971

"Istogrammi", in *Domus*, no. 497, 1971

Nac, no. 5, 1971

"La distruzione degli oggetti", in *In*, no. 3, 1971

VII Biennale de Paris, catalogue, 1971

"Il Monumento continuo, storyboard per il film", in *Casabella*, no. 358, 1971

* *Vita Morte e Miracoli dell'Architettura*, catalogue (Florence, Space Electronic, 9-11 November 1971), S. Space, Florence 1971

"The 12 Ideal Cities", in *Architettural Design*, no. 12, 1971

"Le Dodici Città Ideali", in *Casabella*, no. 361, 1972

"L'Architettura Riflessa", in *Casabella*, no. 363, 1972

"L'Architettura Interplanetaria", in *Casabella*, no. 364, 1972

"L'eliminazione della città, salvataggi dei centri storici", in *In*, no. 5, 1972

"The Misura Series", in *Japan Interior Design*, no. 155, 1972

Italy: The New Domestic Landscape, edited by Emilio Ambasz, exhibition catalogue (New York, MOMA, 26 May-11 September 1972), The Museum of Modern Art, New York 1972.

"Vita, Educazione, Cerimonia, Amore, Morte: Vita", in *Casabella*, no. 367, 1972

"Technomorphous Architecture", in *Perspecta. The Yale Architectural Journal*, nos. 13/14, 1972

"Vita, Educazione, Cerimonia, Amore, Morte: Educazione 2", in *Casabella*, no. 372, 1972

In, no. 8, 1972

"Vita... Morte: Cerimonia", in "Casabella", no. 374, 1973

"Vita... Morte: Amore", in *Casabella*, no. 377, 1973

"Vita... Morte: Morte", in *Casabella*, no. 380, 1973

* *Superstudio - Fragmente aus einem personlichen Museum / Frammenti da un Museo personale / Fragments from a personal Museum* exhibition catalogue (Graz, Neue Galerie am Landemuseum Joanneum, 6 June-1 July 1973), Neue Galerie, Graz, 1973

* Special issue: "Sottsass & Superstudio: mindscapes", in *Design quarterly*, special issue, no.89, 1973

Architettura Razionale di M. Scolari, XV Triennale di Milano, 1973

P. Navone - B. Orlandini, "Architettura Radicale", in *Casabella*, no. 38, 1974

"Global Tools", in *Bollettino*, no. 1 Ed. L'Uomo e l'Arte, 1974

Avanguardia e cultura popolare, Comune di Bologna, Galleria D'arte Moderna, Bologna 1975

"Global Tools", in *Bollettino*, no. 2, Ed. L'Uomo e l'Arte, 1975

Com'era bella l'architettura nel 1966... (Superstudio e l'architettura radicale dieci anni dopo), in *Spazio Arte*, nos. 10-11, 1977

Sala del Pellegrino, Santuario di Montenero, Livorno (IT), 1997-2000

Shopping centre in Empoli, Florence (IT), 1998-2007

Uffizi Museum, Florence (IT), 1998-2004

Dock redevelopment project in Ferrara (IT), 1999-2009

B. Orlandoni - G. Vallino, *Dalla città al cucchiaio: saggi sulle nuove avanguardie nell'architettatura e nel design*, Studio Forma, Turin 1977

* *Superstudio*, Catalogo della personale di Architetti all'In-arch Roma, Centro DÌ, Florence 1978

"Viaggio con la matita tra gli artefatti del mondo contadino", in *Modo*, no. 7, 1978

* A. Natalini, *Adolfo Natalini: La memoria invece*: tre mostre allo Studio Franca Pisani: Firenze, maggio 1978, I quaderni bianchi, Studio Franca Pisani, Florence 1978

* *Superstudio - La moglie di Lot e La coscienza di Zeno* exhibition catalogue (Venice, Biennale, 1978), I quaderni bianchi, Florence 1978

Topologia e morfogenesi. Utopia e crisi dell'antinatura. Momenti delle intenzioni architettoniche in Italia, edited by L. V. Masini, Ed La Biennale di Venezia-Electa, Venice/Milan 1978

Immaginazione megastrutturale dal Futurismo a oggi. Utopia e crisi dell'antinatura. Momenti delle intenzioni architettoniche in Italia, edited by E. Crispolti, Ed La Biennale di Venezia-Electa, Venice/Milan 1978

M. De Lucchi, "Architetture di quaderni (I diari-progetto di Adolfo Natalini)", in *Modo*, no. 19, 1979

* *Superstudio. Storie con figure 1966-1973*, edited by A. Natalini (Una raccolta di Storie), I quaderni bianchi, Florence 1979

"Una casa fatta (anche) di memorie", in *Casa Vogue*, no. 98, 1979

* *Superstudio: ein Haus (auch)aus Erinnerungen* Luebbecke Wstf, I quaderni bianchi, Florence 1979

E. Ruthenfranz, "Ein kùhner Bau", in *ART*, aprile, 1980

"Postmodernismus -Alles geht wieder", in *Schòner Wohnen*, no. 12, 1980

* *Adolfo Natalini/ Superstudio, Römerberg Projekt*, I quaderni bianchi, Florence 1980

Dom-Ròmerberg Bereich Wettbewerb, Stadt Frankfut a/M, Braunschweig/Wiesbaden, 1980

Umanesimo, disumanesimo nell'arte europea. 1890-1980: dai simbolisti al nouveau realisme: 10 installazioni di artisti europei in un percorso storico di Firenze, edited by L. V. Masini, Silvana, Milan 1980.

Cronografie: il tempo e la memoria nella società contemporanea: Chiesa di San Lorenzo, Venice Biennale, Special Projects Section, 1980, Venice 1980

"Per il Römerberg fuori concorso", in *Domus*, no. 613, gennaio, 1981

"Adolfo Natalini/ Superstudio, Römerberg Projekt", in *Parametro*, no. 99, 1981

"Adolfo Natalini/Superstudio, Saalgasse Nr. 4", in *Lotus*, no. 31, 1981

Inventionen- Piranesi und Arbitekturphantasien in der Gegenwart, exhibition catalogue (Hanover, Kunstverein, December 13, 1981 - February 10 1982), Kunstverein, Hanover 1982.

"Adolfo Natalini/ Superstudio, Ròmerberg Projekt", in *Lotus*, no. 32, 1982

* *Metaphors and allegories: Superstudio Firenze*, exhibition catalogue (Jerusalem, Israel Museum, March-May 1982), Israel Museum, Jerusalem 1982

* *Superstudio, 1966-82: storie, figure, architettura*, edited by G. Pettena, Electa, Florence 1982

* *Superstudio & radicals*, a cura di Superstudio & the Moriyama Editors Studio, Japan Interior Inc., Tokyo 1982

L'accesso al Muro del Pianto, in "Lotus", no. 35, 1982

"Edificio a doppia maniera", in *Lotus*, no. 37, 1983

* *Cultura materiale extraurbana*, edited by A. Natalini, L. Netti, A. Poli, C. Toraldo Di Francia, Alinea, Florence 1983

* Adolfo Natalini, *Figure di pietra*, Electa, Milan 1984

Le città immaginate: un viaggio in Italia, exhibition catalogue XVII Triennale di Milano, Electa, Milan 1987

* "Il Teatro della Compagnia", in *Anfione Zeto*, no. 0, 1988

Progetti per la Biennale di Venezia, Electa, Milan 1988

"Non sarà facile trovarlo", in *Lotus*, no. 58, 1988

* A. Natalini, *Adolfo Natalini. Architetture raccontate*, Electa, Milan 1989

"Radicamenti e Straniamenti", in *A.U.*, no. 35, 1989

"Intervista", in *l'Architettura*, no. 3, 1991

'Un progetto per Siena' Il Concorso Nazionale per Piazza Matteotti La Lizza, Electa, Milan 1992

"La Persistenza dell'Archetipo", in *Lotus*, no. 74, 1992

"Un Progetto per la Waagstraat", in *Archi & Colonne*, no. 10, 1992

* *Appunti Costruttivi*, Il Ferrone, Florence 1992

A. Acocella, *L'Architettura dei Luoghi*, Laterconsult, Rome 1992

* *Adolfo Natalini*, exhibition catalogue, Cologne 1993

A. Natalini, in *Salisburgo la verde*, edited by R. Capezzuto, M. Lupano, Electa, Milan 1993

"Dialogo con Adolfo Natalini", in *Costruire in Laterizio*, no. 38, 1994

A. Belluzzi, *Architettura Italiana 1944-1994*, Laterza, Rome 1994

"Den Haag Groningen Leipzig Berlin", in *Lotus*, no. 83, 1995

* *Il Museo dell'Opificio a Firenze rinnovato da Adolfo Natalini*, Sillabe, Florence 1995

* A. Natalini, *Adolfo Natalini: Natalini Architetti, nuove architetture raccontate*, edited by V. Savi, Electa, Milano 1996

XIX Triennale, 'Identità e differenze' Padiglione Italia Electa, Milan 1996

* A. Natalini, *Adolfo Natalini. Avvicinamenti all'architettura*, edited by A. Boschi, A. Castellana, S. Follerà, Pontecorboli ("Quaderni di progetto", 2), Florence 1996

* Adolfo Natalini, *Avvicinamenti all'architettura*, edited by A. Boschi, A. Castellana, S. Follesa, Pontecorboli, Florence 1996

* *De Waagstraat*, Groningen, 1996

"Waagstraat and Surroundings", in *Architectuur in Nederland: Jaarboek 1995-1996*, edited by R. Brouwers, Nai Uitgevers, Rotterdam 1996

* *Sopralluoghi*, Octavo, Florence 1997

* *Novoli-Berlino*, Octavo, Florence 1998

"Waagstraat, Groningen", in *Lotus*, no. 96, 1998

"Centro Commerciale I Gigli", in *Abitare*, no. 373, 1998

"Progetti per Lipsia", in *Area*, no. 36, January-February 1998

"Isolato sulla Manetstrasse a Lipsia", in *L'industria delle Costruzioni*, no. 324, 1998

"Isolato sulla Manetstrasse a Lipsia' – 'Edificio per abitazioni a Bergamo' 'Ultimi racconti di architettura', intervista", in *Costruire in Laterizio*, no. 63, 1998

"Polo Universitario a Porta Tufi", in *Costruire in Laterizio*, n. 68, 1999

* A. Natalini, *Artisti carissimi: (Racconto breve per un libriccino di disegni)*, Pananti, Florence 2000

"Angolo Ferrarese", in *Area*, no. 51, 2000

* *Adolfo Natalini – Temporanea Occupazione*, exhibition catalogue Padiglione de l'Esprit Noveau Bologna, Alinea, Florence 2000

"Ricostruzione di un isolato nel centro storico di Ferrara", in *L'industria delle Costruzioni*, no. 335, 2001

"Ricostruzione della Waagstraat a Groningen' 'Boscotondo: il progetto della città' 'Lo standard costruttivo'", in *Costruire in Laterizio*, no. 81, 2001

Multipurpose building in Uden (NL), 1999-2005

Police headquarters and Prefecture in Pistoia (IT), 2001-2014

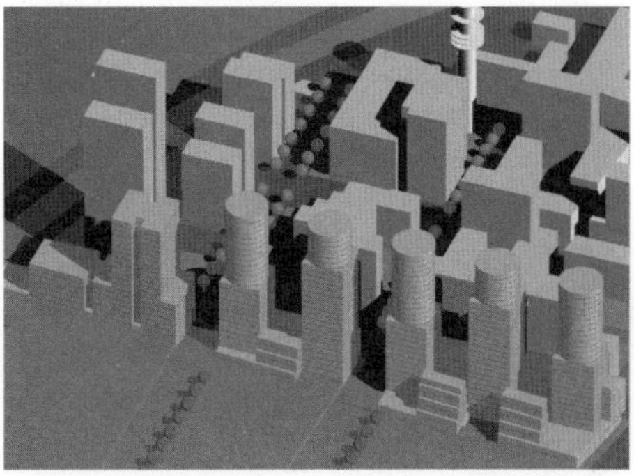
Guideline project, Drentepark, Amsterdam (NL), 2001

Competition project for high-speed railway station in Florence (IT), 2002

"Boscotondo Helmond", in *Stedebouw*, no. 383, 2001

"Concorso per insediamento universitario", in *Parametro*, no. 236, 2001

Architettura del 900 – La Toscana, Polistampa, Florence 2002

Continuità. Arte in Toscana 1945-1967, exhibition catalogue, edited by A. Boatto, M&M, Montecatini 2002

Tra Terra e Cielo, Diabasis, Parma 2002

Het Oude Eiland, Zwolle, 2002

* *Natalini Architetti - un Edificio Senese*, Gli Ori, Pistoia 2002

Toscana Contemporanea 1980-2001, Maschietto, Pistoia 2002

"Utopia a Siena", in *Domus* no. 845, 2002

"L'Architettura del Buon Governo", in *Aion*, no. 1, 2002

* *Adolfo Natalini Disegni 1976-2001*, Motta, Milan 2002

* *Adolfo Natalini Architettore*, Fondazione Ragghianti, Lucca 2002

U. Buscioni - A. Natalini, *Un epistolario dell'anima. Lettere 1991-2002*, Einaudi, Turin 2002

"Adolfo Natalini – Album Olandese", in *Aion*, no. 3, 2003

* P. Lang - W.Menking, *Superstudio: life without objects*, Skira, Milan 2003

* *Adolfo Natalini – Album Olandese*, Aion Edizioni, Florence 2004

* "Natalini Architetti, numero monografico" in *Costruire in Laterizio*, no. 97, 2004

"Sul colle di Montenero", in *Aion*, no. 6, 2004

H. Ibelings, *Unmodern Architecture*, Rotterdam 2004

* "Natalini Architetti, numero monografico" in *Modulo*, no. 311, 2005

"Natalini Architetti + Schrauwen, Boscotondo", in *Area*, no. 47, 2005

* *Adolfo Natalini Quaderni Olandesi*, Aion Edizioni, Florence 2005

Architettura Contemporanea in Italia – Conflitti, Skira, Milan 2005

* *Superstudio: the Middleburg lectures*, a cura di V. Byvanck, De Vleeshal: Zeeuws Museum, Middelburg 2005

"Natalini Architetti Album Fiorentino", in *Aion*, no. 11, 2006

"Natalini Architetti - Gavinana Shopping Center", in *Materia*, no. 52, 2006

"Adolfo Natalini - Punta Perotti", in *Città di Pietra*, Marsilio, Venice 2006

"Teatro della Compagnia" in M. Narpozzi, *Teatri*, Motta, Milan 2006

"Adolfo Natalini - Tra Acque e Cielo", in *Firenze Architettura*, no. 2, 2006

"Natalini Architetti - La Costruzione della Città", in *Aion*, no. 13, 2006

* AA.VV. Il Teatro Politeama, Poggibonsi, 2006

"Conversazione con Adolfo Natalini Pittore e Disegnatore", in *Il Fuoco*, nos. 12/13, 2006/07

"Natalini - Progetti Olandesi", in *Abitare la Terra*, no. 6, 2007

A. Natalini, "Note in margine al progetto dei nuovi Uffizi" in *Cantiere Uffizi*, edited by R. Cecchi, A. Paolucci, Gangemi, Rome 2007

D. Ricchi, "Adolfo Natalini intervista", in *And*, no. 10, 2007

R. Butini, "Architettura e città Due progetti senesi", in *Opere*, no. 16, 2007

P. Gossel, "Voce Natalini", in *The A-Z of modern architecture*, Taschen, Hong Kong 2007

Voci: "Natalini, Radicale, Superstudio", Voce Utopia, in *Enciclopedia dell'architettura*, Motta Architettura, Milan 2008

"Superstudio" in *Megastructure Reloaded. Visionary Architecture and Urban Design of the Sixties Reflected by Contemporary Artists*, Hatje Cants, Berlin 2008

* M.T. Stauffer, *Superstudio Archizoom. Figurationen des Utopischen*, Deutscher Kunstverlag, 2008

"Complesso residenziale a San Casciano Val di Pesa", in *Identità dell'architettura italiana*, no. 6, 2008

* *Radici Radicali 1965-1975. Archizoom Pettena Superstudio Ufo*, Florence 2009

"Forlì. Ex Orsi Mangelli. Piano particolareggiato – 1993/2006. Ferrara. Via Darsena. Piano particolareggiato – 1998/in corso", in *Ottagono*, no. 218, 2009

"Luchtig gespitst", in *Stedenbouwn*, no. 678, 2009

"L'anello e il parco di via Marina", in *Identità dell'architettura italiana*, no. 7, 2009

A. Natalini, in *L'architettura italiana per la città cinese*, Gangemi, Rome 2010

Un progetto per l'università di Novoli in *Firenze il progetto urbanistico. Scritti e contributi 1975-2010*, edited by P. Giorgieri, Alinea, Florence 2010

"Superstudio. Restauri di centri storici Italia Vostra 1972", in *Dreamlands. Des parcs d'attractions aux cités du future*, Centre Pompidou, Paris 2010

F. Gottardo, "Racconti urbani nel recupero della tradizione", in *Abitare la terra*, no. 27, 2010

"Natalini Architetti, recupero della zona stazione a Calenzano, Firenze", in *Costruire in Laterizio*, no. 137, 2010

F. Gurrieri - A. Natalini, F. Purini, *L'architettura invincibile*, Le Lettere, Florence 2010

"Toren met dubbele spinse bekroning van zink", in *Dakenraad*, no. 94, 2010

A. Natalini, "Completamento del Cimitero della Misericordia di Santa Maria dell'Antella", in *Identità dell'architettura italiana*, no. 8, 2010

* R. Gargiani - B. Lampariello, *Superstudio*, Laterza, Bari 2010

"Megastruttures", in *Icon*, no. 097, luglio 2011

A. Natalini, "Architetture per il pubblico e architetture didattiche", in *Architetti Catanzaro*, News 03/2011

* "ADOLFO NATALINI," in *Architetture e città del terzo millennio*, no. 3, 2011

A. Natalini, "Autobiografia architettonica (la scala di ponente nei Nuovi Uffizi)", in *Aion*, 2011

Natalini Architetti, "Uffizi Scala di ponente", in *Lotus*, no. 151, 2012

* "Adolfo Natalini – Il sogno del reale", in *Paletot*, no. 10, 2012

Doesburg Een Historische Stad in Beeld Diepenmaat, Dieren 2012

"All Things Super (intervista a Adolfo Natalini)", in *MacMag*, no. 37, 2012

A. Natalini, "La scala di ponente degli Uffizi, Firenze", in *Identità dell'Architettura Italiana*, no. 10, 2012

A. F. L. Baratta, "Adolfo Natalini il progetto della copertura", in *Costruire in Laterizio*, no. 150, 2012

Tante immagini per il museo – i progetti del concorso per l'allestimento del Museo Civico nel Palazzo Pretorio (progetto del gruppo Adolfo Natalini, I classificato), Prato 2012

A. Midal, *Politique Fiction*, Saint Étienne, 2013

G. Mastrigli, "Meditazioni sul deserto Superstudio e il Monumento Continuo", in *La città nuova* edited by M. de Michelis (exhibition catalogue *La città nuova oltre Sant'Elia* Como), Silvana, Milan 2013

* *Linea d'ombra: 1978-1984; Adolfo Natalini tra il Superstudio e l'architettura*, edited by M. Navarra, Lettera22, Syracuse 2013

Adolfo Natalini, "Un hotel sulle rovine", in *Domus*, no. 977, 2014

* *Superstudio: the secret life of Continuous Monument*, edited by G. Mastrigli, Venice Biennale, Quodlibet, Macerata 2014

Exhibitions

—

SUPERSTUDIO/ ADOLFO NATALINI/ NATALINI ARCHITETTI / SELECTION 1966-2014

* Monographic and main exhibitions

* *Superarchitettura*, Galleria Jolly 2, Pistoia (IT), 1966

* *Superarchitettura*, Galleria Comunale, Modena (IT), 1967

Per un antiquariato definito, Biennale dell'Antiquariato, Palazzo Strozzi, Florence (IT) (Archizoom and Superstudio), 1969

Italien Jugoslawien Österreich dreiländerbiennale Trigon '69 Architektur und Freiheit, Künstlerhaus Graz, Burgring Graz (AT), 1969

* *Superstudio*, Dept. of Architecture, Rhode Island School of Design, Providence, Rhode Island (US), 1970

* *The Continuous Monument*, Galleria Milano, Milan (IT), 1971

* *VII Biennale di Parigi*, partecipazione italiana, Musée d'Art Moderne de la ville de Paris, Paris (FR), 1971

* *Le 12 Città Ideali*, Architettura Interplanetaria, Galleria Mana, Rome (IT), 1971

* *Notizie sulla presenza italiana. Incontri Internazionali dell'arte*, Palazzo Taverna, Rome (IT), 1971

* *Superstudio Antologia*, Galleria Schema, Florence (IT), 1972

* *Superstudio Antologia*, Galleria Lia Rumma, Naples (IT), 1972

* *Italy: The New Domestic Landscape*, Museum of Modern Art, New York (US) (A large exhibition on Italian design with twelve environments. Superstudio presents Microevent/Microenvironment with the film *Life-Supersurface*), 1972

Architecture 1962-72 (with R. Abraham, F. St. Florian, M. Webb), Bell Memorial Art Gallery, Providence, Rhode Island (US), 1972

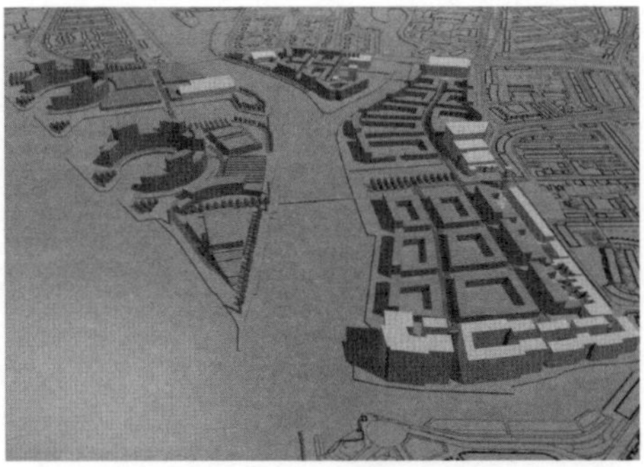

Restoration of the Castello dei Pio in Carpi, Modena (IT), 2002-2008

Guideline project, Stadswerven Dordrecht (NL), 2002

Project for the Chiesa del Sacro Cuore in Pompei, Naples (IT), 2003

University campus in Vicenza (IT), 2004-2009

Guideline project for Saint Gobain in Pisa, Porta a Mare, Pisa (IT), 2004-

Guideline project, viale Europa in Cesena (IT), 2004-

Restructuration of Palazzo de' Rossi, Pistoia (IT), 2005-2012

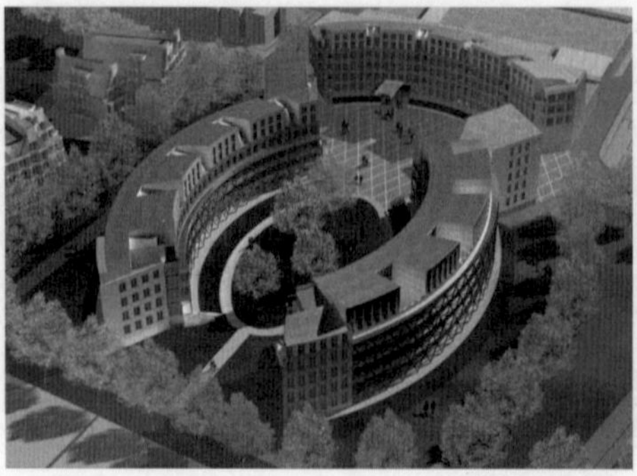

Princenlant, Boxtel (NL), 2005-2012

Princenlant, Boxtel (NL), 2005-2012

Princenlant, Boxtel (NL), 2005-2012

Utopie, Technische Hogeschool, Eindhoven (NL), 1973

* *Superstudio. Fragmente aus einem persönlichen Museum*, Neue Galerie am Landesmuseum Joanneum, Graz (AT), (personal travelling exhibition), 1973

Design als Postulat/ am Beispiel Italien, Internazionales Design Zentrum, Berlin (DE), 1973

* *Sottsass & Superstudio: Mindscapes*, Walker Art Center, Minneapolis (US), (personal travelling exhibition), 1973

Graphic Image '73, Tokyo Central Museum of Arts, Tokyo (JP), 1973

XV Triennale di Milano, Lo spazio abitabile: Esposizione internazionale delle arti decorative e industriali moderne e dell'architettura moderna, Palazzo dell'Arte, Milano (IT), (Superstudio Partecipated with two different environments: *La cassa della sopravvivenza* in the section coordinated by Ettore Sottsass, and a series of projects in the section by A. Rossi), 1973

* *Superstudio. Fragmente aus einem persönlichen Museum*, Galerie nächst St. Stephan, Vienna, Galerie im Taxispalais, Innsbruck (AT), (personal travelling exhibition), 1973

* *Sottsass & Superstudio: Mindscapes*, Contemporary Arts Center, Cincinnati (Ohio); Everson Museum of Art, Syracuse (New York); Herbert F. Johnson Museum of Art, Cornell University, Ithaca (New York); Art Museum of South Texas, Corpus Christi (Texas), Fort Worth Art Center Museum, Fort Worth (Texas), Long Beach Art Museum, Long Beach (California); Joslyn Art Museum, Omaha (Nebraska) (US). (Double personal travelling exhibition by Sottsass and Superstudio), 1974

* *Superstudio*, EPF, Lausanne (CH), 1975

Architectural Studies and Projects, Museum of Modern Art, New York (US), 1975

* *Avanguardia e cultura popolare*, Galleria d'arte moderna, Bologna (IT) (Superstudio exhibited extra-urban material culture research), 1975

* *Superstudio*, Art Net, London (GB) , 1975

Terra I, Krakòv (PL), 1975

Supersommer, Vienna City Festival, Naschmarkt, Vienna (AT), (Superstudio "Memoria per Vienna" and "Le sbarre della memoria"), 1976

Grafica 80 Architettura, Galleria Jannone, Milan (IT), 1977

* *Assenza/Presenza*, Galleria d'arte moderna, Bologna (IT), 1977

* *Superstudio*, Inarch - Palazzo Taverna, Rome (IT), 1978

Seven new design powers, Design Gallery, Tokyo (JP), 1978

* *La memoria invece della Vita; La memoria invece degli Oggetti; La memoria invece dell'Architettura*, Three exhibitions by AdolfoNatalini at the Studio Franca Pisani, Studio Franca Pisani, Florence (IT), 1978

* *Utopia e crisi dell'antinatura. Intenzioni architettoniche in Italia*, Venice Biennale, Magazzini del Sale, Venice (IT), 1978. (Large exhibition of *Architettura Radicale*. Superstudio showed the works, *Lot's wife* and *Zeno's conscience*)

Immaginazione Megastrutturale dal Futurismo a oggi, Venice Biennale, Magazzini del Sale, Venice (IT), 1978

Sesta Biennale internazionale della Grafica, Palazzo Strozzi, Florence (IT), 1978

28/78 Architettura. 50 anni di architettura in Italia, Palazzo delle Stelline, Milan (IT), 1979

* *Romerberg Bebauung/ Superstudio*, Frankfurter Künstverein, Frankfurt (DE), 1979

Fuori della città: le altre culture, Centro Internazionale di Brera, Milan (IT), 1979

* *Superstudio: sei progetti non costruiti*, Galleria Vera Biondi, Florence (IT), 1979

Competition project
for Henan Publishing Co.
in Zhengzhou (CN), 2005-

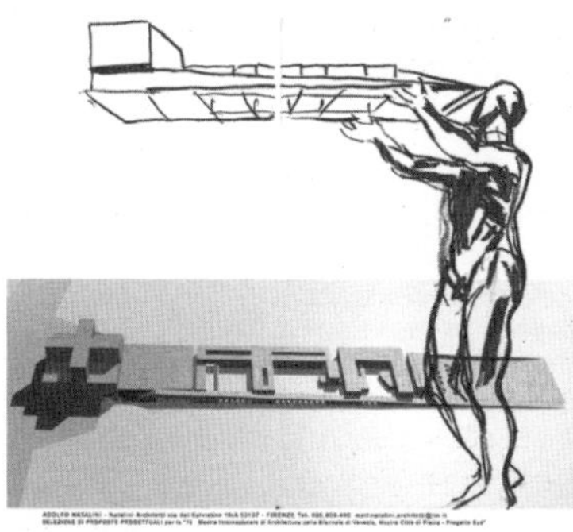

Competition project
for Città di Pietra, Bari (IT),
Stone Lion at the Venice
Biennale, 2006

Competition project for
Oostdijk, Rotterdam (NL),
2007

Corte Italia in Yerevan (AM),
2007-2010

Piazza della Stazione
in Fidenza (IT), 2007-2012

Competition project
for the Parco della Musica
in Florence (IT), 2007

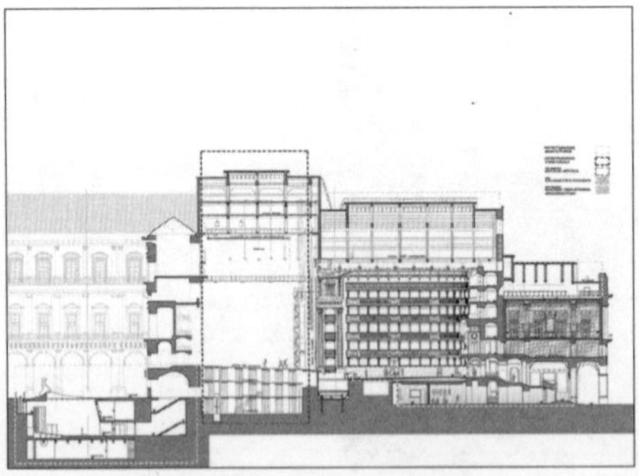

Competition project for the Teatro San Carlo in Naples (IT), 2008-2010

Project for Corte Italia, Roustaveli in Tbilisi (GE), 2009

Project for Corte Italia, Roustaveli in Tbilisi (GE), 2009

XVI Triennale di Milano, Città, architettura, design, moda, audiovisivi: Esposizione internazionale delle arti decorative e industriali moderne e dell'architettura moderna, Palazzo dell'Arte, Milan (IT), 1979

Ricerche sulle Culture Popolari, Palazzo Comunale, Todi, Perugia (IT), 1979

La coscienza di Zeno: tre proposte di analisi su fenomeni delle Culture Marginali, Palazzo Comunale, Bibbiena, Arezzo (IT), 1979

* *Umanesimo, Disumanesimo nell' Arte Europea Contemporanea 1890/1980*, Palagio di Parte Guelfa and other areas in the historical centre, Florence (IT), 1980

* *Cronografie. Il Tempo e la Memoria nella società contemporanea*, Venice Biennale, Chiesa di S.Lorenzo, Venice (IT), 1980

Cronografie, Rotonda della Besana, Milan (IT), 1980

Stanze/un'idea per la casa, Istituto italiano di cultura, Warsaw (PL), 1981

* *Ugo La Pietra/Superstudio*, Galleria Incontro, Imola (IT), 1981

* *Superstudio/Disegni di Architettura 1966-81*, Temple Gallery, Rome (IT), 1981

* *Inventionen - Piranesi und Architekturphantasiien in der Gegenwart*, Künstverein, Hanover (Natalini, Abraham, Cook, Koolhaas, Libeskind), 1981

* *Metaphors and Allegories/ Superstudio Florence*, Israel Museum, Jerusalem (IL), 1981

Nuove intenzioni del design, Sala Comunale delle Esposizioni, Reggio Emilia (IT), 1982

Stadt und Utopie, Staatliche Kunsthalle, Berlin (DE), 1982

* *Superstudio 1966-82, Storie, figure, architetture*, Accademia delle Arti del Disegno, Florence (IT), 1982

La rinascita della città, Centro Oikos, Bologna (IT), 1983

Progetti per la nuova stazione di Bologna, Bologna (IT), 1983

Bauen für Frankfurt, Frankfurt (DE) (and later in USA and in Canada), 1984

* *Revision der Moderne*, Deutsches Architekturmuseum, Frankfurt (DE), 1984

* *Adolfo Natalini - Figure di Pietra*, Studio Marconi, Milan (IT), 1984

Images et imaginaires d'architecture, Centre G. Pompidou, Paris (FR), 1984

Idee, Prozess, Ergebnis, Martin Gropius Bau, IBA, Berlin (DE), 1984

* *Adolfo Natalini. Obras y proyectos*, 1978-1984, Colegio Oficial de Arquitectos, Madrid (ES), 1985

* *Le Affinità Elettive. Ventuno progettisti ricercano le proprie affinità*, XVII Triennale di Milano, Milan (IT), 1985

La ricostruzione della città, XVII Triennale di Milano, Milan (IT), 1985

Il Mestiere di Architetto. La Macchina per Abitare, Palazzo dei Diamanti, Ferrara (IT), 1985

* *III Mostra Internazionale di Architettura. Progetto Venezia*, Venice Biennale, Venice (IT), 1985

Neue Neue Frankfurt. Nuova architettura e contesto storico, Verona (IT), 1985

* *Quadriennale Internationale de design: Caravelles*. Mendini, Natalini, Branzi, Sottsass, Musée St. Pierre, Lyon (FR), Musée des Arts Decoratifs, Paris (FR), 1986

* *Revision der Modern Postmodern Architektur 1960-1986*, The National Museum of Modern Art, Tokyo (JP), 1986

* *Adolfo Natalini*, Premio TERCAS Architettura, Teramo (IT), 1986

* *Le Città immaginate. Nove progetti per nove città*, XVIII Triennale di Milano, Milan (IT), 1987

Architetture di pietra, Ultime dimore, 25° Marmomacchine, Verona Fair (IT), 1987

* *Die Revision der Moderne*, Williams College Museum of Art, Williamstown, Massachusetts (US), 1987

* *Archeologia Museo Architettura*, Tour Fromage, Aosta (IT), 1987

* *Un'idea per le Murate*, Santa Verdiana, Florence (IT), 1988

* *Padiglione Italia. 12 progetti per la Biennale di Venezia*, Palazzo Ducale, Venice (IT), 1988

* *Adolfo Natalini - Architetture 1979-89*, Chiesa di San Giovanni Battista, Pistoia (IT), 1989

Collezione permanente C.C.I., Centre G. Pompidou, Paris (FR), 1989

* *V Mostra Internazionale di Architettura*, (Padiglione Italia) Venice Biennale, Venice (IT), 1991

Herbstucke - Eredità - Pièces d'Héritage, Landespavillon Baden Wurttenberg, Stuttgart (DE), 1992

Vision of Europe, San Giorgio in Poggiale, Bologna (IT), 1992

Architectonicum. Immagini dall'architettura italiana 1970-1990, travelling exhibition around the capitals of Eastern Europe, 1992

Rimini Terzo Millennio, Sala dell'Arengo, Rimini, 1992

* *Adolfo Natalini*, Atelier Foik, Cologne Furniture Faire, Cologne (DE), 1993

Vision urbaines, Centre G. Pompidou, Paris (FR), 1994

European Architecture 1984 - 1994. Ten years of the Mies van der Rohe Pavilion Award, curated by Fundaciò Mies van der Rohe, Deutsches Architekturmuseum, Frankfurt (DE), 1995

Gli anni '60. Le immagini al potere, Fondazione Antonio Mazzotta, Milan (IT), 1996

* *Identità e differenze*, XIX Triennale di Milano (IT), 1996

European Architecture 1984-1994, Fundaciò Joan Mirò, Barcelona (ES), 1996

Visioni, utopie, tecniche, Wiener Festwoche, Vienna (AT), 1996

Architetture del Novecento in Toscana, Fondazione Michelucci, Pistoia (IT), 1998

Le architetture dello spazio pubblico, Galleria della Triennale, Milan (IT), 1998

La Arquitectura del espacio publico, Convento de Nuestra Señora, Seville (ES), febbraio 1999

* *Archipelago Architettura sperimentale 1959-1999*, Palazzo Fabroni, Pistoia (IT), 1999

Nuove Chiese Italiane, Museo Diocesano Tridentino, Trent (IT), 2000

Artisti carissimi, collective exhibition at the Galleria Pananti, Florence (IT), 2000

Superstudio: Monument Continu, Centre George Pompidou, Paris (FR), 2000

* *Quattro da Pistoia, uno da New York*, Galleria Fantacci, Agliana, Pistoia (IT), 2000

Lo spazio condiviso. Artisti e architetti, Palazzo delle Papesse, Siena (IT), 2000

* *Architecture Radicale*, travelling exhibition, Cologne, Villeurbanne, Lyon, Gran Canaria, Valencia, 2000–2001

* *Collezione permanente, nuove acquisizioni*, Centre G. Pompidou, MNAM-CCI Paris with two rooms dedicated to Superstudio, Paris (FR), 2001

* *Continuità. Arte in Toscana 1945-1967*, Palazzo Strozzi, Florence (IT), 2002

Continuità. Arte in Toscana 1968-1989, Palazzo Fabroni, Pistoia (IT), 2002

The changing of the Avant-garde. Visionary Architectural Drawings from the Howard Gilman Collection, The Museum of Modern Art Queens, New York (US), 2003

* *Adolfo Natalini Architettore*, Fondazione Ragghianti, Lucca (IT), 2003

Visionen und Utopien, Schirn Kunstahalle, Frankfurt (DE), 2003

La ciudad radiante, Madrid (ES), 2003

* *Superstudio. Life without objects*, Design Museum, travelling exhibition: Design Museum, London (GB), Pratt Art Gallery, Artists Space, Storefront in New York (US) 2003, Williamson Gallery, Pasadena, Cal. (US), and Vleeshal, Middelburg (NL), 2004

Dal Futurismo al futuro possibile, Tokyo (JP), 2003; Kobe (JP), 2003; Kuala Lumpur (MY), 2003; Brussels (BE), 2004

Radical Italy – Frac Centre Collection, Frac Centre, Orléans (FR), 2003

* *Fantasy Architecture 1500-2036*, Hayward Gallery, London (GB); Northern Gallery for Contemporary Art, Sunderland (GB), 2004

* *Metamorph*, IX Venice Biennale of Architecture, 2004: Metamorphosisraele - Back to the see

* *Arti e Architettura. 1900/2004*, Palazzo Ducale, Genoa (IT), 2004–2005

Archilab new experiments in Architecture, Art and the City, Mori Art Museum, Tokyo (JP), 2004–2005

Pop Art Italia. 1958–1968, Galleria Civica, Modena (IT), 2005

* *Adolfo Natalini – Roberto Barni: De IJsselkade en Andere projecten*, Doesburg (NL) 2006

* *Future City – Experiment and Utopia in Architecture 1956-2006*, Barbican Art Gallery, London (GB), 2006

* *Città di pietra – Cities of stone*, X international architectural exhibition, Venice Biennale, Venice (IT), 2006

Oeuvres choises la collection du Centre Pompidou, MNAM/CCI Centre Pompidou, Paris, (FR), 2007

* *Superarchitettura*, Galleria Carla Sozzani, Milan (IT), 2007

Quaranta Nuove Chiese Italiane 4, Scala Santa, Rome (IT), 2008

Cold War Modern-Design 1945-70, Victoria and Albert Museum, London (GB), 2008

* *Radici Radicali Archizoom Pettena Superstudio Ufo 1965-75*, Galleria il Ponte, Florence (IT), 2009

La Guerra Fredda – Cold War Arte e Design in un mondo diviso 1945-1970, Mart Rovereto (IT), 2009 and National Museum of Lithuania, Vilnius (LT), 2009

* *Marine Hugonnier-Superstudio's misura furniture series again: a model for a revolt*, Villa Romana, Florence (IT), 2009

Il Grande Gioco-Forme d'Arte in Italia 1947-1989, GAMeC, Bergamo–Milan (IT), 2010

Quali cose siamo, Triennale Design Museum, Milan (IT), 2010

* *L'architettura italiana per la città cinese*, Italian Pavilion at the World Exposition in Shangai, 2010 Accademia Nazionale di San Luca, Rome, (IT) 2010-11

* *Superstudio, 5 Atti fondamentali*, Bienal de São Paulo, São Paulo (BR), 2011

* *Superstudio*, MAXXI, Rome (IT), 2011

Invito al viaggio parte 1, Centro Pecci, Prato (IT), 2010-2011

Invito al viaggio parte 3, Centro Pecci, Milan (IT), 2010-2011

* *Superstudio/Backstage*, edited by S. Pezzato and C. Toraldo di Francia, Spazio CID/Arti Visive, Centro per l'Arte contemporanea Luigi Pecci, Prato (IT), 2011-2012

La città radicale, edited by E. Piccardo, Centro Pecci, Milan (IT), 2011

Superstudio/Surface radicale, edited by A. Midal, Haed-Geneva, Design Project Room, Geneva (CH) 2012

Politique fiction, Cité du design, Saint-Etienne (FR), 2012

9+1 ways of Being Political, MOMA, New York (US), 2012-2013

Pop Art in Western Europe, Museum Het Valkhof, Nijmegen (NL), 2012-2013

* *La città nuova. Oltre Sant'Elia. Cento anni di visioni urbane 1913-2013*, Como (IT), 2013

* *Superstudio-Backstage 1966-1978*, Centro Arti Visive Pescheria, Pesaro (IT), 2013

* *Adolfo Natalini- Disegni di architettura*, Galleria dell'architettura italiana, Florence (IT), 2013

* *Adolfo Natalini-Linea d'ombra*, SDS di Architettura, Syracuse (IT), 2013

* *Superstudio-La vita segreta del Movimento Continuo*, Venice Biennale, Venice (IT), 2014

Natalini Architetti, *Relais San Lorenzo, Innesti/Grafting*, Venice Biennale, Venice (IT), 2014

Collaborators

SUPERSTUDIO
1967-82

Fabrizio Natalini
Manlio Brunetti
Eleonora Pallotta
Andrea Noferi
Aldo Roda
Fabrizia Scassellati
Lorenzo Netti
Lucia Ascani

Carlo Chiappi
Alì Navai
Marianne Burkhalter
Frances Brunton
Leonardo Baglioni
Arno Grünberger
Giampaolo Fici
Guido Biancalani
Stefano Parigi
Michele De Lucchi
Mario Ciampi
Gianvittorio Falcucci
Jamie Cali

ADOLFO NATALINI
1979-89

Michele De Lucchi
Mario Ciampi
Nazario Scelsi
Fabrizio Natalini
Luisella Casubolo
Ilaria Andreini
Marc Schmidt
Stephen Schmitz
Herman Scheidt

Martine Bedin
Madlenka Dabac
Monique Bonadei
David Palterer
Guglielmo Renzi
Carla Schorn
Vittorio Santoianni
Marco Matteini
Axel Müller Schöll
Susanne Stihl
Antonio Ravalli
Andrea Aleardi

NATALINI ARCHITETTI
AT SALVIATINO
1990-

Nazario Scelsi
Adrian Blanchard
Damiano Pica
Tommaso Brilli
Giulia Bianchi
Eleonora Pallotta

Marco Magni
Gaetano Martella
Giovanna Potestà
Stefano Tozzi
Ilaria Andreini
Corinne Schrauwen
Donatella Brandi
Angelo Torre
Giulia Chiappi
Tommaso Barni
Giovanni Santini
Matteo Baralli

SCHRAUWEN
ARCHITECTEN
1994-2007

Werner van den Belt
Jaela van Tijn
Flavia Bindo
Fedele Canosa
Menno Trautwein
Kieke Gravemaker
Troy Wener
Joost Kolk
Jutta Hinterleitner
Janfrans van der Eerden
René Kooijman
Cristina Antonini
Agda van Heeringen
Michiel Steltenpöhl
Renate Dekker
Uriel Aboim
Daan ten Kroode
Ilaria Bartoli.

ABKEN SCHRAUWEN
ARCHITECTEN
2008-2012

Wout van Vliet
Jos van der Burg
Theo van den Berg
Martijn van Dijk

Thanks

When I began to assemble the material for this book in September 2014, I felt it was an umpteenth (and ever-futile) reorganisation of my archives.
I thought it would be easy to choose projects and writings, but the operation became more difficult each day. Now that the book is finished, the only task that remains is to write a page of thanks, with a sense of guilt for not having listed all the people who have been close to me during these long years of work:
Roberto Barni, artist and life-long friend who has always encouraged and challenged me with his words and work; my family (Frances Brunton, Arabella Solange and lastly, Arno) who have always surrounded me with affection; my friends and colleagues from Superstudio (Cristiano Toraldo di Francia, Roberto Magris, Giampiero Frassinelli and Alessandro Magris) who shared the worries and enthusiasm of our approach to architecture between 1966 and 1986; Fabrizio Natalini ("same name but not related", as I always wrote in my monographies, but who has become far more than a relative) who has been by my side since 1971 and continues to sustain me on the difficult path of construction; all those who have collaborated with me, first at Superstudio, then at the studio in via San Gallo 96, and lastly those at Natalini Architetti in via Salviatino who have been an essential part of a long story. Vittorio Savi, who involved me in long conversations between our two neighbouring houses on the hill at Doccia...
Buildings/constructions transformed in image by Mario Ciampi and Pietro Savorelli.
And last of all, those who put this book together:
Giulia Bianchi who put my texts in order, Tommaso Brilli who cleaned up the drawings, Elisa Balducci, for her endless patience in creating the layout and repaging the book, Laura Andreini and Forma who edited the publication, and Marco Casamonti who incited me to keep on with the work.

This volume was printed in November 2015 by Forma Edizioni, Italy